MONTY HALL

—

TV'S BIG DEALER

BY MONTY HALL

WITH BILL LIBBY AND ADAM NEDEFF

BearManor Media

Orlando, Florida

Monty Hall: Big Dealer
© 2021 Monty Hall. All Rights Reserved.

No portion of this publication may be reproduced, stored, and/or copied electronically (except for academic use as a source), nor transmitted in any form or by any means without the prior written permission of the publisher and/or author.

Published in the USA by
BearManor Media
1317 Edgewater Dr. #110
Orlando, FL 32804
www.BearManorMedia.com

Softcover Edition
ISBN: 000

Printed in the United States of America

Table of Contents

Acknowledgments vii
Introduction ix

PART 1 – EMCEE MONTY HALL

1. Chapter One *1*
2. Chapter Two *33*
3. Chapter Three *49*
4. Chapter Four *61*
5. Chapter Five *73*
6. Chapter Six *87*
7. Chapter Seven *97*
8. Chapter Eight *107*
9. Chapter Nine *117*
10. Chapter Ten *127*
11. Chapter Eleven *149*
12. Chapter Twelve *191*
13. Chapter Thirteen *217*
14. Chapter Fourteen *229*
15. Chapter Fifteen *243*
16. Chapter Sixteen *263*
17. Chapter Seventeen *273*
18. Chapter Eighteen *293*

PART 2 – CITIZEN MONTY HALL

1. Chapter Nineteen *307*
2. Chapter Twenty *347*
3. Chapter Twenty-One *361*
4. Chapter Twenty-Two *385*
5. Chapter Twenty-Three *419*
6. Chapter Twenty-Four *437*
7. Chapter Twenty-Five *453*
8. Chapter Twenty-Six *463*
9. Chapter Twenty-Seven *471*

Bibliography 491
Endnotes 497

To those who cared, who helped, who encouraged, who had faith: my father, my friends, sometimes complete strangers, my children, and, especially, the two women of my life—my mother and my wife.

M.H.

ACKNOWLEDGMENTS

The co-author wishes to thank, for their help in making this book as good and honest as he could make it, Monty and Marilyn Hall, his entire family, his *Let's Make a Deal* family, many other television executives and performers, many photographers, and the noted transcriber Mrs. Glenn Miller (Jacquelynn Kaysene).

B.L.

Introduction
by Adam Nedeff

"I know deep in my heart that the performance I do on television is a sincere professional effort. The man who is executing this performance is orchestrating all those people in crazy hats in a very articulate manner in a difficult arena. There is a lot more to Monty Hall. He happens to be a well-educated, serious man in his personal life."

This quote, given by Monty Hall in a 1974 interview, serves as something of a mission statement for this book. A year earlier, he had released his autobiography, *Emcee Monty Hall*, a collaboration with co-author Bill Libby, for publishers Grosset & Dunlap. The problem, as it turned out, was that Monty didn't like the finished product. The 800 or so pages he and Libby originally submitted were condensed down to 279 pages—"the *Reader's Digest* version of my life" as Monty called it.

Then there was the persistent nagging feeling Monty felt about writing his life story when he was only 52. The biggest hit of his career was still on the air. His youngest daughter hadn't turned ten yet. He was writing it when he was at a crossroads in his career; he was anticipating drastic changes coming within the next two years or so. How could he call this his "life story" when there was still so much of his life to come? It was a question Monty asked himself so much at age 52, one that becomes more profound when considering that he lived to see his 96th birthday, a month before his death on September 30, 2017. Do the math—more years of Monty Hall's adult life followed his autobiography than preceded it. He hadn't even met some of the most important people in his life. Some of them hadn't been born yet. *Emcee Monty Hall* was an incomplete book.

Bob Boden—once my boss, always my friend—suggested writing an updated version of the original biography. Writing a new book felt strange the longer I thought about it. *Emcee Monty Hall* was thorough enough that I knew I'd be cribbing from large portions of it anyway, so it seemed the most logical thing was to forget writing an entirely new book and just use the original text.

The following book is divided into two halves. The first half is *Emcee Monty Hall*, enhanced with new interviews and research to fill in the blanks that editing created (the original 800-page manuscript has been lost). The second half covers the events of Monty's life after 1973, with help from family, friends, and collaborators.

Now, a word about the format of the book. The original book was told in Monty's own first-person perspective, with co-author Bill Libby occasionally stepping in to offer his perspective on then-recent events in Monty's life. For obvious reasons, I immediately found it awkward to try to shoehorn my own new research and interviews into Monty's own words from 1973.

Because of that, I opted for an "oral history" format for the book. It's not accurate at all to call this book an oral history—many of the newly added quotes are culled from newspaper and magazine articles, which I've threaded into the revised book with some narrative passages where needed. The faux-oral history format, I feel, is the most cohesive way of presenting this new version of the story.

Providing new interviews specifically for this re-worked version of the book: Stu Billett, Bob Boden, Rabbi Sharon Braus, Brian Cummings, Dan Farrell, Dean Goss, Ron Greenberg, Richard Hall, Robert Hall, Sharon Hall, Tom Kennedy, Henry Koval, Karen LaPierre, Carol Merrill, Phil Moore, David Narz, John Schott, and Lloyd Schwartz.

PART 1: EMCEE MONTY HALL

Author's collection

CHAPTER ONE

BILL LIBBY'S INTRODUCTION TO *EMCEE MONTY HALL*, 1973

They have waited two or three years for tickets, these 350 people, and many of them have been standing in the street outside ABC's Hollywood studios for three hours. Ordinarily they are housewives, students, businessmen, doctors, teachers, but for this one incredible evening in their lives they are dressed as rabbits and hunters, as wine bottles and tubes of toothpaste, as ministers and policemen, as baseball players and baseballs. They have come with makeup and paint smeared on their faces and with hand-painted signs proclaiming they are prepared to make almost any kind of deal on earth.

The show is *Let's Make a Deal,* one of the most popular and longest running game shows in the history of television. Three nights a week during most of the year, shows are taped, two to an evening, some 271 shows every year. And 350 persons are sent tickets to each night's taping of two shows… Now they have come from all over the country to be contestants. They have watched the program, of course, and they know that by guessing the prices of items or by trading outright gifts of cash for what may be in a box or behind a curtain, they may win prizes of clothing, furniture, appliances, cars, boats, and all-expenses-paid trips around the world. Though they hope to win prizes, they know they may make the wrong trade and win nothing, or, perhaps worse, win a "Zonk," a gag prize, such as a couple of cows or sway-backed horses or a year's supply of spinach. But they are there, they say, really for the fun of it more than anything else.

Only a few admit to embarrassment at their outlandish costumes. They know that all of them cannot be on the show. Only thirty-one will be picked to go on the trading floor… They don't know how the contestants are selected, and they don't like to think about it. They admit they will be disappointed if they don't make it, but most agreed that it will be fun just to be in the audience and watch the show's main attraction, emcee Monty Hall.

Ushers appear and walk up and down telling the people that the selections will soon be made and please don't wave their signs to call attention to themselves and hit the men who make the choices with them because they would not be apt to pick someone who has just poked out their eyes. Everyone thinks that is funny, but when the men come out to make their choices, the people, desperate to call attention to themselves, start to wave their signs and hit them anyway.

Two of the show's writers, Alan Gilbert and Bernie Gould, make the choices. They walk up and down the line looking at the people and their costumes, and the people jump up and down and smile broadly and shout that they want to be picked. Now and then a writer points at someone and he is picked, and he jumps with joy. An usher hands the lucky person a special ticket and hurries him out of line and into a special room where the contestants wait for further instructions.

The scene is incredible, like some sort of flesh market. Everyone yearns to be picked, and two men are walking up and down wielding an enormous power to choose and exercising it with swift jabs of a finger.

The writers say they don't care so much about the costumes or signs; everyone comes with costumes and signs. They are looking for lively, animated people, but they are also looking for a cross section of America—black, and white, young and old, fat and thin, attractive and plain. What they do not want are those who are overenthusiastic, because someone who puts on a performance in the line may be just too obstreperous on the air; and already they know how ordinary people react, in this arena of excitement and emotion. To place a wild extrovert onto that stage is to look for trouble.

There are no rules to guide them. They have been making the selections since the show began nearly ten years ago, and their record in picking people who have worn well on camera has been good enough for them to go on doing it in this way.

In less than half an hour the selections are made. The writers disappear. And those who have not been picked look stunned, as though it had never really occurred to them that they might not be chosen. A strange silence falls over them. A man in a Tarzan outfit puts his sign down and leans back against a wall and closes his eyes. They will have to sit and watch others go for the cars and the trips around the world. They say it was all right. They knew it would happen. They are disappointed, naturally, but it is just one of those things.

In a studio dressing room, Monty Hall lies on a couch, resting from a day at the office and preparing to resume his role as a performer. Hall is a major television personality. In 1972, a respected poll rated him the public's favorite emcee by a wide margin over Ed McMahon, Johnny Carson, Dick Cavett, Merv Griffin, Mike Douglas, and the others. He is tall, slender, dark-haired, and handsome. He is no longer a boy, but he still looks boyish and has a boyish charm. He has an easy smile and an easy way with people. Win or lose, the ladies kiss him on the show. He kids that when he comes home after a hard night at the studio with lipstick on his cheek and his collar, he looks as if he has had a head-on collision with an Avon lady. Women also kiss him in supermarkets and airports and restaurants and wherever else they encounter him. Men admire him, too. He is a television star, but he is approachable. He talks to his fans. He says he loves people and adds that if he didn't, he wouldn't be nearly as successful as he is.

It is a tough show to do. It looks easy, but it is hard. And the people in the profession understand this. With some shows, the show is the thing. With this show Monty Hall is the show.

Hall is up now, changing from casual clothes to the finery he will wear on camera, and Stefan Hatos, his partner, an intense, articulate, tough veteran from the heyday of radio and the early days of television, reviews the format of the night's show with him.

A merchandising department has rounded up the prizes. More than $15 million in prizes were given away in the first nine years of the show. The prizes offered, however, amount to more, some $3 million a season on the daytime shows, and $1.5 million on the nighttime shows. This is approximately $10,000 a show daytime and $25,000 nighttime. The top prize daytime may top $4,000, the top prize nighttime $14,000. More than half the prizes offered are won.

With the review finished, Hatos and Hall walk into the studio and run through limited rehearsals, because there are, as yet, no contestants reacting to the events of the show. Monty must know the sequence of stunts, the flow of the show, and what is in every box and behind every curtain. Still, he rehearses only the nighttime show.

The show this night starts the way it has for more than nine years and 2,700 performances. Jay Stewart, a pioneer announcer of radio and television, chats with the audience to warm them up. The bright, hot television lights go on, and the cameras swing into place. There is a timpani roll. A studio monitor reveals the costumed audience on the trading floor.

From backstage, Stewart announces: "These people, dressed as they are, come from all over the United States to make deals here in the marketplace of America." The timpani roll again. "And now…here is America's top trader, TV's big dealer…MONTY HALL!"

Monty greets one and all with a bright smile and a promise of fun and money, and the show is on. Between spiels for the products and commercials, the contestants make their pitches for prizes. Monty moves among them, selecting those who will get their chances. A lady in a football helmet opens a chest containing three $100 bills and after much hesitation takes a chance on trading them for what is in a bigger box, which turns out to be a $1,000 coat. She shouts with glee and hugs and kisses Hall. A man in a clown costume works his way up to $1,700, then swaps it for whatever is behind a curtain. It turns out to be a couple of cows. He shrugs and smiles wistfully. Well, he came here with nothing. An elderly black lady trades for something behind a curtain and wins an all-terrain vehicle—just what she always wanted. Contestants cannot trade in their prizes and must pay taxes on prizes worth $600 or more.

They cannot resell them to the manufacturer, though they may sell them to friends. But whatever they win, it is better than nothing and may be something special. A fat couple costumed as farmers wins a set of furniture and appliances simply by making the right selections of boxes and curtains. They go wild and the audience screams hysterically at their hysterics and Monty collects another kiss.

A man dressed as a devil picks a wallet packet containing $100 and is offered a trade for a large box. Before he can take the trade, Monty offers instead to pay him $200, then $400, $800, finally $1,000. The poor devil is tempted, but the box is a greater temptation. He takes it and winds up with a thousand lollipops. The audience thinks it is funny. The man smiles thinly and shakes Hall's hand.

The show proceeds smoothly to the big deal "worth $14,000!" The night's two biggest winners are pulled into the aisle to risk, if they wish, their winnings for whatever is behind three numbered curtains. Neither chooses to keep what he had. A bird in the hand… Intensely nervous, they make their selections. Unselected is a curtain that, rolled back, reveals a houseful of furniture; selected, a second curtain reveals an oxcart. Oh, well.

As the tension grows, one competitor, her husband beside her, and one curtain remain. It rolls back; a picture of an airplane. No, she has not won a picture—she has won a trip around the world, complete with cash for expenses, which Monty peels from his pocket. She screams and throws her arms to the heavens, then embraces Hall and kisses him. Tears slide down her chubby cheeks. A large lady with a hefty husband who runs a filling station has won a trip around the world. Unable to contain their excitement, they scream, laugh, and cry. The audience applauds mightily. And Hall appears pleased, as if he himself had won.

As the show ends and titles roll across the screen, Hall is paying a lady dressed as Cleopatra a dollar for every bobby-pin in her purse and a man costumed as a chicken $20 for every egg he has in his pockets.

Let's Make a Deal is a target for the TV critics. For years everyone has taken a potshot at the program, but the ratings stay up there, and in its tenth year are higher than at any time in history. With the new three-year contract that starts in January 1974, you would think that Hall was beyond the critics' barbs, but he is not.

"I have never maintained that we should get a Peabody Award for our show. We make no such pretensions. But we are in the entertainment business; and for what we do, we are the best. It is a costume show with people having a good time. They wait a long time for tickets. They come down to the show, and the excitement mounts. By the time the selections are made and the show starts, the air is fitted with emotion and tension. When I point my finger at a contestant, she doesn't remember what her name is. Now they embark on a series of trades and gambles that may result in a very big score—or nothing. And at this point the most important refutation to the critics; claim of greed occurs. The woman looks at the five donkeys which she won instead of the car, turns and kisses me. We have had some fun. They have gambled and either lost or won, and for thirty minutes we have entertained them and the millions at home who play along with them. Doctors, lawyers, psychiatrists, as well as plumbers, policemen, and firemen, comprise our studio audience. And from my hundreds of personal appearances, I have discovered that they also comprise the viewing audience. Surely, we must be doing something right. As I said, we are in the entertainment business, and we entertain!"

The costumed crowd that convenes on those studio streets three times a week celebrates Monty Hall. The critics do not. He is a game show emcee. But he is more than just that. And whatever he is now, he has had a long, hard time getting there.

MONTY HALL

I will try to tell it all, all the things that seem to time to be of importance in my life, as openly as I can, without wanting to hurt anyone, but without wanting to be dishonest about how it was, and how I saw it as I remember it and feel it now. Being honest and open is the most important thing, so that is the way I will go, letting others have their say, and having my own.

It began for me in Winnipeg, Canada. My father's parents and my mother's parents were among many Russian immigrants who settled in Canada around the turn of the century, driven from their homeland by prejudiced, oppressive practices against Jews. They settled in Winnipeg, where there was not a large Jewish population and where they and their children, who were my parents, and their children, of whom I was one, were often subjected to ridicule and discrimination. When I was young, my family moved a lot and into sections of the city where there probably were few Jewish families. I was a sickly child and fair game for the bullies. I lost many a fist fight until I could gain acceptance from my peers. These early memories serve vividly to remind me of my heritage. This, together with my mother's dedication, no doubt contributed to my own dedication today.

(Hall Family collection)

Winnipeg [in 1973] is a city of around a half million persons, but it was only about half that when I was growing up. It was and is a tough town, a manufacturing and railroad center, strong on sports, with an increasing interest in the arts. Life there for me and my family was hard.

Oddly, there were nine children in both my father's family and my mother's. My father, the second oldest in his family, was born Maurice Halparin in 1899; my mother, the third oldest, was born Rose Rusen in 1900. My father's family had been in the cattle business for generations and they went into that in Canada, too. My mother's father, arriving penniless from Russia, turned to fruit peddling.

My paternal grandfather, Isaac Halparin, a hard man, strong and stern, was successful in business, and reared his three sons and six daughters in comfortable circumstances. Most of his daughters became schoolteachers. His two oldest sons, my father and his older brother, went to work for him early in their lives. He was a taskmaster. And my father's older brother was, too, in a way. As hard as nails and of very grim demeanor, he took a savage delight in beating the hell out of people—anybody, and he practiced on my father. It is claimed by many who knew him that in the proper surroundings, with the proper training, he might well have become a lightweight boxing champion. My dad tells stories of his youth that illustrate this toughness. When walking down a street, his brother would deliberately flirt with somebody else's girl or subtly elbow someone in passing, merely to provoke an incident. The incident would lead to words, and in a matter of moments, it was *smack* and wallop—and somebody was lying on the ground—but definitely not my uncle. In later years, proud as punch, tough and weather-beaten, he would lead parades on his palomino, ever the cowboy with his "I-can-lick-anybody-in-the-house" attitude. The two boys, with their father, ran cattle from fifty or more miles out of town into Winnipeg and they went on cattle-buying trips throughout Manitoba and Saskatchewan. It toughened my father, this male-dominated life.

Maurice & Rose Halparin with Baby Monte. (Hall Family Archive)

MAURICE HALPARIN, Monty's father

I remember the day Monty was born. It was the proudest day of my life. To become a father with a son was something to me…My own father originally was going to be a rabbi. He got a Hebrew education but wound up going into business. He was a Russian who went to Winnipeg at forty with a family of nine. He supported his family, but he had no warmth left over in him for them. He was from a stern, old-fashioned sort of background and demanded discipline and respect and did not know how to love. He disciplined with a strap. He used to beat us badly. It made my older brother tough. It hurt me. He was a cattle buyer who dealt in wholesale meat. It was rugged outdoor work, and he took me and my brother with him. I was not cut out for it, but I could not get out of it.

I met Monty's mother when we both were in third grade. We were to go through life together. I found warmth and love in her house. She had a warm, loving family. Rose was a remarkable woman. Everyone knew that right from the time she was a young girl. She was outstanding in every way, bright and talented, a leader. Why she bothered with me, I'll never know. Love, of course. We loved each other.

Rose must have bothered Maurice quite a bit, and he must have loved her quite a bit. They were married on February 15, 1921, when Rose was already three months pregnant. Monte Halparin was born on August 25, 1921. From his mother, Monte inherited olive eyes and a proud smile that dug deep into the cheeks. His father provided the nose and a flawless head of thick onyx hair.

(Hall Family collection)

MONTY HALL

My maternal grandfather, David Rusen, had five sons and four daughters. He became one of the major fruit wholesalers in western Canada. By contrast with my other grandfather, he was a gentle man, who made a home of love and warmth for his children and did nothing to drive them out into the world, who stressed academic scholarship rather than studies in the school of hard knocks. Most of his children went to college, rather than right to work. Some of the sons became attorneys, doctors, dentists.

My mother became a teacher in the first part of her adult life. She and my father really began their romance when they were twelve. They were only friends then, but my father spent as much time in my mother's house as he could, preferring it to his own. He tried to stay out of the way of his father and older brother and away from their house of tension as much as he could. He partly grew up in my mother's house, where there was warmth, laughter, and singing.

My mother was the oldest girl and the third oldest child in the Rusen family. As a young girl, she was something of a tomboy, an athlete who played baseball with the boys. She had great talent as a singer and an actress and played the leads in all the student productions as she grew up. She was the president of every organization to which she belonged, from the time she was twelve until, who knows, until she died.

Once when a group of youngsters were forming a new club in high school, they came to her and asked her, "Rose, do you want to join our club?"

She answered, "Yes, if I am president."

And she was. There was some driving force in her that compelled her to leadership. She was a dynamic person with a charming personality from her pre-teen days. She was the heart of her family.

My mother was a schoolteacher by the time she and my father became engaged to be married. She gave up teaching with her marriage and the pregnancy that soon followed. And she gave up much of her home life when my father became sick and was unable to work for a year and she had to go out to work to support us. And later she joined him in his work at the butcher shop, helping him without complaint. She still found time to play a part in the social and charitable life of Winnipeg, and she was a hearty humorist and superb storyteller, a prominent club woman who presided over organizations, starred in stage productions, and headed fund-raising drives to benefit the needy. She was away so much speaking for charities that I later joked I was an organizational orphan. She was not a beautiful woman but a handsome one. She had a personality many remember as the most compelling they ever knew. She had great strength, physically and psychologically. An unusual woman, she influenced me enormously.

Rose had once been a member of a USO troupe, entertaining soldiers during World War II with variety shows. It was Rose who put her son on stage for the first time, in a small role for one of her plays.

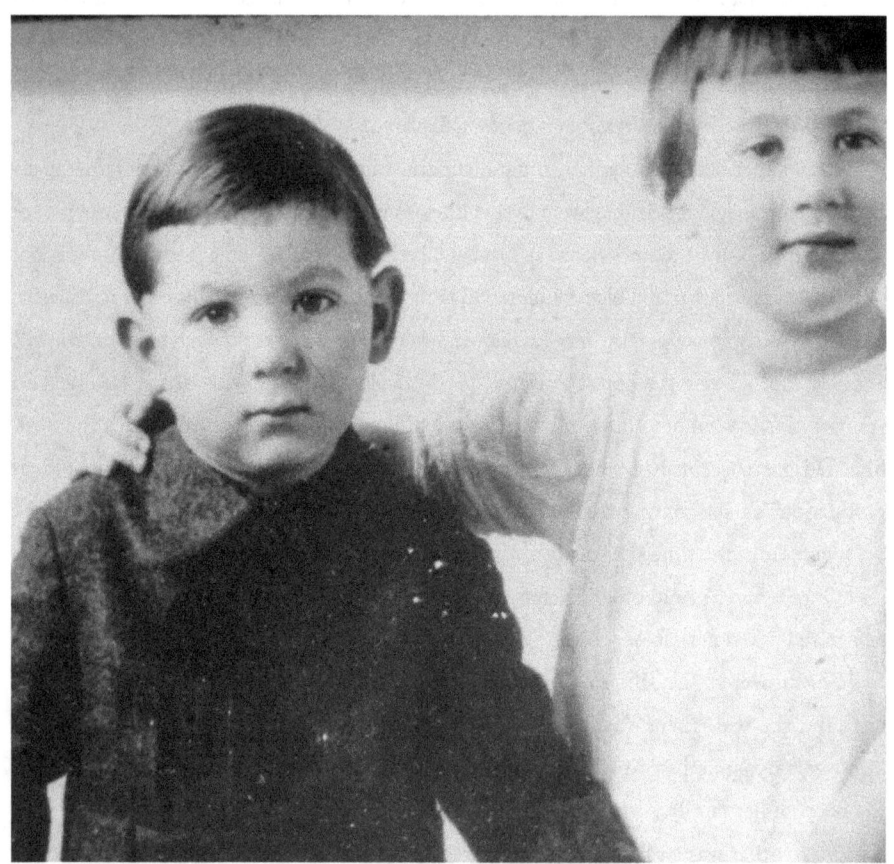

(Hall Family collection)

MONTY HALL[i]

I had no lines. I just had to stand there. All I knew was I had to go to the bathroom something awful. And she wouldn't let me leave. It was dreadful. I had to go in the worst way. Yeah, I held out. Later, I asked her why I couldn't just run offstage.

She said, "When you're onstage, you've got to stay out there. That's what acting is all about."

Rose Halperin's influence on her son can be detected in a 1940 piece in The Winnipeg Tribune. *The National Council of Jewish Women staged a variety show for an audience of 600 homeless people, who were treated to free food and drink while enjoying the performance by volunteer entertainers. Among those who took the stage that night: a youngster named Monte Halperin.*

MONTY HALL

Mother had a remarkable equanimity no matter what the situation. She covered for my father or anyone else. She had a defense for the actions of all friends or family, her basic argument being, "We must love one another no matter what."

Hence she was the mediator, the placator, the negotiator. I recall that couples came to her to try to solve marital disputes. Businessmen called her into their plants or offices to settle employee problems. When people were ill, they invariably called for my mother as well as the doctor. And when a telegram came to a neighbor during World War II saying that a son was missing in action, the first call came to my mother. At a dinner honoring her in 1961 in Winnipeg, my brother referred to her as a lawyer who never attended law school, a doctor without a medical degree, a psychiatrist without a couch, a labor negotiator without a college background, a wife, a mother, an actress, a speaker, a playwright, an athlete—a woman for all seasons. She was this—and more.

We had our arguments. I wanted to follow in her footsteps, to be the storyteller, the actor, the singer she was. But this had brought her nothing. Later, when I went to college and started to study for a career in medicine, this pleased her; when I turned from medicine to the entertainment business, she regretted the decision but never offered one word of criticism. However, when I succeeded, she got great satisfaction from it. Still, she did not take me as seriously as I took myself.

Once a reporter said, "Mrs. Halparin, I understand you are Monty Hall's mother."

She replied, "Young man, where I come from, he's still known as Rose Halparin's son."

Years later, when my parents came to New York to see me do a TV show called *Keep Talking*, they waited while I signed autographs under the theater marquee, which had my name in lights. I kept glancing at them to see if they were impressed.

When I got to them, I said, "Well, Mother, what do you think of your star now?"

And she said, "By me, when you replace Ed Sullivan, you'll be a star."

Growing up, I always felt closer to my mother than my father. My personality was nearer hers, just as my son's now is closer to his mother's.

My father was a fine man who was frustrated by the fates. The roughness of his early life and the failures he experienced later stirred tensions and tempers that caused us to withdraw from him. Yet I remember respecting him, because no matter how hard he made me work in his store, he worked harder. He always found time to take me and my younger brother to hockey and baseball games or boxing bouts. It was a great treat when he came home and said, "How about taking in a hockey game?" And off we'd go, father and son, racing each other to the hockey rink.

(Hall Family Archive)

My father left high school early and fled from his father and older brother and their harsh ways. At sixteen he caught a cattle train for Chicago and made it without any problem. There he wandered the streets looking for work. He soon ran out of money and resorted to sleeping under stoops and eating buns stolen from bakery windows. During one of the latter escalades a big Irish cop caught him and hauled him out of the bakery. Instead of rushing him off to the nearest juvenile judge, the big ruddy-faced policeman took him to a coffee shop, fed him, gave him some fatherly advice, doled out carfare to the outskirts of town, and my father hitchhiked back to Winnipeg. His arrival there was greeted with the kind of reception that warped him for years to come. His mother cried—and his father beat hell out of him for running away.

The next year my father used the family association with a cattle customer in Saskatchewan to change his life again. My grandfather had done business with the Doukhobors, a religious sect. Peter Verigan, the head of the sect, and known as king, remembered my father and gave him a job in the community, allowing my father to practice his own form of religion and ethics by living by himself in a hotel while working in the commune. However, a year of this, interrupted by occasional sojourns to Winnipeg to see my mother, was enough. He returned to Winnipeg, where he was fortunate to find a job as a bookkeeper with a lumber firm, since he loved working with figures. He worked indoors in clean surroundings. He was able to dress well. At twenty, his life was going well, and he became engaged to my mother. A year later, they married and started their family. Then the reversals came.

He began to suffer from severe migraine headaches. A doctor told him he did not have the eyesight for bookkeeping and would have to give up such work or risk blindness. He accepted the advice and returned to the cattle business, the only other job he knew. But he worked with an uncle, not his father. Unfortunately, he did not make it with his uncle and was forced to return to his father and brother. He did not make it with them, either. Ridiculed by them for having dared try to make it without them, he was driven to go out on his own again. For a time, he drifted from one job to another.

All of this has been passed on to me. My earliest memories of my father date from his middle twenties, when he had managed to acquire a little delivery truck and was running his own small meat wholesale business. This truck became the family car. We went everywhere jammed in the upright front seat of that little delivery truck. Its main use was in his business. He would go out, early in the morning, to the stockyards, buy meat from the slaughterhouse, and resell it to retail stores around the city.

When I was three or four years old, he often took me with him on his rounds. I kept him company. Although it is over forty years since I made those trips to the slaughterhouse in St. Boniface, a suburb where the stockyards were located, the stench has not left my nostrils to this day. There is a peculiar odor that is as foreign to our olfactory glands as any. It strikes you on your approach from miles away, and the closer you get, the worse it is. Inside, coupled with the squealing of the animals left on their way to extinction, it is almost unbearable, a combination of sight and sound that never ingratiated itself upon my senses.

In his late twenties, my father was stricken with an awful attack of boils. For a year he was unable to work, and my mother had to support the family. It was dreadfully dispiriting for a man, and it almost broke him. He used to sit in our tiny living room listening to the radio and staring straight ahead. Sometimes he would lie in bed, staring at the ceiling, in intense pain, unable to stand or move around. He was deeply depressed because he had been invalided and his position as the head of the household had been curtailed.

When he was able to work again, he landed at a butcher counter, which he ran as a sort of concession in the corner of a delicatessen. He learned to cut meat. It was difficult for him, but he learned. It was the largest part of his life—or, at least, his profession, such as it was.

He was by nature something of a dandy. He was an extremely handsome young man, small physically, but powerful. He had been toughened by his upbringing, but he also had been bruised by it. He had no stomach for hurting anyone, for tackling trouble. And his yearlong sickness seemed to sap his spirit. After that he found something to do. He did not like it, but he did it.

He dressed more like a banker than a butcher. He wore suits and stiff-collared shirts to the shop as though he was going to an office. He did not shave himself, but went to a barber, though he could not afford it. He had his nails manicured. How many manicured butchers have you ever known? He insisted that his shop be spotless beyond reason. I know, because I had to clean it, scrubbing the block, washing the machines, and the rest. He kept his own books and prided himself on them, on the rows of pleat, precise figures and the beautiful balances he struck. But he seldom cleared more than twenty-five to thirty dollars a week.

Monty's massive family assembled for this group shot. The family was so big that later in life, when Monty saw this photo, he struggled to remember which one was him. His best guess was that he was the boy in the striped shirt. (Hall Family Archive)

ROBERT HALL, Monty's brother (1983)[ii]

…[H]e made it the fanciest kosher butcher shop in town. I wore a silk shirt…My mother, who at one time was a school teacher, was ashamed of living a double life. Before the High Holidays, she'd be up all night gutting, cleaning, and packing 150 chickens. Next day, she'd slip into her finest clothes and mingle with the high society of Hadassah.

MONTY HALL

And he took this money and he went to the races or to his social club for long sessions at the poker table—always in quest of the killing, the big score that would buy him out of the butcher shop and give his family a better way of life. It was a killing that never came, a score he never made; and it frustrated him, as his life in the butcher shop frustrated him.

Many of the friends he had grown up with had gone on to become doctors, dentists, lawyers, successful merchants, and they were always aware of the gulf between him and them. They teased him, calling him "Butch," and that tormented him. He was unhappy, short-tempered, and given to excesses of emotion.

MAURICE HALPARIN

I never liked being a butcher. For some men, it is fine, but it was not for me. Still, I labored at it. I was lucky to bring home $25 a week. I could not afford a delivery boy, so I had to use my son. He must have known I did not want to. But how else could we eat and pay the rent and buy clothing if we did not scrimp every penny? He worked hard, I know that. I pushed him. I had no choice. My temper was short.

MONTY HALL

During one difficult period we lived with another family, relatives named the Spectors, who had two small children. The two families were forced to share one house to make ends meet. The two boys became like brothers to me. The younger, Joseph, was shot down in World War II. I still carry his picture in my wallet. And my Aunt Elizabeth is very special to me. Then my family moved in and out of a series of small apartments, always struggling to raise the rent. Before my brother Robert was born, six years after I was, we moved in with my mother's parents. They had what seemed like a large house. There were four bedrooms and another room which could be used as a bedroom. But living there were my mother's paternal grandfather and grandmother, her mother and father, my mother and father, six of her brothers and sisters, and myself. That was thirteen people living in that one house—and it had one bathroom. Somehow, we managed to share it. Today we have five bathrooms, and when my three children are at home with my wife and myself, they always seem to be in use at the same time. Our standards have changed. We no longer know what patience is.

ROBERT HALL (2019)

All those people and one bathroom. You know how we did it? We all learned how to whistle. There was no lock on the bathroom door, so when you were in there, you tried to whistle the whole time to let people know it was in use.

I don't want to dwell so much on the hardships though, like having the electricity turned off or being in such a crowded house because it sounds like we were miserable all the time, and we weren't. That house was filled with love. There was always music playing. The adults would sit around telling stories to each other, and there was just constant laughter with 12-15 people sitting in there. If the kids didn't want to listen to stories, you paired up with another kid and you ran off and went outside and played. There was a warmth in that house that I think Monty carried in his spirit, and I hope I can say I carried it in mine.

MONTY HALL

We spent several years in my mother's home, and the experience made a deep impression on me. The family house was located on Hallet Street, which, when we lived there, was a lower-middle-class area; but a generation, before it had been populated by rather comfortable citizens, including Premier Norquay of the Province of Manitoba. The street was about three hundred yards long, a sedate and genteel neighborhood which was going through a melting pot change. On this small street resided Jewish families, Ukrainian families, a Chinese family, old aristocrats, and new immigrants. Today, when I revisit Hallet Street, it is purely ethnic, mostly Ukrainian, still neat and orderly, but so miniaturized to my eye. And as I look at Number 107, I don't see how so many people could live in one house with grace.

My mother's brothers were not much older than I was, so they were and are more like brothers than uncles. I was like the tenth child and treated accordingly. Their family life was conducted in a hierarchy.

I clearly remember my grandmother yelling to one of the boys, "Sonny, go to the corner store for some milk."

And Sonny would turn and yell to the next youngest brother, "Charley, go to the store for milk for Mama."

Charley would yell, "Sam…"

When they got to "Monte…" there was no one left for me to turn to and I would have to go. That is, I went until Robert was old enough.

That system is strong. And it seems to me somehow right and good. Growing up with grandparents had a profound effect on me. It is something my children have missed. It is respect. Not a pretense of respect. Real respect.

How can you explain to a child what it is like to live with great-grandparents in their eighties, to try to understand them and try to make yourself understood by them? Their hearing was failing. You had to work at talking to them. Their sight was failing. So, the one who was nearly blind would feed the other who was blind; and you would help, learning to accept their infirmities. You had to help them upstairs. Youngsters today tend to turn from such tasks, but yesterday, when I was a youngster, I was warmed by it.

How can I describe to the kids today what it was like to take a ninety-year-old great-grandfather by the hand and walk him at a snail's pace to the synagogue on a Saturday morning? I talked very little to the old man; he talked less. My task was to deliver him; and if it took an hour to traverse the mile, then that's the way it was. In that mild walk I learned patience, tolerance, and respect. At the end of services, I was to bring him back to Hallet Street. Again, slowly, foot by foot, we made our way home, all the time a raging fire ready to explode inside me, because it was Saturday, a day when I could go to the movies—but something I couldn't do until the mission was completed. The old man would sense my anxiety. When we crossed Main Street, a very wide and busy thoroughfare with streetcars, there was only a half mile left to go. Then he would look down at me and, patting me on the shoulder, say, "Go now, go now." He could make the rest of the way on his own. I would run to my grandmother's house, have lunch, and with my three young uncles be on my way to the movies as the old man was still shuffling his last few steps home.

I can still see my great-grandfather at the age of 90, patiently, tenderly feeding my great-grandmother, who was 88 and blind. They had 70 years together. And I remember many nights after dinner looking up from my homework to see my grandfather and grandmother sitting together on the couch holding hands. They had more than 50 years together[iii]

My grandfather, as the years progressed, brought out from Russia the members of his own family—sisters and brothers, nieces and nephews, and, eventually, countless other residents of Pavelitch, the small town whence he had come. Every year we children looked forward to the annual Pavelitcher picnic. Scores of friends and relatives all descended on Kildonan Park. The first order of business was to organize the soccer and softball games. Every member under the age of sixty was enthusiastically involved. After the games the participants moved to their own family picnic tables. Cloths were unfolded and spread on wooden benches. From huge baskets, epicurean delights miraculously appeared in an unending flow. Chicken and fish and salads and fruit. Pickles, dilled to perfection, and an assortment of Jewish delicacies, blintzes and knishes, were majestically arrayed before the expectant diners. Some tables exchanged goodies. The excitement was contagious. What a feast! And for dessert, we children were given nickels to run to the pavilion where we bought ice cream cones. Overfed and overtired, we boarded the family cars or trucks and wended our way homeward to revel in what was the most glorious of days. There were other times when just the four of us went on a picnic—Mother, Dad, Bob, and myself. We played ball and ate and laughed. It was the best of times. To this day, mention a picnic to me and my eyes get misty.

When I saw the musical *Fiddler on the Roof*, I said to myself, "That's it! That's my family!"

And in my imagination, I see that even now, we are playing out the sequel of what happened after Tevye and his brood left their small Russian village of Anatevka—only our Russian village was named Pavelitch.[iv]

Pavelitch, the town of Monte Halparin's roots, has, at various points, been a part of Lithuania, Poland, Ukraine, and Russia. In the 1830s, it was ruled by Russia's Tsar Nicholas I. Under Nicholas, Jews were restricted in where they could live, work, and attend school. The only thing the battle-hungry Nicholas didn't restrict for Jews was military service, dispatching "happers" into villages to round up Jewish boys for enlistment. Nicholas' rationale was that, if the Jews won battles, it was more land for him; if they lost, it meant fewer Jews. Keeping kosher was prohibited, as was honoring the Sabbath. At the end of a ten-hour march, recruits were ordered to kneel until they converted to Christianity. Some committed suicide rather than convert.

Nicholas I was killed in battle and succeeded by Tsar Alexander II. Alexander II was more benevolent toward Jews, halting forced military enrollment, allowing Jews more freedom in choosing their homes and schools, and even opening up the city of Kiev, which had once been off-limits for Jews. But when Alexander was killed by an explosion, a whisper campaign blamed the Jews, leading to riots. Homes and businesses were looted and destroyed, while police stood by and did nothing. Anti-Semitic legislation called May Laws were enacted, and Jews again were treated as strangers in their own land. Though it was originally claimed that the May Laws were temporary, they remained in effect for over 30 years.

At the end of the 19th Century, with no sign of a better life for Jews ahead in Pavelitch, citizens began looking west toward the United States of America. As rumor had it, Americans became wealthy so easily that everyone in the nation ate meat every day. Word was that education was free and mandatory in the United States, which meant Jews could have any career they wanted.

Faiga Shnier was the granddaughter of Bluma, a shopkeeper, and her husband Mendel, who spent most of the day in the local synagogue, which doubled as a social club. In 1895, Faiga married Dudi Rusen in Pavelitch. Dudi's sister was married shortly thereafter, and the four of them lived more comfortably, relatively speaking, by sharing a house with one bedroom, and a curtain hanging in the middle of the room to divide the two beds. Faiga laughed years later when sharing her family history, acknowledging that the curtain wasn't quite enough; the two newlywed couples were very aware of each other in that bedroom.

But when pressed for details about her family history, Faiga never had much to say. "We just existed."

Dudi dreamt of going to America with his brother Moishe to start a new life. Advertisements in Yiddish newspapers from Jewish relief organizations, urging Russian Jews to come to America, made Dudi feel more and more pressed to make the move. Dudi left Pavelitch in 1901 while his wife and new daughter stayed behind, waiting for him to send for them. Dudi traveled first to Germany, venturing from village to village on carriages and then onto a ship departing for North America. After a week of huddling in the third-class cabin, Dudi Rusen arrived in Halifax, Nova Scotia. Once in Halifax, he was told that immigrants with papers could travel to Toronto or Montreal, the two biggest cities in Canada. Immigrants traveling without papers had to take a train to Winnipeg, Manitoba. The unusual instructions were part of an effort by Canada to spread out new arrivals in the underpopulated country. Canada was urging immigrants to settle in the middle of the nation, using farmland as an incentive, selling it at bargain prices.

Dudi stepped off the train in Winnipeg, the full weight of what he had done just sinking in. He knew no English and he had abandoned his homeland with an idea of what he wanted to do, but with no plan in place. Dudi remembered later how terrifying that moment was. But to his surprise, he heard a voice yelling in Yiddish. "Se du Yidden?"—"Are there any Jews here?" Dudi rushed to the man doing the yelling and replied in Yiddish, "I am a Jew." A group of five families in Winnipeg, sensing that immigrants would be terrified as they took their first steps in their new hometown, regularly posted volunteers at the train station to look out for Jewish immigrants, intercept them, and help them get comfortable in their new surroundings. The man, whose name turned out to be Weidman, took Dudi to his house and fed him his first hot meal since he had departed for the long voyage.

The next morning, Dudi was taken to the Jewish Free Loan Society, where he received a five-dollar loan. Dudi spent one dollar as a payment on a room in a boarding house. Then he went to a market and spent the remaining money on a pushcart. With the help of strangers, Dudi Rusen had found a home and a job within 24 hours of his arrival.

The Halparin family, based in Gomel, Mohyliv in Ukraine, spent most of the 19th century in the cattle business. Their business model was a little strange—they made it a point to own only one cow at a time—but they lived somewhat comfortably, although they got into quite a few adventures. Monty listened to their memories as a child and acknowledged as an adult that he could never be sure which stories were real and which stories were works of fiction, but Halparin family history tended to be exciting.

MONTY HALL[v]

My great grandfather and my grandfather stopped off at an inn…and they asked for dinner and a place to sleep. My great grandfather, because it was Friday night, put on his tallit and started to pray in the corner of the restaurant. A couple of hooligans came and started tugging at him and took his tallit. They tore his tallit. But my great grandfather was a brute of a man and he grabbed one of these guys and attacked him. He hit the man so badly that he fell down, hit his head, and died.

My great grandfather was taken to court in the Ukraine. Now what chance do you think a Jew had in a small area of the Ukraine after he killed a non-Jew?

Amazingly, the judge said, "The worst thing that you can do is insult a man about his religion at a time when he is praying."

And he would not convict him, but he warned my grandfather, "If you ever raise your hand again, that will be the end for you."

In 1905, the Halparins decided, as the Rusens had, that better fortunes awaited them in North America. The Halparins arrived in Winnipeg and picked up where they left off, bringing their cattle business to their new homeland.

Dudi Rusen, meanwhile, had sent back for his family and supported them in Winnipeg with his pushcart, selling fruits and vegetables on a street corner. He had enough success that eventually he combined resources with another friend operating a pushcart and they replaced the pushcart with a truck. A few years later, the business was thriving to the point that they outgrew the truck.

MONTY HALL[vi]

It came time for [my grandfather and his friend] to have a building, because business was really booming. He went to the bank—Alloway and Champlain, I still remember the name of it—and he met the manager. Now, my grandfather didn't speak the language too well.

The bank manager said, "Mr. Rusen, you want a $5,000 loan to buy this building. What have you got for collateral?"

My grandfather said, "What means it, collateral? What are you talking about?"

The bank manager said, "Well, you have to have some asset in the event that you default on the loan."

My grandfather said, "I tell you Mr. Bank Manager what I got for collateral. What I know up here [pointing to head], and what I tell you from here [pointing to heart]."

And the bank manager said, "That's good enough for me."

That was the way it was done in those days.…That was the contract, that was the way they did business.

From a handshake backed only by knowledge of his business, Alloway and Champlain's $5,000 loan helped Dudi Rusen build a thriving, profitable fruit wholesaling company. The family moved into a large house in a nice part of Winnipeg and enjoyed such financial security that Dudi eagerly made plans for helping Faiga's cousins, the Margolis family, move to Canada. Due to administrative errors in paperwork, the plan was delayed for several years, until most of the family received clearance to board a ship and go to Canada.

The move culminated in a warm memory that Monte carried for his entire life. When he was six years old, the Halparin family sat down for the traditional Passover meal of Seder. The dinner was interrupted by the ringing of the phone in the next room. Monte's grandfather took the call.

It was the stationmaster at the Canadian Pacific Railroad. "I have a family here that had this phone number. It's the Margolis family from Russia. What will I do with them?"

Monte's grandfather answered, "Put them in a cab and send them to 107 Hallet right away!"

Monte's grandfather returned to the room and announced to his wife, "Your family is here! Your cousins are on their way!"

The family happily, but frantically, left their meal for the moment and prepared the house for the arrival of six visitors: Moishe Margolis and his wife, the former Babtsy Shnier, and their four children, Kiva, Aaron, Marion, and Nuchem. A devout Jewish family that had endured generations of oppression had made their way to a new land to start a new life, and on their first night, they joined their family to celebrate a sacred Jewish ritual, openly, without having to look over their shoulders. They were safe. They were home.

Monte's family had fled Ukraine due to generations of being treated as outcasts. But so many Jewish immigrants had flocked to Winnipeg that Monte generally never experienced that sort of treatment growing up. Winnipeg and its devout Jewish citizens fostered a strong sense of community.

MONTY HALL[vii]

Let me explain the culture in Winnipeg.…First of all, it was a very highly cultural Yiddish community. Tremendous population. When I was growing up, there were 250,000 people in Winnipeg, and 25,000 of them were Jews. They were ten percent of the whole population. That was a very big Jewish population, in one area of the city, mostly. There were synagogues all over the place…everybody went to a shul.

Culturally, there were two types of Jews: the ful shul Jews and the parashul Jews. The people at the ful shul were the normal people; they came and had their plays and so on. But the parashul people…considered themselves a cut above, because they discussed much deeper [subjects], authors, literature, politics, and so on. But the culture! There were Jewish bookstores, a Jewish theater—a wonderful, thriving Jewish Theater…of which my mother was an integral part.

What bothered me about that Yiddish Theater was that they had plays where they needed youngsters. And I so desperately wanted to be one of them. But I was a sickly child. I couldn't make it. My close friend got the job. I hated him. His name was Murray Nathanson and he got the job. And then I became the actor and he didn't. He went into the mattress business.

When I was growing up in that large Jewish community, it was a given that you went to normal English school and afterward you went to your Jewish school. At four o'clock, you went to the cheder. And you knew all the holidays, you went to shul on Saturday mornings. It was a given. It was also a given that in a community where there was tremendous anti-Semitism, you knew who you were. Because they let you know who you were.

That community sustained the Halparins in many ways—emotionally, spiritually, and mentally—throughout Monte's childhood, and he needed it. Life at home was difficult and insecure for everyone.

MONTY HALL

Eventually we had to leave my grandfather's house, and we moved first to an apartment, then to a small house. We still had little money and it was a terrible struggle to pay the rent, to meet the bills, to have enough left over for food. There were times when the lights and gas were turned off in our home because we weren't able to pay the bills. Every Friday night we went to dinner at my maternal grandparents' house. Every Sunday we spent the day and had lunch and dinner there. These were our best meals of the week. And before, during, and after the meals was the family comedy hour. Laughter sustained us. At home, we often made a meal of porridge. We sometimes did not have enough wood for the furnace. Our warm clothing was old and well-worn. When the rent was due, there was terrible tension between my parents.

Aside from the meals, my grandparents rarely helped us. In later years I asked my family why, and no one seemed to know. Apparently, my parents were too proud to ask, and my grandparents were too busy with their own problems to think to offer. In those days it was accepted that people made their own way.

I was a bright child. My mother had been a teacher and I was brought up among people who were interested in education and willing to work with me. In my first year of school, I skipped from grade one to grade two. When we moved from my grandfather's house, I entered a new school and was put back to grade one. This lasted one day. They put me in grade two. This lasted one day. Then they put me in grade three. At the end of the year they put me in the fourth grade. I still was only six. When I was seven, I missed half a year of school because of two serious ailments. At first, they tried to put me back, but finally they advanced me to grade five at the age of eight. I ended up finishing high school at fourteen.

The studies came easy, but other things came hard. Because I was ahead of others my age in school, I was always the smallest or one of the smallest boys in my class. I was put down a lot. Brightness seldom is admired by other young boys. Toughness is preferred. I, too, wanted to be tough, but I wasn't. I was always being moved to a new area and a new school and always had to make new friends the hard way, in the crucible of hard knocks.

The first of my two misfortunes as a seven-year-old came when I was playing in the kitchen with a cousin. We stacked up some furniture and placed a rocking chair atop it all. There always seemed to be a pot of soup boiling on our stove, and somehow the rocking chair hit the handle of the pot and flipped the boiling soup over my head. I screamed. I can still hear the scream. I was severely scalded and in terrible pain. My mother ripped my clothes off and smeared butter all over my body.

My face was wrapped in bandages, and I was fed through straws for four or five weeks. At the end of that time, the doctor came to my house to remove the bandages. There was great apprehension that I might be scarred, and my skin discolored for life, and my parents concealed this fear from me. But when the doctor unwrapped one arm and my parents saw that it was horribly, violently red, they recoiled.

My mother rushed the doctor from the room. Years later she said she simply was stalling because she was afraid of what my face would be like. Many are not as fortunate as I was, however. My mother returned with the doctor, who resumed the ordeal of the bandages. As he finished, there were gasps and tears of joy. I was rushed to a mirror. My face was fine. The skin came out smooth.

One sidelight is significant to me: My father used to nag my mother about keeping the boiling soup on the stove and letting me play nearby. But after the accident he never said anything to her or in any way blamed her for the mishap. To me this is remarkable.

At the time, I weighed forty pounds. Sipping meals through a straw did not build me up, and I probably started to go out on the streets with the kids sooner than I should have. One night I got up feeling sick and, going to the head of the stairs and seeing what I thought was my uncle Sonny, called for help.

"Uncle Sonny, Uncle Sonny," I yelled desperately. But it was not Uncle Sonny, only a coat hanging on a stand at the foot of the stairs.

They found me in the morning, huddled up at the bottom of the stairs with a raging fever. An ambulance was called to take me to the hospital. In the ambulance, the doctor told my mother, "I don't think he's going to survive."

I had double pneumonia. I was in an oxygen tent for seven days, delirious the whole time, I recognized my mother, but not my father or anyone else. It was touch and go for a while, but I pulled through. I returned home thin and weak, lucky to be alive.

The rest of the year, I was kept home from school. From the time I was burned until my recovery from pneumonia I spent most of four or five months in bed. As it turned out, this was a productive and not unpleasant period for me. My mother, the former teacher, tutored me. My father, the former bookkeeper, challenged me at arithmetic. We put a large blackboard by my bed. My mother would write a long list of figures on the board and my father and I would race to see who could add them up faster in his head. I went on to multiplying, dividing, and subtracting in my head. I became a very fast reader and a whiz at math. Once, in my freshman year at college, a professor asked me why I was not writing down a trigonometry problem as the rest were. He didn't believe me when I said I already had worked out the problem in my mind, and he was startled when I gave him the correct answer.

About the only practical use I've ever found for this ability has been on *Let's Make a Deal* whenever contestants must guess the price of various products and the amount they are off must be subtracted from the money they started with. I am always able to throw the dollar-forty-nines and the twenty-seven cents and the four-ninety-eights around in my head and provide accurate accountings while announcer Jay Stewart is writing things down and figuring them out. I have never yet been found wrong. The fellows in the control room try to catch me, but they haven't yet.

Lying alone in bed while I recuperated, I invented football, baseball, and hockey games that could be played with a deck of cards, a piece of paper, and a pencil. Later, I created "playing fields" on which "players" might be moved with everything from Mah-Jongg pieces to tea service. Unfortunately, I never patented them—they were similar to games devised and sold successfully in later years. They were a satisfying diversion, however, and when I started to play outside again and couldn't keep up with the other kids, I used these games to lure them back to my house.

My father was intrigued by my ability to read the racing form and select winners. He would play this game with me each night and challenge me to dope the races. The boy genius did just that, juggling the speed ratings and past performances and class of competition and jockey's abilities and coming out with a remarkable record of winners. At home, that is. When I was taken to the track, I lost the skill, and was wiped out. No one beats the races—not even a smart-aleck kid.

We moved to the Elmwood section of Winnipeg and I started at Lord Selkirk School. The kids in that area were rougher and tougher than any I had experienced, and they took turns beating the hell out of me. My classmates were older and bigger, and I was overwhelmed outside the schoolroom. I had nothing. Every year I looked forward to the annual show put on in an arena by the Native Sons of Canada. They staged amateur boxing bouts and gave free hot dogs and soft drinks to the kids. That was the highlight of my life then.

When my father was sidelined with boils, my mother went to work selling life insurance and advertising for a local newspaper. After he recovered and became a butcher, she helped in the store. And so did I. The conditions were dreadful. The money I earned was for the family, not for myself. Sometimes I worked as the delivery boy so my father would not have to pay another helper. I never had the ice skates I wanted, or the bicycle, or the new leather jacket. My folks gave me what they could, but they could not give me much.

Actually, I started helping my father when he began as a butcher and was running the concession counter at the delicatessen. Soon I spent my lunchtime there, then my time after school and my weekends. Using a wagon in the summer and a sled in the winter, I made deliveries to nearby customers, while he took the truck to make more distant deliveries. After he got his own shop, he no longer had his truck—it had broken down, I suppose—and he had to borrow a car from relatives.

Soon he got me a bicycle so I could make deliveries all over town. I was eleven or twelve years old and considered strong enough. I weighed less than a hundred pounds and used to pile more than a hundred pounds of meat into a large carrier on the front of my bike and start off. I could make the north end deliveries in a series of short runs, but the south end deliveries had to be made in one long trip, which included twenty to thirty stops and took several hours.

MAURICE HALPARIN
I didn't want to give my son a hard time, but those were bad times for us. We needed his

help, and he resented some having to give it. I don't blame him, but I couldn't admit it at the time, which frustrated me and made my temper short and words often sharp.

ROBERT HALL (1973)

Monty can remember harder times than I can—he helped our family out of them. Monty can remember the rent collector coming and our dad hiding out back because we could not pay him. Monty can remember when dad had to drive him at the butcher shop because he needed his help. Monty retains resentments of those early days I never formed. I think he was wrong, and I have told him so. But then I was six years younger and never took the full brunt.

MONTY HALL

It always seemed to me I covered a hundred miles a trip. In recent years I returned to my old route, went over it in a car, and found that it ran somewhere between sixteen and twenty miles. I remember sweating in the summer heat, and much worse, freezing in winter temperatures that sometimes dropped to forty below zero. I wore moccasins and heavy breeches and a winter jacket of some sort, and what we used to call an aviation helmet, like those worn by pilots in World War I. It came right down over my ears and buckled under my chin. But it couldn't keep the cold out. My nose ran, my eyes watered, my feet and fingers grew numb.

ROBERT HALL (1983)[viii]

At first, I did the deliveries on a bicycle, with a bushel basket in the carrier piled high with parcels. In a winter blizzard, the wheels would get caught in the streetcar tracks. All my meat and me would go sprawling on the icy roads in a tumble.

MONTY HALL

I would sneak into stores to warm up along the way. A few customers were kind enough to invite me in and give me something hot to drink. Others couldn't care less. They would leave me standing outside while they closed the door and took their time getting the money together. I remember all of them, the ones who were kind and the ones who were not, and some of them come up to me now and are surprised that I remember them, their names, even their addresses. One thing I never will forget is making those deliveries on my bike in the bitter cold. I still feel that cold. I remember those years all too well, and it is not a pleasant memory. I hated those days.

RICHARD HALL, son (2019)

Being poor really left its mark on my dad. Even when he was an adult, and he became comfortable, and then he became wealthy, he still thought like a poor person. My mother would cook dinner and my father would be shocked by the portion sizes sometimes. "You cooked too much food! Look at how wasteful that is! So much waste!" We had a gardener and he'd get charged for the gardener. "It's so much money! Why are we spending so much money for this?!" Well, Dad, it's because he's a gardener and we're in Beverly Hills.

Long distance phone calls, too. You had to speak in a very efficient way if you made a long distance call in our house. You had to keep it short, and Dad would grill you if he saw a call on the bill that took more than a few minutes. Don't even think of leaving a room without turning off the light.

SHARON HALL, daughter (2019)

"Why is the heater turned on?!" That was another big part of our childhood.

My dad wasn't cheap, but he was thrifty. Soap was a running joke in our family because my dad saved the soap and shampoo from every hotel he ever stayed in, and he was always trying to get us to stop spending money on soap and shampoo. He'd try to pawn off his soap from the hotel to us instead.

I had a chance to go see all the sights from my dad's childhood. I saw the site where the butcher shop used to be—it's gone now—and I saw Haslet Street, where he grew up. No offense to my Winnipeg cousins and friends, but it's easy to look around and imagine that when my dad was a kid, it must have been a one-cow town. It's flat, it's sprawling. It blew my mind that he was loading his bicycle on the north end and then spanning the entire town with deliveries when he was just a sick little kid.

RICHARD HALL (2019)

It's possible that I'm reading too much into this, but my dad never rode a bike during my life. Now granted, by the time I came along, there was no reason for him to do that. He had a car, he got other kinds of exercise. But he told us all about his childhood, having to pedal that bike through the streets of Winnipeg in the winter, and that sticks out to me when I look back on it. Once my dad was an adult, he never, ever rode a bicycle again.

MONTY HALL

When I was about thirteen and in the tenth grade, my father bought a 1929 Whippit, a little four-cylinder car that had to be cranked up when it wouldn't start. The car cost $150, and my father swung it by borrowing $50 apiece from three friends. Our business had grown some, and customers complained I was getting their deliveries to them fast enough with a bicycle. My father figured I would do better with an auto, although I was not legally old enough and so small I could hardly see over the steering wheel. My father took one day to teach me how to drive.

He put me in the car and he said, "Here's the gas pedal and here's the brake and here's the clutch. Here's how you shift into first, second, third, and reverse. Now you get behind the wheel and you do it."

I did it terribly, and he yelled at me a lot, but soon he decided I was set.

That very day he drove me back to the butcher shop and he gave me an order for a customer about two blocks away.

"Here, take the car and deliver this," he ordered.

I was scared to death. My mother was scared to death. She screamed, "He can't drive. He could get killed. Or he'll kill someone."

But my father said, "He'll manage. By the time he gets back, one way or another, he'll be driving the car."

So, I got in that car and I went. Somehow, I started it and I bucked and heaved my way down the street. I practically ripped up the gear box. I was terrified, but somehow, I made it. I got back to the butcher shop in one piece without having killed myself or anyone else.

By the time I was fourteen, I had been driving for two months. Strangely, no one ever stopped me. The longer I drove, the better I got, and it made my life much easier. There was a heater in the car, so I froze only when I had to get out to make a delivery. Physically, I was not as exhausted.

ROBERT HALL[ix]

It got lonely making deliveries on a Saturday night and my buddies would always offer to accompany me. Today some of the best-known citizens in Winnipeg claim they got to know the town by riding with the Hall brothers on their meat delivery route.

…It was kind of nice, finishing my Saturday night deliveries, and then staying up until 2 o'clock on Sunday morning, playing pinochle with my mother and father.

Robert, though he found at least a dim flicker of a "bright side" to the experience, still recognized his father's misery in the butcher shop. In rare moments, his father was even able to muster a smile and joke about it. He once asked his dad for a raise to $5 a week. Maurice shot back, "You better shut up or I'll make you a partner in the business!"

ROBERT HALL (1999)[x]

He once said to both of us, "I don't know what you want to do with the rest of your life, but whatever you do, make sure that when you go in for a day's work, that you want to go to work."

MONTY HALL

When I graduated high school at fourteen, I began working full-time in the butcher shop. The boy who had been working part-time was let go so my father could save the six dollars a week he had been paying him. Most of my friends were sixteen or seventeen years old and ready to start college or go to work. I had been able to spend little time with them, and now they began to drift away from me. They joined fraternities and made new friends. For a while I was invited to their parties on Saturday nights, but I usually could not make it because I had to work late at the shop. Soon I was left alone.

I found new friends among others who could not afford to go to college or had not found steady jobs. This was during the depression, and many young men were without much to do. It was like the old song, "Standing on the Corner Watching All the Girls Go By." That's what we did I was beginning to be interested in girls, but few were interested in me. I could not afford them. The girls in my high school group were older than I and by then were dating college boys. So my drifting friends and I patrolled the streets of our neighborhood in the evening and, with ten or fifteen cents in our pockets, ended up at Oscar's delicatessen, where we occupied a booth or two in the back.

We spent half our free time in these booths. Oscar was a kind man. For five cents he gave us a plate full of small slices and crusted ends of rye bread that he otherwise would have thrown away and a thick slice of salami and, for another nickel, a Coke. For ten cents we had a feast with all the free mustard we could use. We talked, we ate, and we sat. And then we went home. Sometimes we went to a movie. But that cost ten or fifteen cents, and when we got older it cost twenty-five cents. We just couldn't afford it very often, that was my life and I didn't like it.

My life revolved around the butcher shop. There I worked hard—without pay—yet I was treated as just another worker. My father was a difficult man to work for. He never hit me, but his temper was like a whip. His voice used to cut me to shreds. He'd buy a small side of beef for as little as possible and have to sell every part of it to come out ahead. But most customers obviously wanted the best parts for the least money. My mother took phone orders and tried to talk customers into taking common cuts. If she failed, my father would be furious and take out on her the wrath he felt for the customer. He was always insulting customers, and my mother was always trying to soothe their ruffled feelings. Customers were important to us.

My mother was the buffer between my father and his customers, between her husband and his sons. She suffered those days in the butcher shop, this brilliant, gifted woman, so she could spend nights with her clubs, with her charities, with the shows she often wrote and produced. This was her social life, because my father refused to share friends.

MAURICE HALPARIN

I am not proud of it. I could not give my son the material things other sons get from their fathers. I hated this. I ran from my life as much as I could, trying to be something even when I had nothing. I had my pride. I always tried to dress nice, to be neat, to leave the stain of the bloody shop behind me, to wash it away. I gambled some. I enjoyed the companionship of other men. I never ran around on my wife. She had her clubs, her charities, her friends, too.

I wish I could have done more, but a man cannot be ashamed of doing as much as he can. I know my son realizes I did all I could do. I was never as close to him as his mother was. They had a very unusual relationship. I never saw so much love between a mother and a son as they had. My son was much like his mother. He is talented and outgoing and confident, as she was.

There's another way that Rose Halparin influenced the man that her son became. In later years, Monty Hall described childhood memories of electricity and water being shut off in his home because his parents were too far behind with their bills. Yet there was always a box for charity money—a Tzedakah box—in the kitchen. No matter how bad things were, Monty was constantly reminded that there was somebody less fortunate.

Rose once confronted a wealthy citizen of Winnipeg who had notoriously never opened his wallet for any worthy causes. Rose caught the man in mid-brag about his son, who had been raised similarly not to contribute any part of the fortune he was inheriting.

"Do you know how much my son is worth?" he asked.

Rose snapped back, "No, it's not how much he's worth, it's how much he's got. He's got $2 million, but he's not worth anything."

MONTY HALL

[My father] suffered those days in the butcher shop, and he lived for those nights at his club. And when he came home late and my mother reproached him, they would argue bitterly. I would hide my head under the pillow so as not to hear them.

Still, she was a diplomat by nature. I remember one Saturday morning, when I was about fourteen years old. My father had been out all Friday night and had not yet come home. My mother was waiting at the window, weeping. Seeing me, she wiped her eyes and called me to her.

She said, "Monty, I want you to do something for me. Your father will be coming home any minute now. He's been out all night playing cards. He does it because he is desperately trying to make some money for his family. And he always fails. We have to show him that he doesn't have to be a big financial success to be a big man to his family.

"When he comes in, I'm going to get into an argument with him because there is no way that I can just let him stay out all night without a word and worry me to death without complaining about it. But after we have been arguing for about ten minutes, I want you to come into the room. I will draw you into the argument. I will say something about how terrible it is to stay out all night, and I'll ask you to tell him how terrible you think his actions are. But, instead, I want you to tell him you think he's right, that he has a right to stay out if he wishes, that he is the man of the house and is just trying to help his family, and that I am wrong for arguing with him and complaining about it. I want you to take his side."

I was too young to understand what she was up to, but I trusted her and she talked me into doing as she asked and also into never telling him about it. When he came home, my mother drew him into the inevitable argument.

After a while I walked into the room and she turned to me and said, "Ask the child, ask him how he feels."

Feeling full well that my mother was right and he was wrong, I said what I had been told to say about the rights of the man of the house. I said, "Daddy's right. I'm on his side."

My father at first seemed stunned, but then swiftly accepted the unexpected and turned triumphantly to my mother and said, "You see, you are wrong. Even the boy says I'm right. So, it shows what you know." And he stormed from the house.

I was almost in tears, but my mother gathered me in her arms and said, "Don't worry. You did your job well. Wait and you will see what happens now."

Ten minutes later my father returned with a quart of ice cream and a big smile on his face. My mother started to smile, and then they both started to cry.

Soon we were seated at the table eating our ice cream happily amid laughter and tears. Slyly, my mother winked at me, warning me. I realized then that somehow, she had handled it just right. I saw how she saved a man's pride and shown him that he was loved. I will never forget it.

ROBERT HALL (1973)

My dad suffered in comparison to my mother. He did not have her personality, her popularity. But my dad was a good family man and father. He suffered frustrations which made him temperamental. But he worked a lifetime at work he loathed, endured the intolerance of others, and gave us everything he could.

Monty favored our mother. He was incredibly close to her. She has been his inspiration above and beyond all others, even his wonderful wife. He became closer to our father in recent years, but he did not give him his due most of his life. I have argued with Monty about this. It is about the only argument we have had.

Monty recognized the hardships that molded his father into the man he became, but somehow, even that made him feel closer to his mother.

MONTY HALL[xi]

My determination to see only good in life came from her. My father saw only bad in life because life treated him badly. My mother loved everyone until proven otherwise. That's the way I am…You can get hurt a lot in life by trusting people, but you sleep a lot better.

CHAPTER TWO

Monte Halparin
who plays Johnny, the student
president. He sings the hit song,
"Tag, You're It".

(Author's collection)

As a teenager, Monty became a fan of radio quiz show called Treasure Trail. *For a genius who was witnessing the world passing him by as he toiled for a meager wage, the idea of a handsome reward for knowing a lot appealed to the young man. Although* Treasure Trail *didn't offer a fortune, Monty at least thought he could make a comfortable chunk of pocket money if he could just be a contestant on the show.*

MONTY HALL[xii]
I was such a brilliant young man, and there was no question I couldn't answer. I listened for 39 weeks and never missed.

Then I got on the show and the host said: "For five silver dollars…" and I thought, "That's a week's pay!"

"Name the Scottish New Year." For 39 weeks, I'd never missed at home. This was my big chance...I couldn't answer it. But if you want to know the answer, I've never forgotten it. Hogmanay.

Even if Monty had won the five dollars, it was only enough to make life easier for a week. The week after that, and the week after that, and the week after that would all be the same as before. It wasn't that Monty lived from day to day not knowing what would happen next. Quite the opposite, he always knew exactly what tomorrow was going to look like. That was the problem.

MONTY HALL

The two years between high school and college were unpleasant. While my friends sit on to college, I worked full time for my father in the butcher shop without pay, unable to participate in a teenager's social activities. On Saturday nights I frequently had to deliver meat to homes where my friends were giving parties. Frequently, too, the kids would sing the old classic, "The butcher boy, the butcher boy, I'm going to marry the butcher boy. Oh, Mama, oh, Mama, how happy I will be. Oh, Mama, oh, Mama, the butcher boy for me."

Too young to handle this embarrassment, I'd hang my head and leave. as fast as I could. I was a, lonely boy who desperately wanted to go to college. I knew my parents could not afford it, but I was determined to raise the money. My mother was all for it and argued with my father, who was more realistic about our finances and who long since had given up on dreams.

Finally, my parents decided to start me off at the University of Manitoba and see how long it could be sustained. Tuition was $150 a year at that time, and the cost of books and student activities was $25. My mother had put aside a lot of twenty-five cent pieces over the years, and these small savings and some money my father raised saw me through the first year of college.

My clothes were a big problem. All my life I had worn hand-me-downs from my mother's younger brothers. I had not had a new suit since I was thirteen, and now that I was seventeen, my mother felt I needed one. My father did not. A new suit at that time cost about $18. A hand-me-down from one of my uncles could be altered to fit me fairly well for $2 or less. In the end my parents compromised and bought me a heavy sports coat and a new pair of slacks. I think I wore that same outfit for three years.

Going to the university was an emancipation. I was freed from the butcher shop. I was back, with my peers, and college excitement loomed ahead. I arose between six and seven in the morning, took a streetcar across town to the university, and did not get home until after six in the evening. My father began to use my younger brother more and more in the store and took on more and more of the side duties himself.

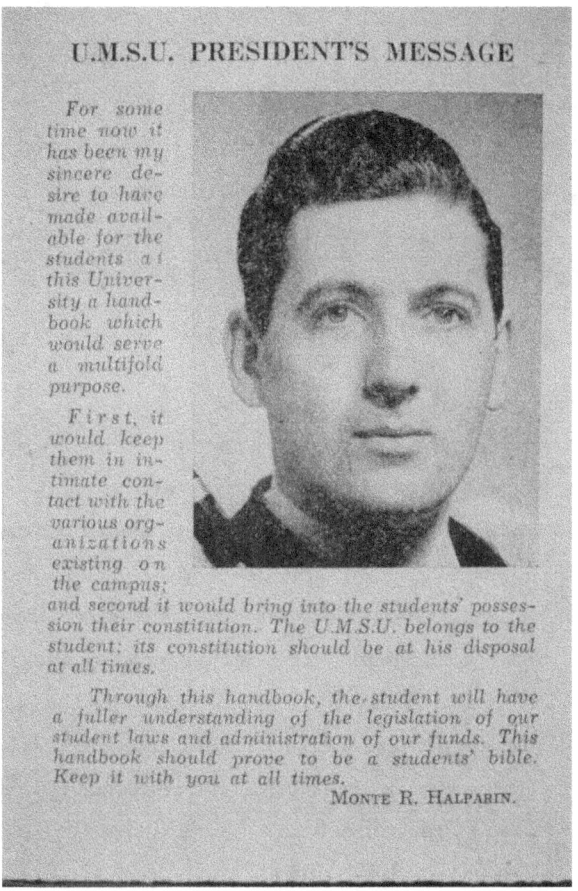

University of Manitoba Student Union President Monte Halperin, as pictured in the school handbook. (Hall Family collection)

I still made deliveries on Saturdays and collections on Sundays, but the butcher shop no longer was my prison. The first year of the university, the equivalent of the last year of high school today, was considered a period of adjustment. The studies were easy, and I had plenty of time to go out for athletic teams and drama programs.

After a summer back in the butcher shop, I was at first relieved to return for the second year of college, then depressed to find it much tougher than the first year had been, simply because I had rushed headlong into extracurricular activities. I wasn't prepared and I began to do poorly. By this time World War II was in its early stages. I was nearing draft age and was serving in the Canadian Officers Training School, a sort of ROTC program. I got the idea it would be glamorous to become a young officer, and I volunteered. When I was turned down, I was deeply disappointed. The war was just starting, and officer selection was still being handled on an elitist basis.

Reluctantly, I returned to my studies. I dropped out before the final examinations, and anyway I had run out of money. It seemed to me that there was no point to going on with college. I had to go to work, but I just did not want to go back to the butcher shop. I took a job in a wholesale clothing house, making nine dollars a week. Lunches cost twenty-five to thirty-five cents a day, and the job was close enough that I could walk to work. Since I lived at home, other expenses weren't high. So, I figured I could save five dollars a week and put my kid brother through college someday.

ROBERT HALL (1973)

Monty has been magnificent to me. There was a fantastic relationship between us despite the difference in our ages as we were growing up. He was my mentor, wanting me to be all the things he had not been able to be. He coached me as a boxer and baseball player. He counseled me. He encouraged me to go to the University of Manitoba, to make as much of myself as possible. He urged me to go back to law school and financed me in the early years.

Whatever I wanted to do, Monty was for it. He represented strength to me. Financially, he was always behind me. I never had to worry about losing out. I remember once he bought an extra car just so there would be one for me to borrow, because he knew I needed one and would not have accepted it as an outright gift. He has always done for others. He did for me, our mother and father, other family and friends, his own family, of course, and countless strangers through countless charities.

When no one could help him, he helped himself. In the early days in Toronto and later in New York when he was not getting anywhere and he had to survive layoffs, he was sure enough of himself, brave enough, tough enough to stay with it. I am proud of that in my brother.

MONTY HALL

If I had been humbled by working for my father at the butcher shop, I was humbled more by working for a stranger. The boss was a hard man who spoke broken English. Receiving an order on the telephone, he would shout out to the help: "Do we got there sufficient sizes?"

He had trouble remembering names, but that didn't bother him. He referred to Mr. McCorkindale, the manager of Eaton's, the finest store in town, as "Mr. McCockendoodle." He didn't even try to remember my name. He asked the accountant what I was called. When the accountant said "Monty," the boss sneered, "What kind of a name is Monty?"

From then on, I was called either "Say" or "Boy." If he wanted me, he'd merely raise his voice and shout, "Say, go get me two boxes of underwear." Or if I was not in sight, he'd yell to someone, "Call me the boy."

My job was to do all the small things others were too big to do. I arrived in the morning before anyone else and swept the floors with a long broom. When I finished, I went upstairs, uncrated clothing, and stacked it onto shelves. Then I made deliveries to department stores. At six, after sweeping all the floors again, I was finished. At night I went out with my young friends and tried to play the man about town on my small wages.

I worked there for a year. Then came the first of two turning points of my life in Winnipeg. One day another clothing man called me and said, "I have a buyer in town I want to do business with, but he has his son with him and I don't know how to get the boy out of the way. I'm sure he'd like to go out, and he's about your age. Get a date for yourself and somebody for him, and take him out. I'll lend you my car and give you enough money to cover your expenses. It'll be a free night out for you and a life-saver for me."

This was a bonanza for me, and I readily agreed. The boy turned out to be a fine young man. I found us a couple of dates, and we had a great time, and laughed the night through. I played the big sport and insisted on picking up all the tabs. He had no idea someone else had paid the bills and thought I was quite a high liver. He called the businessman the next day to tell him how pleased he was to have been entertained by such a splendid lad.

That afternoon my boss decided that the front steps needed washing. "Get the boy and tell him to wash the steps," he ordered.

Soon the boy was on his hands and knees with a bucket scrubbing the steps. As I was working away, a visitor almost stepped on my fingers.

"I'm sorry," he said.

It was the young man. Our eyes met when I looked up, and in a second, we realized the truth about each other. We were both embarrassed, and in another second, he was gone. I never saw him again. But I never forgot him.

This was one of the most humiliating moments of my life. I had pretended to be something I was not, and what I really was, was brought home forcibly to me. A cruel embarrassment. That night, in tears, I told my mother what had happened. She gave me a lecture in pride that I have never forgotten. She pointed out the indignities she had suffered throughout her life and how she had endured them. I realized that this magnificent woman who had achieved much more than I had and who had been subjected to so much more abuse, had learned to handle herself with real dignity.

Now, it may seem corny now, but I will never forget my mother looking into my eyes and saying, "Do you know the Rudyard Kipling poem 'If'? And let me quote the first few lines to you: 'If you can keep your head when all about are losing theirs…'"

Such was her way of restoring my confidence and picking me up.

The episode in the clothing store was a turning point of consequence. All the years of working in the butcher shop, all the hours of wire-brushing bloodstained cutting blocks and delivering heavy loads of meat in below-freezing weather, all the uncrating of clothing, of sweeping floors, of scrubbing steps, of being treated as if I were less than nothing, all the embarrassments I had suffered with my friends—all of it suddenly stiffened my desire to succeed in life.

I determined somehow to make something of myself, to rise in the world and bring my mother, father, and brother up with me. I resolved to return to college and study to be a doctor. But how could I make it? A second turning point provided the answer.

Across the road from the wholesale house in which I worked was another run by a man named Max Freed, who was about ten years older than I was. His father had established the operation and made his son president at twenty-one, and now, at thirty, he was running the business by himself. He ran it well, and it was an enormous success; all of which others overlooked when they criticized him. People said his father had provided him everything, and now he was wasting it. He was a handsome young man and a bachelor, and he was quite a young man about town.

Freed noticed me making deliveries to his plant. One night, when he encountered my father playing poker at a club, he asked him what I was doing. Why, he wondered, was such a fine young man working at such a poor place?

My father said, "It's very simple. He has no money. We have no money. What alternative is there?"

When Freed suggested that I should go to college, my father replied honestly, "I imagine he would like that very much, but what about money?"

Freed said, "Have him come to see me tomorrow."

When my father came home, he told me of the conversation, but I didn't get my hopes up too high. Nevertheless, I went to see Freed the next day. He asked me if I wanted to return to college. I did. What did I wish to study? I mentioned medicine.

"Well, I'm going to arrange it," he said. "You will go back for as many years as you need, taking whatever courses you need. I want you to write down how much money it will take for tuition and books and clothing and your weekly expenses. In a few days, when you have figured it out, show it to me and I will give you the money."

I was stunned. I couldn't believe it was this easy. Why would he do this for me? I went away and made up my list of expenses and kept it modest to make sure it was not too much. I left out the clothing and limited the lunches, streetcar fares, and so forth to $2.50 a week. Nervously, I took the list to him.

Monte, brimming with confidence as he concluded his education. Max Freed's generosity altered the course of his life. (Hall Family collection)

He looked it over and said, "You haven't included anything for clothing."

When I replied that I didn't need any, he said, "I want you to have a couple of nice suits. We'll add that on. And you can't possibly handle your other expenses on $2.50 a week. We'll double that so you can go like a gentleman." It came to about $300 a year.

Then he explained why he was doing this. He said, "I have had everything in life given to me and I want to help people who have nothing. I have already tried it with a couple of others, but they have disappointed me. One showed signs of being a brilliant scholar, but both dropped out. I don't want you to disappoint me. So, there are several strings to my proposition. One, you must report to me monthly and show me you are maintaining a high grade average—or the deal will be dropped. Two, you must promise to eventually pay me back every penny. Three, if you can, you must help others in the same way some day. And, four, you must never tell anyone about this except your parents."

I agreed, and though I never became a doctor, I kept every promise except the last one. I reported regularly and formed a firm friendship with this amazing man. I got high grades. I paid back in full the $900 he advanced me. When I could afford it, I began to help others and have sent several through college. But I could not keep his secret forever. When others criticized him, and put him down as a playboy, I could not resist straightening them out. The so-called playboy had moved into my life where the town's aristocrats had failed me.

In Manitoba, criticism of Max Freed never fully waned. He lived lavishly. He loved golf so much that he founded Glendale Golf Club in 1941. He invested his earnings from his clothing empire in thoroughbred racehorses. He expanded his portfolio to include hotels and poultry farms. Because he was born into such comfort and started his business with his father's money, Freed was scorned for his opulent lifestyle. In reality, he gave quite generously to numerous causes throughout his life but chose not to trumpet his giving, quietly writing checks and tolerating the barbs about the way he lived. Although Monty understood it, he seethed at the criticism for the man who changed the course of his life. Freed held Monty to a promise never to divulge where the money came from, but Monty only kept the promise for 30 years, finally "outing" him when he wrote his autobiography. Monty felt the good deed should be acknowledged, and on a grander scale, he hoped that giving attention to the act would encourage people to be more generous with their fortunes.

SHARON HALL (2019)

I didn't learn until very shortly before the end of my father's life that there was more to this story than he had really been telling. For years, the story that my dad told about Max Freed, in public and to me, had been that Max was a man whose father owned a business across the street from where my father was scrubbing steps.

It turned out there was more. Max and my father were fairly close in age, so Max began inviting him to join him at social events. My father was just riddled with shame at the time because he saw himself as a charity case. But Max worked really hard to develop a relationship with my dad among his own circle of friends, and he helped bring my father into his own with socializing and interacting with people. I didn't know that until my father was on his deathbed, but Max helped him in more ways than just financially. He really brought my father along socially and gave him self-confidence.

ROBERT HALL (2019)

I knew Max Freed a little bit when I was younger because I would go to the club where he and my dad both went to play cards. And Max's mother had been a good friend of my mother because they were both involved with Hadassah in Winnipeg. Max's mother was a member and my mother was president. It's impossible to put into words what Max meant to Monty, though.

MONTY HALL

I had a new outlook because I had a new obligation. Before, my parents had been behind but they had not pushed me. Now, this friend was behind me, too, and he was pushing me hard. I pushed myself. I could attend classes without worrying about how to pay for them, I could live well while pursuing life as a student. I had decent clothes on my back, my hair was cut, and I had a few bucks in my pocket.

Although Freed wanted me to restrict myself to my schooling, I insisted on working at his wholesale house one day a week and at my father's shop on Saturday nights. I picked up other jobs after school every summer to help out as much as I could.

I plunged into university life. I lettered in athletics, wrote for school publications, performed in school shows, headed school organizations. I became, in fact, a "big man on campus." I was spirited. Although I could not be compared to the rebellious youngsters today, I was always an outspoken activist for various campus causes and was frequently in hot water with university officials and my professors.

When I finished my final pre-med semester of studies, I stood in the top ten of those who were applying to medical school, some three hundred in all. But although seventy were accepted, I was not. The explanation: there was a quota system at the time, though no one would talk about it. Winnipeg had a large ethnic population, and many Jewish students applied to med school. The school accepted three or four students from each minority, including women, and gave the rest of the places to Anglo-Saxon Protestants.

When I told Max Freed, who had been so proud of my progress and so sure that admission would be granted me, he was furious. But he encouraged to remain in school and seek admission again.

Disappointed, but intent on making med school the next year, I remained at the university and took another year of science—the recommended procedure for promising rejects. Again, I got good grades, and was elected president of the Science Student Body. The latter was considered the highest honor a student in science could attain. I was called "Senior Stick" and my benefactor and my parents were tremendously proud of me. I was also the president of the University Booster Club and active in athletics. Again, I applied to med school, and again I was not accepted.

The next year I did well a third time, and at the end I was elected president of the entire student body of the university, but I still failed to make med school. Then I decided to remain in school for a fifth and final year—and to fight the med school's prejudiced administrations practices. I joined with several prominent attorneys and businessmen who started to investigate the situation and apply pressure to have it altered.

Meanwhile, as president of the student body, I tried to right other wrongs. At this time, there was considerable public criticism of the university as a hideout for "slackers" from the war effort. Despite the fears of officials, I organized an "open house" at the university campuses. The public was invited to see the university at work. Thousands went through laboratories and classrooms, listened to lectures, watched their young at study, and came away convinced that there was purpose to such endeavor. The press stressed that much of the research being done would benefit the war effort. The open house was a smashing success. But college officials never forgave me for going against their wishes, and this probably resulted in my loss of the alumni medal.

Every year the alumni presented its medal to the outstanding student on campus. At the end of my fourth year, the alumni met and decided that I would be the recipient; but because I elected to go on for a fifth year, they decided not to make the award but save it for my graduation the next spring. As a result, no award was made that year to anyone. When the alumni met with student representatives in my fifth year, I was expected to receive the medal. But the alumni and the professors sitting on the committee had other ideas. They voted the medal to another student. Whatever their reasons for literally stealing my medal away, they remain theirs to this day. When David Robertson, my close friend and my successor as president of the student body, came directly to me to tell me the news, he broke down.

"There was no discussion," he said. "It was a *fait accompli* when I arrived at the meeting."

I was crushed. I had had a great college career, probably one of the greatest any student had ever had at that university; and I was left with the taste of bitter ashes. It is a generation since then, but I have never forgotten.

In my final year I had begun to work for the local radio station. I had a disc jockey show seven nights a week. Before that there were other jobs, and some of them were less than grand.

Monty the surveyor. (Hall Family Archive)

I got a summer job building airfields with the Department of Transport. The fields were strung throughout Canada, and I was assigned to Portage La Prairie. I became a chain man, which is the lowest job on a survey team. Although the temperature was ninety or more, we wore dungarees, heavy shirts, hats, and boots because the air was thick with mosquitos and flies and we usually worked on swampy farmland. The surveyors staked out the land and the airstrip area and used hand signals to instruct us where to string our chain. It was backbreaking work, lasting ten to twelve hours a day and paying forty cents an hour, six days a week. I averaged about sixty-five hours and $25 or $26 a week—out of which I paid $8 or $9 for breakfast and lunch as well as the room I shared with another worker. I had to pay for my suppers. If I wanted to go out on a date or buy a bus or train ticket for a trip home, the rest of my salary was wiped out. I was not saving a dime.

The foreman was tough. One scorching afternoon a truck stopped to dispense lemonade and drinks to the field workers, and the survey gang asked him if we could have some.

He laughed and told us to get it. I could have murdered him on the spot.

When the crew moved to Souris, there were reasonably priced rooming houses, and we had to stay at the hotel. Room and board was $15 a week, which really left little for other expenses. One weekend I went home, and on Sunday night I caught a train from Winnipeg to Brandon, where I expected to make a connection to Souris, thirty miles away. When I got to Brandon, however, I found there was no train to Souris, and no bus until the next morning. It was eleven p.m., and I was due on the job at seven a.m. or I would be fired. I had only enough for a room for the night or any other kind of transportation. So, I started to walk.

I hoped to hitch a ride, but with gas rationing in effect there were few cars on the highway, so I walked on through the dark, deserted lonely night. For a while I whistled. Then I stopped whistling and began to tire. Fortunately, I had no luggage. By six in the morning I had covered eighteen miles, and it was light. A bus bound for Souris came along, and I had enough for a ticket. I arrived at my hotel at seven, just as my roomie was leaving for work.

He said, "Hurry up or you'll be late."

I was too weary to care. "To hell with work," I said, and fell down on the bed. And I added, "To hell with the Department of Transport and to hell with the foreman."

In the late afternoon I woke up and walked over to the office where they were winding up work for the day. The foreman said I was fired. I said I quit. A traveling salesman was parked outside the hotel, and I hitched a ride home to Winnipeg with him.

The summer was far from over, and I needed another job. So, I went to work for the Canadian Wheat Board. At that time there was a surplus of wheat and farmers were being paid by the government to keep their fields unseeded. Inspectors checked out the size of the farm so each farmer could be paid properly. A fellow sitting at one desk read these reports aloud. I sat at the next desk and entered the details in large ledgers. There were rows and rows of us at desks doing the same thing. It may have been the most boring work anyone ever did.

The only break in the monotony came when it was discovered that I had some small theatrical background. Asked to put on the board's annual show for employees, I became the producer and director, and I also took part in it. It was a great success. A few days later, however, I was caught conversing on the job. Other than the reading of official reports, no one was allowed to talk while working. I always talked and I had been warned. This time the straw boss fired me. So that was all for that summer. As a producer-performer, I was accepted; as a talker, I was fired.

During winters I began to work for a troupe that traveled around entertaining at service installations. The war was in full swing, and people put together shows privately and visited bases and hospitals. Harry Zimmerman, an old Chattaqua circuit vaudevillian, came out of semi-retirement to start a troupe with his wife, Elizabeth, and I got a spot with them. Our shows were called "Priorities of 1941" and so on.

After my last class in the afternoon I hurried to catch a bus that rushed us 50 or 100 or 150 miles to an army post or airfield or hospital. We did two shows for the enlisted men and a third for the officers. Then we climbed back on the bus and returned to town. Often, I arrived about seven in the morning and had to go straight to class. It was wearying but exciting. I emceed the show and did comedy routines. I also sang alone and with a girl singer. It was the best training I ever got in show business, and I loved it. Among the local kids in that show were Morley Meredith, now with the Metropolitan Opera, Iva Withers, who headlined on Broadway, and many others who toured in Canada and the States.

Coached and encouraged by my mother, I had been performing in school and club shows since I was a child. In college I played the lead in an original musical comedy *You Can't Beat Fun*. David Yeddeau, who directed the show for us, went on to direct radio shows and asked me if I wanted to work for him. I said I did, and whenever I could get away from classes I worked at Station CKRC, whose studios were in the Royal Alexandra Hotel in Winnipeg.

My first show was a disaster. I had a small dramatic part. After our dress rehearsal we had a half hour until air time. Someone said Lily Pons was in the lobby of the hotel. I had grown up listening to opera records and I idolized the great performers. I rushed to the lobby in hopes of getting a glimpse of Miss Pons. I never found her. Suddenly I remembered the show. Dashing back, I found Yeddeau reading my lines on the air. He froze me with a chilling glance, thrust the script into my hands, and went into the control room while I went on with the rest of the script. Later, other members of the cast took me aside and explained how bad it was to miss a cue, much less a show, without good reason and sufficient warning for a replacement to be found. The director must have assumed I learned a lesson from this mishap because he never said a single word to me about it. I was not fired, as well I might have been, which probably would have nipped my show business career just as it was budding.

ROBERT HALL (2019)

When Monty started in radio, I was still working at the butcher shop. I was close to the end of high school at that point.

I was making deliveries in my dad's car during a rainstorm, and lightning struck the car. I wasn't hurt but it scared the hell out of me. It's funny looking back because you realize we know things now and we didn't know them then. The police were baffled when I explained what happened because the car had tires on it. I'm not joking, at the time, conventional wisdom was that there was something about automobile tires that would prevent lightning from striking a car. The kids at school teased me about it the next day when word got out about what happened. "Bob's got lightning in his pants!" But I laughed it off and forgot about it.

As it happened, after Monty went off to college, business got slightly better for the butcher shop. My dad moved the whole business into a nicer section of Winnipeg and was able to make a living. Never a great living, but a nice living. Things got a little bit easier when he moved the business across town.

Monty's job at CKRC included performing for a different Canadian Army base every Sunday. He'd do three shows, one for the officers and two for the enlisted men.

MONTY HALL[xiii]
That was the best. They talk about comics getting their training in the Borscht Belt? The army shows were my Borscht Belt. You went from one Army camp to the other and at the Army camp before a thousand soldiers, you emceed the show, you did the burlesque bits, you sang the patriotic songs, you did all these things. Then you went and did another show for the officers, and you got on the bus and came home at three in the morning. These were the best audiences in the world…so that was great training for me.

The great training was near constant. Radio in the 1940s commanded such versatility from its performers that it didn't take long for a rookie to become a seasoned veteran.

MONTY HALL
I began to do a great deal of radio work. I pinch-hit as an announcer and did small acting parts. In my last year of college, Esse Ljungh, a prominent producer and director of drama for the Canadian Broadcasting Corporation in Winnipeg, auditioned me and hired me to play the parts of many young men in his shows.

I was young and indoctrinated early into the hard-talking, hard-drinking, free-living life of the broadcasting people of those days. They played a lot of practical jokes on each other, and I took part in them. Our sportscaster, Arthur Morrison, was about seventy years old and fair game. Once, when he sat broadcasting into a mike, we filled a wastebasket with news clips and set them afire at his feet. Our newscaster, Ron Alderson, always had his four o'clock newscast prepared by two o'clock. No matter what happened in the world during the intervening two hours, he was set. Once we inserted a recipe for frying fish into the middle of his copy, and he read most of it before he realized what he was reading.

Another newscaster, Cy Cairns, always was able to make me laugh with a line or a look. It got to the point where he could simply stand in front of me while I was broadcasting and he would break me up. The sponsors started to complain, and I determined to get revenge. Cy did the twelve o'clock news in one of our glass-walled studios. Sitting at his table, he faced directly into a corridor. I put a pile of chairs and junk atop a desk and shoved it all in front of his window while he was broadcasting. I then stood on the desk, stripped off all my clothes, and sat stark naked atop the mountain of rubble. Cy didn't crack a smile. He had anticipated something of the sort, and he had lettered a sign, which he held up as he continued speaking into the mike. I was so surprised by the funny obscenity that I fell to the floor—and limped the rest of the semester.

My work at the station on the six to midnight shift covered lots of different shows—a singing program, a quiz program, and a disc jockey program, along with various acting and announcing roles and the job of directing an ethnic musical show. How I got the singing show is a strange story. I sing, but I'm no Sinatra. The station had a musical program, *Concert at the Console*, which needed a soloist. I had a friend I felt could fill the role and I arranged an audition for him. I went along, and after he had finished, I was asked to sing, too. I did—and I was hired. My friend was not. And that is how I beat out Morley Meredith of the New York Metropolitan Opera for a singing job. It is possible that the people at the station were not the best judges of talent.

I was now making $50 to $60 a week working part-time on radio in Winnipeg while my father was making $25 to $30 a week working full-time in his butcher shop. I had paid my own way through my fifth and last year at the university and wanted to begin repaying Max Freed. I had stirred an investigation into the quota system at the medical school, but after my fifth year I did not bother to apply again. By then I was fed up and finished with that and excited by thoughts of a career in show business.

That year, of 78 or 80 who were accepted for Medical School at the University of Manitoba, I believe 26 were Jewish, and many others were members of other minority groups. My closest friend was among these. But I was not. I was satisfied that I had played a part in righting a situation that was dreadfully wrong.

As so often happens in life, a bad experience had good consequences. I might have been a good doctor. Who knows? I do know that I have been successful in show business and that I am happy with my profession. But at the time I started up the path into show business, I had not the slightest idea how tough the way would be.

CHAPTER THREE

MONTY HALL

Originally it appeared that the world of entertainment would somehow have to wait until I had done a hitch in the service and the war had ended. I had been serving in the university's reserve officer training corps and therefore was protected from having to serve in the regular Army. I did not feel guilty about it, because I'd volunteered at the start of the war and been rejected; and I had later volunteered for the army's entertainment corps and been rejected for that, too. But now, with my college career concluded, it appeared I would be going into the army.

The colonel in charge of our college officer training program was not one of my biggest boosters. In Canada, we had a service review board that was supposed to classify college graduates according to their fields. But as is the case with most such classification systems, the graduates' backgrounds were ignored and they simply were inducted into the infantry. I wrote an editorial in the student newspaper pointing this out and suggesting the board was a waste. The colonel did not like it and threatened to court martial me and strip me of my reserve officer's status.

I then enlisted to serve in the European theater where the Canadian Army and all of the British Empire forces were primarily involved. I was to go to camp as usual for two weeks, after which I would be transferred from the reserves to the regulars.

While we were in camp, V-E Day came. The colonel wanted a solemn ceremony staged at the camp and suggested I put it on. In short order I rounded up some talent, rehearsed a choir, and presented an essentially religious program. Backed by a large chorus, I sang "The Lord's Prayer." Near the end, the colonel was introduced to offer official comments. He gave a speech. It was a great moment in his life, and he wept. The show was well received and later he came to me to tell me all was forgiven.

Then it was discovered that because our enlistment papers had covered only service in the European theater, we had fulfilled out contract and were free of commitment. We were asked to volunteer for the Asian theater, but I declined.

The colonel came to me and said, "Do you realize that as the president of the student body of the college, you are a leader and an example for the others? If you don't sign many of them won't either."

"I don't care what the others do," I replied. "I just want out."

Suddenly, I was back on the outs with him and he was as angry as it is possible to be. But he was also helpless. I was a free man. In his frustration he followed me into civilian life, went to CKRC, spoke to the station manager, Gerry Goetz, and demanded I be dismissed as a slacker. Goetz threw him out of his office—for which I have always loved him.

The colonel's only revenge came when he refused to permit me time off from camp to attend my graduation ceremonies. I received my Bachelor of Science degree anyway and went to work for Goetz and CKRC, beginning my real career in June 1945. My immediate supervisor was program manager Jack Kemp. He was a marvelous man who believed in me. His inspiration carried me through many a frustrating period that year.

I remained on the six-to-midnight stint, but I worked every other shift, too. When I wasn't working, I was at the station helping or trying things out. I did music shows, sports shows, quiz shows, dramatic shows, interview shows, man-on-the-street shows, every single sort of show. On V-J Day, for instance, I reported on the celebration in downtown Winnipeg.

I stood on top of a recording truck and described the incredible scene of celebration. I jumped on a streetcar to interview people. It was a great, wild, exciting day, the most memorable of my life for years. I also learned a lot about how to produce and direct, and I spent a lot of time creating new shows in the hopes they would get on the air someday. I learned some of the engineer's duties. I did everything they threw at me, and loved it all. It was hard to tear me away from the station. I was only making $60 a week or so, but I was satisfied.

I seemed to be making it. At least, I was off to a swift start. I sent Max Freed a $100 check at the end of the first year. I was to send him another $100 check at the end of the second year, and a $700 check at the third year, wiping out the debt. Much later when I was in New York and he wanted World Series tickets for four business friends, I promised to get them for him. I refused to accept any money and willingly paid a scalper $200 for four fine seats, never letting Max know how I got them.

That first year out of college my best friend, who was to start medical school, came to me and asked for help.

He said, "I have enough money for my tuition and just about enough to get through the year, but I haven't enough money for my books or microscopes or other supplies. Now that you're working, could you lend me some money?"

I had $225 in the bank. I withdrew it all and gave it to him. He took it gratefully and returned to school and later repaid the loan. Today he is a successful doctor, and we remain close friends. This was the first interest payment on my promise to Max Freed.

People in my position are constantly asked for cash to cover rent or operations or some need for some desperate circumstance, but obviously we cannot respond to the many problems of strangers. But from the time I had money to give, I have given it to those who seemed deserving. Often, I have been paid back, often I have not.

I was paid little in my early years in radio, and after the first flush of enthusiasm for my new field wore off, I began to feel frustrated. At CKRC the veterans were content to coast and laughed at the hustle of an ambitious youngster like myself. Yet they got the choice jobs and the top money. I was used only as a fill-in. If the sportscaster tied one on and didn't show up, I was rushed in to pinch hit. If the newscaster played sick, I served in his place. Yet they kept their positions, while I couldn't seem to improve mine. One night the Dominion Network blacked out and we had to improvise several hours of programming. I went to my desk and pulled out a quiz show, a sports show, and two musical shows I had worked up and put them on. From 7:30 to 10:30 that night, I was the producer, the director, and the star of all our shows. I was our station. I was proud but received little recognition.

This situation was especially depressing because I had been burying myself in work deliberately. Since the summer of '44, I had been going with the daughter of a Los Angeles couple who returned to Winnipeg each year. After my first date with her, a blind date, I began to see her every day or night, and we swiftly grew serious about each other. So much so that her father checked with friends to find out why I had not been accepted into medical school. He liked me. But his wife did not like the idea of a broadcaster, a son of a butcher, with about $18 in the bank as a prospect for her daughter. She tried to discourage us.

Nevertheless, at summer's end, when she returned to Los Angeles, we had an understanding that we were at least unofficially engaged. If I did not make med school in my last year, I would go to California to work in broadcasting. There I could be near her, and we could pursue our romance. All my final year in college I corresponded with her. But near the end of the school year, she wrote me a "Dear John" letter. She had met someone else; she had fallen in love; she had just become engaged. Shortly thereafter, I heard they were married. I was young, and a romantic, and I was crushed and resentful. So, I plunged deep into my radio work after graduation. And when I swiftly felt frustrated, I acted.

Early in 1946, I went to see Gerry Goetz and told him I thought I rated better than I was getting. He agreed, but he did not offer me more. Instead, to my surprise, he spread a map out on his desk. He said that it was a map of Toronto. I pointed out that my plea had nothing to do with a map of Toronto.

He disagreed. "This is where you have to go. Toronto is the big time for broadcasting in Canada. I've been watching you ever since you began with us and I believe you can make it in the big time. I could give you a few dollars raise or a new show. I don't want to do that because I don't want you to stay here. If you do, you'll become like the other regulars—fat and lazy, and going nowhere. You're young and you're going somewhere. And my advice to you is to go. Go now."

I thought about it. There was nothing to keep me in Winnipeg. Toronto, indeed, was tops in Canadian broadcasting. So why not try there? Why not try Montreal, too—and even New York? I had saved another $250. On the night of my parents' twenty-fifth wedding anniversary, I announced I was on my way. I remember friends and family were there.

I was explaining, "First I go to Toronto and make several calls at stations there for five or six days. Then I go on to Montreal and spend four, or five days visiting stations there. And then I'm going to take a week in New York and try the big city."

And someone asked, "And then what?"

My grandfather interrupted, "And then Monty comes back home to Winnipeg."

And everybody laughed because they all believed that would happen. But I was determined that it would not happen—and it did not. I left Winnipeg and returned thereafter only to visit.

In mid-February 1946, I got on a train with all my belongings easily squeezed into a single valise and went off to Toronto. I moved in with a friend and began to make the rounds. Selling myself was not easy. I was a budding talent but couldn't prove it in a brief interview. I had a good personality, but not the beautiful baritone voice of Orson Welles, Lorne Greene, Joseph Cotton, or Howard Duff, some of whom began as announcers and went on to become actors.

I went to see Andrew Allen, head of CBC Drama in Toronto, and others at the Canadian Broadcasting Corporation. I went to CFRB but received no offers. Then Don Insley offered me a job with CKEY for $175 a month. I thanked him and asked for some time to decide. I went on to see Jack Part at CHUM and he seemed impressed but not enough to make me an offer. I ran out of Toronto stations. Before I went on to Montreal, though, Jack

Part changed his mind and offered me $225 a month to join CHUM. I told him I would let him know. In Montreal, I was asked to work on overseas broadcasts for the CBC's International Division, but that didn't appeal to me. I went to New York and got exactly one interview, which was arranged by a cousin who was working as a writer there.

The man told me, "You're an emcee, are you? Listen, son, when I want emcees I call Danny Kaye or Bing Crosby or Bob Hope, not a kid from Canada."

It scared me half to death. I couldn't even get in to see anyone else. I stood on the sidewalk watching the St. Patrick's Day parade, then went to a telegraph office and wired Jack Part in Toronto, accepting the offer and saying I would report for work at CHUM as soon as possible.

In a few days, I was there. Jack Part was short and stocky with wavy gray hair and the dancing eyes of a pitchman. He owned a patent medicine business, and he recorded programs for his elixirs and placed them stations throughout Canada. His remedies were doing well, but the station was not. CBHK was a daylight station, operating from sunrise to sunset, and it was not making any money. Part, however, was a joy to work for, and we took to each other right away.

One thing Part didn't like was my name. I was Monte Halparin then and he thought I needed something short and sweet. We tried a lot of combinations without hitting on one we liked.

Then I suggested, "How about just cutting my second name in half?"

He said, "Monty Hall, that's fine."

I did not know that he did not know how to spell my first name. I woke up one morning to find billboards all over Toronto announcing a new show with "Monty" Hall. I shrugged and accepted it. Later I had my name legally changed. (My brother, Robert, also changed his name to Hall, not knowing that Robert Hall was a familiar name in clothes in the U.S.)

ROBERT HALL (2019)

I worked in the butcher shop until 1949, when I left Winnipeg and followed my brother to Toronto. I reasoned that people wouldn't understand why two brothers had different last names, so when I arrived in Toronto, I changed my name.

The name change didn't bother our parents in the least. My father had such a terrible relationship with his side of the family and was much closer to my mother's side of the family, the Rusens. So, my parents didn't feel any great attachment to the name Halparin. When Monty broke the news that he was changing his name, they were fine with it. In fact, what made them happy was that he held onto Rusen as a middle name so he always kept a connection that way. His full name was Monty Rusen Hall.

MONTY HALL

Jack Part asked me what sort of show I'd like to do. I had done a musical morning show in Winnipeg with that lovable old pianist-newscaster Cy Cairns, and I said I'd like to do such a show in Toronto. I said I needed a partner who could not only play the piano but sing so we could harmonize some. Part said he had someone who would be almost perfect, a pianist who both sang and wrote his own songs. The problem was that he drank heavily and might not appear every now and then.

I gave him a try anyway, and he turned out to be almost perfect. He didn't mind taking orders from a kid eleven years younger than he, and he did everything beautifully. We called the program *Wake Up and Smile* and it was on seven to nine every morning dispensing songs and snappy patter. Only on the fourth morning he failed to show up, and I had to resort to records. He promised it would never happen again. A week later it happened again. I devised a solution. Every day a taxi picked me up and took to his apartment house, where, hungover or sober, he was roused, showered, rushed to the studio, and shoved behind the piano. This worked for many months.

However, he had another problem. He adored his estranged wife and spent almost all his money phoning her in New York and pleading with her to take him back. One morning I found his apartment empty. There was no word from him for three days. Then he called from New York to say he had gone there to make his pleas in person, but had been refused and was returning. Later he announced that he had accepted an offer to do a show in Winnipeg for more money. So that was that.

I found another partner, a talented man but not an outstanding pianist and it didn't work out well. I tried others, but the chemistry wasn't there. Finally, the program was dropped. Most shows have short lives, and this experience taught me that there are many and varied factors behind their troubles—not all of which are apparent on the air.

Again, there was a silver lining to the cloud. The death of my show probably helped the birth of my marriage. I had begun to go with a lovely young lady named Marilyn and was head over heels in love with her. I suddenly found myself becoming a romantic of ridiculous proportions. I decided I would serenade her every morning on the show, dedicating one or another love song to her. I always asked her later how she'd liked it. She realized it was important to me and tried to be enthusiastic. The problem was she was going to school, working as a radio actress on the side, and going out with me nights. I could get by on four or five hours sleep a night, but she could not. Getting up at seven in the morning to hear me sing "Embraceable You" when her first class didn't start for three hours was beyond love or duty. Fortunately, the show went under before our romance did.

There was no shortage of shows for me. I did radio sports shows and play-by-play. Since my early days back in bed with burns and pneumonia, I had studied sports record books, especially Frank Menke's *Encyclopedia of Sports*, and I was full of trivial facts about sports history. At CHUM, I had a sports quiz show on which people asked me such things as Rogers Hornsby's lifetime batting average and who held the flyweight boxing title in 1907. I could answer almost all the questions then, though I can't now.

I loved doing play-by-play hockey and football games. But I loved even more doing live on-the-spot broadcasts, something that sadly has almost disappeared from radio. With an "actuality" broadcast, you never know what might happen. On a show broadcast from the steps of City Hall called *What Do You Think?* I interviewed passers-by on topics of the day. Larry Mann was my assistant. Larry now is a prominent character actor in Hollywood and remains a close friend. Larry's job was to select interesting-looking persons and talk them into going on mike with me. He was my "grabber." I trusted his judgment.

One day he shoved someone in front of me and I asked: "What do you think about the Hamilton steel strike?"

The man replied with a startling string of obscenities. The show was live and his words were going put over the air. In panic, I turned and started to run from him. He started to chase me, and only Larry's flying tackle saved what was left of the day.

Another time Joe Louis, then still the heavyweight boxing champion of the world, came to Toronto to play a golf exhibition. He said he didn't want to do any interviews, which disappointed the radio men of the area. I figured if I could get to talk with the champ it would be quite a coup. I was young and brash. I raced over to his hotel, went to his room, and announced I had a parcel.

In a big, booming voice, he said, "Come in."

So, I went in, portable recorder in hand instead of a parcel. I said, "I'm sorry for the deception, champ, but I was desperate to see you for an interview."

He growled, "I said, NO interviews."

I said, "I know you did, but I'm a young guy working hard to get ahead and an interview with you would be a big help to me."

He looked at me a moment and then said, "All right," and waved me to a seat.

It was one of my first "scoops." Today Joe is a "greeter" at Caesar's Palace in Las Vegas, and I see him from time to time. He recognizes me, but it must be in television. I'm sure he has no memory of that morning I crashed his room. I call him "champ." Life has turned difficult for him, but he will always be "champ" to me.

I also covered the arrival of Alexander of Tunis, who had become the new Governor-General of Canada. The government gave him a parade, which was to wind up at the 48th Highlanders Building. I found a perch on a wide ledge just above the first story of this building and broadcast from there. To our disappointment there were no speeches. As the parade ended, Alexander was hurried into the Highlanders Building. As I was climbing down, I happened to look into the room below me and there was Alexander and an aide. On impulse I jumped into the room through an open window and went up to Alexander with live microphone in hand.

"Sir, would you be so kind as to say a few words to the people of Toronto?" I asked.

Even as I spoke, I knew something was very wrong. The aide looked terrified. Then I saw that he was holding Alexander upright. I took a closer look at the Governor-General and realized that he was three sheets to the wind. Suddenly, I was terrified. Thanks to my rash act Alexander's reputation was at stake. And I couldn't back out. I had to leave the microphone in front of his face. With the majestic bearing and resourcefulness that had preserved the British Empire for centuries, Alexander somehow rose to the occasion. Drawing himself erect, he gave a glorious, articulate address to the people. All the while his eyes were rolling in his head. Swiftly I thanked him and announced we were returning to the studio. And Alexander collapsed on a couch.

I also broadcast our city's welcome to Field Marshal Montgomery, the Empire's greatest World War warrior. He was paraded to the City Hall, but the caravan was extremely late, and I had to fill in a lot of empty time. I had done my homework and had much material on Montgomery to pass on to the public. My eyes swept over the waiting crowd and saw mothers with babies in their arms, decorated veterans, and other interesting types, and I described the scene as colorfully as I could. There were other stations there, too. They had teams of three or four while I was alone with an engineer. But they weren't as dedicated as I was. Floundering to fill time, one had inched closer to me and was beginning to repeat almost exactly what I said. It was as though I had an echo. Soon, I noticed another moving near him and repeating his words. I was getting angrier and angrier.

Finally, Montgomery arrived and was ushered without a word into the mayor's office. Through a friend in the office, I knew he would be there only briefly. Guessing that the others might not know this, I made a swift decision.

As the cheers of the crowd were dying out, I announced, "And that covers the arrival of Bernard Montgomery of El Alemain to Toronto. I thank you for being with us. We now return you to our station."

The others said some of the same, signed off, and began to pack up. As my engineer prepared to pack up, too, I whispered to him to fake it, and I said quietly into the mike, "However, it is possible the general may return shortly, so we will play some music and we hope you will wait."

The others had packed their gear and were leaving when Montgomery suddenly emerged with the mayor. I was the only one with a live mike and I moved up to them and asked the general, "Sir, would you say a few words to the people of Toronto?"

He did just that, then departed. I had an exclusive interview. The others stood there in surprise—and how they cursed me! I couldn't have cared less.

Jack Part liked me well enough to make me CHUM's program manager at $500 a month. I felt pretty important. But Part also made a fellow named Roly Ford sales manager, and we didn't get along at all. Ford said he couldn't sell the programs I programmed. I said he couldn't sell anything. In radio and television, the sales manager always wins. I'd had my new job for only a few months when Jack Part made Roly Ford the station manager and told me I was to report to him. Roly Ford told me I was no longer the program manager, but I could remain as a performer at $500 a month. Having no alternatives, and no loss of income, I accepted the demotion and continued to work my shows.

There is also a moral here. I have often preached that no matter what jobs you may lose or what conflicts you have with your superiors, "Always leave the door open when you leave." The fact that I accepted Roly Ford as my new superior without a scene resulted in my continuing on without loss of salary.

Esse Ljungh arrived from Winnipeg to take up a new position as a producer for the CBC in Toronto. I applied to him for acting work but was turned down. He told me he didn't want to be accused of using his pets from back home. He didn't have to use me, of course, now that he had the cream of the crop to pick from. At one point, I was asked by John Crosby of Dancer, Fitzgerald and Sample advertising agency in Toronto to emcee the Canadian version of *Truth or Consequences* which Ralph Edwards was emceeing in the U.S. I was excited by the opportunity to do my first national network show, but nothing happened. I checked into it and found that the advertising agency and the CBC were at odds over money, and they also accepted advertising on shows, but they objected to a program that gave away merchandise in exchange for free plugs from companies, which then did not have to buy commercials. This has always been a sore point in the business, and in this case, CBC finally rejected the program.

Disappointed, I went to the CBC to protest to Ernie Bushnell, who was the head of programing and an important man there. I pointed out that I was being deprived of my big break because a show that was considered good enough for the U.S. was not considered good enough for Canada. Bushnell said he was sorry, but that was exactly the case because the CBC had certain standards it felt necessary to uphold.

But he then opened up a folder and pulled out a dossier, and he said, "I've been doing some research on you. Frankly, I feel you have shown enormous ambition, imagination, and talent. I can't imagine why you are worried about losing a job as emcee of a quiz show. You have much greater potential than that. I'm so sure of it I'll bring you into the CBC right now as a producer."

I was stunned. Many men had worked for the CBC for years without attaining that height. As sure of my ability as I was, I would not have even thought of seeking such a position at that point in my career. I was flattered. The CBC was the cultural network in Canada and had a country-wide audience. As a producer, I would have the opportunity to do important shows. Unfortunately, my first reaction was to ask him how much the job would pay. And when he said $4,500, I was disappointed. I had made $4,800 my first year in Toronto and was making $6,000 my second year. At the CBC everybody started at a set salary his particular job called for and got small raises periodically—a typical government operation.

I said, "Mr. Bushnell, you're asking me to go back to making less money than I made in my first year in Toronto broadcasting,"

And he said, "Yes, but look at all the prestige you will get working for the Corporation. This is as high as one can go in in Canada, and you can become a truly creative artist."

And I said, "I am aware of all that, but I have been a poor boy all my life. I hope to become creative in broadcasting, but I must do it on a level in which I can be well paid for my effort and I don't think the CBC answers that need. I am truly grateful for your offer, but I have to decline it."

He seemed astonished. It was the first time but not the last that I looked at a situation and took the road toward greater earning potential rather than creative opportunity.

I must add I never have regretted turning down the CBC offer. Ego didn't enter into it because I would have had much more prestige as a CBC artist than as anything I've been since. I would have liked that, but at that time in my life $6,000 was a lot more money than $4,500 and a lot closer to the $10,000 I was shooting for. If I had taken the Job, who knows, I might still be in Canada earning $15,000 to $18,000 a year and being terribly frustrated because there was insufficient money to produce something the way I wanted. I might be rated a creative talent, perhaps even an artist, but I would not be nearly as happy as I am at present. Today I am making big money, and have had the opportunity to do things for family and friends. But I must admit that if an equally lucrative chance came along, I'd try to escape the game shows and establish myself as an artist in another area of show business.

CHAPTER FOUR

MONTY HALL

I met my wife through a mutual cousin named Norman Shnier. I was a cousin on his father's side, and she was a cousin on his mother's side. Norman had been a prisoner of war in Germany. Released early in 1946, he decided to resume life in Toronto and arrived there when I did. He told me about his other cousin.

He said, "You just have to meet her. She is adorable."

I asked, "How old is she?"

And he said, "She is eighteen, and a senior in high school."

I smirked. "Oh, she's too young for me. I'm a college graduate."

"But she's a radio actress," he added. "You have something in common."

And I said, "My God, if there is any one person I don't want to meet it's some precocious eighteen-year-old radio actress."

MARILYN HALL

I started working young and helped out the family. I accompanied a friend down to a radio station where she was to audition for a dramatic part. After hearing her, they asked if I wanted to read, too. I did, and I won. For some years, in the middle forties, I was one of maybe three ingenue radio actresses in Canada who got most of the major roles available to us. At times I made as much as $140 a week, working with the elite of the business. I did not know if I wanted to act all my life. I was interested in writing, and when the time came, I wanted to go to college.

MONTY HALL

Norman wrangled a dinner invitation to her family's home. While we were standing outside talking, this girl came walking toward the house. It was Marilyn. She had a trench coat draped over her shoulders and a model's even walk, and as she approached, I saw that she had a lovely face. Something inside of me seemed to say, "Look out." She gave me a soft smile and said hello in a gentle, pleasant voice.

We went in. Her parents were separated, I learned. She and a younger sister, Peggy, and a maiden aunt lived with her mother in this small, modest six-room house on Eastbourne Avenue. Marilyn was working as an actress and helped to support the family. She had read about me in an interview printed in *Radio World* Magazine. In the interview I had spoken about being president of the student body at the university, and about all the broadcasting I had done at an early age, and about how I hoped to reach the top in Toronto when I got there. For a guy with a buck and a half in his pocket I exuded confidence to the point of cockiness, and that's the way Marilyn read it. All during dinner she baited me. I didn't expect that from an eighteen-year-old, and some of her needles had sharp points.

She let it be known that while I had been doing bit parts for Esse Ljungh in Winnipeg, she already had acted coast-to-coast as Alice in *Alice in Wonderland* and *Alice Through the Looking Glass*. She still was getting top ingenue parts around Toronto, while I was just breaking in with an early-morning show. She was making as much as $90 a week at eighteen while I was making $60 at twenty-three.

Marilyn had the upper hand on me. She wasn't obnoxious about it, but she did make me feel less mature than I was. Her mother was very nice until she realized I was serious about Marilyn. She wanted more than me for her daughter. Not that her daughter was throwing herself at me. In fact, she refused my first requests for dates and did it like an adult turning down a child.

Once at dinner I sent her a little note asking, "How about going out with me this weekend?"

She passed me back a note saying, "No, I can't."

Then when she saw my expression, she passed me another note that said, "There, there, don't be too upset."

I was being patronized, but I persisted and I finally got a date with her.

By the oddest of coincidences, I had already met Marilyn's father. He had been the Toronto manager of Warner Brothers motion picture company and had been slated to become the Canadian general manager. His separation from his wife disrupted his life, however, and he was passed over in favor of an underling, who promptly fired him. He found a new position as Canadian General Manager of Monogram Pictures, and every morning he had breakfast in the same place I did before doing my show. After I found out that Marilyn was his daughter, he and I began to eat together every morning. As so often happens in such separations, the mother had given Marilyn and her sister a one-sided version of their marital difficulties, and it had turned them against him. He seldom heard from them and was eager to hear what news I could pass on. Whatever the marital troubles, whoever was to blame, he was a nice man who missed his wife and daughters very much.

There still were little things to be settled between him and the family, and Marilyn agreed to go out to dinner with me one night to discuss them. Another night we went to a dance. Later she went away to a camp, where she was a counsellor, but when she came back she wanted to have dinner with me again because I could be the go-between between her family and her father. We went to an Italian restaurant. She looked beautiful to me and I realized how much I had missed her and how much I wanted her. Then she told me she was going to marry someone else.

She said that a fellow she had been dating on and off for a couple of years wanted to announce their engagement when he returned from a business trip.

I said, "Does he know that when he gets home he will have lost his girlfriend?"

Marilyn laughed a little and asked, "What do you mean by that?"

I smiled. "I mean you are going to belong to me."

"Oh, really?" she replied.

"Really," I said. She just laughed again.

We went together all through the rest of that month, getting closer and feeling the love developing between us. We hated to part at night. When we had night broadcasts, we'd often walk back to her home. On one such walk my breakthrough came. Her boyfriend had been away for six weeks and was due back the next day.

I said, "I think it's time you told him about us."

She looked at me a long time, then smiled and said, "All right." The next day she broke the news to him.

Immediately her friends started dropping by her house to tell her she was making a mistake. If I was there, they'd ask her to go outside for a minute so they could talk to her. Some of them, I suppose, were sent by her boyfriend. I laughed it off, figuring that they would not get very far in trying to divert Marilyn from her course. I was right.

Marilyn's mother applied considerably more pressure, however. Other young men were interested in Marilyn. One was heir to a real estate fortune, and another was in medical school. Here was Marilyn, committing herself to a radio announcer without any certain future. Through the next winter Marilyn and I fought all efforts to break up the romance. On May 17, Marilyn's twentieth birthday, I gave her the gold ring that I had received as president of the university student body and we announced our engagement.

MARILYN HALL

When Monty and I met, I was going steady with a boy I had grown up with. We had drifted toward marriage and were almost engaged. But he was out of town and Monty wanted me to go out with him.

I didn't want to just sit home, so I started to go out with him. I had no one to talk to, really, so I talked to Monty. He was a good listener and a good talker. The first thing we found between us, and not the least thing, was that we could talk to one another. He became quite a rock, someone I felt I could trust and lean on.

Monty says he knew all along we'd get married but I sure didn't. When I went away to camp, I left him easily enough, but then there was an emptiness.

I looked forward to going back to be with him. And when I went back, I realized I had fallen in love with him. I was very much at ease with him, and I knew there was a life for the two of us together.

MONTY HALL

Marilyn was at the University of Toronto and was acting on radio on the side. Her mother kept trying to get her to change her mind about me. She enlisted other relatives, who would call up to counsel Marilyn not to act rashly. Marilyn was a strong girl, but that summer she was down to ninety-four pounds and I was worried about her.

We decided on a date to get married and so informed both sets of parents. But Marilyn's mother had one last shot to fire. She called Marilyn's father, buried her pride, and asked him to try to talk his daughter out of it. He wanted us to marry, but I suspect he was willing to do almost anything to win back his wife's favor. So, he telephoned Marilyn and started to talk against the marriage.

Luckily, I happened to be there and I took the telephone from Marilyn and said, "Joe, the wedding is going to take place on September 28 in Winnipeg. We invite you to give the bride away. If you don't come, someone else will. But the wedding will take place, with or without you."

In a sad voice, he said he was sorry for having interfered and he wished us well. Marilyn's mother was out of ammunition.

I felt sorry for him. He kept up a bold front while his life was falling to pieces around him.

Marilyn and I were married on September 28 in Winnipeg, as I had announced. We restricted the guest list to close family and friends, so we had only three hundred or so in attendance, and upset several hundred we didn't invite. My family had lived in Winnipeg since the turn of the century and had spread out in great numbers in that area. Marilyn had family there, too. Her mother and father and sister came. Her father gave the bride away. Marilyn had saved $2,000, and she paid the railway fare from Toronto for herself, her sister, and mother. She also bought her own trousseau and new dresses for her sister and mother. I had about $1,500 saved up and I blew most of it on a second-hand 1941 Ford we called Crasty, short for procrastination, so named because I procrastinated a long time before buying it.

My family gave us $500. I'm sure they didn't have a thousand dollars in the bank, and it was a tremendous gift from two people who were barely getting by. Of course, my father always was a sport, and when it came to the marriage of his first son, he was going to dig deep. It was a grand gesture.

It rained the day of the wedding, and Marilyn, leaving where she was staying to go to the hotel, spilled a suitcase full of everything she had. It looked like a bad day all around. But a friend from my army shows, Harold Green, provided his quintet as a present, and when we walked down the aisle at three on a Sunday afternoon, the sun came out and shone through the windows on us.

We were to have honeymooned in the lake area of Minnesota, but I had just been offered a new radio show which was to start a week after our marriage, and we felt it was wise to cut the trip to a short holiday in the Toronto area.

On our wedding night, we boarded a train for the trip back to Toronto. An uncle was supposed to have booked us a private bedroom compartment, but all he could arrange were upper and lower berths. Boldly, I broke the news to my bride that we were not going to be split up on our wedding night and would share a single berth, no matter how narrow.

It may sound old-fashioned and unlikely, but the truth is Marilyn and I had resisted the terrible temptation of sex throughout our courtship. But now the time had come. Maybe it was not the perfect place, but it was time. I stood outside in the aisle while Marilyn struggled out of her clothes and into a nightgown and robe in the cramped lower berth, and then she waited outside while I struggled out of my clothes and into my pajamas. I called my lovely bride to me and she climbed inside the berth. That was when I saw the face staring at us.

It was a teen-aged girl and she was peering at us from through the curtains of the adjoining berth. I was sure she had seen us come on board with Marilyn wearing a corsage and had guessed we had just gotten married. She was curious and fascinated. I whispered to Marilyn that I was not about to make love to her as long as that girl was watching and listening. Nor were efforts to outstare the girl successful. She just kept staring back. I can still see that face.

So we lay side by side in our little berth and stared out the windows at the rolling prairies of Canada and hoped the girl would go to sleep, but she seemed determined to stick it out to the finish. Every time I opened the curtains, there was the face! Eventually we drifted off to sleep. In the morning, I called the porter aside and asked if our berth could remain a bed for a while and he smiled patiently as if to say even a newlywed must realize there is a limit. He was sorry but he had to fold them up into their daytime seats. It was a one-day, two-night trip from Winnipeg to Toronto. As we entered the dining car for breakfast that morning, I spotted the teenager sitting with her mother. The kid had bloodshot eyes and looked as if she had been up all night, which indeed she had. We sat up all day and talked, and that night when my bride and I got back into our berth, there was that teen-aged face. We didn't even attempt to wait her out this time.

Arriving in Toronto, my bride and I sped off to the Guild Inn in Scarborough, on the outskirts of Toronto. It was the opening day of the World Series. I was a big baseball fan, and I wanted to hear the game. I sat down and pulled a pencil and a paper out of the desk drawer and started to draw lines. Marilyn, who was unpacking, asked me what I was doing.

I said, "I am making up a box score."

I will never forget the expression on her face. She knew nothing about the World Series, and thinking that this was the day that her sex life was to begin, she was stunned.

I reassured her, but insisted on listening to the game. I believe it was the Yankees and the Dodgers. If I remember right, the Yankees won. In any event, after the game we finally won.

We moved into our first home—a bedroom. That was the only room we had. We rented from a couple with a three-bedroom house in the Rosedale section in Toronto. The family had been comfortably fixed until the husband suffered a stroke and the wife had to let out the two smaller bedrooms to make ends meet. She built a tiny bathroom for us on top of the garage. The bathroom was unheated, and we endured some chilling cold that winter. And the night we moved in, part of the bed collapsed under us. We didn't bother to fix it, not that night. Youth can put up with a lot of things.

We made do with a small hot plate and a toaster, which we kept in our room. Every morning Marilyn went down to the kitchen and got our milk and maybe some bacon and eggs from the common refrigerator and made us a hot breakfast. Then we'd go off to our places—me to the radio station, Marilyn to her second year at college.

CHUM assigned Monty and a fellow radio star, Barry Phillips, to do a goodwill performance of sorts for the station, asking them to sing at Toronto's Hospital for Incurable Children. In a time when parents of disabled children tended to keep them hidden from society, Monty had never seen a handicapped person until the day he visited the hospital. He and Barry Phillips enjoyed the experience of performing for the patients so much that rather than be assigned by the station to make an appearance, they started going there in their spare time to put on shows for the kids. Marilyn's father, Joe, learned of Monty's hospital performances and told him about an organization called Variety Club; Joe was a charter member of the Toronto branch.

Variety Club, founded in 1927, had initially been not a charity, but a social group for men in the theater business in Pittsburgh. A year later, the group was in the midst of a friendly card game backstage at a theater when they heard crying. They traced the sound to a baby girl left in the auditorium. Attached was a note from the mother, who said she couldn't afford to care for her new baby, and that she was abandoning her in the theater because she knew entertainers made enough money that they could raise the child. The Variety Club was inspired to do something greater with their resources and turned themselves into a charitable organization. The founders elected not to focus on any one need, or disease, or cause. The Variety Club set out to meet as many needs as possible for children around the world. Monty and Marilyn turned their attention to movie theaters throughout Toronto. Due to "blue laws," most major businesses at that time were closed on Sundays, but theaters could remain open if they didn't charge admission. The Halls arranged with theater owners to show films at no charge on Sundays and instead collect donations. An accordion player and a tap dancer accompanied the Halls. The theater would show half the film, then bring up the lights for a short performance. The accordionist played, Monty sang, and the dancer hoofed it, and then they'd pass the hat as Monty remained at the microphone and described the good deeds of the Variety Club. And then they'd finish the movie. These Sunday afternoon spectaculars would usually raise about $800, and in a way, it was a more lavish incarnation of the cash box that Monty recalled seeing as a child in a house that sometimes had the electricity turned off. He and Marilyn were a young married couple, just barely getting by on their own. But on Sundays, they worked for Variety Club, because somebody needed that money more.

MONTY HALL

One morning we went off without remembering to turn off the hot plate. We returned that night to screams of outrage from our landlady. We had decided to hard-boil some eggs and left in a hurry with the element still on, and they had exploded all over, staining the ceiling. The pot had burned and the room reeked of sulfur. It took days to get rid of the terrible smell and we never did get rid of all the stains. They may be there yet.

After work I picked Marilyn up at the college library and took her out to dinner, though we couldn't afford anything fancy. Afterward we went home to our one-room home, and Marilyn studied and I read or listened to the radio unless I had radio work to do.

It was a confined way of life, but we were young and didn't mind. We paid $87 a month for that one room, and I had to pay $10 more a month to rent a garage for our humpty-dumpty car. We didn't have a lot left.

After a few months we managed to find an apartment in the center of town. Apartments were hard to get, but I managed to find someone who would be an intermediary in the pay-off of $300 key money, divided among the intermediary, the superintendent, and the house mistress. It was torture to pay the $300, but we desperately needed a place to live that at least had a heated bathroom, to say nothing of a kitchen.

The new apartment was across the road from a Catholic boys' school, De la Salle College, and I have three distinct memories of that school. The first is that a rich benefactor died and left the school $5,000 to purchase new brass instruments for its marching band. Every Saturday morning at the crack of dawn the trumpets and cornets started to sound, disrupting my sleep. How I cursed the benefactor! The second is that Marilyn and I used to take a football over to the grounds and play tackle football, rolling over and over in the snow, until we were so fatigued we couldn't move. And the third recollection is that on Sunday afternoons I used to take my ice skates and hockey stick and join the boys in a hockey game. The kids thought I was a member of the faculty and called me "Brother." I hope that when they read this now, they will forgive me. I needed the workout. Come to think of it, they certainly treated their Brother with little respect. More than once they gave me an elbow in the chops and the butt end of a stick in the ribs.

Our apartment was so small that I swear even the mice were hunchbacked. We had one who visited us regularly. We called him "H.B." (short for "hunchback") and he terrorized Marilyn. Coming home from a hockey game one night, I found Marilyn semi-hysterical. With tears streaming down her face she announced, "H.B. was here." I waited for him that night, got him, and gave him a respectful funeral.

We lived there for two years while Marilyn continued her classes and part-time acting. I had left CHUM to freelance, and I often had free time. Frequently, I made our breakfast, made the beds, and cleaned up around the place. Often I could meet her for lunch. She studied a lot in the library, and I passed a lot of time in the local pool hall. A friend and I played what must have been the longest-running billiards series in history. It lasted through two semesters while the girls studied. The loser and his wife were to take the winner and his wife out to dinner at the best restaurant in town. Believe it or not, after six months it came down to the final ball in the final game. I lost, and Marilyn and I had to pop for a fancy meal.

One year a friend told us he could get us a hamburger stand at the Canadian National Exhibition Fair. It may not sound like much, but it presented possibilities. I had worked as a performer for $5 a show almost around the clock during fair week. It was one of the largest fairs in the world, and 250,000 to 350,000 visitors a day had to be fed. Concession locations were hard to land and could be converted into fat profits if you knew what you were doing—which we did not.

We invested in the stand, and my brother Bob joined us to help out. Wes Cox, who had worked for me in radio production, offered to work for me in hamburger production. We decided we needed something different and special to lure customers and Wes came up with an idea in which he sliced a warm hamburger bun in half and ladled cream of mushroom soup over it. Imaginatively, we called it "cream of mushroom on a bun." Later we added "cream of chicken on a bun." We broadcast pitches for our concoctions over a loudspeaker all day long. After the first day, however, we had to make a new tape pitching our hamburgers because so many customers had asked for their money back that we had to discontinue our special snacks.

Marilyn, Wes's wife, Alva, and other relatives helped out at the stand. It turned out to be a tough trick. As we pulled the soft drinks out of the cooler and popped the caps off, water and spray splattered onto the floor, and by evening we were standing ankle deep in slop as we served our customers. Unfortunately, there were not enough of them.

Our biggest days came over the Labor Day weekend. Len Starmer, who now is an executive with the CBC, and his wife and sister came by elegantly dressed and, seeing us swamped, moved right in to help. Len took off his suit coat, rolled up his shirtsleeves and started to sell. His wife and sister took off their white gloves and wide-brimmed hats, sat down on crates behind the shack, and began to peel onions. I will always remember them in their Sunday best, perched on those crates, peeling onions, tears streaming down their faces and messing up their makeup. But what friends!

At the end of each day we would take the cash receipts and compare them with the goods we had used up. They never balanced, not once, not one single day. It was simple to estimate the number of buns and hamburgers sold, but the money always came out short and we never figured out where it had gone. We took whatever money we managed to hang on to, usually a few hundred dollars, home with us at night and hid it. We'd take ice cubes out of the trays and stuff the money in and keep it in the refrigerator. We called it our "cold cash."

There was a sad footnote to this period. Marilyn had become pregnant for the first time that fall, but miscarried. That was a deep disappointment to both of us. She suffered another psychological setback when her father died in Vancouver, a broken man. But tough times matured her a great deal. She buckled down and did exceptionally well during her final year in college. And I bore down, too, and formed my own production company in 1949.

Our first child, Joanne (named after Marilyn's father, Joe), was born in June 1950. My folks had come from Winnipeg to be with us and joined me in a thirty-two-hour vigil. Poor Marilyn was a wreck, and the three of us pacing the waiting room were no better. Finally, Marilyn was taken up to the delivery room, and shortly thereafter a nurse walked down the hall and called out: "Father Hall!" My dad screamed out "Yes!" and ran down the hall toward the nurse. My mother was second, and I placed third. The three of us stood like children at a candy store with their noses pressed up against the window, just gawking. We had a daughter.

Our son Richard was born two years later in June 1952. I was in New York on a three-day conference when I received a call from Marilyn saying she was in labor and my brother was rushing her to the hospital. I forgot about the conference. There was a bus and taxi strike in New York, but some of us at the hotel wanted to get to the airport and hired a limousine for an awesome amount of money. By the time I got to Toronto and the hospital it was evening. But our baby had not yet come. I waited with my mother-in-law until eleven that night, when Ricky arrived. He was born jaundiced. Marilyn has RH negative blood, and it was touch and go for a while, but he made it, and all went well after he survived the early crisis.

We had never definitely picked out a name for the second child because he came three weeks, prematurely; but when I rushed to be beside Marilyn when she came down from the delivery room, she looked up at me, semi-conscious, and said: "We have got our little Richard David." Thus it was decided.

At the time my father's business was not going well in Winnipeg. I helped where I could. My brother, who was now married himself, was still in law school. I flew back to help

Dad move his shop to a different part of town but after a couple of good years, business began to fall off again. He was in his fifties and beginning to feel frightened about the future. I started a small monthly retirement fund for him, and my brother agreed to contribute as soon as his law practice began to pay off. We hoped to see him through his difficulties and wind up with savings of perhaps $25,000.

Eventually, we got him into another business, then retired him and my mother to Palm Springs. But in the early fifties we were all struggling financially and unsure of how well off any of us would be in the future. I was hustling to make my way in radio and by now television. It was an exciting time but an exasperating one.

CHAPTER FIVE

MARILYN HALL

I was a good student. I could have made a career for myself in radio or television, if not as an actress, then as a writer. Monty never discouraged me from it. He worried I would take on too much, but he was proud of me and wanted me to make as much of myself as I could. However, I'm sort of an old-fashioned girl and my family came first. And when Joanne and Richard came along, I drifted out of acting.

When television came along, I lacked the confidence in myself, but I still tried odd things. I remember I did a Kraft cheese commercial in which only my hands were shown on the screen. I ran my hands over some cheese as seductively as I could, and I made $42 a week for it.

But it was Monty's future I was concerned with. I wanted him to get ahead. We talked over whatever he wanted to attempt, but basically, I just supported his decisions. I never even thought about his not making it big. Somehow, I was sure he would. I didn't marry him for that, but even when times were tough, I had that kind of confidence in him. I'd been in show business long enough to know times had to be tough every now and then. It seldom comes easy.

I'm a cowboy. I'll go anywhere and do anything if it's what my husband wants and it's a new adventure. We moved around a great deal as he made his way up the ladder—six times in nine years. Often, he had such deep disappointments I don't know how he endured them and kept going back for more. But he wouldn't give up, as so many others did, and he got it, as so few ever really do. I was with him most of the way, and I know how rough a road it was.

We fit together. We always could talk to each other and still can. We could always both see humor in life and we laughed together. We always have been able to confide in each other. Our love has lasted. Most couples have times when their marriage threatens to come apart, but I don't think we ever have.

MONTY HALL

The radio show I emceed after my wedding trip was called *The Auctioneer*. We auctioned, traded, and dealt things in much the same way we do now on *Let's Make a Deal*.

While Monty seemed to forget a name as he recounted the story later, he happily gave credit for the nucleic form of Let's Make a Deal *to an anonymous staffer at CFRB who suggested that for the last ten minutes of* The Auctioneer, *Monty should go into the audience. Most radio hosts kept the audience at a distance. The staffer proposed it might be different for Monty to interact with them face-to-face, likening it to a "medicine man" selling his potions out of a wagon by appealing directly to one buyer in the crowd he had drawn.*

The Auctioneer *premiered and as advised, Monty spent ten minutes of each show going into the audience and offering money for oddball items. By the end of the second week, people were showing up with handbaskets overflowing with odds and ends collected from around the house, in anticipation of every possible thing Monty might ask for that day.*

MONTY HALL

The Auctioneer lasted only a year, but most shows I did then—most shows anyone did then or do now on radio or television—only lasted one year or twenty-six weeks or thirteen weeks. You have to realize that and accept it. Shows flop, but that doesn't make you a failure. No one knows for sure what makes a successful show. They didn't know then and they don't now. If they did, you wouldn't have so many shows going off every year. You can copy a successful format and put the finest people into it and it probably will still fail.

I learned fast that you try your best, and if it doesn't work, you try your best at something else. In this business you're involved with one show for a while, then another, and then another. That's what makes *Let's Make a Deal* so remarkable. Ten years on the air for one show is a rarity.

In Toronto in those days shows came and went at a rapid rate. I did a lot of different programs for CHUM, but after the sales manager and I had disagreements and he became the station manager, there was a bad situation between us. We both thought we knew it all, and we rubbed each other wrong. I got a few offers from other studios to do other shows, but I decided to freelance for a while.

For a time, I did commentary for the Canadian Broadcasting Corporation. Among other things I did two special programs. On one I covered happenings in Toronto for the evening news. The other was an overseas broadcast in which I covered happenings in Canada for transmission to the British Broadcasting Company. I also cut some singing transcriptions and made guest appearances on various shows. But I really did not do much, and soon I was just eking out a living and beginning to figure out that freelancing was a hard way to go.

Then Rai Purdy called and asked if I would like to emcee not just one but two shows. It was an unusually good break in this business to be offered two shows at the same time—and they were my first national network shows in Canada. One was a quiz program, and the second was a musical variety show. Both lasted one season. The variety show starred Mildred Morey, who was a sort of Martha Raye or Gracie Fields, a big girl with a big voice and a broad sense of comedy. I emceed, sang some duets with Mildred, and served as her foil in some comedy sketches. They brought in an American writer, Sid Resnick, and he wrote a good show.

I was paid $75 for each show, and the $150 a week I made on top of my other work brought my income up quite a bit. No matter how hard times were, I always managed to make a little more each year In Toronto. I made around $4,500 my first year, $6,000 my second, and close to $8,000 my third year. This was not a lot of money, but it was not a little, either, at that time for a journeyman who was still far from stardom. Marilyn and I had been collaborating on some scripts for a dramatic show, *Curtain Time,* and one week we sold two for $300 each. That same week I cut some commercials for the Canadian Department of Health and got $250 for these. With the $150 I was making from my shows, I was up over $1,000 for that week.

I sent a telegram home to Winnipeg: "Dear Folks. Am now making $1,000 a week. This week. Monty."

They got a kick out of it. So did I. It was the first week I'd made that much—and the last for a long time.

Early in 1949, I decided to make a serious attempt to develop and sell new shows through my own packaging house, Monty Hall Productions. At Community Chest meetings, I had met my future collaborator in the hamburger business, Wes Cox, a bright young man who'd been editing a newspaper covering high school activities in the area and doing some broadcasting. I considered him brilliant and enlisted his help. My brother pitched in, too. I hired a secretary who was willing to work whenever there was work to be done and at a very modest salary. The office was my apartment. Several of us worked up show ideas, and I hustled our products from station to station.

I thought we had a shot at success if we weren't shot down by starvation first. I needed a helping hand. Unbelievably, another benefactor came into my life. He was a banker, of all things, and his name was Mr. Houston. I had always thought that bankers were cold, tight-fisted businessmen. Mr. Houston was in his sixties when I met him. I had been using his bank, the Imperial Bank of Canada, since I had arrived in Toronto, and I went to him when I sought a loan. I sat down and told him my background. I said I was starting my own production company, had a few employees, and needed money to sustain us while we sought to sell some shows. I pointed out that we had no production companies in Canada at the time, and that there seemed to be a need for one. I explained that the stations were developing their own shows, but they were not specialists. CBC was doing its own things, and the rest were relying on U.S. transcriptions of shows like *The Lone Ranger* and *The Green Hornet*. There was no Canadian origination of shows especially suited to Canadians.

"How much money do you think you'll need?" he asked.

I braced myself and said, "$2,500." I had figured that with the secretary making $25 a week or so, my brother $15, Wes $50, and myself $75, and with an office I had found for $250 a month, this much money might sustain us for two or three months. By that time, I could be in business. I figured Mr. Houston I would fall off his chair when he was asked for that amount. I thought I'd be fortunate to get anything.

He asked me more about the business, however; then he asked me what I had for collateral. I hadn't thought of that.

I said, "Collateral?"

And he said, "Yes, what have you got to put up to protect your investment in case your plan should fail?"

And I said, "Mr. Houston, I don't have anything. I don't own anything of value. My business has no inventory. All I've got is what is here in my mind and here in my heart. I have ideas and ambition and a willingness to work hard to make this business work and enough experience in the field to know It can work. And I am an honest man. I have never defaulted on a debt in my life."

He seemed to be studying me as I made my plea, which I hadn't prepared and which surprised even me. When I was done, he was silent.

Then he smiled and said, "Maybe it's not the best business for a banker, but bankers are human. We have to take chances on people from time to time even if they don't meet all our standards for loans and such things. You meet a man and you make a judgment on him. I believe you have potential, and I feel you are to be trusted. So, I'm going to take a chance on you. Only one thing—I won't lend you $2,500. I'll lend you $5,000 and put it in a special account for you. I want you to be free from worry for longer than a few months."

I was amazed. I thanked him as gratefully as I could and I promised to do my best by him. But he was not through helping me.

Many months later he called and said, "Monty, have you noticed your overdraft?"

My heart sank. I had not been aware of it.

And he said, "Well, you had $5,000 in the account, and you have sent checks for $5,600."

I felt terrible and I said, "I'm sorry. We've been careful, but we haven't had any money coming in yet, although I think we are on the verge of big things."

Very quickly he said, "Hold on, I wasn't calling you to put pressure on you. I called because I was concerned that you might be upset about it."

I said, "Well, I certainly am now."

He replied, "Well, don't worry. I have confidence in you and I'm standing behind you. We'll just say the loan was a little larger than originally planned."

So, there it was. I had only dreams, ambition, and who knows how much ability? And here was this man who, like other men before him, was willing to be my benefactor. Looking back on it, it is hard to believe. But I can tell you that there are people like this in the world if you are fortunate enough to find them—and you can never repay them enough. I repaid the loan in full, incidentally, but I don't know if I ever made this man realize what he meant to me, to my career, to my philosophy of life, as others, beginning with Max Freed, had meant to me.

We moved into an office that consisted of one large room and four smaller ones in a building owned by a chiropractor in downtown Toronto. We took on two more writers: Leonard Starmer, who was to become one of the top in the variety field at the CBC, and John Ellsworth, who later teamed up with Frank Peppiatt to form one of the better writing and producing teams in the United States, turning out all sorts of things from *Hee Haw* to Frank Sinatra specials. There were a lot of talented young people around who were hustling for a chance. We couldn't afford another writer, but Ellsworth was willing to come on without pay just for the opportunity to create a product that might make it. Len also doubled as a bookkeeper—as if we had any accounts. We were thinking big, anyway, which is the way in this business.

(Author's collection)

At the start we put together a program called *Who Am I?*, on which I gave clues in rhyme about a mystery person and the audience mailed in their guesses. We kept adding clues until we opened an envelope with the correct answer on the air and the prize was given away. We convinced CFRB in put the show on the air for a short time as a test, but it was understood that if it was not sold to a sponsor it would be taken off. I went to a friend, Clare Appel, who was in charge of advertising for the Odeon Theater chain, and convinced him to take a partial sponsorship to encourage the station to keep us on while I sought full sponsorship. This kept us going for a few weeks.

One day I played the show for McLaren's Advertising Agency. That evening Hugh Horler, head of the agency's radio department, called and said, "We're taking the show. People's Credit Jewelers is going to sponsor it."

Marilyn and I whooped with joy and went out that night to celebrate with a steak dinner. We weren't eating much steak in those days. First thing in the morning, however, Horler called to say that the owner of the jewelry company had a change of heart, they weren't going to sponsor the show after all. Suddenly we were sunk into depression. I remember thinking, well, at least we had the steak dinner and a few hours of happiness. These things were very important to us. This was my life. After weeks and weeks of trying to sell the show, then finally selling it, then having it unsold overnight—it was disappointing to say the least.

I decided to try all the advertising agencies is Toronto. I got the idea to simply take a telephone book, turn to the advertising agencies, start with "A," and work my way right through the alphabet if necessary. Well, I went from "A" to "G" and got two appointments, neither of which led to anything. Then I reached H and what I shall call the Hennessy Agency. Hennessy went for the show and came up with the idea of selling it taped to a national network made up of any stations that would buy it.

The CBC was the only real network in Canada, and they wouldn't use game shows with giveaway prizes. Other shows had been transcribed onto records and sold to various stations around the country for use whenever each station wished. But ours was the first show to be taped and sold for simultaneous airing across Canada. We formed the first tape network in our nation's broadcasting history.

We used two cities as a test market—Toronto and smaller Sarnia, not too far away—to see what sort of response we received. It was tremendous. We signed up fifty-six stations, and Colgate agreed to sponsor us nationally. The show was a success right from the start, and more stations signed up. I had my first hit —for which Hennessy paid me the grand total of $300 a week, which came to $15,000 a year. Out of this, I had to pay all salaries and expenses and get by myself, but I had no choice. Hennessy had created a network for the show and was in control. Either I worked for him at his price or I didn't work.

Hennessy also had me do other shows for him, including the *Colgate Carnival*, which was a quiz show, a Colgate sports show, and *The Roy Rogers Show* for kids. I did them because I thought they would lead to more money. Some of these programs didn't last very long, but there were always others to take their places. After I had begun to do a lot of these, I suggested to Hennessy that we ought to reach some sort of agreement.

"Yes," he said, "I'm going to sign you to a contract which will guarantee you $20,000 a year and you can do *Who Am I?* and these other shows."

I said that would be fine, but I never got the contract.

When my first weekly check came, it was for $300 instead of the $385 or so it should have been.

"There must be some mistake," I told Hennessy. "I'm still being paid at my old rate instead of the $20,000 you promised me."

He said, "I've changed my mind. I just took one of the four shows off the air, so I don't see any point in paying $20,000. I'm going to keep you at $15,600 until we see what develops."

I should have walked out on him then and there, but I was in debt and desperate for the guaranteed income. I could have called him on his promise, but I was afraid. And no matter how many more shows I took on for him, I never got any kind of an increase.

Hennessy, a smallish, red-haired Irishman, was the toughest, roughest boss I've ever known. I was not rough and tough enough to stand up to him, not then. No matter what I did, it never was enough. He never gave anyone any credit, and he demeaned his employees in every way he could. He was always threatening to fire us, and he was always agreeing to do things for us and then changing his mind. He was the sort of boss you avoid as much as possible, the kind you dread having to deal with. He made my life miserable. I worried and suffered and developed intestinal problems. Nevertheless, I was working regularly and paying off my debts. And *Who Am I?* continued to grow yearly, increasing my national popularity. Eventually it ran 1875 performances over more than ten years.

We had a couple of young, mischievous engineers we called the Katzenjammer Kids—Bill Bodington and Francis Van Rassel. Hennessy built his own studio and installed a sound system in his office so he could hear everything that was said. All day long he would call down and say that we were doing this wrong or that wrong, and it drove us up the walls. Then Bodington and Van Rassel figured out a way to reverse the wires so they could hear everything that went on in his private office, too. The Katzenjammer Kids enjoyed these private broadcasts enormously. As much as I might have wanted to join in this private escapade, I put an end to the eavesdropping. It was an invasion of the man's privacy, and it could have cost us our jobs.

When our second child was born in 1952, Hennessy, in a burst of generosity, decided to give us a present. He knew we were living in an apartment asked me if we had a washing machine at home. When I said we didn't, he said we soon would have. I was surprised and I thanked him. And after it arrived, my wife sent him a note thanking him again. The machine, however, proved to be the cheapest one on the market—we were giving it away as a prize on one of our shows and Hennessy may have gotten one for free—and Marilyn was disappointed that it wasn't the new automatic type. I called an appliance store and arranged to trade the old-fashioned wringer machine in on an automatic model.

Then Hennessy came to dinner. He just came right out and asked me why I didn't invite him over some time so he could meet my wife and see my children. So, of course, I had to ask him right away. Just before he arrived, Marilyn remembered our new washer and realized that when we showed him our small apartment, he might notice that the machine was not the one he had given us. But there was no way out. It was like a silly situation comedy. We gave him the grand tour, physically twisting him away from the washer to show him something on the other side of the room. Every time he went near the kitchen, we headed him off. At one point, my wife did a sort of matador's flourish with her apron to conceal the washer. We got away with it, and afterward we collapsed with laughter.

I worked hard for that man and I had to keep catering to him to hold my position, which left me with little pride. After Rickey was born, Marilyn and I decided to take our long-postponed honeymoon. I was producing or performing in all sorts of shows at the time. I was weary and wanted a break. I informed Hennessy in advance that I had vacation time coming and that I'd get ahead in my schedule as much as I could. He raised no objection, so we planned a trip through Montreal, New England, and New York.

The week we were to leave, Hennessy sent word through his secretary that I couldn't go. I told his secretary, "You tell Mr. Hennessy I'm going."

She returned with his message: "If you go, *Who Am I?* goes off the air and you're finished here." I sent back word, "It's OK with me."

And when I told Marilyn, she said, "It's OK with me, too."

So off we went, scared but determined. I was frightened enough to tell Hennessy that I'd fly back for a few days in mid-vacation to record some additional shows, which I did. But we did have our honeymoon, though my nervousness spoiled a lot of it. When I came back, nothing was said. *Who Am I?* remained on the air and I continued to work for Hennessy, turning out show after show. I guess I should have stood up to him more often. But I was an insecure person at the time.

It soon became clear, however, that I had to get away from Hennessy. I had learned a lot from him. I had learned that a dime is not worth a nickel to you if you pay too much for it. I had learned that no shot at success is worth failing as a person when going after it. I learned that no work is worthwhile if you dread doing it day after day. I was determined never to suffer abuse again—ever! Somehow, I would manage to feed my family, but I would never do anything that degraded me again. If I didn't have my self-respect, I didn't have anything.

I had a home. It was small, but splendid. It had cost only $16,125 to build it in a tract of similar homes. And I needed $5,000 for the down payment. Even with what I made from Hennessy, and having paid back my debts, I did not have that amount. So I asked Hennessy if I could have the money as an advance on my salary to be paid back $100 a week through the year. And he said OK. But then, after I had signed the papers, he changed his mind, he said he'd decided against it.

"I just can't see my way to such a large advance at this time," he said.

So, I was on a spot. But then my mother-in-law came through and loaned me $2,000. And while Mr. Houston had retired, his replacement at the bank loaned me the remaining $3,000 on the strength of the good credit rating I'd established. And I repaid them both. It was just another little thing which turned me out of my rut. I had to screw up my courage and get away. It took years, years I'm ashamed of, years when my career drifted instead of rising. I'm left with a souvenir—stomach trouble that remains to this day.

It was at this time, too, that I almost acquired a less desirable benefactor. After working as emcee at a benefit baseball game for the Variety Club, I walked under the stands of Maple Leaf Stadium to get a Coke before the game began. A heavy-set man approached me, and in a voice that resembled a steamroller going over gravel, he said, "Kid, you know who I am?"

I certainly did. He was a prominent gambler and underworld character from Winnipeg, and I stammered out my recognition.

He grabbed me by the shoulders and said, "When you talked about dem crippled kids tonight, you turned my spine to jelly. You got to have lunch with me tomorrow, you and the missus."

Since one did not say no to this person, Marilyn and I showed up for lunch at the Horseshoe Tavern the next day. The gambler spent an hour telling me how great I was; then, edging closer, he said, "I want to do something for you."

I could only imagine, as he reached for his wallet, that he was going to slip me a couple of thousand dollars, and in my desperate financial circumstances, I am sure I would have accepted. But the problem proved academic. He reached into his wallet, pulled out a card, wrote something on the back, and handed it to me.

I didn't dare look at the card until lunch was over. After saying our goodbyes, I drove two blocks away, pulled the car over to the side, and immediately fished out the card with trembling hands. On one side it said, "Margaret Rose Tea Room," with an address in Winnipeg. And on the back, he had scribbled, "Good for two free teacup readings." I was so incensed that Marilyn had to restrain me from returning suicidally to the restaurant to hurl abuse at the character.

I tried to branch into television, which by then was coming in and replacing radio. In the early days of television in Canada, we did not have independent stations or networks to approach. The CBC controlled the medium, so I laid siege to the CBC. I had made a name for myself in radio, and I felt I could make it on camera, too. I was full of ideas and high hopes. It was like starting all over again, but it was the medium of the future and had to be conquered.

I started doing my first TV show, *Matinee Party*, on the CBC. I developed an idea for a late-night talk-and-talent program based on *The Tonight Show*, which Steve Allen was hosting at that time on NBC-TV in New York. My idea was different enough to be original. I wrote a sample show and got money from the CBC for a pilot. Drew Crossan produced and directed a kinescope with me as host and with a trio and a girl singer as well as guests. I was called in by Don Hudson, a top executive at the CBC. Hudson said that the CBC had its own writers, directors, and producers and wasn't interested in my package. But, he said, the show might work anyway, and if they decided to do it, I could audition to be the host. When I objected, he offered me $200 royalty.

I said, "You won't let me do anything but audition to emcee my own show, but you'll give me $200 a week royalty for it?"

He said, "Not $200 a week. I said $200 period."

I said, "Forget it," and left.

Angry, I went to Hudson's superior, Harry Boyle, the head of programming for the CBC. Boyle said it was Hudson's decision. Later the CBC went ahead and made their own pilot of my show, using my material, the same trio and singer, but a different host, and started to show it around. When I found out, I rushed back to Boyle, but he shrugged his shoulders and said there wasn't anything to be done about it. What he meant was there wasn't anything he dared do about it. He'd been a big man when radio was king, but now television was in control and he had lost his power. (After almost fifteen years in limbo he regained a top position.)

I went back to Don Hudson and told him, "You can't do this with my show."

And Don Hudson told me, "We at the corporation can do anything we want with any show that is presented to us."

It was very much like a commissar in Moscow telling someone, "You better like it, buddy boy, or it's Siberia for you." This is not a bad parallel, because the CBC always has operated like a powerful state organization that is accountable only to itself. Its building on Jarvis Street in Toronto is called "The Kremlin."

The men who rose to power there had civil service-type jobs that did not pay much money but put them in positions of power and provided them immense security. They could push writers, performers, producers, and directors around like so many pawns. They could make or break a man's career with a snap of the finger.

Of course, story ideas are always being lifted in broadcasting. There just isn't any way to prove someone else's show was really your brainchild. Sometimes just a part of an idea is lifted. Sometimes your idea may not have been drastically different from their idea in the first place, and they just found a little something of yours they could add to theirs.

Mine was an extreme case of total theft, however, and I screamed bloody murder, which didn't help my standing at the CBC. I was not only doing the show *Matinee Party* but had been approached about a new quiz show. Shortly after my debacle with Hudson, the quiz show idea was dropped, and so was *Matinee Party*. From three shows on the network, I was down to none. I started knocking on doors—on what seemed to be a revolving stage. Everyone was evasive.

I remember lower-echelon officers at the Kremlin saying, "Maybe somebody up there doesn't like you," and those in the upper echelons saying, "Somebody down there doesn't like you, I guess."

After Stewart Griffith assumed a position of authority in the corporation, he gave me an appointment. I got to his office on time but was kept waiting outside almost forever. When I finally got inside, he immediately left. I waited a half hour before he came back. When I finally got to talk to him briefly, he said, "Is it possible that somebody out there doesn't like you?"

I have never forgotten Griffith's rudeness—or that of others like him. People in positions of power in the entertainment business tend to have enormous egos, and many of them are among the rudest people on earth. I have a pretty big ego myself, but I remember when I was demeaned, and as a result I may be the easiest person in television for someone else in this business to speak to on the phone or see in person. I am courteous to everybody and try to help anyone I can. I remember all too well how it was when I went hat in hand begging for a hearing, in Toronto and later in New York. I hadn't yet made my move to New York, but I was fast being driven to it.

The middle fifties were tough times for me in Toronto. *Who Am I?* endured and sustained me along with other shows and jobs I picked up from time to time. At one point I took a Variety Club vaudeville show on tour around eastern Canada. The star was George Formby, a great figure in English music halls and motion pictures, and we had solid supporting acts, I emceed, sang, and did a little bit of everything.

After the show appeared in Ottawa, Ernie Bushnell came backstage to see me and invited me out to lunch with him the next day. I'd stayed friendly with Ernie I and played cards with him many times at the Variety Club in Toronto. But then Ernie moved to Ottawa and became the top man in programing for the CBC.

I knew he had influence, and I went to lunch wondering if I could make use of any of it. Right away he said, "Gee, it's wonderful seeing you, Monty. My wife was saying at the show last night that it's certainly good to see Monty Hall performing again. And she asked me why we didn't see you on television. And I didn't know what to tell her. Why don't we?"

I looked at him and said, "Ernie, you've got to be kidding. You're the head man. If you don't know why I'm not on television, who does? Did you think I'd retired? I'm a bit young for that. I've been trying to get a show from your people in Toronto without any luck."

I told him about the show I'd created and how it was taken from me. I told him how I'd raised hell about it and wound up being blackballed. I added that I was thinking of leaving Canada and trying New York.

Ernie listened sympathetically to the wail and said, "I'm very distressed to hear all this. I've been a booster of yours for years and I believe you belong in radio and television in this country. Canada desperately needs performers of your caliber, and I'm going to look into this situation and see what can be done about it."

Well, he certainly boosted my spirits. As busy as he was, he kept the luncheon talk going for three hours and filled it with praise of me and promises for the future. I left him with my feet hardly touching the ground.

Very soon afterward I got a call from Fergus Mutrie of the CBC in Toronto saying that he'd heard from Ernie Bushnell and that he wanted to meet with me as soon as possible. We went to lunch and he asked me for details, so I repeated the whole story. He said, "I promise you, Monty, I will look into this, and I'm going to find out why you haven't been able to get work." Again, I left buoyed with new hope.

Then, about ten days later, Mutrie called me a second time. "Monty," he said, "I've investigated the whole situation and I've found you haven't been treated any differently from anyone else."

I was stunned. I asked, "Did you talk to the people who stole my show? Did you talk to the people who wouldn't give me the time of day? If you did, what did you expect them to say?"

He said, "I talked to everyone and they all agreed they have treated you just as they treat any other talent seeking employment. They just have not had anything suitable for you."

"Are you telling me I don't have the talent?" I asked.

"I'm not saying that," he replied, "but I am saying our people simply feel they have found nothing suitable for your talent."

So I said, "Well, I'm sorry," and he said, "I'm sorry, too."

I left, and that was that.

It was a dead end, after all. I was convinced then I had to get away from Canada and the CBC. I didn't know what sort of talent I had, but I knew the CBC didn't know either. I had tried and been turned away. I had to go to where there were greater opportunities. Now was the time to try New York.

CHAPTER SIX

MONTY HALL

There really was no strong reason for me to believe I could beat the odds and break into big-time television in New York. The facts were that I had left I Winnipeg without having established myself as any sort of sensation, and though I had made something of a name for myself in radio in Toronto, I had failed to make it in television there. Frustration was forcing my move. Having been beaten up a bit by a couple of contenders, I now felt qualified to take on the champion. Chalk it up to youthful enthusiasm—or desperation. It was a rough, tough fight, I'll tell you. I kept getting knocked down, but I kept getting up swinging.

I made my move on the first of July 1955. Marilyn and I had agreed I would spend at least two months in New York to see what would develop. She was willing to remain behind with our children, who were five and three, and bear all the responsibilities of our home and family. Otherwise I never could have attempted the venture.

I rounded up a couple of other Canadians who were bound for New York—Albert Shea, who was in the research business and planned only a short stay, and John Drainie, a fine radio actor who also felt he had reached his limit in Canada—and we made the trip in my car.

We had not arranged for a place to stay in the big town, and on our arrival, I looked through some ads and was struck by one for the Shoreham Hotel on West 55th Street. We could have a one-bedroom apartment with twin beds and a kitchen for $360 a month. That was a lot, especially at that time, and Shea chose to stay elsewhere. But there were benefits, such as a telephone answering service, and I figured it would work out. Drainie and I agreed to share all expenses, and the adventure began.

We each had lists of people we wanted to see, and every morning we would call some and seek appointments. After a time, we were batting the same—zero. We simply could not get interviews with most of the people we wanted to see, and those people we did see were not especially interested in us. We pounded the pavements and took a pounding ourselves.

I wasn't surprised. Naturally, it was discouraging, but I had expected it to be tough and I planned to keep at it until it worked. But Drainie's discouragement began to depress him after a few weeks. He was a superb radio actor with a thousand voices, but he had a bad limp, and that didn't help his chances in television. He began to figure he was beaten.

One day I was reading a story in *Life* magazine about Sylvester "Pat" Weaver, the president of NBC, who had been stirring up television with his daring innovations. On radio he had created *Monitor*, the weekend program, and *The Weekday Show*. In television he started *The Today Show*, *The Tonight Show*, *The Home Show*, which Arlene Francis hosted, and many others. The story said that Weaver was a man with a feel for the unusual. I was struck with an inspiration. I would try the unusual; I would send him a telegram pleading my case.

As I started to compose the wire, Drainie asked me what I was doing. I said, "I'm composing a wire to Pat Weaver at NBC."

Drainie was amused. "Why not send one to General Sarnoff, too?"

I said, "Nothing else has worked so far, so I can't lose anything by trying this."

The wire went something like this: "This may be a daring and presumptuous thing to do, but, according to *Life* magazine, that is Pat Weaver's sort of thing, and if it's good enough for him, it's good enough for me. My name is Monty Hall. I am an emcee and producer from Toronto and I think I have a lot to offer, but I haven't been able to impress this on anyone. I have been trying to see the executives at NBC but can't get past their secretaries. Anything you can do to help me see them will be deeply appreciated. I will be grateful to you for your consideration…"

I read it to Drainie; he roared with laughter. I took the wire to Western Union; the operator read it and started to smile.

"Are you sure you want to send this?" she asked.

"Just tell me how much it is and send it," I retorted.

I went back to the Shoreham and tried to forget it. A few days later, Drainie answered the telephone.

"It's Pat Weaver's secretary," he announced.

He laughed as he said it because he must have figured somebody was putting me on. I grabbed the phone, and it really was Pat Weaver's secretary. She said that Mr. Weaver was quite taken with the telegram and would very much like to meet the man who sent it. Could I see him Friday at three? I assured her I could.

She added, "Incidentally, I'm sorry it has taken us so long to get back to you, but Mr. Weaver just returned from the West Coast."

I told her I hadn't minded the wait at all.

The few days to Friday passed slowly. Now that I'd talked myself into an interview with one of the great men of the industry, how could I back it up? I showed up at Weaver's office early, waited, and just before three an aide grabbed me by the arm, exclaimed, "Now!" and hustled me into an enormous office.

Weaver looked at me and said, "Your wire was great. But I only have ten minutes now before I have to catch a flight, so please tell me everything you can in that time."

He listened to everything I said, and at the end of ten minutes he turned to his assistant and ordered, "See to it that Mr. Hall gets to see everyone he wants to see here and then give me a full report on the interviews."

Then he jumped up and left. The assistant took me out to his secretary. We drew a list of the people in power at NBC, and she made me a series of appointments for the following week. I walked out wide-eyed and phoned my wife the news.

Of course, the natural ending to such a tale is that the doors of stardom opened me. They did not. I saw everyone who was anyone at NBC. Everyone treated me courteously and heard me out and promised to get back to me—but not one of them ever did. There was nothing whatsoever, not one single nibble. I didn't even get to audition for a job.

The telegram remains famous in the industry. Almost everyone assumes that it gave me my first break, but it didn't give me anything except a good story to tell later.

Drainie's wife came to visit him one weekend, and I moved out to give them some privacy. She soon went back to Toronto, and Drainie was lonely without her. Shortly thereafter he gave up and returned to Toronto. I didn't give up, but I was tempted to many times. Each morning I would make about ten or twelve phone calls requesting appointments. Then I would wait to get calls back. I'd be lucky if I got one or two calls, and luckier still if I made any appointments at all. Sometimes the phone would not ring for hours, and I would sit staring at it. If I did get an appointment, I would walk to it, even if it was ten or twenty blocks away, because I couldn't afford to spend my dwindling money on taxis. It was midsummer and dreadfully hot, and by the time I arrived, I was barely presentable. Then I had two minutes to tell some executive all about myself. He would say he'd let me know, and that would be the last I'd ever hear from him. He had another appointment, I'd go home to shower and change because I had to look presentable even if I couldn't afford dry-cleaning and laundry bills. Then I'd walk to my other appointment, get another two minutes that came to nothing, and return to my apartment. If there were no messages, I'd sit by the phone and wait and hope.

For the performer the telephone can be an instrument of torture. He is afraid to leave it for fear of missing out on a call that may mean a job, maybe the best of his career. I had an answering service backing me up. Still, it made me nervous. What if the service missed a call or made a mistake? What if I got back too late to reach the caller that day and it cost me a job? To this day I am unable to ignore the ringing of a phone because this built-in fear has become part of me. I can't break a habit as strong as this. You answer your phone. You had better be there to answer your phone. When you're there, it never rings. The minute you go out, it always rings.

The nights were lonely. I had a few friends and relatives in New York and I visited them occasionally. Their family life made me even lonelier. I missed Marilyn and the babies badly and called them every other night. My only income was from the tapes of *Who Am I?* that I cut in New York and sent back to Toronto. Baseball was a blessing. There still were three teams in New York at the time, and they televised all their home games and some of their road games. Sometimes I watched three games a day. Afterward I went to bed and waited for morning—when the whole routine of making calls and hoping for appointments began all over again.

During this time, I saw agents who didn't want to handle me and producers who didn't want to cast me, and all sorts of executives who had no interest in me. I would call up some bigwig and ask his secretary, "Is Mr. Smith in?"

And she'd ask, "Who is calling?"

I'd say, "Monty Hall."

She'd say, "Marty who?"

I'd say, "No, not Marty. Monty…Monty Hall."

And she'd say, "You're from Montreal?"

And I'd say, "No, my name is Monty Hall and I'm from Toronto." I would almost be in tears by this time.

She'd say, "Does Mr. Smith know you?"

And I'd have to reply, "No, but I'm a performer and a producer and I'd like an interview for a job."

And she'd say, "Well, Mr. Smith is busy right now, but if you'll leave your name and number I'll give him your message. Now that was Marty who?" I became known to my friends as "Marty who."

Often when I did get an appointment, I'd go in and find that it had been made for a Marty Hull from Montreal. Then I'd have to explain my name all over again. At first, I had to wait anywhere from fifteen minutes to an hour and a half beyond my scheduled appointment. One thing I am, and that's an independent cuss, job or no job. So, when I was kept waiting longer than twenty minutes, I would rear up and tell the secretary or receptionist, "I'm sorry, but I can't wait any longer. If Mr. Smith is not going to see me in the next five minutes, please let me know so that I can leave and come again another time."

Some people feel they have to make other people wait; they feel they have to impress the little guys with their power. By keeping you waiting, they wield some power. They put you on the defensive.

Executives have many tricks, and I saw a lot of them. The executive's chair is almost always higher than the visitor's chair, He is looking down on you and you are looking up at him. He is a king, and you are at most a member of his court and at worst merely one of the rabble. And the executive swivels. He has a swivel chair and you do not. He swivels around looking at everything but you, while you have to follow him with your eyes, locked in your face. The executive fiddles with papers on his desk. The more papers, the more important he is supposed to be. Often, he takes a lot of telephone calls while you are in the office. The more calls he gets the more important he is. The executive seldom cuts off his calls or apologizes for taking them. He just interrupts the conversation and ignores you. In a ten-minute interview you are lucky to talk for two minutes, and that comes to starts and stops. You have no reason to believe the executive is listening.

One executive who received me was decorating his new office. The whole time I was with him, he was busy examining the pictures he wanted to hang on his walls. He never looked at me once or said a single intelligible word. He'd grunt "uh-huh" and keep on studying his pictures. When I was done, he finally spoke to me. "Which of these do you like best?"

As Monty drifted from office to office in search of one executive, any executive, who would at least give him the time of day, Marilyn raised two children by herself in Toronto. Her faith in Monty and his dreams was so unwavering that when young Joanne suffered a hemorrhage, Marilyn elected not to tell her husband about it. She reasoned that Monty already had enough to think about, and she didn't want anything to distract him when success could be right around the corner.

MONTY HALL

Years later I was selected emcee of the CBS show *Keep Talking*. After our premiere, Lester Gottlieb, an executive of CBS, toasted me at a dinner at Danny's Hideaway. He told of how he remembered this kid from Canada coming into his office and telling him cockily how he was going to lick this town, and now, by golly, here he was heading for the top. What I remembered as I sat there listening to him was how terribly nervous I had been at our first meeting, how I sat in his office crushing my hat between twitching fingers. Yet now, in the flush of success, he was picturing me as "cocky." So what was the point of his story, and what was its meaning for me? Simply that when you are on your way up, everybody "discovered" you, and everybody has anecdotes, almost always apocryphal. To further prove my point, eight weeks later, when *Keep Talking* did not obtain high ratings, I was fired. A friend of mine met Gottlieb in the halls of CBS and asked him why I had been dismissed.

Gottlieb's answer was, "Oh, him and that damn Canadian accent of his!"

Gottlieb is not a bad guy, and, in fact, I was always fond of him and still am. But I tell the story to demonstrate that there is one kind of story for the guy going up and another kind for the guy going down.

Some years later, after his career had recovered from the blow of being dismissed from Keep Talking, *he spoke out in defense of his damn Canadian accent.*

MONTY HALL[xiv]

The appearances and vocal qualities of most Canadians are not limited to particular accents identifiable to specific regions in the United States. We have no regional peculiarity of speech. You might say the closest we come to an accent is to that of your Midwestern citizens, who have practically no accent at all.

For this reason, it's not only difficult to distinguish a newly arrived Canadian from a U.S. citizen, but many people, as in my case, can't figure even a guess as to what part of the United States I might hail from. Did you know that many U.S. radio and TV networks import Canadian announcers for that very reason? Without an identifiable accent, they have broad appeal to every listener.

STU BILLETT, producer

I was a production assistant—a gofer—for the company that did *The $64,000 Question* in the 1950s. We were pitching a new series for the network. The guy who was supposed to be our master of ceremonies calls us that morning. He's been in a car accident; he won't make it there.

Steve Carlin, the big boss, tells me, "Call Monty Hall. He'll come and do it."

I didn't know who Monty Hall was. But I had all the things set up for this run-through, I called this Monty Hall guy and explained the situation and he said, "I'll be right over."

When he got there, he said to me, "Tell me what the show is."

I said, "But I've got all these things set up. Let me show you…"

He says, "Just tell me what the show is."

I explain it to him, and he says, "Okay, I've got it. Give me the material. I'm ready."

I couldn't believe it. He just did it like that. And every network and producer used Monty for that. If they needed a guest host because someone was sick, they'd call Monty. If there was a run-through coming, the producers would call Monty and ask him to host the run-through. He was amazing at hosting run-throughs.

He never got his own show, though. I believe there were two reasons for it. The first was, if Monty got his own show, they couldn't use him for run-through work anymore. Every producer wanted Monty available for that part of the process because he was so good at it.

The other reason was he was too Jewish. They would tell him, "It's that Canadian accent," but they actually thought of it as a Jewish accent. In television, anything that's not midwestern is Jewish. TV networks at that time wanted their hosts to look the way that Tom Kennedy and Jack Narz looked—white, American, nothing regional in their speech, nothing distinctive in their features. And Monty was Jewish, and at that time, he had a bit of a hook in his nose.

Steve Carlin, by chance, met Monty's rabbi at a party once. They began talking about him, and Steve leveled with the rabbi and said, "Look, you want to do Monty a favor? Have a talk with him and tell him to do something about his nose."

Monty got his nose fixed. They still didn't give him a show.

MONTY HALL

Keep Talking was my first big network television show in the States. Up till then I had been a replacement for others. I was crazy about the format and loved being a moderator, especially because the show had a great inventive comedy flavor.

When I got a few laughs myself, Herb Wolf, the producer, took me aside and said: "I've had a complaint from one of the comics on the panel. He told me to tell you that he'll get the laughs and you just stick to moderating."

Being practically a freshman in the big time, I heeded the advice and played it straight. I shouldn't have. If I was going to go down, I should have died as a lion, not as a lamb.

I was replaced by Jackie Cooper for a couple of weeks, and then Carl Reiner for the balance of the season. The show changed networks and used Merv Griffin as the host, but it never got a rating. It was just too sophisticated for the audience. My only consolation was that the change in emcees never added a point to the ratings. Two years later Mike Dann of CBS hired me to do *Video Village.*

He sent me a note which said: "We may have been wrong when we let you go from *Keep Talking,* but I know damn well we're right this time!" I appreciated that.

Show business is at once the best and the worst of businesses. If you are on top, it can be the best in almost every way. If you are not, it can be the worst in any way. It is referred to as a profession, but it is not a profession. A profession is a skill you have learned and can prove. If you study to become a doctor and get your license, you are a doctor forever. You can put M.D. after your name and hang out your shingle and wait for patients to appear. Anyone in the entertainment business has no letters to prove his profession and no shingle to hang up. Instead of waiting for people to come to him, he has to go to others for work. And he is only a professional while he is working.

You go in to executives and say, "I'm a director." But you can prove it only by things you've directed. If you haven't had any experience, you're not a director. A director directs. A writer writes. It's only when you sell something that you are proving yourself. And it only lasts as long as the things you've sold lasts. And nothing lasts forever in this business. Jobs come and go. Your profession is unemployment marked by periods of employment. Most people in show business—even stars—are out of work most of the time.

You live in fear. I have never met one single person in this business who has not been afraid at one time or another. They wouldn't all admit it, but they all showed it in one way or another. There aren't any of us who are any bigger than the show we have going at the moment. If the show fails, we are failures. We have no guarantees there will be another show. It doesn't matter how long we've been on or how successful we've been, today is all that counts, and our world may crash around our shoulders tonight.

Jerry Lewis is big in movies, but has failed several times on television. Vince Edwards had one of the most successful shows in television history, *Ben Casey,* but when it went off, he dropped out of sight for years; it had nothing to do with how good he was —only with the fact that he had not come up with another *Ben Casey*. Milton Berle was "Mr. Television"—until television forgot him. Sid Caesar, Red Buttons, and so on—the roll call of great talent ignored in the shuffle is almost endless.

Even the biggest names suffer for fear it will end tomorrow. It's in the nature of the performer. The contract I had with Hennessy to do the Colgate show, which was sustaining me in my early days, was like a lifeline. I took everything the man dished out, because the job was all I had, and the thought that I might lose it turned my insides into jelly. I've never seen the fear on my own face, then or since, but I know it has been there.

I fought fear through those dreadful days and lonely nights in New York. I hated the city. It terrified me. I wanted to go home to friends and family a hero. In the mornings I'd make fifteen calls and fourteen wouldn't answer, and the fifteenth would see me and reject me. And another day was done. The struggle is worse than most realize. And the ending is usually unhappy.

CHAPTER SEVEN

ROBERT HALL (2019)

One of the things that helped keep my brother afloat while he was struggling in New York was that we went into business together in Toronto. We owned a restaurant there. We bought a place, we named it Kingburger, and we made it a drive-in restaurant. The only downside was drive-in restaurants became popular hangouts in that era for motorcycle gangs. Every once in a while, I'd get a call. "Bob, there's a rumble breaking out, you'd better get down here."

Monty and I also owned the first Colonel Sanders franchise in Toronto, which was very popular, but two restaurants stretched us a bit thin. And honestly, the Colonel Sanders franchise drove us a little crazy anyway. The franchise fees were so expensive, and the corporation overcharged us for everything. The fees for the eleven secret herbs and spices were ridiculous because you could buy them anywhere.

One day, we got a call from a company that wanted to buy the rights to the name Kingburger. We thought it was such an odd business deal. They didn't want to own the restaurant, they just wanted to buy the name, and we could continue operating the restaurant under a different name after that if we wanted. We had a lawyer look into it to figure out why they wanted this. It was Burger King in America. They were planning on opening franchises in Canada and they wanted to buy the name Kingburger just so they didn't have to worry about any legal issues. We made the deal and changed the name of our place. It stayed open a few more years.

MONTY HALL

If many people were cruel to me in those months in New York, many more were not, and

I must be forever grateful to them. One was Sam Rosenwasser. He was a cousin of my mother's and lived in Brooklyn. When I arrived in New York for my first visit in 1946, he was out, and I left a message and went to bed. The next thing I knew, he was pounding on my door at the Edison Hotel, dragging me out of bed, pushing me into some clothes, and taking me to the Carnival nightclub to see Milton Berle. Sam was my father's age, but we became true and devoted friends. In the summer of 1955, when I was walking the streets of New York looking for work, and long after that, Sam and his wife, Ada, took me into their home and their hearts. Sam's usual way of handling me was to call from Brooklyn to ask, "What are you doing for dinner?" When I said I was free for the evening, he would say, "Be in front of your hotel in an hour." Dinner with Sam and Ada always consisted of too much food (they must have thought I was starving) served amid a barrage of solicitous questions: "Who are you seeing?" "What can I do for you?" "Where do you want to go?" "How about a Broadway show?" There wasn't anything that this magnificent man wouldn't do for me. And to this day there isn't anything in the world I wouldn't do for him.

Sam was a relative, but there were friends who were closer than relatives could be—like Eugene and Emily Grant. Marilyn and Emily had been close girl friends in Toronto; and after Emily's marriage to Gene, all four of us became close. It was only natural that I would spend a lot of time with them in Mamaroneck. They gave me moral support, Gene became like a brother to me. When Marilyn and the kids joined me in New York, we settled in Westchester County just to be near the Grants. And today, though we live three thousand miles apart, we still fly back and forth to be with one another on happy occasions and for just plain visits.

I met Deke Hayward, who was a writer for Garry Moore at the time. Deke introduced me to Bill Bratter, his lawyer, and Bill and I took to each other immediately. Bill offered to represent me for free in any legal matters, saying, "I'm going to represent you now, and someday you're going to be big and I'm going to make a lot of money off you."

Through my contacts with Colgate in Toronto, I got to see the Colgate people in the New York area. They were in Jersey City, and they set up an appointment with me to meet Walt Framer, who at the time was producing *Strike It Rich* and *The Big Payoff*. Framer was a busy man, and he conducted other business the whole time I was in his office. He apologized for it, and he let me stay a long while, talking to me between calls. He invited me back for a second visit, and then he and his wife took me to dinner at a fashionable New York restaurant. I have always thought this was an extraordinarily nice thing for him to do. He had no work for me at the time, but he had plans for other shows, and I got the feeling he might have plans for me. At that point, an occasional good feeling was about as much as I ever had.

For eight weeks I did not see Marilyn. We decided she would come to visit me on my birthday, August 25. About that time, Hurricane Hazel struck the Northeast and floods devastated Connecticut. Jerry Danzig, an NBC executive I'd talked to, asked me if I would emcee a telethon in the Hartford-New Britain area to raise funds for the flood victims. I said I'd be delighted. Unfortunately, the telethon was to run from late the night of August 24 to early the evening of the 25, when my wife was due in New York. Danzig said he would arrange for a private plane to fly me from Hartford to New York and a limousine to drive me to the hotel for my meeting with Marilyn. I was dying to show somebody what I could do, so I readily accepted.

The telethon starred Raymond Massey, Robert Strauss, Eddie Fisher, Lanny Ross, and other performers. I served as emcee for eighteen long hours and felt I did very well, and we raised a lot of money. Danzig was impressed with me, but at the time he had little power at NBC. Norman Lear, creator of *All in the Family*, also saw the show. Norman had gone home to Connecticut to help his mother bail out during the floods and had watched the telethon for many hours. Years later I met him in the halls at NBC, and he told me of this incident from eight years before.

He said, "The funny thing about it was that I always remembered this Canadian kid doing a sensational one-man show all night and all day long; but when it was over, I never saw him again, and I wondered what had happened to him."

So much of this business is timing. You can impress the right people at the wrong time, and the wrong people at the right time.

I left the studio exhausted but exhilarated. I'd needed that opportunity to perform. I was driven to a private airfield where the plane was ready but the pilot was not. His son, a youngster of sixteen or seventeen, said, "My dad is busy, but I'll fly you."

I said, "Can you?"

He replied, "Sure, I've been flying for years."

The man who had driven me to the airport appeared worried as he told me, "Listen, you don't have to go if you don't want to."

And I said, "I want to. My wife is waiting. I haven't seen her in eight weeks. If he's willing, I am."

We walked to the plane—and my heart sank. It resembled a large orange crate with wings attacked.

The kid started the engine, we bumped down the runway, and suddenly we were aloft. We flew at altitudes of 500 to 1500 feet, which was like driving a little high off the road. He kept glancing at the instrument panel with a worried look, and I was too concerned about my own discomfort to ask him what worried him. My knuckles were white from gripping the door handle, and I kept saying improvised prayers in my mind. It was a short flight, and finally we reached LaGuardia Airport, coming in right through the telephone wires, it seemed. We made it, and I blessed the boy silently. The limousine was waiting and got me to the hotel before my wife arrived.

Marilyn's plane had ridden the tail end of the hurricane into New York, and she was pale and nervous. We clutched each other, cried and kissed, and then she ran to the bathroom to throw up. She couldn't eat that night, I couldn't sleep, though I had been up for forty-eight hours straight. It was not a particularly romantic reunion. The next day was much better, but then it was over and time for her to return to Toronto and our children.

I knew we couldn't go on this way, but we also decided I shouldn't give up on New York. We agreed that after Labor Day I would return to Toronto and then start commuting—one week in Toronto, one week in New York—and we would manage the money somehow. So she went back and I started to wait for the Labor Day weekend, while continuing to make the usual useless rounds. God, how I missed those children!

When the appointed weekend came, I decided to drive the car back. Leaving late on Friday afternoon I drove hard until around midnight, when I sacked out in a motel. Early the next morning I resumed my drive. The closer I got to Toronto, the more anxious I became, and before I realized it, I was driving ninety miles an hour. On the Queen Elizabeth Highway between Hamilton and Toronto, the four-lane highway suddenly becomes a divided highway. The change makes a driver come unexpectedly upon a divider with a heavy stanchion at its foot. I had forgotten about the road and was thinking only of my family when suddenly I was speeding directly at the divider. I swerved, missing it by inches.

The near-accident scared hell out of me, and I slowed down to a sane speed. I reached Toronto and drove to my house and up the driveway. Six or seven boys and girls were playing on the grass. But after ten weeks without them, I wasn't sure which of the children were mine. Then two of them came running toward the car crying out, "Daddy! Daddy!" and I was so shaken I could not even get out of the car. All the love I had stored up in New York welled up in me, and I just sat there with tears streaming down my face. I finally got out of the car and clasped the kids to me. Marilyn came out of the house and started to cry watching Daddy with his daughter and his son.

I had my reunion with my family and my week at home, and then it was time to fly back to New York for my week of telephone calls and pounding pavements and making office calls. It became a regular routine. I did my shows in advance in Toronto and on Sunday I'd fly back to New York for five days; on Friday night I'd fly back to Toronto and wait by the telephone for the next week. September passed, and October, and November. Through Danzig I was offered $600 a week to do a show in Chicago. Well, I wanted the money, I wanted the show, but I didn't want Chicago. From Toronto to New York is a vertical move; from Toronto to Chicago is a lateral move.

To keep up my contacts, I hit upon the idea of sending a mimeographed news sheet of my doings, *A Memo from Monty*, to those network and agency folks I had met—even briefly. To my surprise they actually seemed to enjoy them. Once I missed a weekly mailing, and Steve Krantz, program director of WNBC in New York, asked me "What happened to the latest *Memo from Monty*? I missed it."

I laughed and said, "I guess I was too busy, although I don't know what I could have been doing."

"Are you too busy for lunch?" he asked. I was not, and we went.

Krantz told me he was having trouble with a show, *The Sky's the Limit*.

"You seem to have some good ideas," he said. "I want you to watch the show and tell me what you think is wrong and what can be done to fix it up."

I watched the show every day for a week, and I found a lot wrong with it. At the end of the week, I wrote a long dissertation, touching on the show's structure, production, personnel, prizes, everything. I mailed it to Krantz and forgot about it.

Shortly thereafter Colgate-Palmolive stopped sponsoring my show in Canada and I was cast adrift. What else did I have? Early in December, I was sitting at home in Toronto wondering what to do when my world turned around. The date, I remember, was December 7, 1955. Steve Krantz called me from New York.

"Monty," he said, "Your report on the show was brilliant. I think your ideas will work. I'm ready to make you an offer to start work immediately as both producer and emcee of *The Sky's the Limit*."

Finally, my first chance had come. Excitedly, I said, "I accept." Then I added, "I really don't know if I'm ready to handle the dual role of producer and emcee."

And he said, "Well, take a day or two and think about it and then we'll negotiate."

"Fine," I blurted.

I hung up and danced Marilyn around the room.

Again, the phone rang. And again, it was long distance from New York. I couldn't believe it. It was Walt Framer.

"Monty, Warren Hull is taking a vacation from *Strike It Rich*, and I thought maybe you'd like to do the show for a few days while he is gone."

"You bet I would," I told him.

When we hung up, I turned to my wife and heaped this new bit of heaven on her, and we went on dancing around the room.

Less than an hour later the phone rang a third time. It was Gordon Keeble, who was working with an independent agency in Toronto.

"Good news," he said. "I've sold *Who Am I?* to Canada Packers. It can go right back on the air because they're ready to back it immediately, let's lock it up."

I was overwhelmed. One hour earlier I had nothing. Now I had a New York show to do, a stint on U.S. network, and a new sponsor for my radio show in Canada. After all that time, good fortune had struck three times on a single day.

I called my friend Bill Bratter in New York, told him the developments, and admitted that I had not even thought of asking what sort of money was involved.

He advised me, "Just take whatever they offer at this stage. We'll worry about more later. But don't sign anything until I've seen it."

"Fine," I said.

And from that time Bratter was my official representative. I got $500 to do the Hull shows and $450 a week on *The Sky's the Limit* and $300 a week for *Who I Am I?*

I wanted to start paying Bratter, but he said, "Forget it for now. You've been starving too long, and I'm not in need. When you catch up and get ahead, then I'll start taking fees from you. You're going to make a lot of money. I'm not going to lose I out on anything."

I decided against taking the producer's job on *The Sky's the Limit*. I wanted to be free to do as many other things as possible. We set December 30 as the date for my first show. In the meantime, I did the three *Strike It Rich* shows, and everyone seemed to think they went well.

The Sky's the Limit began life as a children's game show, but the format changes when Monty became involved were significant—and somewhat familiar. Each episode now concluded with Monty wandering through the bleachers and playing small games with members of the studio audience, mostly Monty asking trivia questions and offering $5 for a correct answer.

For months, Monty noticed the same elderly woman was sitting in the audience for every episode, but he never picked her because for the longest time, something about her gave him the impression that she didn't speak English fluently, and he was didn't want to accidentally embarrass her somehow if he picked her to play a trivia game.

Monty began to worry that she'd catch on to the way he was avoiding her and that such a realization would be equally embarrassing, so he made up his mind once that today would be the day that he'd pick her for the trivia game. To minimize potential embarrassment, Monty decided to ask her the easiest trivia question he could think of, and to make it up to her for all the times he hadn't picked her, he'd offer her fifty bucks for the correct answer.

"Sweetheart," Monty addressed her. "Who was the first man?"

The little old lady, misunderstanding what Monty meant, replied, "Darling, I wouldn't give you that answer for $1,000!"

I was at the U.S. Immigration Office in Toronto getting a resident alien visa so I could work in New York on a steady basis when my wife phoned to tell me to get in touch with Bill Bratter. I wound up in a three-way conference call with Ed Wolf, a New York producer and packager, who was in Phoenix at the time. He had seen me on *Strike It Rich* and wanted me to host a new national show called *Twenty Steps to a Million*. I told them I was certainly interested.

If I could add a regular national show to my local New York program, I'd really be on my way. Scheduling conflicts would have to be worked out, but that wasn't an immediate problem. *Twenty Steps to a Million* was only in the formative stage, and I went over to Wolf's office whenever I could to help shape it up. Almost everyone in the office was a relative of Ed's, and I was quickly accepted into the "family." Meanwhile, I did *The Sky's the Limit* five days a week and worked hard to dig it out of the hole it was buried in. Its ratings had gone way down, and we had to attract a new audience, which is difficult with an old show.

The keeping-up-with-the-Joneses scheduling practices of the major networks were in full force in 1956, and as a result, Twenty Steps to a Million *received quite a bit of attention for a show that never made it on the air, with press releases touting that it would be premiering "in the fall of 1956, if not sooner." The premise of the program was that five contestants would compete against each other in a series of games that would span a full twenty episodes, with the winner after the twentieth week receiving a million dollars, guaranteed.*

Creator Ed Wolf maintained that he had been developing the show with his staff for over two years, and because Raleigh Cigarettes was holding out for an ideal time slot, both NBC and CBS were laying claim to the show, battling with each other to find the best spot on their own schedules. The fact that the issue hadn't been resolved didn't discourage anyone from hyping the impending arrival of the series. Everyone just presumed it was a sure thing.

MONTY HALL
One sidelight: Steve Krantz said I could do pretty much what I wanted to do to improve [*The Sky's the Limit*]. I had taken over for Gene Rayburn as emcee, and I wanted to replace

the lovely young lady who was assisting him on the air because I thought I could work better with a lively male announcer, as I do now with Jay Stewart on *Let's Make a Deal* and as Johnny Carson does with Ed McMahon on *The Tonight Show*. I hired Bill Wendell, and he worked out well. The lady I fired to make room for Bill was Hope Lange, who was to become a most successful movie and television actress.

It was great to be working—especially now that the other show was in the works, too. Every Friday afternoon I'd leave the studio and fly home to Toronto for the weekend to be with my family and to tape *Who Am I?*

This schedule was very tight. Each week the same cabbie rushed me to the airport. I never had time for lunch, and he was kind enough to pick up a carton of milk, a couple of hardboiled eggs, and some bread and butter from a local beanery, and they would be waiting on the seat for me.

On Sunday evening I'd catch a plane back to New York in time to get a night's sleep before beginning the new week's work on Monday, but I was weary of being apart from my family for so long. And Marilyn was starting to say that my visits were like having a soldier home on forty-eight-hour pass. It certainly seemed time for me to move the family to New York. So, in May 1956, when Joanne finished kindergarten, we made the move. We sold our home in Toronto, but I was wary of buying a house in New York right away. With the help of the Grants I rented a three-story house in suburban Mount Vernon.

Our house in Toronto had been small but new and modern. The Mount Vernon house was large but old-fashioned. It had heavy drapes and heavy furniture, and everything creaked. Marilyn was excited as I drove her and the kids to it for the first time, then obviously disappointed when she saw it.

She said, "When you told me you'd found a house in Mount Vernon, I thought it was the Mount Vernon where George Washington lived. Now that I've seen the house, I wonder if George is still living here."

Well, we had lived apart for almost a year since I embarked on my mission to Manhattan, and old house or not, at least we were together. Soon we began to get postcards reading, "Dear Alien. Classes in English will be taught at Mount Vernon High School. Please attend."

The day we moved into our new home *The Sky's the Limit* was canceled. Some timing. The show had improved, but it was just buried too deep to be saved. A few days later Ed Wolf sadly informed me that Raleigh Cigarettes, which had all but bought *Twenty Steps to a Million*, had decided against it at the last minute because CBS would not give them a better time period, and finding another sponsor seemed unlikely. Suddenly, I had nothing again. I had moved my family to New York, and now my only job was back in Toronto. Tough times loomed ahead.

In a desperate search for a bright side to all this, Monty quickly realized that he had a lot of free time now.

MONTY HALL[xv]

I said, "Kids, this is your new home, in your new country: The United States of America."

And we go inside, the phone is ringing. It's NBC. "Your show is cancelled."

I'm in a new country with my family and I'm unemployed. You know what I did? I said to Marilyn, "I saved up a couple of thousand dollars. We're going to Miami on a vacation!"

My friends said, "How can you go? You're unemployed!"

I said, "I was unemployed before, I'll be unemployed again. I'll come back and we'll start all over again. But we're going to have our vacation."

So, we went to Florida, got sunburned, came back, and started all over again.

Then Mort Werner called me from NBC to say the network was pleased with my work on the local show and was interested in putting me on a network program. Steve Allen's *Tonight Show* was doing well Monday through Friday nights, he said, and they had a similar show planned for Saturdays. They needed a fresh personality like me to do it; the producer should meet me, more as a formality than anything else; and it was all but set. I was thrilled. I had become a specialist in game shows and I enjoyed doing them, but this was a chance to host a variety-talk show, and I thought it would be perfect for me, the kind of show I wanted to do more than any other— and still do.

When I walked into the producer's office, he asked, "What can I do for you?"

I said, "Mort Werner felt I should meet with you. Didn't he tell you I was coming?"

And he said, "Well, he told me you were coming in, but he didn't tell me what for."

When I told him it was about the Saturday night show, he drew back and his eyes narrowed. "What about the Saturday night show?"

I was surprised and I stammered. "Well, he said he wanted us to talk about my emceeing it."

His expression turned hard and hostile. "I don't know anything about that. I do know you're not anywhere in my plans."

I couldn't believe I had been sent on such a wild goose chase. One moment I was a star, the next moment a piece of dirt. How often we ride a rollercoaster in show business, up and down in seconds.

CHAPTER EIGHT

(Author's collection)

MONTY HALL

It was back to the telephone and the streets and the offices and making the rounds one way or another. But now there was a big difference. I was known and I could get in to see people, even if there wasn't much for me. I did manage to land part-time work on NBC's *Monitor*, pinch-hitting for fellows who for one reason or another were absent. Occasionally I'd do a few bits on my own, but it wasn't anything I could count on, and the pay was uneven.

One day Mort Werner, who clearly cared, called me in again and assured me that NBC had high hopes for me as an emcee, which made me feel better, and wanted to put some eating money in my hands while waiting for the right opening to develop, which made me feel even better.

He said, "You've been pinch-hitting on *Monitor*. I'd like you to be a regular. That will pay $161.60 a week. And then we're putting on a Saturday morning cowboy movie. We want you to dress up in a checked shirt and host the show. I realize it's not a prestige thing, but it will pay $500 a week. Add that to your *Monitor* pay and you have $661 a week. Does that sound like eating money?"

It certainly did. With the $300 from my Canadian show, and with an odd job here and there, I averaged around $1,000 a week for a time.

Monitor presented news, music, and a lot of special features, including live on-the-scene broadcasts and interviews with personalities. Originally the program stressed these live segments, but as time passed they started to tape a lot because it was easier to insert taped segments whenever they wanted instead of constantly disrupting the schedule by shifting to live reports.

The original idea was better. It packed more punch. In the early years we always tried to make things lively. Occasionally we tried too hard. One time, NBC sent Merrill Muller and Jinx Falkenberg to cover a visit of Queen Elizabeth and Prince Philip to Ottawa. Morgan Beatty and I were co-hosting the show from New York, and Murray Burnett was producing.

Burnett got a call from Muller asking, "How would you like an interview with the Queen?"

"Fantastic," Murray said, and told me to announce to the audience that shortly we would be presenting a live interview with Queen Elizabeth.

"Murray," I said, "you're kidding. The Queen doesn't grant interviews."

Murray replied, "If Muller says he can get one, he can get one."

"Look, Murray," I protested, "I'm a Canadian and I know about the protocol of British royalty. There is no way Muller is going to get an interview with the Queen." At which point Murray told me to do as I was told.

So, Beatty went on with the show and every five or ten minutes I came on to announce that shortly we would be having an interview with the Queen. Twenty minutes passed, then forty, and still no interview. The switchboard began to light up with calls from listeners wondering what had happened. Meanwhile Muller and Jinx were broadcasting the reception ceremonies in Ottawa, but without the interview. Then Murray got Muller on the phone.

"Don't worry," Muller said. "I'll get to her any time now. Just play records and tapes and fill in until I can get it."

Monty, one of the many legendary Communicators who took the microphone for NBC's *Monitor*. (Author's collection)

Apparently, someone had told him he could get to the Queen, but as I expected, it wasn't happening.

An hour passed. By now everybody up to General Sarnoff was calling us. The network executives who had been listening in were worried, and worrying Murray, who was starting to sweat heavily, but I kept making the announcements and telling Murray I had told him so. Which, of course, endeared me to him. Jinx described the Queen's entrance into a ballroom.

I couldn't resist making a suggestion to Murray: "Tell her to grab Philip, and say, 'Hey, Prince-baby, how about a few words?'"

And Murray replied, "A few more words from you and your head will roll."

Then Muller called and said, "I understand the Queen has gone to sleep. I guess there won't be an interview." Murray just stared at the phone in disbelief.

Desperate, his job at stake, Murray was suddenly struck with an inspiration. Urgently, he huddled with Beatty and wrote something out for him. Then he told me to introduce Beatty and the interview. I was dumbfounded but did as he asked.

"And now," I said, "here is Morgan Beatty to bring you Merrill Muller's interview with Queen Elizabeth from Ottawa."

And Beatty said, "Ladies and gentlemen, we have Jinx Falkenberg and Merrill Muller on the line from Ottawa and Merrill has Queen Elizabeth with him for an interview. Hello there, Jinx. Jinx?...Jinx? *Jinx? Are you there, Jinx?...The line is dead.*" He was reading it slowly, like a child reciting aloud. "I'm sorry…ladies and gentlemen…the line to Ottawa must be down…We cannot continue our conversation with Merrill Muller and the Queen of England in Ottawa…If it can be repaired in time, we will return to it…And now…"

The show went on, but not with me. I was laughing too hard.

Murray Burnett was quite a character. We used to broadcast a harness race from Roosevelt Raceway every Saturday, and Burnett started to book our bets. Since most of us knew nothing about trotters, we each bet a different horse. If one of us won, Murray would pay off the price announced by the track, but he always came out ahead. This went on for weeks.

One night I came in with a tip on a hot horse. I told the others, and we all put our money on the same horse. Murray was surprised by that and not sure he liked it. When the horse finished first, he was sure he didn't like it. When we went to collect, he refused. The payoff was $8 or so, but with all the winners, he owed us a pile.

He said, "Nothing doing. You guys ganged up on me. I'll refund your bets, but I'll be damned if I'll be taken."

So, he stopped booking bets and we stopped betting.

When I began *Cowboy Theater*, I met with the producer and we discussed my background. He wanted to westernize me, of course, and he was delighted to learn I was from cattle country in western Canada. I told him how my grandfather had practically ridden the range and now my father and uncle had helped him. I told him my uncle owned a string of horses and wild west ponies and at one time led parades at the Calgary Stampede. He sent all this information to the publicity department, which worked up some exotic releases. Then he took me to a specialty store on Fifth Avenue and bought me some expensive cowboy-style shirts.

There I was, Mr. Wild West himself. I didn't have to wear cowboy pants or boots on the air because I was seen only from the waist up. The studio was not much bigger than an outhouse, and they paneled the walls and hung up some guns and portraits of wild geese in flight. I'd sit there and announce the movie, which usually was 1930s vintage and starred Charles Starrett or Buck Jones. I got pretty damn tired of the chase scenes—but it was a wonderful show, nevertheless, with that son of the Old West, Monty Hall, sitting there in that Old West outhouse telling everyone what they were watching and making pitches for a toy company every five minutes. An actor couldn't make a fast draw before it was time for another commercial. He'd be halfway through the draw, and I'd throw in a commercial; he'd complete the draw and I'd throw in another commercial. I was at the peak of my profession, all right. But then I guess Ronald Reagan did much the same thing as host of *Death Valley Days*.

Monty, on NBC's *Cowboy Theater*. (Author's collection)

The show started in September, and about a month before Thanksgiving a member of our sales department called me and said, "Monty, great news. We have just made a deal with Macy's. Guess who is going to be the number one man in their Thanksgiving Day Parade and ride the horse right at the front? Monty Hall, that's who! You're going to be grand marshall of the parade."

"You're kidding," I said.

"Who could be more natural than Monty Hall?" he replied. "Star of *Cowboy Theater*, descended from a long line of horsemen and ranchers? What a boost it will be for you and the show."

I said, "Look, there's something I have to tell you. I've never been on a horse in my life."

There was a long silence on the other end of the line. It was his turn to say, "You're kidding."

"What made you think I had?" I asked.

"Your publicity," he said.

"Oh, that," I replied. "Well, it was true as far as it went. But as for me, I never rode a horse outside of a carousel. I never rustled a steer or did anything like that."

He said, "It would be such good publicity."

I said, "I think it would be bad publicity to have old Cowboy Monty thrown from his horse while it was standing still in front of the parade and in front of millions of people. There is no way I am going to make a fool of myself by trying to ride a horse for the first time at the head of a parade."

"No way?" he asked.

"No way," I answered. And he never spoke to me again.

The show lasted twenty-six weeks, which was routine, and when it was over I was out the $500 a week and back looking for a new show while living on my paychecks from *Monitor* and *Who Am I?* Despite the ups and downs, we had bought a house in New Rochelle, figuring it was foolish to pay rent when we could be building up equity in a house of our own. So now I had a fairly fancy place, but I didn't have the jobs to support it in style. So we took a Florida vacation. In this business the only time you have for vacations is when you're unemployed. A tan means you're "at liberty."

In some ways the period I entered into next was the worst of my professional life. I was known and should have been able to make it, but I couldn't. There was nothing for me. I came close to a few things, but I missed out. Walt Framer once called me in to meet Bess Myerson. They had been working together on *The Big Payoff,* and it had gone off the air. He was trying to come up with a new show for her, and he wanted a man to be emcee. Bess, of course, is a former Miss America, a beautiful woman —and tall, more than six feet in high heels. I'm a little under six feet, and when we met, I looked up at her. I talked to her on tiptoe for a while.

Finally, I laughed and said, "Bess, if we do this show, you're going to have to work in your stocking feet."

She looked down at me and replied, "No chance. Bess Myerson does not work in her stocking feet." That was that.

Though I didn't have anything to do, I kept going into New York every day anyway. As the saying goes, Marilyn had married me for better or worse, but not for lunch. I had seen all the people I had to see, and they all knew I wanted work. Marilyn saw that hanging around the house was torture for me. So, she threw me out, and I was glad to go. She urged me to get on the commuter train and ride into the city every day and visit people and keep in touch and let them know I was still around. And so, I put in a nine-to-five day in the city just like all the working people. I'd check in with Marilyn a couple of times a day to see if there had been any calls. There never seemed to be any.

I'd go into the RCA Building and go up to the NBC studios and walk through the office and kibitz with the *Monitor* production staff. Or I'd go up to Ed Wolf's offices, because I felt like a member of the family. Ed had a sister on the switchboard, and a nephew, a son, an uncle, and a brother-in-law on his staff. He always had people around because it was a comfortable place to be. I always was welcome in whatever meeting was taking place, and I sat and listened and once in a while made a suggestion. When they had lunch, I was always invited. I was treated wonderfully. No one there ever put me down or said anything about my situation. I guess they realized I had to have some place to go, some place where I felt I belonged, at least on the fringes.

As the weeks went by, it got harder to endure this existence, and the rejections got harder to accept.

I remember Mort Werner one day saying, "I think I've got something for you. We're going to revive the *Bride and Groom* show, and we're thinking of you as the emcee. I want you to go and meet the producer, Roger Gimbel."

All this sounded sadly familiar to me, but what choice did I have? I made an appointment and went to see Roger Gimbel.

I had never met him. His office walls didn't reach the ceiling, and from where a visitor waited by the receptionist's desk, you could hear some of the talk coming from inside. I was on time but kept waiting, as usual.

He was with someone else, and his secretary hadn't even announced me when I caught part of his telephone conversation: "Yes, we're trying to revive *Bride and Groom,* and we need an emcee. But the toughest thing of all is to find an emcee. Every time I start looking for one, the program department always sends me the same five or six old names—Bill Cullen, Bert Parks, Dennis James, Monty Hall, Bud Collyer...."

I sat straight up, almost in shock. What the hell was this? How many shows had I done? How many weeks had I been on the air? How could I possibly be classified as one of the same old names? I had never even met the man, much less auditioned for him or worked for him.

"Yeah, the same old names. They never find me anybody new and that's what you need—someone new. The public is tired of the same damn faces all the time."

I was new, even if he didn't know it. Nationally, the public had hardly seen my face. I was being damned for having been around a while looking for work, even if I seldom got any. As I listened to him, I got madder and madder.

Finally, his visitor left, and his secretary told him his next appointment was waiting. She neglected to say who it was, however. He looked at me, and he obviously didn't know who I was.

I said, "You don't know who I am, do you? Well, I'm one of those old faces you're getting tired of having suggested to you for your shows. I'm Monty Hall and I'm number four on your list...."

I had caught him off guard, and he apologized. "Look, no offense meant, but every time we do a show, the program department sends us a list of names; and although I've never met you, I guess, seeing your name on that list all the time, I automatically put you in the same category as the others."

Maybe his embarrassment turned to anger at having been embarrassed. In any event, I never heard from him again. Robert Paige, the former movie actor, was brought in to emcee the show, but it went off after a short run. I have no idea whether I could have made it a better or more successful show. Naturally, I feel I could have. In this business, if you don't think you can, you can't. You need confidence. A good-sized ego is almost indispensable. You have to sell yourself, your personality, to the public. But first you must sell yourself to the network or the agency. If I won a lot of auditions and lost a lot of shows because I wasn't a big name, or the producer preferred a friend. By God, I was good at this, and I had proven it. But I couldn't get a chance then, and it was tough to be shut off for the wrong reasons.

I feel for all the good actors who are always out of work. There are talented performers tending bar or running liquor stores or selling shoes or real estate or insurance all over Hollywood. You run into these familiar faces all the time, and it embarrasses you and makes you feel sad for them.

I was deeply depressed. I stopped going into the city and sat home. My brother wrote me. He had established his legal practice during the time I had gotten next to nowhere in show business. He knew I was struggling again.

"You've got it," he wrote, "but they don't seem to want it, so why suffer their refusals and insults? Why is it so important to be a performer? It's time you gave your family some security. My practice is going well. Why not join me? You're still young enough to go back to school. Together, the Hall brothers will be invincible."

I thought about it for months. I knew I would make a good lawyer, and I would enjoy practicing with my brother. I would have a profession that no one could ever take from me. I would never have to face long layoffs and uncertainty, and I would never again have to sit at home waiting for the phone to ring. I thought about it for a long time. It was the only thing that made any sense—but I couldn't do it. I was a performer and I had to perform.

CHAPTER NINE

(Author's collection)

MONTY HALL

I wasn't starving, of course. With *Monitor* and *Who Am I?* and an odd job here and there I was making around $500 a week, and we were able to live well on that. But I didn't have anything solid and I wasn't getting anywhere.

One day in late 1957, Steve Krantz said to me, "I've an idea for a show, and I want you to emcee and produce it. We're going to play Bingo on television, with the home audience. People at home will use the digits in their telephone numbers. We'll pulled numbered balls out of a machine in the studio until we get calls from winners whose telephone number matches what we pull. We'll take the call on the air, check out the numbers in a telephone book, and award prizes. Channel Five is interested in it as a local show, but if it works, I think we can syndicate It across the country." I wasn't refusing any reasonable offers, so I told him to count me in.

Through Bill Bratter, I had managed to get MCA, the biggest talent agency in the country, to represent me. Dick Rubin became my personal representative and he got me $600 a week from Channel Five, with a year guaranteed, and 10 percent of any syndication. The program was called *Bingo at Home* and went on the air early in 1958. Our first show must have jammed every switchboard on the east side of Manhattan. We hadn't realized how many thousands of people might get to a winning total at the same time.

For the premiere broadcast on WABD Channel 5 in New York, a total of 40,000 people called the station during a single hour, jamming phone lines so severely that the entire YUkon exchange in the city was knocked out of service.

MONTY HALL

The next morning the telephone company came up and ripped out every line to our studio. That was the end of the telephone game. We had to improvise a new form of Bingo by that afternoon. We still used phone numbers but decided to do it by mail. We'd limit the amount of numbers on each show, wait for letters or postcards from winners, check them out, and reward them. We still had thousands of winners each show.

The reason for the unexpectedly large number of winners was that viewers figured out quickly that you just needed a telephone number, not necessarily your own telephone number. And since you had until midnight to mail in your postcard, a number of viewers would scour phone books until they found a winning number and mailed that one in.

The show changed the rules of the contest once more, telling viewers that they could only use phone numbers from the column of the phone book in which their own name appeared. This still gave a person about 100 opportunities per game to win something. But the new rule drew the ire of viewers with unlisted numbers, and viewers who didn't own phones, because it was exclusionary. The show amended the rules one more time, encouraging the phoneless and unlisted to mail in a request to have a column of the phone book assigned to them. 35,000 people sent in requests. Once the format stabilized, the mail whittled down to about 1,500 postcards per day; not nearly as many as they had to deal with in the beginning, but still far more than the show could really handle.

Monty demonstrates how to make a bingo card using your phone number at the opening of *Bingo at Home*. He thought it was the dullest thing he ever did on television. (Author's collection)

Game shows are constantly defending itself from accusations that they celebrate avarice. Viewers like game shows for a number of reasons—they like playing along with the game and comparing their own abilities to the players onstage; they like the personalities of the hosts and the players; the vicarious thrill that comes with a big win...But Bingo at Home *was such an unremarkable program that it irked critics because there truly was no reason to tune in other than to try to win something yourself.*

Bingo at Home *found a small but loyal audience. While it was easy to find Bingo games at any number of churches and social organizations,* Bingo at Home *attracted quite a following among viewers in poor health. It was a daily habit for long-term hospital patients who would gather together to watch the show. A 78-year-old woman wrote a thank-you note to the station, saying that she enjoys Bingo but that she can't spare the money to buy a card at local games, so the show made her feel included.*

Little did the viewers realize they had more enthusiasm for the show than the man calling the numbers. Monty, whom one critic likened to a tobacco auctioneer, was given a format that left him with little to do other than call out numbers one at a time. Monty ("not likely to cause John Daly or even Hal March any anguish" sneered columnist Jack O'Brian) did all he could in that limited role, calling out numbers in rhyme ("Under the B, man alive it's five…Under the G, ain't it great, number eight…") and even locking in on one unique bit of lingo to spin into a catch phrase. This version of Bingo included a zero under the O, which Monty would ominously call when it was pulled as "Uh-oh, it's oh-oh!" with the in-studio audience chiming in and saying it along. It breathed a little life into a show that was rather dull and repetitive.

MONTY HALL

It was a terrible program, boring as could be, and I hated it. But it caught on. Not that anyone at the networks realized it. The ratings showed no one was watching. Still, we were getting 200,000 postcards or letters a week. You have to live by ratings in this business. There is no real replacement for them as a measurement of your show's appeal to the public. If ratings are good, you believe them. If they are bad, you doubt them.

Bingo was the lowest rated show in its time slot, but the mailmen were bringing us bundles of mail daily. We made all the papers and *Life* ran a full-page picture of me holding a numbered ping-pong ball. But the show died of its own devices. There were too many prizes. We couldn't keep up with them. Also, scores of people complained that we hadn't responded to their winning cards. Finally, we surrendered.

Before *Bingo* went off, I landed two important network shows. I was asked to substitute for Jack Barry on *Twenty One*, which was the number-one rated program in the country at the time. Game show or not, this show, along with *The $64,000 Question*, had a tremendous following of fans who wanted to see whether an average person could answer awesome questions on the way to wealth. I did well, and the Barry-Enright office called to ask me to replace Barry for a few weeks while he went on a nightclub tour. Later, they asked if I'd be interested in taking over full-time because Barry wanted to continue in his new career. I almost knocked them over accepting. It was worth $1,000 a week to me, and it put me on coast to coast.

At the same time, Ed Wolf had made me emcee of *Keep Talking* on the CBS network. That was worth another $1,000 a week. Suddenly, I had two national shows, a local show, and a Canadian show. Monday nights, I did *Twenty One*. Tuesday nights, I did *Keep Talking*. Every afternoon, Monday through Friday I did *Bingo*. Saturdays, I did *Monitor*. Sundays, I did my Canadian show, *Who Am I?* I was a busy guy that month and in the $150,000-a-year bracket.

Keep Talking was an unorthodox game show; no real contestants, no prizes, and a game that involved a strong level of imagination. Teams of comedians & actors would compete against each other. One team had to improvise a story with two stringent guidelines. They were shown a secret sentence—example: "The proper way for porcupines to kiss is very carefully"—and Monty would announce a completely unrelated sentence. The team had to improvise a story that started with Monty's sentence and, at some point, included the secret sentence. After hearing the story, the opposing team had to guess which part of the story was the required sentence.

Game shows traditionally garnered terrible reviews from critics, even in the earliest years of television, but because Keep Talking was such an odd entry, and virtually not a game show, it was one of the rarities to enjoy positive feedback.

"CBS-TV's Keep Talking *is a welcome oasis in summer TV's Sahara. It has no isolation booths, no electronic switchboards, and most unbelievably at all, no cash prizes. Instead, some wise old soul reasoned that to gather together such raconteurs and comedians as Ilka Chase, Martyn Green, and Joey Bishop and allow them to free play with themselves and the language might be fun.*" –Broadcasting Magazine

Keep Talking wasn't getting good ratings and after a few weeks I was fired. Herb took some of us to lunch at Longchamps and broke it there. "You know how it is, kid," he said. "The show's in trouble and we got orders to shake it up—new emcee, new panelists. Nothing personal, you know, but we got to let you go."

And I smiled and said, "Oh hell, I know how it is. Don't worry about me. Right after I enjoy these oysters Rockefeller, I'm going to commit suicide." I put up a big front, but I wasn't fooling anyone. It was a kick in the ego, and it hurt.

Then I received another blow. I had been subbing for Barry on *Twenty-One* and was about to take over for him permanently when a report hit the newspapers that the show was fixed. A former contestant named Herb Stempel said that he had been offered a job with [Barry & Enright Productions] if he would lose and clear the way for a more popular contestant. He said he lost but didn't get the job. So he went to the D.A. He also charged that the contestants were given answers in advance. *Twenty One* was not alone. Other big-money shows, such as *The $64,000 Question*, *The $64,000 Challenge*, and *Tic Tac Dough*, either already had been accused of fixing or were soon to be.

I couldn't bring myself to believe the charge. I never had knowledge of any such set-ups on any show I'd emceed, including *Twenty One*. If it had been done, it had been engineered without my knowledge. Maybe they wouldn't have wanted the emcee to know about it so his reactions would be real and he wouldn't do anything to make anyone suspicious.

In the coming years, Monty learned more and more about his experience on Twenty One. *During his brief tenure as guest host, he was brought into an office with a large safe. The safe would be unlocked, the questions for the next episode were removed, and Monty was allowed to sort through them and make sure he was comfortable with the pronunciations of everything he needed to say. Then he'd put the questions back in the safe, re-lock it, and leave. Monty later learned that the moment he was gone, a contestant would be brought into the same office, and the safe would be unlocked for them.*

In Monty's own words about the experience, "I was a patsy."

MONTY HALL

In any event, the Parkson Advertising Agency called me in and said they were sorry, but Barry was going to have to take over again at once because it was felt it would look bad if he wasn't on the air while investigations were taking place. The fix scandals spread and the big money giveaways folded fast. Some leading men in the business, including Barry, were out of work in the industry in many years.

I do recognize that the guilty seriously abused the public trust. Still, I think people like Barry were dealt with harshly. No one was really hurt. It was a deception, but so are wrestling and roller derbies, all done in the name of entertainment. The punishment didn't fit the crime. I'd have put the guilty on probation. Bank robbers and muggers usually get second chances, and often a lot faster than the Barrys.

In the wake of those scandals, the shows I work on now have built-in safeguards. The networks police the shows closely. Producers and employees are liable, and the rules are followed to the letter. In the case of our shows, we would not jeopardize our position and success by any kind of hanky-panky, and I am sure that this holds for the entire industry today.

When *Bingo* was bounced, I suddenly was left without a show in America again. But the Channel Five producers had been pleased with my work, and Bennett Korn, the general manager, asked me what sort of show I'd like to do in that same one p.m. time period. When I suggested an interview show, he created *By-Line: Monty Hall*. It was a sort of *Tonight Show* in the afternoon. Every weekday, I sat around a coffee table with actors, scientists, ministers, politicians —people from almost every field—and discussed their work and the world around them for a half-hour. I pride myself on my wide interests and ability to talk to people on any subject, so this was a tough test for me. I feel I passed even if the program did not. Our ratings showed no one was watching, although our mail showed many were…But the sponsors were dissatisfied with the ratings, and we went off the air.

As I have said before, I have made many compromises in my career, and experiences like *By-Line* inly reinforce my belief that before one can become a patron of the arts, he had better get himself some wherewithal. In other words, the first step toward becoming a philanthropist is to earn some money. At this stage of my life, that seemed to be the paramount issue.

With the demise of *By-Line* I was willing to do any kind of show at all to take its place. I had a contract with Channel Five to fulfill, and I did anything they wanted me to, including announcing wrestling matches.

The wrestling was a farce. I broadcast these shows every week from Sunnyside Gardens in Queens. I just did them straight and didn't hoke them up the way others did. It was a job. Every match was scheduled to be the best of three falls, but we had arranged that every match would go the limit. That way we could get in more commercials.

The fans were frightening because most of them believed in it, although the fakery was transparent to anyone with eyesight. A friend of mine, Dr. Abe Kroll, a dentist and man of many talents and much intelligence, was hooked on wrestling. He used to plead with me to take him to one of the shows. I kept saying that if he did go, he would see how phony they were and be disappointed. But he didn't want to hear about the phoniness, he just wanted to go. So, one night I took him. I showed him the briefing room where wrestlers were getting their instructions. I told him exactly what would happen. I let him sit near me at ringside to see it happen exactly as predicted. We ran far overdue on a commercial and I signaled to the referee several times before he finally simply disqualified both contestants to give us a break. The good dentist saw it all.

As we drove home, I said, "Abe, I'm sorry, but now you must see it for what it is."

And Abe said, "What it is, is the most exciting thing going. I don't care about the side stuff. I enjoyed every minute of it. I want to go again." Well, there is one born every minute.

I heard there was a job open with the New York Rangers as color man on their hockey broadcasts. Les Keiter of WINS was impressed enough with me and my knowledge of the game to hire me without an audition. Because of my other commitments in town, I could only work the home games. This made it pretty tough on Jim Gordon, the play-by-play man, because he had to do both play-by-play and color on the road. I got a fast fifty a game for my Wednesday and Sunday nights in Madison Square Garden. But as a Canadian, I had come to love the game, and I might have gone on for nothing if asked. I did the games for two seasons, but had to resign when I started *Video Village*.

As a result of his duties as a color man for Rangers hockey games, Monty is a footnote in a night when professional hockey history was made: November 1, 1959.

MONTY HALL[xvi]

The Montreal Canadiens are visiting. In the pre-game warm-up, Jacques Plante, the goalkeeper for Montreal, is wearing a mask. They didn't wear masks in those days. But he wore it in the warm-up. Now the game starts, and no more than three minutes into the game, a puck hits him in the forehead and he's bleeding profusely. They take him off the ice to stitch him up.

They didn't carry two goaltenders in those days as they do now. So I have to fill fifteen, twenty minutes while they're stitching him up.

I say, "It wouldn't surprise me if, when he comes back on the ice, because of that injury, he'll be wearing a mask. And if that's so, it will be the first time in National Hockey League history that a goaltender will wear a mask."

Sure enough, twenty minutes later, he comes onto the ice, he returns to his position, he's wearing a mask, and 15,000 people in Madison Square Garden got to their feet and booed him! They were all macho. They booed him. But I predicted it, he wore it, and it made National Hockey League history.

Some years after Monty finished his autobiography, he found himself seated next to Les Keiter on an airplane. Monty confessed that he harbored a nagging feeling about his job calling Rangers hockey. He had been collecting $75 per game, which he had been told was the allotted talent fee.

Without revealing why he was asking, Monty asked Les Keiter, "What was the real talent fee for that job?"

Keiter, without hesitation, confessed, "It was $250. I was paying you $75 and keeping the rest for myself."

Monty laughed and told Keiter he had only cheated himself. "I love hockey. I would have done that job for free."

MONTY HALL

My strongest memory of this show was when I got the team's coach, Phil Watson, fired. I had Watson on between periods, of one of the Rangers' worst games and asked him why the team was playing so badly. Phil, a fiery fellow, told me why right out, ripping each player in turn.

He started out, "Well, take Worsley [the goalie,] with that beer belly on him. He couldn't stop a barrel from rolling into the net."

He went on from there: this player was selfish and another was lazy and that one had no ability and another was wasting his energy chasing broads. Muzz Patrick, the Ranger general manager, was listening, and as soon as we were off the air Watson was no longer coach.

That summer I got a job telecasting International Soccer League games from the Polo Grounds over WPIX. There were teams from Germany, Italy, Hungary, Yugoslavia, England, Scotland, Brazil, and so forth, but despite New York's enormous ethnic population from countries where soccer was the top sport, no one came to the games.

I enjoyed these play-by-play telecasts because they required fast thinking and apt description. I have never believed that a play-by-play announcer should relate only what is happening on the field, but as a reporter should try to convey to the audience the nuances: "What is the strategy now? What is the manager thinking of? What would you do in this situation?" This draws the listeners or viewer into the action and gives him a chance to be an armchair quarterback. So, I never missed an opportunity to interpret an action. For example, soccer players have a marvelous tendency to showboat. When injured, they swoon and lie on the field immobile. After eliciting the crowd's sympathy, they jump miraculously to their feet and resume two-way action at top speed.

Accordingly, when I saw a player go into a Sarah Bernhardt, I couldn't resist saying: "Keep your eyes on Stanislaus. He's lying there like dead, but I guarantee he'll be on his feet in sixty seconds." And he always was.

Among the incidents I recall is one that arose when the Yugoslavian team was playing Brazil. Before the game could start, we had to have first the United States national anthem, followed by the national anthems of the two visiting countries. After "The Star-Spangled Banner" and the Brazilian anthem, the Polo Grounds public address system started on the Yugoslavian anthem. The very courteous audience in the stands was appalled to see the Yugoslavian team break ranks and start to kick the ball around. They booed the athletes for their disrespect.

Knowing there had to be a reason, I surmised over the air, "The only thing I can think of, folks, is that these players are all Titoists, and the only record we have here is the national anthem that was played under Mihailovich." After the game, I found I was right.

I received some great compliments for my soccer reporting. The president of the Scottish team Kilmarnock wrote a letter to the soccer league saying that I was the best soccer announcer he had ever heard. A *Cue Magazine* critic called me one of the best play-by-play men he'd come across in any sport. It may be hard to forget criticism, but it is easy to remember compliments.

About this time, I gave up *Who Am I?* It had been on the air for ten years, but I couldn't continue without returning to Canada. As the show went off, my bank account began to shrink. A Channel Five executive called to remind me that the station had a contract with me calling for $800 a week until the end of the year and that they wanted me to do something to earn it. I agreed that was fair enough.

He said they wanted me to do a children's show. My blood ran cold. If there was one thing I didn't want, it was a children's show.

He said, "You'll record the show during the week and it'll play for three hours on Saturday mornings."

To me it was like the end of the world. I ran cartoons and educational films and I played games with the kids. I sat around and talked with them and felt like a fool every minute. After four or five weeks I quit. No weekly paycheck was worth that to me.

I don't remember the name of the show, and neither does Marilyn. I don't want to remember. That was the ebb of my career, worse even than doing the wrestling.

An odd blessing emerged, however. I used to have the cameras pan across the faces of the children in the audience and linger on a closeup on each one, figuring that this would be a thrill for their relatives. After the show had been off the air a while, I met a woman at a party.

She said, "I want to thank you for the warmest moment of my life. My mother was in the hospital dying of an incurable disease. More than anything, she wanted to see my little boy, her only grandson, but children were not permitted to visit patients in the hospital. My son was going to be on your show. I knew you put a picture of each child on and prayed you would do so with my son this time. So, we brought a TV set into Mother's room. As your show came on, she was in a coma, but the moment you put a picture of her grandson on, her eyes opened. She saw her grandson, smiled, and died hours later. Thanks to you, my last memory of my mother is with a smile on her face."

Performers occasionally have a frightening emotional impact on the public, and it is a large responsibility. I hated that show, yet in a few seconds I gave two women something almost supernatural. And it be that those moments make it all worthwhile.

During that period, Bill Bratter died of a heart attack. When I got word of his death, I went to the funeral parlor in Manhattan to pay my respects. There I saw grown men sit and cry, for he had helped others as he had helped me. I could have used a Bill Bratter in my life during the tumultuous is times that were to come.

CHAPTER TEN

(Author's collection)

MONTY HALL

While I had *Twenty-One, Keep Talking, Bingo, Monitor,* and *Who Am I?* all going at once, I heard that Jack Paar was going to take a week's vacation from *The Tonight Show*. I asked my agent if he could get the week for me. He looked at me as if I were crazy and exclaimed,

"You!" That was a great boost to my ego.

Some agents are marvelous. When you need them, they couldn't care less. When you don't need them, they care. I remember sitting in the office of an MCA agent who was handling Red Buttons. Red had been big on TV for a couple of seasons, but his show had gone off. A secretary buzzed the agent to tell him Red was calling.

The agent said, "Oh, for Christ's sake, get rid of him. Who needs him?"

Then he turned back to me. He didn't need me, either.

In the 1950's, Bill Bratter had talked MCA into giving me an agent on a three-year contract. The agent didn't do a thing for me, and I'm sure he didn't even try. He never called me. About three years later I figured I'd try to get someone else, and I called the agency to find out when my contract was up.

The secretary said, "You've been finished with us for three months."

That hit me pretty hard. They hadn't even bothered to call or send a note. I had been removed from their roster, from the face of the earth.

My morale really hit rock bottom when all my shows went off the air. For a time, my friends and I tried to develop ideas for shows in hopes that we would hit the jackpot. One of my co-workers at *Monitor* was Bernie Kahn. He had a friend, Nat Ligerman, who ran a laundromat in Greenwich Village to keep body and soul together. Nat had a sign in his shop that read: "You don't know what you're missing until you use my laundromat."

And to prove it, every one of his customers missed something. Nat had three sons at the time, and keeping them in clothing was difficult. His customers made unscheduled contributions. Among his clientele were such stars as Anthony Franciosa and Jason Robards, Jr. To this day, they don't realize that their underwear was being worn by assorted Ligerman children.

Bernie and Nat used to bring me ideas, and I would reject them. Nat wanted to be in show business even if it meant sweeping up after the elephant in the circus. He operated his thirty-two machine laundromat only because it brought in a buck. It also brought in television people who lived in the area, and he could try out ideas on them or ask them for jobs. He used to send ideas and scripts to the network executives, and he called himself Nat Ligerman Productions.

One day Nat answered the phone with his usual bark: "Laundromat!"

The caller turned out to be a partner at Doyle, Dane, Bernbach advertising agency. One of Nat's submissions intrigued him. He asked, "Incidentally, did you say 'laundromat'?" Nat immediately changed direction:

"No, no! I said 'Ligerman Productions.'"

At that moment washing machine number 16 started spilling suds, flooding the store.

Nat's only assistant, a Puerto Rican boy by the name of Chico, was in the back of the shop sorting out the stolen socks.

"Chico!" Nat screamed, searching desperately for someone to help him, since he could not and would not dare leave the telephone. He turned back to his caller for a moment and then again desperately shrieked "Chico!"

At the third summons a head peeked around the barrier and answered, "What ees eet, Nat?"

Ligerman, having a prospective client on the phone and unwilling to reveal the true nature of his predicament, shouted, "Camera 16's gone crazy!"

The man on the other end was stunned. "Sixteen cameras?" he asked.

Nat regained his composure. "I got thirty-two!" he said proudly. The show didn't sell, but Camera 16 was fixed so it stopped flooding.

One day Nat and his buddy Bernie brought me an idea, but I didn't go for it and had to reject it. As they were leaving, Ligerman paused and asked, "What's the first thing you'd say if I said the word 'black'?"

I said, "White."

Ligerman said, "Yes, but maybe someone else could say 'cat' or 'dark' or 'night.'"

"Come back in here," I said. He returned, grinning.

He said, "I wanted to try that on you because maybe there is a show in free association." And that was the beginning of a program we called *First Impressions*—and, for that matter, several other shows.

I spent weeks developing the idea, and came up with a two-part program. In the first part the audience would be shown key words, and contestants came up with answers based on clue words. In the second part married couples would answer the clue word separately, and if they matched them in free association, they would get points toward a winner's prize.

A friend of mine did some artwork and I arranged an appointment to discuss the show with Oscar Katz, head of daytime programming at CBS. Nat Ligerman, desperate to get into show business fulltime, called me nightly from the laundromat to see what progress we were making with the show. When he heard I had an audience with a CBS executive, he begged to go along.

I said, "No, Nat. You have no experience in television or in meetings like this. You're overanxious, and you're liable to say something that will screw us up."

He said, "No, I won't, I swear it. I just want to tag along. I've got a good suit. I'll shave. I'll sit in a corner and never open my mouth." Reluctantly, I agreed.

The next day we went to 485 Madison Avenue, and I made the presentation to Katz.

Nat, true to his word, sat silently in a corner. Oscar was interested and proposed what is called a "step deal."

He said, "We'll give you some offices next door at 501 Madison and we'll give you some money to prepare an audio tape. If it looks good, we'll shoot a pilot. If that works, we'll go on the air. To begin with, we'll give you, let's say, $8,000 as work-up money."

Nat, who never in his life had heard of so much money being given out at one time, jumped out of his seat and shouted "Eight thousand dollars!"

Oscar Katz, who was really interested in the show and thought my partner was outraged by the size of the offer, leaped from his seat and shouted back, "All right, make it $12,000."

I couldn't believe it. "Sold!" I yelled, and hustled Ligerman out of there before Katz found out what had hit him.

I said, "Damn it, Nat, you almost blew it."

"Did I?" he asked. He wasn't sure what had happened.

I told him, "Hell no, you got us four grand extra."

We produced an audio, but CBS didn't buy it. I took it to a friend, Bob Stewart, who worked for Goodson-Todman, the game show people. He took it down the hall to show Mark Goodson. When Stewart returned, he suggested some changes. I went home and worked on it, came back, and talked over the changes with Stewart. He went down the hall and talked them over with Goodson. Then he returned with more refinements. This routine went on for weeks. I was never permitted to see Goodson. Stewart would suggest changes. I'd go home, work on them, and bring them back. Then Goodson would always suggest still other refinements.

Stewart finally talked Goodson into trying our idea out on *I've Got a Secret*, Garry Moore, who was the emcee at that time, told his celebrity panel, "I'm going to try an experiment on you. I will say something to you, and you give me the first thing that comes to mind."

I forget the words involved, but it went well under the circumstances. But it didn't seem to sell Goodson and I got tired of my trips to see Stewart and his invisible boss, so I gave up on that end.

Another friend, Perry Leff of the Frank Cooper Agency, put me in touch with a New York producer named Art Stark, who took a shine to the show and suggested we try to work out a format that would use a celebrity panel. By that time, I was willing to try anything, so I invited Art to be my partner in the project. We started to develop the show along new lines and soon we arranged a run-through for CBS.

Stark was working on a show titled *Who Do You Trust?* with Johnny Carson as emcee.

It's good to be the mayor. Monty Hall takes over as host of *Video Village*.
(Hall Family collection)

We got Carson, columnist Murray Kempton, and some others as a panel. They had to identify celebrity guests through free association of words and hints. Joan Fontaine, Jan Murray, and Louella Parsons were the guests. On the day of the run-through New York was hit with one of the biggest snowstorms in its history. It looked as if we were lost, but we hired bulldozers to dig people out of the suburbs and somehow got Oscar Katz and other executives in the studio. Only Jan Murray, in Scarsdale, couldn't make it, so we did his bit by telephone. The show went off all right, but nothing came of it. That was not unusual. Most television series take a lot of selling, because no one is sure what will succeed. Even if a network or sponsor falls in love with a show, they aren't sure that the public will.

In September 1960, something solid turned up at last. One day Alden Schwimmer of the Ted Ashley agency was driving me home from the golf course when I saw my wife and my car going the other way on the parkway.

"What is she doing?" I wondered aloud.

I found out twenty minutes later when Alden dropped me off and Marilyn returned. She had been searching for me desperately. I was wanted as a rush replacement for a show in New York.

When I returned their call, they said, "Thank God we've reached you. You've got to do this show tomorrow morning. Can you do it?"

Without hesitation, I said "I'll try." Then I said, "What show?"

They said, "*Video Village*. Do you know the show?"

"I have to be honest," I admitted. "I've never even seen it. You show me how and I'll do it."

They told me to come on in, so I drove into New York.

CBS, which was significantly wounded in the quiz show scandals, had purged programs like The $64,000 Question *and its spinoff,* The $64,000 Challenge, *at the end of the 1950s. The network held onto three panel shows,* What's My Line?, I've Got a Secret, *and* To Tell the Truth, *from Mark Goodson-Bill Todman Productions. Goodson-Todman was virtually the only game show house to emerge from the scandals with no accusations, and the three panel shows had such modest prize money that fixing them didn't seem terribly logical anyway. In 1959, CBS unveiled* G.E. College Bowl, *a venerable team trivia competition where the prize money was awarded not to the contestants, but to the scholarship funds of the schools they represented.*

In 1961, the network seemed ready to gamble on game shows again, introducing four new daytime games, while making it a point to tell any reporter who would listen that the network was now enforcing some very tight controls. To offset accusations that game show producers would gather prizes, but then fix the games to prevent them from being won and keep the prizes for themselves (an accusation that was never really proven on any show during the scandals, but the networks were now wary), a rule was in place that the networks would acquire prizes themselves, or from an outside agency hired specifically to do so. A further rule was enforced saying that either the prize had to be offered until somebody won it, or if it went unclaimed, it had to be returned directly to the manufacturer.

In the case particularly of their new show Video Village, *CBS had two more safeguards that seemed to ensure no chicanery behind the scenes. The game relied so heavily on luck, with rolls of a die determining contestants' fates on each turn, that on its face there didn't appear to be a means* of rigging it. More importantly, CBS, in sharp contrast to the way they boasted about the largesse offered on big money quiz shows just a few years earlier, enthusiastically touted that the prize budget for Video Village *would be "modest." And how…on the premiere broadcast, the winning contestant came away with a grand total of $15.*

MONTY HALL

That summer, CBS had bought a show called *Video Village* and made Jack Narz emcee. Narz, however, was having domestic difficulties. He had a wife and a home in California and a five-day-a-week live show in New York. His wife wanted him to stay home. He had asked CBS to shift the show to California, but they had not agreed. Now he had suddenly gone back home to talk matters over with his wife, and someone had to be found to do the program the very next day.

The show was like a Parcheesi game. It was laid out on a large board and the contestants moved up and down the board by rolling dice. The show's originators, Merrill Heatter and Bob Quigley, laid out the board in a hotel meeting room, and we went over and over it. The next morning at CBS I did a couple of rehearsals. We went on the air at 10:30, and it worked. I saved the day. The Heatter and Quigley people poured praise all over me. They were very grateful and I was elated.

That afternoon Narz called and said he was giving up the show to save his marriage. I was asked to carry on for a few days. After those programs went well, they asked me if I would be willing to do it permanently. I said I would, and they went to the CBS brass and asked permission to make me the permanent emcee.

Jim Aubrey, then the big boss at the network, was leaving for Hawaii. He said he had someone else in mind for the spot, an old friend from California named Red Rowe. Heatter and Quigley argued that I'd pulled them through in a pinch and deserved the job. But Aubrey insisted on his man, and Rowe came in and worked a couple of shows.

But Perry Leff, who was representing me, and Heatter and Quigley were persistent. They went to Larry White, head of daytime programing, and said, "Tell Aubrey we want Hall."

White courageously made the decision while his boss was away. Aubrey returned and apparently gave in. I suppose he had done what he felt was the honorable thing for his old friend, and then had decided to do what was best for the show. So, I got a national network program, at $1,250 a week, with my name up in lights on the marquee outside Theater 52 just off Broadway.

Several ironic twists followed. Despite his return to California, Narz's marriage ended within months. Then in February CBS decided to move the show to California as Narz had wanted them to do originally.

Video Village's *move from New York to California was a logistical issue. Television in New York was predominantly done in repurposed Broadway theaters, many of which had surprisingly tiny stages that couldn't accommodate the increasingly elaborate sets designed for television. In Los Angeles,* Video Village *would be taped inside the massive CBS facility known as Television City, which was more accommodating of the sprawling miniature town on which the game was played. The set consisted of three streets: Money Street, Bridge Street, and Magic Mile. There was a jail, a row of shops, a bridge, and even a little bus which Monty would steer to take the contestants from the Finish Line all the way back to the Video Village Visualizer Wonder Window to start the next game.*

Monty was originally joined by a lovely assistant, "Associate Mayor" Joanne Copeland, but when the show moved west, Copeland resigned from office and remained in New York City, where she'd become the second Mrs. Johnny Carson.

In Los Angeles, the new Associate Mayor was Eileen Barton, an upbeat singer/actress who would join Monty in a duet on the Village bus. The show actually had a more impressive musical pedigree than your average game show. Barton had a number-one hit with "If I Knew You Were Comin' I'd've Baked a Cake," and each game was underscored with live music provided by musical director Sid Wayne, who had penned 13 songs for Elvis Presley.

Barton made a number of fans on the show, included a dedicated eight-year-old who decided he wanted to meet her, so he mailed two cereal box tops into the program. The show never made any such offer, but the boy had seen so many TV shows that made special offers in exchange for the sponsor's box tops that he reasoned he could get whatever he wanted by doing so. Monty was so amused by the effort that he read the boy's fan letter on the air, showed off the box tops, and quipped, "Sorry, meeting Eileen takes three box tops."

When the boy wrote a second letter and included another box top, Barton decided he had at least earned a phone call and chatted with her fan for a while.

MONTY HALL

I decided to go along with the show, since it was becoming clear to everyone in the business that the bulk of the television production was shifting to Los Angeles. Anyway, aside from *Monitor*, I had nothing to give up. Marilyn agreed.

Then, just before I was to leave for the coast, Bob Stewart called me for the first time in months and invited me to lunch at the Stage Delicatessen. He said, "That idea of yours,

First Impressions, is still the best idea that's come across my desk in a long time, and I've finally got Mark Goodson interested enough so that we can go ahead and start working on it together." I told him I had already made a deal with Art Stark, was going to California, and it was too late.

"Well, that's too bad," he said.

In March, Marilyn and I left the kids with a sitter and went west. It was warm when we arrived in Los Angeles, and we were wearing heavy winter coats. When I stepped off the plane, I took off my coat and said, "That's it. No more coats. I'm staying." We fell in love with sunny southern California right then. Once I got there, I never wanted to leave. You live better—it's that simple.

We didn't feel secure enough to buy a house right away, but we rented a lovely place in the hills of Laurel Canyon for $600 a month. It was like living in the country. I had to do five *Video Village* shows and one *Kideo Village* show, a Saturday children's version, weekly, but we started to tape and wrapped them up in three days. The rest of the time I lay around the pool or played golf. It was such a different way of life, half vacation all the time.

I remember the first day I went to work in Los Angeles. I rented a little Corvair and drove up to the CBS gate in a line of large cars. Right ahead of me was the producer of *Video Village* in a Rolls Royce, the director in a Jaguar, and my assistant, Eileen Barton, a prominent singer, in a Cadillac. As each pulled up to the gate, the car was waved right in. When I pulled up in the Corvair, I was stopped and the guard asked who I was. I said, "Look, buddy. You waved all the others in without asking that question. But I've got news for you. If you don't let me in, Corvair or not, there's no show today!" After he found out who I was, he let me in. I get in easier now.

I always have enjoyed studio work. It may be the same old show, but every time you do one it's new and offers something different. I enjoy the camaraderie of the crew. I have never had an argument of any kind with anyone on the floor of one of my shows. We may not agree on how everything should be done, but we work it out. I'm not temperamental. It takes a lot of people doing many jobs will to make a show successful. Any one of them can mess it up, but most of them don't. There are a lot of pros in television who work hard but who do not get rich or famous, and l appreciate them.

In the summer of that year, I began to have severe abdominal pains. The doctor whom I consulted said I had an infection and needed surgery, which he later performed, but after six months l was so little improved I went to another doctor. He said that the surgery had been a waste of time. My problem stemmed from a slight perforation of the small intestine, and as long as the intestine leaked, the infection would re-form. Just when it seemed that more surgery was needed, almost miraculously, the perforation sealed and the infection drained away.

I continued to have severe stomach distress from time to time, and further examination by a gastroenterologist revealed that I had ileitis. Because of my stomach trouble and the problems I've had with my back, some have labeled me a hypochondriac. But I have missed only twenty shows in ten years on *Let's Make a Deal* and none on *Video Village* for two years.

That first winter I worked in constant pain, but I tried not to impose my discomfort on anyone else. At Christmas time a very nice thing happened to me. The producers and performers always throw parties or give gifts to their crews. It's a custom, and crews expect it. They are never expected to respond in kind, and they almost never do. One day I was lying down in my dressing room during the lunch break when there was a knock at the door. I asked who it was but couldn't make out the name. Wearily, I got up and open the door.

There standing before me with wide smiles on their faces were fifteen or twenty members of the CBS crew. They handed me a box, and some of them shouted.

"Open it up…open it up!"

I opened the package and there was a tall, handsomely carved wooden pepper mill with a crown on it.

"Read the card…read the card," they yelled.

It had been specially prepared by the art department, and it read, "To the King of Television from all his Crew." They had all signed their names to it.

I was deeply touched. One of the old hands, a little guy who always wore a hat, said, "Son, this is an important thing we just done for you. To tell you how important it is, we've only done it once before, and that was for Jimmy Durante. So, I wanted you to know this is kind of important to us as well as to you." He didn't have to tell me.

I hadn't ever really given up hope on *First Impressions* and still hoped to sell it somehow. Shortly after my surgery, I read an item in the trade papers that Mark Goodson and Bill Todman were starting a new show called *Password* on CBS. It sounded suspiciously like what I had been trying to sell them earlier. My lawyer, Roy Blakeman, who had taken over my affairs after Bill Blatter died, was also the lawyer for Goodson-Todman, and I asked him about the new show.

He said, "I knew you'd read the item and wonder about it, but it's absolutely not the same thing you showed to Mark. Don't get excited about it. Call Bob Stewart first thing in the morning."

I called Bob Stewart. It was one of the most painful calls I've ever experienced.

He said, "Yes, Monty, what can I do for you?"

I said, "Didn't Roy Blakeman tell you I was going to call?"

He said. "No, he didn't. Why are you calling?"

I said, "I'm calling because I heard about *Password*."

And he said, "Monty, I knew you were going to call about that. I knew it would upset you." I was getting very upset.

"Look," he said, "I'll level with you, but it's just between us. When I had that last conversation with you and you told me you were no longer interested in working with us on your show, I reported it to Mark. He said, 'Well, we're going to go to work on this idea anyhow.' We changed it and worked up a sale. I said, 'Don't you think we ought to cut Monty in on this because he brought the show to us in the first place?' And he said, 'No, Freud was with us long before Monty Hall.' So that's it. I wanted you to know how it is. But I will not repeat it publicly. I'm sorry."

I'm sure he was, for Bob Stewart is a decent fellow. He was, in essence, telling me where his loyalties lay. I couldn't blame him. Show business is a jungle. Survival of the fittest.

I called Blakeman back and told him what Stewart had told me. He said only that he was headed back to New York and would look into the matter there.

A few days later he called me and said, "Mark wants you to come to New York."

I said, "Well that's more like it."

"Wait a minute," he said. "He wants you to come to New York to prove to you that he had this idea long before you brought it to him."

I replied angrily, "You mean he wants me to go all the way to New York just to tell me I'm wrong?"

Roy said, "Yes, he says you're wrong. He claims that he had the idea before you ever entered the office."

"Well, then, I'm going to sue him," I said.

Roy pointed out that he also represented Mark and would have to withdraw from the case. I told him I'd get another lawyer. And I did.

Meanwhile, NBC started another Goodson-Todman show called *The Match Game* in which three contestants wrote down their reactions to a word and if they matched with one another they received points toward prizes. Since this procedure was outlined in the second half of my original show, I figured I had a second lawsuit to file. And now NBC would be involved, too.

However, Larry White at CBS told me, "Look, you're working here as an emcee on our network. It wouldn't look good for you to be suing another packager on our network and to be biting the hand that's feeding you."

But then, right in the middle of the controversy, NBC turned around and bought my own program *First Impressions*. I was delighted but perplexed. Some of my friends said I should go ahead with the suits. People at the networks obviously urged me not to. An idea is an idea, they said. We all have them. You can't prove one belonged to you. If you want to keep working in the business, you can't sue people.

In the end, I did not pursue the lawsuits. I was a little man in the business, and I would have been bucking the big shots. I could never have gotten ownership of the shows; the most I could have gotten was some money, perhaps royalties. I wanted to get ahead, and suits would have alienated people.

I am not unfamiliar with suits myself. Since becoming a successful producer, I have had countless people pounding at the door to show their ideas. As a favor to some friends, I have met with a few. Nothing has ever come of it. But as soon as a new show is started, inevitably a phone call comes from a lawyer, saying, "You stole this from my client!"

"What on earth did we steal?" I ask.

The lawyers answers, "Well, his show also has three panelists!"

Such suits are always dropped. A dentist who came to visit me one day insisted he had the greatest panel show of all time. He explained that three celebrity panelists tried to identify a man's occupation by interrogating him. I looked at him with uplifted eyebrows.

"That's it?" I asked.

"That's it," he replied.

"Haven't you ever heard of *What's My Line?*" I queried.

"What the hell's that?" he shot back.

I said, "Well, it's only been on CBS Sunday nights a dozen years or more!"

The dentist was furious. "The hell you say," he muttered, taking up his portfolio and leaving the office in a huff.

Three shows developed out of the idea of a free association game. *Password* has been a great hit and remains on the air to this day. *Match Game* had its success, and so did *First Impressions*. Selling it was a thrill, though the experience was diluted by the heartbreak of all that went with it. After I flew back to New York, Art Stark and I signed the contracts, and I had made my first major sale in this country. Since the show was to be done in California, we offered to move all those who had helped us put it together in New York. Bernie Kahn came out as a writer. Nat Ligerman wanted to go more than anyone, but as what?

"As anything," he said. "I'll sweep the floors. I'll run messages. I just want to get out of the laundry business and into show business, and this is the chance."

So, I told Nat to come out. I made him a production assistant, and later an associate producer. He's been with me ever since.

We took offices in the NBC Building at Sunset and Vine and set up shop in November 1961. The title of the show was changed to *Your First Impression* because *First Impressions* is a subtitle of *Little Women,* and the network, like all networks, was nervous about anything that could cause any complications.

There were problems with the show from the start. Among those who had come with us from New York was Fred Stettner, who was a brother-in-law of Dan Enright—and thus involved by association it the quiz show scandals of 1958 along with Barry & Enright. Some people at NBC remained determined that none of these people would ever work in television again. However, I would not fire him. An hour before the first show was to go on the air, we got a call from an NBC executive in New York telling us not to use Stettner's name in the credits or the show would be taken off the air.

I told Stettner and he said if his name were removed, he would sue. I knew he had a case. I asked him to let it go for now so we could get through our first show and I'd fight the good fight for him the following week, but he refused. He was fighting for his life—and I was fighting for my show. In desperation, I got on the phone. It was past quitting time in New York, and I had to track down NBC executives at their homes, but I did obtain permission to use the credit.

Afterward I was angry with the NBC executives who had posed this problem in the first place, and I was angry, too, with Stettner, for not backing down briefly. He was and is a friend, but I still think he was wrong in this case. In this business, the show is the thing. What the hell does principle do for you if you screw up the show? Putting on these shows is a team effort, and we all have to pull together. This was opening night. And it damn near was closing night at the same time.

The incident goes to show how this business bends you. I admire men of principle and have fought for my own. Maybe I was wrong to ask Stettner to lower his fists even for a minute. But we all run scared in television. He was. And I was. We didn't have positions of power; we had few weapons; we were desperate for survival. It's easier to fight when you're not afraid, when a failure doesn't threaten to finish you.

Bill Leyden, host of Monty's production *Your First Impression*. (Author's collection)

Your First Impression started off struggling. The format wasn't working right, and there were personnel problems. Art Stark started to telephone every day to offer advice. Then Bob Aaron of NBC started to call from New York with his own daily observations. Somehow, we got through the first thirteen weeks, and our option was picked up for another thirteen weeks, but I knew we were in trouble. I flew back to New York to meet with Stark and Aaron, and I laid down the law. This was my show and I was not going to see it destroyed. They could call and make suggestions, but as long as they were in New York and I was in L.A. I was not going to spend all my time on the phone with them. I told them I was going to make the final decisions, I needed a new producer, and I was going to change the format: the first half of the show would have celebrities as usual, but the second half would have ordinary contestants.

In a newspaper profile, Monty admitted to being overwhelmed, trying to produce one show while hosting another.

MONTY HALL[xvii]

When you're a producer, you have all the headaches. When your show is on the air and something goes wrong, you're powerless. On *Video Village*, I'm on top of the show constantly and I have a good working relationship with my producers. Yes, I tell you, a producer is a worrisome thing.

Coming to realize he was in over his head, Monty sought out a business partner. He found that plus a kindred spirit in Stefan Hatos. Like Monty, he was a poor boy trapped in a successful man's body.

STEFAN HATOS[xviii]

I always knew that someday I would wind up with what I had envisioned for myself. But if you mean material things, they're not important to me anymore. I have 50 to 75 pairs of shoes, 50 to 100 suits. When I was in high school during the midst of the Depression, I only had one pair of shoes, and it was terribly embarrassing for me…when I sat in the shoemaker's shop, everybody knew why I was in there. I only had one pair of shoes. I had to wait until he repaired them. So the first money I ever made, I bought shoes and clothes. I figured if there was going to be another depression, I'd be well-shoed.

Hatos brought some extensive experience into his new role. He began as a radio announcer before drifting into script-writing, penning episodes of The Lone Ranger, The Green Hornet, *and even Orson Welles'* Mercury Theater of the Air. *He created one of ABC's first game shows,* Fun for the Money. *After a two-year break to command a PT boat in World War II, he returned to radio as a director for* Lucky Strike Hit Parade. *Hatos moved onto television, earning a Peabody Award for a whimsical series,* The *Adventures of Uncle Mistletoe, about an office assistant at the North Pole. He produced Bob Hope's specials for a time before taking a position with Ralph Edwards Productions.*

MONTY HALL

I wanted Stefan Hatos as producer. Hatos had produced *It Could Be You*, with Ralph Edwards, which had been in our time slot before we took over. (Our emcee, Bill Leyden, had come from that show.) I met with Hatos and he struck me as a shrewd, sharp, no-nonsense man with great experience. But Stettner was still on staff as our producer. I explained the problem to Hatos and offered him the title of consultant and a position of responsibility. He accepted, and I then made it clear to everyone on the staff that he had a lot of authority. Hatos smoothed off all sorts of rough edges. For instance, he saw that all the work and advance interviews were finished on time and that there were scripts for each show. Up to then we had been working from notes made on the backs of envelopes.

Stettner soon was dissatisfied with his diminished stature. He was handling administrative details, while Hatos had taken over the creative function. NBC still wanted Stettner out, but I stuck with him. I offered to give him my own title of executive producer, but he saw this for the gesture it was and finally quit, I watched him go with mixed feelings. I loved the guy and liked his work, but he wasn't right for this show and it hadn't worked with him.

There are shows and shows and performers and performers, and none of us is right for all of them. Bill Leyden wasn't right for *Your First Impression*. Bill, who died of a brain hemorrhage a few years ago, was a friend and a fine performer. He had done *It Could Be You* for six years, and everything had focused on him. He worked with the audience, he was on all the time, and he did beautifully. But on *Your First Impression,* he just sat in the emcee's chair and funneled the free association flow among contestants. He had no chance to express himself and he didn't like it. He didn't work well with our celebrity panelists. I was a referee more than an executive producer.

The game wasn't simple enough and was ahead of its time. It was psychological and revealed a lot about those who played it. We asked people to respond instantly and to really let themselves go. When they did, it seemed to stir up storms.

One day Cathy Nolan of *The Real McCoys* came on in a mean mood. She completed one phrase, "I wouldn't walk a mile for…any man," and another, "The problem with this country is…President Kennedy." We got 7,000 letters from those two lines alone. The country wasn't ready for such frank irreverence. Another time Joanie Sommers threw the network censors into an uproar with "I won't…go to bed with every Tom, Dick, and Harry." Unfortunately, few were as free with their feelings.

"People bother me when…they don't know who I am." –Milton Berle

"I'd like to put a stop to people who…keep insisting I take a drink when I think it tastes like medicine." –Connie Francis

"When I was a child, I was…lonely." –Joan Crawford

"There ought to be a law against…people who eat candy during a show and rattle the bags." –Edward Everett Horton

"I can't stand a man who…doesn't look." –Marie Wilson

We also had a mystery guest. The panel was shown five pictures of celebrities and told that the mystery guest was one of the five. They then had to guess which one by the responses the guest made. When Hugh O'Brian was the mystery guest, the late Inger Stevens was a panelist. She took his answers and made a brilliant but brutal analysis.

She said something like, "Well, whoever he is, he sounds to me like a man who needs the love of a woman badly. He must be a bachelor. He refers to living alone with his dog and enjoying the company of the dog. He plays baseball with the boys. I think the kind of person who lives this way must be Hugh O'Brian. And if he is the kind of person I think he is, I would like to be the person to give him what he needs."

Well, instead of taking these remarks as a compliment, Hugh was insulted and demanded the tape be destroyed. We were in no position to throw away shows, so it went on as it was.

Monty was proud of Your First Impression. Selling any TV show is reason to be proud, but Monty was particularly delighted that he was able to close the deal for such an odd show. For one thing, there were no big paydays. There were no prizes, period, just a game, and the fact that it attracted any type of audience at all, Monty said later, was a valuable lesson.

MONTY HALL

I learned more about human reactions on that show than in a college psychology course. A successful game show requires two things to really appeal to the viewers. They want to see how the contestants come out, and they get involved with playing along at home… thinking, "Now if I was there, I'd do this or say that." The size of the prize didn't figure into it.

The questions were deep and probing. Psychological analysis and free associating were significant parts of the show, which opened it up to some startling honesty from all players. Cathy Nolan and Joanie Summers' bluntness made it on the air, but there were occasions when the show was so taken aback by what the stars said that they got out the scissors before letting the nation see the game.

One celebrity (not identified when Monty retold the story) was given the statement "Fat men are…" and completed it, "…overbearing and pugnacious like William Morris agents."

When Dinah Shore stood in the show's booth as mystery guest, one of the panelists, trying to sort out hints in the statements she had made so far, said, "It couldn't be Dinah Shore, because this person loves her husband, and Dinah Shore couldn't care if her husband lived or died."

A movie star on the downward slope of his career was waiting for his identity to be guessed when another panelist pontificated, "This person is either very old or very dull."

MONTY HALL

On another occasion, Dennis James, a member of our panel, said of the mystery guest, "I don't know who she is, but she sounds over the hill." Nina Foch emerged from the booth and threw a punch at him.

Some guests were gracious. Joan Crawford was our mystery personality on one show, and Archie Moore, the light-heavyweight boxing champion at the time, was also on the show. When Archie found out she was there, he said he was a great fan of hers and asked to be introduced to her. Warily, I promised to try to arrange it. After the show, I went to Joan's room and asked if she would mind waiting around to meet Moore. She said, "Why, I'll do better than that." Finding that he was on the next floor of the studio, she bounded up a flight of stairs and swept into his room with a wide smile and outstretched hand. He was surprised and delighted.

Richard Nixon was a guest on the show when he was running for governor of California. He had lost his bid for the Presidency to John F. Kennedy two years earlier, and he was waging a losing battle to beat Pat Brown. He was highly, explosively nervous, and we had to lay everything out for him very carefully. He was worried about his television image, which had been criticized in his campaign against Kennedy, and he was worried he would say something he shouldn't. But he got through the program all right. He even came up with a clever line: "I wish that I…had been a P.T. boat captain." That wowed the audience, and he was very pleased with himself.

NBC, however, felt we had to cancel that show rather than show favoritism to one of the candidates. When I telephoned Nixon to tell him, he got quite upset and went into a tirade against the network. He really wanted that guest appearance to go out over the air. Later, I thought about his outburst when he lost the election and told the press on camera, "Well, you won't have Richard Nixon to kick around anymore"—and again, when he became President and Vice President Agnew began to blast the media. His *Your First Impression* show did go on, however, because Pat Brown appeared on another broadcast.

Your First Impression stayed on the air for two and a half years, but never got super ratings. We just got by, slipping from a 30 percent share of the audience to 28, to 27, to 26; and twenty-six weeks into the 1964 season, the show was canceled. The share is the percentage of the viewing audience that is watching television at that time, as contrasted to pure ratings, which show the number of people who are watching out of all television households available.

The game was good for a laugh every day…sitting on the *Your First Impression* panel are Monty's close friend Dennis James and the queen of game shows, Betty White. (Micki James collection)

In a 1963 interview, Monty offhandedly explained a hitch that hadn't occurred to him when he first created the show. You can only ask a celebrity guest so many probing questions before you run out of things to ask, so Your First Impression *didn't really lend itself to repeat appearances. After two years on the air, the show had welcomed 500 celebrities, and amassed a long list of celebrities who declared they didn't feel comfortable doing the program.*

One cowboy film star told Monty, "I wouldn't go in that booth and reveal anything."

A film actress came to a similar conclusion, telling him, "I wouldn't put myself through that for all the money in the world."

Even Dr. Joyce Brothers lamented, "You know I'm going to lose my standing?"

And the show had plenty of guests that they wouldn't have wanted back anyway. Your First Impression *tried to round up plenty of bright young stars and rising names in show business, but to everyone's frustration, those guests tended to be very protective of whatever image they had, to the point that they'd stonewall any effort to make them open up.* Comedians of the day, Monty found, were just as bad. From Monty's point of view, the best celebrity guests the show had were much older stars, the ones who had already experienced the peak of success and solidified their public images. Those stars tended to say anything; they just didn't seem to care.

Though Monty was half-joking when he relayed this problem, the truth was he really did have to look ahead to his next career move. Your First Impression *wasn't a concept that was built to last forever.*

MONTY HALL

But as an owner and co-producer of the program, I had finally made enough money to get some security for myself and for my family. In September 1962 we had bought the Spanish-style home we still occupy on a quiet street in Beverly Hills and I was turning a corner toward bigger and better things.

SHARON HALL (2019)

In a lot of ways, my parents were careful about not letting success change them, and that was one big way. They bought that house and stayed in it until they died.

MONTY HALL

Stefan Hatos and I had become partners, and we were dreaming up shows and packaging them. For me, this was an old story, of course, but this time it had a happy ending. Hatos and I were concentrating on a new show I would emcee. It was called *Let's Make a Deal*.

One of these weeks or months, Monty Hall will have another new NBC game on the board, with Monty Hall as host—a host who will play the "good-natured con man" trying to convince members of the audience that they should trade something they've already won for a mysterious something behind the curtains up there on the stage. Fast, wild trading is the idea, and Hall will play the entire show in the audience. –Alan Gill, August 20, 1963

(Author's collection)

CHAPTER ELEVEN

Going into 1964, Monty Hall, who used to beg for meetings in which he'd be subjected to power trip tactics from executives who'd make a show of ignoring him, reflected on how he was able to measure his success in recent years by how those people in power greeted him when they saw each other socially. They had gone first from ignoring Monty to nodding their heads. Somewhere along the way, the nodding gave way to a verbal acknowledgment, usually a simple hello. Now, Monty found, they skipped the hellos and engaged Monty in a full conversation.

MONTY HALL

Even while Stefan Hatos and I were turning out *Your First Impression*, we were trying to create other shows that could be sold to the networks. I emceed some of his run-throughs and asked his advice on some of mine. It was only natural that we would get together to try it as a team. In Hatos-Hall Productions, we became equal partners.

One of the shows which did not sell, but which should have, was *Three of a Kind*, in which teams of three butchers or three truck-drivers faced teams of three schoolteachers or three waitresses in battles of wits. Another was *Chain Letter*, which eventually did sell but did not last long. (Incidentally, *Three of a Kind* led us to *Split Second*, which sold in 1971 and is a smash destined for a long run.)

Another show was *Let's Make a Deal*.

I told Stefan about *The Auctioneer,* which I had done in Canada. I worked directly with many members of the audience in this show, not just with contestants or a panel. Although I'd never been able to convince a TV executive, I thought there were possibilities in a format in which the emcee operated in the arena, right out among the people.

On *The Auctioneer*, I asked members of the audience for articles such as postage stamps or silver dollars, and I offered $5 or $10 for each item they happened to have. On another part of the show we auctioned off items. Both features were enormously well-received, and I told Hatos I thought they would work in a TV game show.

Monty on the set of *Your First Impression*. Not content with just one successful show, Monty and partner Stefan Hatos were breathing life into a new idea at club meetings across Los Angeles. (Author's collection)

He worked on a show called *Ladies Be Seated*, in which the emcee, Johnny Olsen, bought items from members of the audience and offered to trade the contents of a box for cash. This show had stemmed from one called *Super Market*, in which contestants had to guess the retail price of items. Stefan felt both these procedures would fit our new program.

We felt we had something, and we did. Eventually we incorporated these and other stunts into a format that concluded with a "Lady and the Tiger" trick in which two contestants got the opportunity to trade what they had won for whatever was behind one of three curtains, at least one of which was sure to conceal the largest prize on the program.

As we practiced it on ourselves and others on our staff, we sensed that there ought to be a fair amount of excitement as the contestants proceeded through various stages. They always had to risk something to get something, maybe nothing. Originally it was determined they would have to bring something, anything to trade to get into the game.

Acting like a carnival barker or a commercial pitchman, I'd say things like "I'll tell you what I'm gonna do. I'll offer you fifty bucks for that. Is it a deal? Let's make a deal. I'll trade you what's in this box for that watch."

We agreed that *Let's Make a Deal* was a great title. It was Stefan's idea. I think he had used the term "Zonk" on a previous show to represent some sort of booby prize, and that's what we called our "losers."

We didn't realize how good a show we had at first. We decided to work up a run-through that we could try out on clubs and organizations that had written NBC asking for group tickets to other shows. We rated them as audiences—good, fair, or lousy. We tried the good ones first. We asked them if we could try out a TV show idea as the entertainment for one of their meetings, and a lot of them invited us to come.

We'd finish taping *Your First Impression* at nine o'clock at night and jump in our cars and get to a meeting at ten or so and perform until around ten-thirty. We didn't use prizes or props or anything. We had cards with the prizes spelled out on them— $200 or a $1,000 set of furniture or a $3,000 car or a five-cent comb—and the people had to use their imagination.

We played all over the Los Angeles area. I remember we did a show for TOPS—Take Off Pounds Sensibly—in a meeting room on top of a supermarket, of all places. We often had to go in the back door like delivery boys. Some meetings lasted so long we didn't get on until nearly midnight.

But the reaction was the same every time everywhere—a smash hit. Even without props or prizes, the audiences reacted with enthusiasm and excitement. We couldn't believe how good the response was. We started to play some of the groups rated as "fair" audiences, and again the response was great. So, we tried groups that were rated "lousy." Some of them seemed to resent our even taking up their time, but, sure enough, the show caught them, and they reacted enthusiastically.

After a while, we decided we were ready to try the big time. First, we contacted Armand Grant at ABC, and he agreed to look at a full-scale run-through. So, we hired a big NBC studio at Sunset and Vine and invited impartial groups to act as an audience and be called on as contestants. We had a few props, but again we used only pieces of paper as prizes.

It was a sensation. The audience reaction was wild.

I finished with these words . . . "and so this is Monty Hall saying as the old traveling salesman used to say, 'caveat emptor—let the buyer beware.'" I bare all farewell and faded behind the curtain to a thunderous ovation with my heart pounding. I knew we had just demonstrated to a network executive a show so certain of success that it would be easy to sell.

Happily, I joined Stefan Hatos and our agent, Jimmy Saphier, who were talking with Army Grant and his assistant, Dick Dunn. I was surprised to see long faces. I asked Saphier, "What's the matter?"

"He didn't like it," he answered.

I turned to Army Grant and I said, "You must be kidding. Didn't you see what I saw out there? That wasn't a rigged audience. They roared. They cheered us to the rafters."

And he said, "Yes, that's all right, but what could you do tomorrow?"

I replied, "We'd do more of the same thing we did today. And variations of the same thing day after day. That's the way you do any game show. Only the contestants change. And the questions. As far as that goes, what has Bob Hope done for thirty years? Or Jack Benny for forty years? If it's good today, it'll be good tomorrow."

Army said, "No, you'd just repeat yourself and it wouldn't be any good. I can't see any future for it."

I walked away in disbelief. Dick Dunn came up to me and said, "I thought it was sensational. Absolutely sensational. I'm as surprised as you that he doesn't like it."

I thanked him, but his opinion wasn't the one that counted. I went off with Hatos and had a couple of drinks and expressed my rage, sorrow, and frustration. I've done many run-throughs for many people in my time, and I have done some so badly that I was ready to beat the buyer out of the room. But when you do one this good and have it rejected, it is almost more than you can bear because those moments of triumph are the ones you live for. We decided there was nothing we could do differently, except to do the same show for a different man.

Two months later we set up a run-through for Bob Aaron, the head of NBC daytime television, and Jerry Chester, his immediate boss. We did the same show with another neutral audience and we got exactly the same great reaction. I walked off feeling this time had to be it. I walked up to Jerry Chester, and, incredibly, his reaction was almost exactly the same as Army Grant's—word for word—"What do you do the next day?"

Steve and Jimmy and I looked at one another in shock. The same thoughts passed through our minds—was it possible that the three of us, with our experience with audiences, and feel for the business, were wrong? Or were they, having emerged briefly from their ivory towers, out of step with the public? It was easy to blame the executives. Now, for the first time, our confidence in our judgment was shaken.

I don't think we would have given up on the show. Certainly, we would have tried CBS, although they were leery of giveaway shows since the scandals. But this wasn't that sort of show. We had many different contestants, and not one of them won anything unreal. It was the reactions of the contestants that made our show, not the prizes. It was the games they played, which each viewer could vicariously play along with them.

We didn't have to worry. By the strangest sort of coincidence, as Jerry Chester's reaction had been as bad as Army Grant's, Bob Aaron's was as good as Dick Dunn's. And Aaron, unlike Dunn, was in a position to argue with Chester, and he did.

Jimmy Saphier went right to Jerry's superior, Mort Werner, and said, "Look, we have a sensational show. Jerry Chester doesn't think so, but Bob Aaron does. We wouldn't tout a show if we didn't feel it was a winner. All we want you to do is check with Bob Aaron as well as with Jerry Chester and then see it for yourself."

Mort did and came back and said, "All right, let's get up a pilot so we can really see what you have. We'll pay for it."

STU BILLETT

Monty created *Your First Impression*. And he wanted to host it himself, but NBC wouldn't let him. They wouldn't give it to Monty and it was Monty's show! Monty goes into business with Stefan Hatos, and they create *Let's Make a Deal*. They didn't want Monty to host that either.

But then the network couldn't find anybody else to do it! It's a tough show. There's numbers to keep track of in your head as you're talking to the contestants; you have to change the direction of the deal based on what they do. They had no choice; they had to let Monty do the show because none of the other hosts could handle it.

Let's Make a Deal slowly came together during 1963. *As the sets were being built, Stefan Hatos and Monty Hall began assembling the staff of the show brick by brick. They hired a director. And a note from that director led to someone else being brought on board.*

Monty and Carol Merrill in one of the first publicity stills snapped for *Let's Make a Deal*. Director Joe Behar claimed credit for recognizing that the show needed a model to show off the prizes. (Author's collection)

JOE BEHAR, director[xix]

I was doing a soap opera around '59 or '60 for CBS called *Clear Horizon*. And that went off the air, but I got to know the people at CBS. They had a guy there named Red Rowe… and they did a game show called *Face the Facts*…It was the first game show I ever did. And I got to know the head of daytime at CBS. NBC was going to do the pilot for *Let's Make a Deal*, and the head of daytime at CBS recommended me. I interviewed…and I got the job.

And it wasn't an easy job to do. That was a complicated show! The whole thing was all reactions. Once the reaction was gone, if you didn't catch it, there's no way of editing or re-doing it. But I knew how to do that stuff. There was a lot of action going on. I knew how to do that from doing football and baseball…I'm a wiz at doing stuff that's all tumultuous at the same time and catching it all. I just have a knack for that, so I was perfect for that show.

I never had any contribution about the concept of it, but the first time we did the show…we had the prizes behind the curtains and the prizes behind these big boxes, and we'd have a stagehand behind the box who would whisk the box away, and the TV set would be there, and we'd shoot the close-up and say "You've won this TV set…"

And the first time I saw it…I went to them and said, "This isn't right the way you're doing this. There's no relationship to the size of anything if you don't have a person there. If you don't have a person by those curtains…until you open it and see the car behind it, you don't know what it is. And when you see a TV set, you don't understand how big it is."

[Stefan Hatos] said, "No, no, we don't need a person." He didn't want to spend the money for a model.

I said, "I'm telling you, it's going to look better, especially when you show the curtain. Because you don't know if it's a little one or anything."

He said, "As soon as we open it, they'll know."

I said, "But not beforehand."

Monty agreed with me, and the next day, we went out and got Carol Merrill.

CAROL MERRILL

I was born in Grantsburg, Wisconsin, near Frederick. My name was Carol Hiller. My father was a farmer, with 140 acres and our own lake. When I was five years old, my parents decided to go west and they auctioned off the farm. They chose southern California because my mother had two sisters there. But what would happen for the rest of my childhood was my mother would get homesick. So, we'd move back to Wisconsin or Minnesota. After being there, my mother would get an urge to go back to California, and we'd go back to California. She'd get homesick again, so it was back to Minnesota or Wisconsin. We moved every time Mom got homesick. My father was so adaptable and so willing to please my mom that he went along with this, even though he would have been more comfortable just staying on the farm. We moved 30 times and I went to sixteen different schools. I was never attached to any one place, but that was fine because it actually made me more outgoing. I had to keep making new friends, so I was always very eager to meet people.

By the time I got to high school, my mother settled down enough that I got to go to the same school all the way through 9th, 10th, and 11th grades. That was Citrus Union High School in Glendora. I got picked for varsity cheerleading squad, which was a big deal for me, and then my parents suddenly told me we were moving to San Diego for my senior year. I attended school in San Diego for one day, went home, and announced, "I want to go back to Glendora." So, my parents found a family in Glendora for me to stay with, and my dad paid them $10 a day to look after me.

I got an after-school job at a shop called Azusa Fashions. The owner of the shop was fond of me. At one point, the owner encouraged me to round up my favorite outfits that we had on sale and sent me to a tea room to model them. That was the start of my modeling career. I enrolled in a modeling school. I still remember the lessons we had. How to walk with one foot in front of the other, and—this is going to sound ridiculous now—how to smoke in a lady-like fashion. I didn't smoke, but they wanted you to look good if the client wanted you to do that.

I got married for the first time in 1960, to Tom Merrill, which is how I ended up with my name. Tom was friends with Gardner McKay, a very handsome actor who starred on a show called *Adventures in Paradise*. I found out that Tom co-owned a modeling agency called Flair. They were a big agency in LA at the time. Gardner was a talented photographer in his own right, so he took photos of me himself and took them straight to the agency, and they said, "Yeah, let's sign her."

Flair got me booked on a game show called *Your Surprise Package* on CBS. Allan Sherman, a very sweet man, was the producer. The host was George Fenneman, also a very sweet man. Flair got me booked for the initial pilot, but when CBS bought the series, they made a strange blunder. Flair didn't put anything in writing with the producers for some reason, so when the show got picked up, they didn't make any money from me for it, so they were unhappy with that.

I've heard two different versions of how I got hired for *Let's Make a Deal*. I had a friend named Ted Walsh, who worked in Standards & Practices at ABC, and he was a friend of Stefan Hatos, so when he found out Stefan was looking for a model, he recommended me. Stef told me years later he was considering using Suzy Parker or Lauren Hutton.

Monty's version of how I got hired was that Stefan walked into his office and told him to watch some videotapes of models.

Monty told me he said, "The last one impressed me the most."

Stefan said, "I agree. I was hoping you'd say that."

The last tape was my tape. I'm not sure what's true in all that, but those are the versions of how I got hired that I've heard over the years.

Little did she realize what a cultural icon she'd become, and she had Monty to thank for that, not just for hiring her. For some reason, Monty couldn't just bring himself to ask a contestant, "Would you like the curtain?"

He always said, "Would you like the curtain that Carol Merrill is standing in front of?"

When he looked back on his career decades later, Monty made a joke that wasn't exactly a joke; he said he couldn't recall ever uttering a sentence that contained the word "curtain" but didn't contain the name "Carol Merrill."

CAROL MERRILL

When Stef called me, I thought I was coming in for an interview. He said, "No, you're it. We're calling you because we're hiring you. You've already got the job."

I got the impression that I was being brought on board very last-minute. I found out later that I was right. I heard the whole story of Joe Behar telling Stefan Hatos that they needed a model. But I told Stefan about the issues I had with Flair when I worked on *Your Surprise Package*. Stefan called Flair directly and said, "Listen, instead of collecting your percentage, I'm just going to pay you out of pocket directly, and it'll just be a fee for using Carol on our show. It's easier for all of us that way, I think." He ended up cutting a check every week for fourteen years.

I liked Monty and Stef both from the moment I met them. Both of them showed confidence in me and respected me, and I appreciated that. Joe Behar was the same way. He was respectful and gave me a lot of freedom. In the days leading up to the first taping, he'd make a suggestion from the booth, like, "Take a step to the left" or something basic like that. But what he kept saying repeatedly was "Do what you do." And he would let me go and do what I had to do. I had experience as a model. I had already worked for a year on a game show. He respected me and felt I knew how to do the job.

MONTY HALL

So we prepared a pilot. It was by far the best pilot I had ever made for any game show. It worked well as this show always works.

HENRY KOVAL, Assistant to the Producers, later Executive in Charge of Production for *Let's Make a Deal*

We did the rehearsal for the pilot in the hallway between Studios 2 and 4 at NBC. We had no space or time allotted for a studio that day. The pilot went through the roof, but Army Grant made that infamous statement. "What do you do the next day?"

Jimmy Saphier deserves so much credit. He met with NBC executives in New York and worked very, very hard to get the show greenlighted.

"Next day on your dressing room, they've hung a star." Monty, despite NBC's reservations, got the nod to host his own creation. (Author's collection)

MONTY HALL

We sent it to New York, and this time Mort Werner, other studio executives, and the advertising agency people who were brought in to see agreed that it was the most exciting pilot of this kind of show they had ever seen. We knew we had a sale.

The NBC people took an option on the show, and we signed a contract for $25,000 a week for five shows each week. Of that, about $13,000 went to us, and out of it we had to provide prizes and pay our staff, including ourselves. NBC took $11,190 for its studio and personnel costs. The rest went for commissions. This was not a lot for a show such as ours, but it was a start.

We had some problems getting a network time period. Our show was put in the 2:00 p.m. time slot opposite, ironically, *Password*, which was a big hit for CBS.

HENRY KOVAL

To be honest, a lot of us thought that we were there as a replacement show. NBC was so unenthusiastic when they first signed on for the show, they gave us a 13-week commitment against a top show on a competing network. We figured we were there as a placeholder until NBC found something they actually liked.

Monty with Wendell Niles, his announcer on *Your First Impression*. Niles also served as Monty's roving assistant for the *Let's Make a Deal* pilot, but surprisingly, he opted not to join Monty full-time for the new series. (Author's collection)

Monty had one more piece of business before starting production. On the pilot, Wendell Niles had been the announcer who roved through the audience with Monty, carrying boxes and popping up behind the doors for Zonks. Once the series was sold, though, and Monty realized that the new show was complex enough that anybody who was a part of it had to be fully committed to it, he approached Niles again and laid out his options.

MONTY HALL[x]

Wendell Niles was the announcer on *Your First Impression*. I said to Wendell, "Do you want to go with the new show or stay with the old show?"

He says, "I'd better stay with the old show because it's nice to have a show on the air."

So, we went out and got what turned out to be a tremendous choice: Jay Stewart. Jay Stewart turned out to be not only an announcer on the show, but also a co-performer, a co-star, and he was delightful to work with.

The 2:00 p.m. time slot meant the odds were very, very against Let's Make a Deal. *In the two years since* Password *had premiered, four shows had come & gone in that time slot on*

NBC, and sight unseen, there was no reason to believe that Let's Make a Deal wouldn't be number five. Monty, however, brimmed with confidence when discussing the new game with a reporter, pointing out that Let's Make a Deal hadn't been "woodshedded" in executive offices, with employees popping in to serve as contestants and audience for test games. The beta testing for Let's Make a Deal had been done with members of the general public. Monty believed that the average viewer would like the new show because he had already shown it to the average viewer.

MONTY HALL[xxi]

December 16, 1963…

I remember that day. I had a little bit of a cold…I'm nervously walking up and down backstage. I open up a new package of Marlboro cigarettes. I take out a cigarette, I light it up. I got a cold, it doesn't taste good, I throw it down, I stomp on the cigarette.

Nat Ligerman, one of my assistants [walks by]. I said, "Nat, here's the pack of cigarettes. I'm not going to smoke for the duration of this contract. 13 weeks. I'm not gonna smoke for 13 weeks."

Monty orchestrates a deal with help from Jay Stewart. Although many sources would refer to him as "assistant" or "announcer," Monty would always view him as a co-star. (Author's collection)

After months of workshopping and tinkering, of Weight Watchers meetings and knitting groups, of stalled negotiations and "What do you do the next day?," Let's Make a Deal finally aired its first episode on December 30, 1963.

The action of Let's Make a Deal *took place on "the trading floor," a section of the studio audience seating that held 36 people chosen in advance by the show's staff. This was a matter of logistics; it would have been time-consuming for Monty to try to walk throughout the 400 seats in the studio to find contestants at random, so as a time-saving measure, 36 people were picked and seated in that special section close to the stage, and those were the only people that Monty would talk to during the show.*

Monty picked people on the trading floor and what followed was basically a series of this-or-that choices. Here's a small box of candy, but there's something else in it. Do you want that or the much larger box on the display floor?...One curtain has a sign that says "gold," another curtain has "silver." The signs are a hint about what's behind each curtain, so which one do you want? Okay, now, would you accept $200 to just forget about the deal and not take either curtain?...Here's a prize, and it's all yours without having to do anything, unless you want to give it back and take what's hidden under the box on this tray.

Toward the end of the show, Monty would offer the Big Deal of the Day; each of the three numbered doors was hiding a prize package, but one was the Big Deal, worth thousands and thousands of dollars. Monty rattled off a roll call of the contestants he had already picked that day, starting with the one who had won the most and working his way down the list, until two contestants had agreed to forfeit what they had already won in exchange for a pick of one of the doors.

At the end, as the credits rolled and the theme music played, Monty engaged in a series of what became known as "quickie deals," approaching people on the trading floor he hadn't picked during the show and offering them money for any objects that they might happen to have on them. "If you have a postage stamp, I'll give you $50. I'll tell you what, if you have an envelope to put it on, I'll give you another $50...You, for every dime you have, I'll trade it for a ten dollar bill!" Or Monty's favorite request, "$50 for a hard boiled egg!" He asked for it so often that alert viewers began coming to the studio with hard-boiled eggs in their purses.

MONTY HALL

Let's Make a Deal worked wonderfully well right from the start, but it had to win a new audience and do it against a show that had a hold on more than half the viewers. We started with a 17 percent share of the audience and inched up week by week, to 20 percent and then to 25 percent. Meanwhile, *Password* went down to 50 percent and then to 40 percent. We were renewed after 13 weeks and again after 26 weeks. We had knocked ten points off *Password* and made NBC competitive. It was a strain waiting out those 13-week cycles. What sort of security is that for a man to live with?

The first few times that NBC renewed the show, Monty made a point of renewing his no-smoking pledge along with it. But life without cigarettes became easier and easier for Monty and he didn't need a 13-week contract to get him through it. He didn't smoke for the rest of his life.

13 weeks down, and many more to go. Monty lines up more mystery boxes and more prizes for the years to come on *Let's Make a Deal*. (Author's collection)

MONTY HALL

Then NBC moved us to the 1:30 slot, which posed a new problem. This period had been station option time throughout the network, and the individual stations had been providing their own programs to fill the half-hour. Many of these shows had been successful locally for years, and now the stations were being asked to remove them to take our show. They did not have to do it, and many didn't, so we were without a full line-up of stations with which to get viewers. To top it off, we were thrown up against the sturdiest soap opera in television history, *As the World Turns*, on CBS, which had a tight hold on over 50 percent of the audience. Nevertheless, we got right at them. We added stations and got our ratings up to more than 30 percent, while *As the World Turns* dropped to less than 40 percent.

Suddenly, we were secure. If we hadn't whipped the opposition, we had caught up with them and brought NBC up to CBS. Also, our success helped the show that replaced us at two p.m. We were making money for the network, and we continued on that level for five years.

The "What do you do tomorrow?" concern went away and in time, the naysayers realized that Monty's answer—"More of the same"—really was the correct one. It wasn't strictly the same. By Monty's estimate in an early profile of the show, the program had about 20 unique core ideas for deals, with a team of writers that simply rotated between the ideas and then, not-so-simply, brainstormed minor variations so each of the 20 would look different whenever they used it.

Monty and the writers tried to add as much as they could to every show but adhered to a few rules for themselves. Though only human and prone to being overwhelmed by the excitement of his own creation, Monty tried to limit the volume of his voice as much as possible and attempted not to raise his voice. He injected some "sleazy car salesman" attitude in his performance, merely as a means of keeping contestants on their toes, but tried to maintain some semblance of good taste. The writers, meanwhile, had a hard and fast rule about Monty's role in deals:

ALAN GILBERT, writer[xxiii]

Monty never tells a lie on the show. He may never tell the whole truth about what's behind the curtain, but he never lies. If he says an envelope has money in it, there's money in it. If he says something behind a curtain is not half-bad, it may be all-bad or it may be all-good.

HENRY KOVAL

In show business, I'm what's known as a hyphenate. I was a writer-executive in charge of production. We eventually built the show up to 50 ideas or so that we cycled through. Once in a while someone thought of something new, but there was never an urgent need for anything new. No one ever said, "We have to do something different!" The contestants were what kept it fresh. We had different contestants and they made different decisions every time. So that's what kept it new.

Monty looks ahead to the next deal. The show's staff of writers actually weren't looking for new things to do, but rather for new ways to do what they already thought of. (Author's collection)

Monty, while always comfortable as a master of ceremonies on anything he hosted, but quickly realized that being the boss as well as the host made the job even easier. One of his favorite types of deals was what he called "the turn of the screw." He'd give the contestant the curtain without telling them what was behind it. Then he'd offer to buy the curtain right back for $100. Or $200...or how about $300? Will you sell it for $400?...

Had Monty been only the host hired for the show and nothing more, somebody might have made it a point to tell him right before the segment started, "Make sure you stop when the money reaches $500."

But Monty, mindful of his own budgeting and his own show's needs, felt freedom to go as far as he needed with the deal before the contestant finally cracked. He considered himself a *good reader of people, and when asked how he controlled the budget for the show, he used the "turn of the screw" as an example of how to keep the show's money in check, describing what sounded like a shockingly imprecise science. If he needed to keep an eye on the budget, he'd play with a contestant whose face looked like they'd be prone to caving in sooner, so he'd only give away $100 or $200.*

The longer the show stayed on the air, the more difficult it became to brainstorm simplistic variations on themes, so deals became more intricate.

Monty picks a man and offers a him the box on Jay Stewart's tray. Then he picks a woman a few steps away and hands her $300. He goes a few more steps and gives another woman $300. He offers the second woman the curtain that Carol Merrill is standing in front of if she gives back her $300. She gives up the money and ends up with a washer/dryer combo and a sewing machine. Monty returns to the first woman and offers her the giant box on the display floor for her $300. She gives up her money and wins china, plus a dishwasher. He returns to the man with Jay Stewart's box and offers him his choice of anything he's already seen in the deal; the money, or the washer/dryer combo and sewing machine, or the china & dishwasher. He chooses Jay Stewart's box. Monty switches his offer from "anything" to "everything," putting up the $600, plus the sewing machine and the washer/dryer. The man sticks with the box and ends up with a talking doll. Although Let's Make a Deal *thrived on spontaneity, Stefan Hatos insisted on having scripts prepared so everyone on the staff could keep track of what was going on. The scripts took on the form of flow charts, with directions reading "If contestant says NO" and "If contestant says YES" guiding everyone to the next thing Monty had to do if that particular scenario presented itself.*

For another deal later, Monty hands a woman a handbag with money in it, but he won't say how much. Jay Stewart has a box on his tray again. She has to decide whether to keep the handbag or the box for herself, with another contestant getting whatever she doesn't pick. She takes the handbag, so a man gets the box, unless he wants to part with it for $400. He takes the box and gets a camera and a diamond watch. Now it's time for the first dealer to open her handbag, unless she wants the box on the floor. She declines. Monty picks a third dealer and gives her the box that the first dealer said no to, but offers to buy it right back for $500. She takes the box and wins appliances and 50 cans of Shasta. Monty returns to the first dealer and asks if they'll surrender the handbag for a generous supply of Mallo cups and something behind it. She keeps the handbag and learns that all she missed out on was Baby Jay Stewart's oversized high chair. The purse was hiding $1200, and it's all hers.

CAROL MERRILL

In the beginning, I didn't realize how complicated the show would become. I watch the pilot episode now and I laugh to myself because I'm wearing the same outfit through the entire pilot, which certainly wasn't how we ended up doing things. I had a screen for making quick wardrobe changes backstage, and *Let's Make a Deal* became so complicated that I began pinning outlines and script pages to that screen, and I would read as I was changing my outfit. I'd remind myself where to walk if the contestant did this, or if they did that.

Monty could handle it. Racing his father to solve math problems as a child, the complicated card games he had devised for himself; all of it exercised Monty's mind so well that he could adapt to the increasing complexity of the show. Besides, as Monty noted later, he had created the show. He felt so in tune with it as a result that he felt comfortable with whatever the writers devised for him. He was the coach and the quarterback; it was his game.

What Monty didn't realize was how utterly indispensable he was making himself because of that skill. He also didn't realize what a problem that would be for him in the years to come.

Monty Hall and Carol Merrill led many contestants to the end of the rainbow on *Let's Make a Deal*. (Author's collection)

CAROL MERRILL

At the time, I just thought of it as a gig, as I thought of any other job I'd take. I never even bothered considering if I thought the show might be a hit or might be a flop. So when I'm asked a question about the beginning of the series, I don't really have an answer because at the beginning, it was just this thing I got booked for.

I look back at the tapes of the earliest episodes now and I think, "Come on, how could this not be a hit!" Monty was charming and quick-witted, and we had these fun-loving people who showed up to be in the audience. Monty was great at eliciting responses from them, and really brought out the best qualities in them. He was darling.

HENRY KOVAL

Carol was the first big model on TV. She got more oomph out of raising her hand and twisting her wrist than your average announcer could get out of reading a script.

MONTY HALL

From the time I arrived in California my life had changed around enormously. Although Stefan Hatos and I were not getting very rich, we were doing all right because, as the producer and the emcee, we did not have to pay others to do these jobs. Our audience grew yearly. There was no way we could fail. What would we do the next day? We would be better, and better every day after that, too It was an enormously exciting time.

STU BILLETT

I could spend hours breaking down why *Let's Make a Deal* was a hit, but I'll try to keep this short. I got my start in television on *The $64,000 Question* in the 1950s. Contestant wins $8,000, has to decide whether to take it or leave it and go for $16,000. A week later, they have to decide whether to take or leave the $16,000 to go for $32,000, then the next week, take or leave the $32,000 and go for $64,000.

It aired on Tuesday nights and there were only three channels in those days. On Wednesday mornings in the 1950s, wherever I went, I overheard conversations between people. "I couldn't believe she quit with $16,000! She knew so much about that subject, she should have gone for $32,000." "That fella shoulda quit with the $8,000. He didn't seem very sure of himself. If I was as nervous as he looked, I would have quit."

That was the conversation. The choice the contestant had to make and how it turned out. Monty built a show that was just that one piece—the choice—and made it the entire show. It's one choice right after another. "Do you want the box or the curtain? Okay, you chose the box, it turns out it's a set of designer leather goods, but now there's a much bigger box on the floor. Do you want the leather goods or what's behind the bigger box?" Anybody who watches the show can play along with it, they get that feeling of reward when they choose what turns out to be the better option, and then there's an altogether new choice and they get the same feeling from that. Brilliant.

In this early episode, Monty makes a deal with an audience member who came to the studio wearing a nice sweater. Contestant wardrobes would soon go in a direction that even Stefan Hatos and Monty Hall never anticipated. (Author's collection)

Of his own creation, Monty once remarked, "I don't expect a Pulitzer Prize, but it is the best of what it is."

Barely two months on the air with Let's Make a Deal, Monty would have his first encounter with the disrespect for game shows that he'd soon become accustomed to. The National Academy for Television Arts & Sciences announced in February 1964 that they were eliminating the Emmy categories recognizing game shows. It was a slight that Monty, and many others, felt was rooted in the Academy thinking that game shows weren't dignified enough to merit recognition.

John Guedel, a trustee in the Academy who had enjoyed enormous success collaborating on *game shows with Art Linkletter and Groucho Marx, said that he objected purely for pragmatic reasons—there were more game shows on the air than there were other genres that got to keep their categories, so eliminating the awards for game shows was ignoring a fairly significant chunk of programming. Johnny Carson, a former game show host and panelist who had been sitting in the host chair for* The Tonight Show *barely over a year, gave his support to his old friends, saying on the air one night, "To look at a show like* What's My Line? *and say it doesn't deserve an award is ridiculous."*

Game show mogul Mark Goodson, who was always fighting for recognition and respect, was so offended by the decision that he resigned from the Academy. Monty Hall, on the other hand, remained in the Academy, saying that he felt he could accomplish more by being "a thorn on the inside."

To show that his objection wasn't purely self-interest, Monty used his own competition to argue that game shows deserved the acknowledgment. "Take Password. *It might be called educational. At least it brings better language into the house than* Beverly Hillbillies.*"*

Monty remained blunt, drawing attention to other categories that he felt lacked prestige. "Okay, if it is prestige the academy wants, then why not toss out categories like 'Supporting Actor'? I mean, they give it to Don Knotts every year anyway. Isn't that a little ridiculous? What Don doesn't get, E.G. Marshall does."

Monty was also eager to point out (without naming names) that many of the Academy members who supported dumping the category were people who had appeared on game shows themselves and been paid handsomely for it. In some cases, Monty said, the people who wanted the game show categories jettisoned were people who had come to his office to pitch game show ideas in recent years, unsuccessfully.

Monty would even argue that the Academy should just jettison categories altogether and announce what shows and performers they felt deserved recognition, and hand the Emmys out without regard to what categories they belonged in.

For the even-tempered arguments Monty had, he acknowledged that yes, he wanted to be considered for an award, only because anybody else in his shoes would feel the same way. "I'm like a father in a neighborhood that's giving a picnic, and if everybody else's kid is going to that picnic, I want my kid there, too."

The Academy of Television Arts & Sciences would finally establish a separate Emmy ceremony for daytime television programming in 1974, at which point game shows were finally once again eligible for awards. Let's Make a Deal *starring Monty Hall, however, would never receive an Emmy.*

The contestants are still wearing their Sunday best, but a sign of things to come looms in the background. (Author's collection)

MONTY HALL

When we sold the show *Chain Letter* to NBC for $20,000 a week, and when it folded after 15 weeks, we weren't worried. I had been working too hard, anyway, emceeing *Let's Make a Deal* and producing *Chain Letter* at the same time. I wanted to enjoy the fruits of all I had put into getting to the top. My only annoyance was that NBC was not properly appreciative. They acknowledged the success of our show and how it had boosted their daytime schedule, but it seemed to be beneath their dignity to praise a game show. They were getting $7,400 per commercial minute and were sold out. Critics panned the program. But the people loved it. I asked Herb Schlosser to renegotiate a new and better contract for us and he refused.

He said, "We expect you to live up to your present pact for five years."

The origin of the costumes has been thoroughly documented over the years because it was such an unusual gimmick that Monty was asked about it constantly. It made the roots of it rather hard to forget. In the beginning, contestants for Let's Make a Deal showed up in their Sunday best—the men donned suits and ties, the ladies wore nice dresses. One day, a woman showed up with a sign on her neck. She had written a short poem on it: "Roses are red, violets are blue, I came here to deal with you!"

The sign delighted Monty so much that he picked the woman and made a deal with her. Evidently, a sizable number of future studio audience members watched the show that day, because in the coming weeks, an increasing number of people were coming to the studio still in their Sunday best, but with signs around their necks with a variety of messages on them. Let's Make a Deal quickly became "that game show where the contestants wear signs around their necks."

Well, if everyone has a sign around their neck, it's a little harder to stand out, so eventually a woman showed up with a sign around her neck, AND a gawdy-looking hat. Monty was taken aback by the hat, and since it grabbed his attention, he picked her. In a matter of weeks, everybody in the audience had accessorized their Sunday best with odd-looking hats. Let's Make a Deal was now "that game show where the contestants have signs around their necks and wear ugly hats."

The audience is still wearing their nicest outfits, but notice the hats and signs that are now dotting the landscape. (Author's collection)

It just snowballed from there until contestants were showing up in full-blown costumes; the audience was chockful of ballerinas, hobos, Charlie Chaplins and Groucho Marxes, baseball players and kitty cats. This development didn't initially please everyone. As a line gathered outside one day for a taping of Let's Make a Deal, Stefan Hatos and Monty Hall received an irked phone call from an NBC executive who just arrived at the complex.

"You need to put a stop to this! Have you looked outside? It looks like there's a Halloween party on the sidewalk!"

Stefan Hatos reluctantly called a staff meeting to announce that going forward, costumes were banned, and any audience member wearing a costume would be denied entry.

A staff member raised his hand and asked, "Why?"

Hatos didn't think of an answer for that.

The staff member persisted. "Don't you realize there's never been a show like this before? People are dressing up...and it makes the screen come alive."

Stefan Hatos overruled himself and allowed the costumes to continue unimpeded, and the staff, as well as Monty, would marvel in the coming years at how dedicated some of the contestants were.

HENRY KOVAL

I can still remember the first costume I ever saw. It was a man dressed as the Jolly Green Giant. As I recall, he kept showing up on every taping day and getting tickets at the booth, dressed as the Jolly Green Giant. Looking back, I don't understand why they kept letting him in. It had reached that point where the audience had signs hanging around their necks and wearing funny hats, but a guy wearing the Jolly Green Giant was still pretty different from what everyone else was doing.

We finally put him on the trading floor one day. As I recall, the thinking was that we were putting him down there to get rid of him. "Give him what he wants and let him be there with Monty and then he'll go away."

Well, Monty was so intrigued by him that he made a deal with the guy. And then that episode aired, and at the next taping, everybody showed up wearing a costume.

The costumes gave Let's Make a Deal a gimmick that made it easily identified—a viewer turning the dial on the TV could see a man in a suit standing among a sea of pirates, bears, and baseball players, and realize, "Oh, this is Let's Make a Deal."

Those remarkable costumes gave Monty some of the most memorable conversations of his life.

One woman stood up, covered in gift-wrapping paper. Monty asked if she was a present for him. She answered breathily, "Yes, and if you want it you can have it!"

Monty blushed lightly before coming up with the perfect line. *"Do not open until Christmas."*

With too many costumes to count over the years, Monty was surprisingly quick to answer when he was asked later in life to name his favorite costume. It was, surprisingly, a woman on the trading floor that he didn't pick. He regretted it when he realized what she was wearing.

MONTY HALL[xxiii]

The cleverest costume I ever saw…a lady came and I didn't pick her. But at the end of the show, everybody said, "Look at this lady, look what she had!"

She had in front of her a mock-up of the *Let's Make a Deal* set. There was a stage with three doors, and she would press a button on Door #1. A little Monty Hall walked out and walked back in. Door #2, a little Jay Stewart walked out with money in his hand, turned around, and walked back in. Door #3, a little Carol Merrill walked out.

Her husband was an electrical engineer and he made this fantastic set! And I didn't pick her! That was the most inventive, brilliant thing I ever saw.

Done deal. The clown and the rag doll sitting side-by-side are signs of *Let's Make a Deal's* completed evolution. (Author's collection)

Least-favorite costume was also a no-brainer. Monty was stunned at how often he saw grown men in "baby costumes" that consisted of little more than a diaper. He once warned his staff that if they ever put a man in a diaper on the trading floor, he'd fire them.

CAROL MERRILL

I loved the men who showed up in diapers. The sight of hairy legs stretching out of a big floppy diaper is just always funny. But what I loved was what it said to me. Here's a man who's a good sport and he's committed to getting into the spirit of the show.

I don't have a favorite costume. I was always more dazzled just by the effort in general than the actual costumes themselves. To look into that audience and see the Jolly Green Giant and Raggedy Ann and Cinderella...you could just see that these people had worked for hours and hours and hours on their costumes just for our show.

The contestants were getting more elaborate with other elements of the show. In the early years of Let's Make a Deal, contestants had to bring something to give to Monty before he would make a deal. It was always made extremely clear that this was just a gimmick in keeping with the concept of trading things to earn prizes, and nobody was expected to bring anything of value. Monty, who referred to the audience members' items as "white elephants" to demonstrate that he didn't actually expect nice gifts, would make trades for something as insignificant as an old tin can or a button.

But as Let's Make a Deal morphed into a daily costume party, the contestants also got more and more imaginative with their white elephant trades. Monty picked a contestant who stood up and produced a fully cooked seven-course Italian dinner. Baked goods became so common that Monty said he had the best-fed crew of any show on television. One day, he asked a woman what she brought to trade, and seemingly on cue, a live bird flew out of her hair. When contestants brought items that were determined to actually have some value, those items would be given to charity. So many people brought small toys to trade away that the staff put them in storage and distributed them to needy children at Christmas.

There were a few restrictions in place for the white elephant trades. Anything that appeared to be a legitimate weapon had to be discarded before entering the studio, and the woman who showed up with a boa constrictor wrapped around her was asked to leave it in the car.

Audience members also started showing up very well-prepared for Monty's quickie deals at the end of the show, very much the way they had prepared for coming to his radio show in Canada.

MONTY HALL[xxiv]

Well, I had a whole array of things I could ask for. Sometimes I had to invent some as I was going along. That last three minutes of the show was sometimes every bit as exciting as giving away a car. If they could fool me by producing a paper clip or a ball or a hard-boiled egg, they put one over on me as it were.

The reaction from the audience from that person getting $200 for producing that hard-boiled egg was just as big as they gave me for the new car that was won just five minutes prior. I think there was a time when I said, "I'll give you $20 for every dime you have" and the person pulled out a roll of 40 or 50 dimes and he got $1,000. The excitement of that audience, that roar, you could have heard three blocks away. It's the time you pulled one over on Monty: "I had what he was asking for."

Not surprised, because they came with baskets full of stuff, purses, huge purses full of stuff. When I asked for something and they couldn't find it right away, they'd empty the purse on the steps and they'd be searching through all the stuff. "I know I've got it here. I know I've got it here." Those were fun parts.

BOB BODEN, friend of the Hall family

I always loved *Let's Make a Deal*. I'm a game show lover through and through, but *Let's Make a Deal* was structured as multiple games within a single show, and I loved that. It was a constant flow of new ideas and fresh presentations. You never knew what specifically you'd see on any given day. And I think that's why it endures to this day. It's a variety show.

I remember watching it when I was very young, and I was captivated. I loved that there were different games every day. I loved the costumes. We had a color TV and I was a young kid, so this show was Halloween every day for me. It was a dress-up parade with real people making simple choices that a kid could follow, but such compelling choices. It was good television.

As Monty gained more experience dealing with more and more ordinary people in extraordinary outfits, he became something of an amateur psychologist, able to anticipate what different contestants might do, and sometimes why they would do it. He pontificated about contestant psychology in 1965.

MONTY HALL[xxv]

If the Big Dealer said, "Now you have St. Louis, do you want to try for the Rocky Mountains?," most Americans would say "Yes." They always want to know what's over the next hill. If we were doing *Let's Make a Deal* in England, I suspect that once an Englishman won ten pounds, he'd take it and go home.

People are out to win something, true, but *Let's Make a Deal* isn't based entirely on greed. People are exercising their gambling instinct. Remember, no one gambles anything of value of their own. They gamble only with what they've won from us.

Women risk more than men. The husbands back away once they won something, but women get a gleam in their eye and want to try for more…

It's a funny thing, but why does the average woman complain about three cents overcharge on a bottle of milk, but gamble all the way on our show? It's probably the one time in her life when she can shoot craps at these stakes. With her it is all or nothing. Will she risk a bird in the hand for an unknown? Usually she does.

It was one of the first times Monty had to address the issue of greed on his show—one that he grew understandably weary of. Giving a contestant a prize, asking if they wanted to try to win more, and then presenting a box or curtain that may contain more just smacked of greed to many observers. Wasn't that first prize enough?

MONTY HALL[xxvi]

The show combines the unexpected, the emotion involved in taking a risk and the hope of making a big strike. The show is very real, these are everyday people, dressed as if they were going to a costume party and faced with an exciting situation. The fascinating part is watching each individual's reaction.

If there's one thing I've learned it's that basically we are all the same in the respect that we all have a great desire to win something. We all have an emotional quotient that comes out under periods of excitement.

It's a people show. Under those baby diapers may be a district attorney and his wife. These are simply nice people who have come to be entertained and are amazingly good sports. Even when they are hit between the eyes by trading a $4,000 car for a camel, the vast majority of them have the attitude that 'I came with nothing' and leave with a fun experience.

Monty argued early on that the very presence of the Zonks was proof that the show didn't celebrate greed. A greed show would be one where the contestant was offered bigger and bigger prizes, with no risk, and asked to "say when" once they felt they didn't need to own any more stuff. On Let's Make a Deal, *sometimes the next prize was nice, sometimes it wasn't, which meant that when contestants were offered anything at all, they had to stop and think about what they had already won and consider if it was enough. And the answer absolutely could be "yes."*

Monty never forgot a woman that he picked for a deal one day. She talked about how she had boarded a Greyhound bus and traveled through several states to get to the studio. Monty gladly handed over $200 and walked her through what turned out to be an uneventful deal. He offered her a box. Not interested. How about the curtain that Carol Merrill is standing in front of? No thanks. How about the box on the display floor? No. Every one of these dilemmas was supposed to lead to a new scenario, but the woman would hear none of it. She kept her $200, and when Monty was out of offers to make her, she smiled, thanked him, and sat down. After the show, she reiterated to the mystified staff that she really just wanted to see the show, and with her tax forms filled out, she walked straight from the studio to a bus stop to begin the long journey home. Nobody could say she was motivated by greed.

Moreover, Monty and his business partner both pointed out, the show wouldn't even be interesting if it celebrated greed. If contestants were just given prize after prize after prize, one right after another until they decided they didn't need any more, how fun would that be?

STEFAN HATOS[xxvii]

If we didn't have the pitfalls, the jeopardy, the show would become Pollyanna and nobody would watch it. When you do watch it, you're either feeling superior because you outguessed the guy who chose he wrong curtain, or you're happy with him because he just won a new car. The name of this show is action and reaction, and the reaction for a $6,500 Pontiac Grand Am is no greater than for a $3,500 Chevrolet.

CAROL MERRILL

The "greed" criticism was just silly. Everybody feels the same way those contestants do. Everybody wants to win. Everybody wants to do well when they play a game. If somebody had a legitimate complaint about *Let's Make a Deal*, maybe it would have hurt my feelings, but that was just such a weak reason for saying you didn't like the show.

Of course, Monty couldn't control what the contestants did, and occasionally they surprised him. A contestant bluntly revealed that he was unemployed, so when Monty made him a deal that resulted in a $800 cash payout, and then offered him a curtain, Monty was sure the man would say no and take a seat. Monty was flabbergasted when the man forked over the $800 and ended up with a bicycle. Moments like that gave critics as much ammo as they needed.

Monty, on the other hand, preferred to remember a moment where a woman made a deal and ended up with $1,000. The cash was all hers, and when Monty asked what she was going to do with the money, she surprised the host and the audience by explaining that she was using the money to adopt a baby.

Monty also was quick to point out that it couldn't be a celebration of greed if the people who ended up with Zonks didn't seem all that bothered by it. Each day on Let's Make a Deal, losers smiled broadly at the moth-eaten curtains, donkeys, and broken wagon wheels that they were saddled with by way of a bad trade. One contestant traded away $750 and discovered he ended up with three stuffed toy dogs; he broke into a broad smile, telling Monty that he had three little girls at home and he was happy to end up with an armful of presents for them. How could the show be celebrating greed when it was obvious that the losers really didn't care?

Monty and Carol take their opening bow for the new nighttime version of *Let's Make a Deal*. It should have been a triumph, but instead, it signaled the beginning of the end of Monty's relationship with NBC. (Author's collection)

MONTY HALL[xxviii]

There has never been an angry loser...because they wait for weeks, sometimes months, to come here. They get all dressed up in wild costumes, bring strange objects, such as a white rat or a bag of rags, to trade and bargain with. It's like coming to a costume party. It's not so much winning prizes as the fun and the game of trying to out-psyche me.

Perhaps the most remarkable proof that the contestants weren't greedy, in Monty's eyes: to his astonishment, the network censors never had to edit anyone's reaction to getting a Zonk.

Still, the show's popularity with viewers couldn't be denied...even though NBC was trying to deny it.

Monty said in 1967, "From the very beginning, I've hoped to get this show on at night. That just hasn't been an idealistic wish to hit the big time. I know this show appeals to men and I know this show can go at night because it's very entertaining. We always have a very good rating, but on holidays such as July 4th and Labor Day, when husbands are home and the whole family can watch, our rating goes right through the roof."

In 1967, Monty finally got his wish, even though, as he acknowledged at the time, he didn't exactly get on his knees and beg for the slot he was offered for the show.

MONTY HALL

In 1967, Proctor and Gamble canceled a show in the eight p.m. Sunday slot and wanted us to fill in while they were readying a new program. NBC didn't want to broadcast game shows at night, no matter how much larger the audience they might reach than dramatic or variety shows, but they didn't want to lose P&G. We did the show for buttons, and against awesome opposition—*The Ed Sullivan Show* on CBS and *The FBI* on ABC. Sullivan had more than a 40 percent share of audience, *The FBI* more than 33 per cent, NBC less than 28 percent. At the end of our stint we had the lead, 32.9 to 32.7 for *The FBI* to 31.5 for *Sullivan*. It was an astonishing upset, although almost no one noticed. NBC didn't even say, "Nice going, fellas."

When I think of the top people who had flopped opposite Sullivan, such as Steve Allen, it irks me that they shrugged off our success, but they did. P&G did congratulate us, however.

An executive told me, "We are absolutely delighted with your success this summer. We're sorry to see it go. If we weren't committed to our new show, we'd be happy to continue with you." They should have.

Later in the fall, *My Mother, the Car* turned out to be a disaster, and NBC asked us if we were prepared to put *Let's Make a Deal* on at night again in January. By now we were a proven nighttime entry, and we felt we were entitled to more money. We asked for a $6,000 raise. NBC said to forget it. They bought *Hollywood Squares* instead. We were hung out to dry—and damned disturbed.

HENRY KOVAL

People at NBC said the network was embarrassed that we beat Ed Sullivan. I have never heard anyone at a network say something like that, and I still don't understand it. There were people at NBC who were angry that we beat Ed Sullivan on CBS.

Monty and Carol pack up their wares. It was time to shop around for a new home, Monty concluded. (Author's collection)

In an interview by Dick Kleiner in late 1967, Monty acknowledged that he had asked NBC for more money. It was one of the first times he acknowledged publicly that he was growing restless as master of ceremonies for a top-rated game show.

Monty said at that time, "I should be a happy man. I'm one of the top men in my field, I have a hit show, plenty of money. But I'm not happy. There are frustrations. What I'd really like to do is emcee a talk show, and I'd like to act, too. Why is everybody surprised when an emcee wants to act? Hal March is a pretty good actor. Bob Crane is a pretty good actor. I get out there and I perform every day of my life. I may feel sick but I go out there and I'm performing just as much as any actor."

A number of game show hosts had been able to indulge the acting bug through summer stock—regional performances of plays at theaters that only operated during the summer months. Game show hosts like Allen Ludden and Gene Rayburn would spend the bulk of their summer away from home, performing plays and musicals for large audiences, flying back to New York for one day a week to tape five episodes of their game shows, and returning to continue the theater engagement.

Because the complexity of Let's Make a Deal rendered it impossible to rehearse and tape five episodes in a single day, Monty was never able to perform in summer stock productions, much to the chagrin of numerous producers and directors who had the same brilliant idea. On multiple occasions, Monty was forced to politely decline offers to portray Professor Harold Hill in The Music Man.

At the same time, Monty was also finding that his plan to be "a thorn on the inside" for the Academy of Television Arts & Sciences hadn't succeeded, and there was still no recognition forthcoming for all the effort he put into cultivating a popular show and becoming one of the top hosts in the industry. He expressed his frustrations in a newspaper essay.

DAYTIME TELEVISION IS THAT POOR OUT-OF-TOWN COUSIN WHOSE VISIT IS UNWELCOME

By Monty Hall

For a number of years now, the Academy of Television Arts and Sciences has been passing out Emmy awards for excellence in categories by methods that are in a continual state of change.

Television at its best is a difficult medium to break down into neat categories, yet the Academy continues to try. In its attempts it has always insulted thousands of talented people and their shows by lumping them into one category called "Daytime Programming."

Giving an award to a Sunday afternoon children's show as the winner in "Daytime Programming" is as ridiculous as it would be to present an award to The Monkees to the exclusion of other nighttime entertainment.

The shunting aside of programs that provide good entertainment five days a week, week in and week out, is a slap in the face to not only the people who pour all of their creative energies and talents into the shows, but to the millions of viewers who derive entertainment and enjoyment from these programs.

There is no valid reason why daytime programming should be made the "poor relative" the TV Academy would rather not talk about.

The networks count heavily on daytime television for revenues. The competition to get shows on the air during the matinee hours is as fierce as the competition to get them on at night. To stay on the air, a show must produce or off it goes to be replaced by another.

In discussions of entertainment value and production quality, the daytime programs can hold their own quite well with the shows that appear in the so-called prime time hours.

Mike Douglas presents just as much charm in the daytime as Johnny Carson at night. And As the World Turns or Days of Our Lives *is just as powerful as* Peyton Place.

Let's Make a Deal *creates as much excitement as* Bonanza, Beverly Hillbillies, *and* Batman. *The proof of that is the large audience* Let's Make a Deal *has obtained in its Sunday evening spot.*

But so stuffy is the TV Academy that it continues to ignore this large segment of the television industry. And when it does let it in, it must enter through the back door.

The crushing blow occurred this year when Mike Douglas, on winning the Daytime Personality Emmy, was not even given the dignifying tribute of being called to the stage for the presentation. The award was made verbally, not physically, and was almost obscured by a commercial break.

Television has a long way to go to match the maturity of her motion picture brothers who learned long ago that, in making awards, the documentary and the short subject were every bit as important as the foreign film, the Disney animations, and the multi-million dollar blockbuster.

MONTY HALL

So, we moved into 1968, the fifth and final year on our NBC contract. Now five years is a tremendous run in television, even for a daytime show, and we had proved we could do the job at night, too. We knew that we would be renewed and that we'd have to negotiate our new contract by the fall since our old pact would expire in December 1968. We decided we wanted $28,000-$30,000 total per week daytime, for five years, with two years guaranteed, an opportunity to prove ourselves again at night at about $30,000 a week, and some fringe benefits.

Early in the year, NBC said they would like to start discussing the possibility of a renewal. We said that was fine with us. In the spring, a negotiator met with Steve and me in Jimmy Saphier's office.

He came in, smiled, opened up his briefcase and said, "Well, gentlemen, have you given some thought to what you might like to ask for?"

Saphier said, "Yes, we want $30,000 a week."

The negotiator stood up, snapped shut his briefcase, and said, "That's impossible. There's no point in opening negotiations at that figure. I'll return when you decide on a more moderate figure."

And he left. We had mentioned only the daytime figure, none of the other things we wanted, but we knew how these people operated and weren't upset. He came back a month later and asked us if we had come to our senses yet. We said that we felt our figure was sensible, and he left again. By then we had begun to be disturbed.

In June, the day after Bobby Kennedy was shot, the negotiator returned for another try. We were in no mood for any more nonsense. We were entitled to a large raise. Other game shows were getting $30,000 and even $40,000 a week. NBC had not even pitched a proposal at us.

"What do you really want?" the man asked.

We said that we wanted just what we asked for.

"Well," he replied, "then I have no recourse but to go back and tell Larry White [the vice president for daytime programming] to find some new program for your time slot for next year."

I said, "You do that."

And, as he got to the door, he turned around and "You certainly have my regrets," as though he were a doctor giving the last bad news to the widow.

Angrily, I wheeled on him and snapped, "Save your regrets for someone who needs it. There are more important problems in the world today than the fate of this show."

We began to think about switching to another network. We had had feelers from ABC, which, of course, had turned us down originally, and also, rather surprisingly, from CBS but we hadn't taken these too seriously. Most feelers are just talk. One network wishes it had some show another network has, and from time to time, one of its executives may say, "Hey, if you'd consider coming over to us, you call me, right?" And the owner of the show will say sure. But nothing much usually comes of it. I knew NBC wasn't worried about any feelers we'd had. They knew CBS wasn't taking on any prize shows, and they figured ABC was so far behind that an owner of a successful show would have to be insane to bury himself over there. But we weren't so sure. We had faith in our work and felt it would work anywhere.

Elton Rule, who had just become the head man at ABC, invited me to come to New York to talk to him. He wasn't personally negotiating for his daytime programming, but he wanted to meet me and perhaps probe the possibilities of my shifting our show. I met with him in July.

He said, "We know we can't open formal negotiations with you until ninety days before the expiration of your contract, but I want you to know we are definitely interested and my checkbook is open and I am ready to write in some interesting figures." I said I would certainly consider it.

I did not keep my visit to New York any secret. When Larry White at NBC learned about it, he immediately arranged a luncheon to be hosted by Don Durgin, one of the network's top executives, in the executive suite. I had been with the network on and off for many years with many shows, small and large, but this was the first time I had been given this sort of treatment. In addition to Durgin, many other executive superstars were present and ready to romance me. I wasn't given a key to the washroom, but I was served first, and the small talk centered on Monty and his show, good old Monty, one of the oldest and most valued members of the team. My advice was asked on everything from problems of industry to the Vietnam war. Everyone hung on good old Monty's words of wisdom. I was sparring with them. I wasn't going to be a sucker for their trap.

Eventually, Don Durgin turned to me and said, "I understand that Jimmy Saphier was not happy when we did not sign *Let's Make a Deal* as a midseason replacement for *My Mother, the Car*. You realize it was economics, not program content that dictated that decision. We could get *Hollywood Squares* for very little money, and your price had gone up. We were forced into making a decision that upset Mr. Saphier."

I looked at him, and I said loud enough for the others to hear, "Because of the proprietary interest that Mr. Saphier has in *Let's Make a Deal* and that which I and my partner have, let's say that Mr. Saphier suffered only ten percent of the hurt."

Durgin stopped the preliminary sparring and moved into the main event. Larry White had quarterbacked the team to this point and now the coach was taking over.

Durgin declared elegantly, "I hope we will have no argument when it comes to re-signing *Let's Make a Deal* for another five years."

I said, "Well, of course, this is a matter for Mr. Saphier to negotiate. He is our agent and he does our negotiating. I am not going to negotiate at lunch. We have let NBC know the sort of money we want, but your negotiator declined to discuss it. There are many things we want and have not been offered. I would suggest that if things are to work out for us next January, a better attempt be made by NBC to go into these matters. And for now, I prefer to leave it at that." The lunch was over.

Going down in the elevator, I found myself next to Larry White. He whispered, "You're a son of a bitch, but a brilliant one."

I followed him into his office and asked him what he meant by that. He smiled and said that it was the coolest performance he'd seen.

Then he said, "Now, just what in hell do you want?"

"Look, Larry," I replied, "you know your man hasn't treated us well at all. He hangs around only long enough to open and close his briefcase and offer us his sympathy. We've been dealing like enemies."

He sighed and said, "Suppose I gave you thirteen weeks of nighttime, would that close the deal?"

I told him that wasn't the main point. We wanted a large increase in our weekly money, at least twenty-six weeks at night, some rerun rights, and ownership of our tapes.

I said, "Why don't you get together with your people and see how much you can give us and then meet with us instead of all this nonsense."

He answered, "I'll do that. I'm making a trip to Europe in September and I'd like to see this settled by then."

I said, "It's up to you." And I left.

After my return home, we began to get calls from NBC executives in California assuring us that everything would work out. Then the offers began to come in. Every week, someone from NBC in New York called to offer us a thousand dollars a week more than the original offer. By the end of the month we were up $4,000, but still $5,000 to $7,000 short of what we wanted. And they still were offering only thirteen weeks nighttime. I discussed every step with Steve and Jimmy, and we were in absolute agreement about standing firm.

Then NBC sent us a new negotiator who said, "Let's start from scratch"—which, of course, was absurd. Jimmy Saphier told him that we would continue from where we were and suggested that instead of trying to nickel and dime us to death, they get serious: time was getting short. He also reminded him that we could begin negotiating with another network ninety days prior to the expiration of our contract.

Larry White, about to leave on his trip, called to remind me how *The Price Is Right* had failed after switching to "that other" network. I told him I didn't care what had happened to any other program. I had faith in the show, and If we could get a better contract from another network, I'd have to consider it.

I told him, "You have yet to begin to negotiate with us on a reasonable level. Let me put it to you this way: If you're not getting any loving at home, then the hussy across the street is going to start looking better to you."

And off we went to negotiate with ABC. Their first offer was, if I remember correctly, around $25,000 a week for the five daytime shows, twenty shows a year cleared for reruns, one nighttime show a week for twenty-six weeks guaranteed at $20,000 each, and ownership of all tapes. The contract was to be for five years, with the first year guaranteed. It was not all we wanted, but it was a lot closer than NBC had come. And it was straight out. We told them we would think about it.

We thought we might have a shot at CBS too. Fred Silverman, their vice president of daytime programing, had taken Stefan and me to dinner and said he wanted us very much and would go high to get us —thirty to forty grand a week—if he could get his superiors to rescind a rule, that limited a contestant's winnings to $500 on any single show. He couldn't, however, and that took care of CBS.

ABC went up to $29,500 daytime and $30,000 nighttime. NBC inched up but still wasn't that high, and time was running out. One week I flew to Montreal to be the guest of honor at a United Nations dinner. When I got back to L.A., we were right up against the deadline. I was surprised when I was met at the airport by Stefan Hatos instead of the usual limousine driver.

He said, "We've got things to discuss." It was all very dramatic—it was our future.

Steve told me that Saphier had been on the phone from New York. NBC had come up with the same sort of money ABC had offered.

"What about nighttime?" I asked.

He said, "No, they're still at thirteen weeks."

I said, "What about reruns?"

"No," he replied.

I asked, "What about ownership of the tapes?"

"No," he answered.

"Well," I concluded, "It seems to me we're still further apart from NBC than we are from ABC."

Hatos said, "Jimmy feels that if the daytime offer is equal we should stick to NBC."

And I said, "The nighttime may not mean much to Jimmy, but it means a lot to you and me in professional standing as well as in our bank accounts. And I think the other things are important too."

And he said, "'I agree with you 100 percent."

We got to my house late in the evening and telephoned Jimmy to tell him that Stefan and I agreed the other factors were too important to ignore. He tried to talk them down, but we stuck to our guns. I knew he had tried for a two-year guarantee and been refused by both networks, but I suggested now was the time to tell ABC that if it guaranteed if it guaranteed us the two years—104 weeks daytime and fifty-two weeks nighttime—it would seal the deal. Saphier said he would try. He called back in a little while to say Elton Rule might go along but that Rule needed the approval of the board of directors and they were not all available and would have to be reached. Steve and I sat back, ate tuna sandwiches, drank coffee, and waited while our fate was being decided across the country.

About an hour later, Jimmy called and said, "The board at ABC has accepted. What do we do?"

Stefan and I smiled at each other and in unison said, "Sign!"

Jimmy asked, "What about NBC?"

We said, "Tell NBC we're sorry, but we've signed with ABC. They had plenty of time to satisfy us and didn't try very hard. Their last offer was topped by a lot."

And Stefan and I shook hands and toasted each other with coffee.

Just before quitting time that day, Jimmy signed for us with ABC. Before he could call NBC, NBC called him. He was asked to lunch with Robert Sarnoff, chairman of the board, and Bob Stone, president of the NBC associated companies.

"For what reason?" Jimmy asked.

"It's time to finally put this *Let's Make a Deal* thing to bed," said the NBC man.

Jimmy replied, "It was put to bed at five yesterday afternoon. We signed a paper with ABC. We're moving."

There was stunned silence, followed by flustered roars of upset. It hit 30 Rockefeller Plaza hard. The rest of the day I got more phone calls than I've ever gotten in one day.

The executives from NBC moaned, "How could you do this to us?"

And I said, "I'm sorry, but you did it to yourself."

The performers I worked with chortled, "You fired a network. You've struck a blow for all the underdogs."

Herb Schlosser called and said, "You've made a mistake. NBC will kill you. You'll be left with nothing."

I replied, "Maybe and maybe not, but the two years we're guaranteed will be enough to take care of us for a long time."

He insisted we hadn't been fair to them, but later he called back and said, "I want to apologize. I talked to the people in New York, and I know now they did not treat you right. I had been assured over these past months that everything was being done to satisfy you, but I now know otherwise. We here in California were told to sit back and let New York take care of it. Well, we did, and I'm sorry we did. You played fair. Jimmy Saphier negotiated in good faith. I admire you enormously. I wish you the best of luck with your new network, and I hope some day you'll be back on NBC."

He was a damned good sport. I thanked him, and sincerely, too.

(Author's collection)

CHAPTER TWELVE

In addition to the extra dollars and cents and the nighttime version that came with the ABC deal, Monty's contract for jumping ship included at least three pilots for additional ABC-TV shows; as the contract spelled it out, one pilot would be a game show, one would be a variety show, and one would be whatever other genre Monty wanted to try. Monty would also get to star in a primetime special, as himself, doing something significantly different from his previous work. ABC opened more doors for Monty to showcase his talents. He'd appear in ABC sitcoms to stretch his acting muscles, and talk & variety shows, where he could sing. He even got to guest-host The Joey Bishop Show *for a few nights.*

Possibly the best part of the move to ABC was that, at least for a little while, Monty had a ready-made retort to the accusations of greed that he was already tired of addressing. It was known that he was uprooting the show for a sizable raise, so when interviewers invariably asked, "Isn't it true that Let's Make a Deal *promotes greed?," Monty's ready answer was, "The only greed on the show is <u>mine</u>."*

For historical perspective, ABC wasn't just the third-place network in 1968. It was a distant third—even if the battle for ratings in those days was a three-horse race, ABC was seemingly in fifth place. Their programming was low prestige, often low budget. It may sound arrogant, but if CBS wasn't interested in Let's Make a Deal, *then it could explain why NBC's negotiators didn't try very hard to hang on to Monty Hall. ABC looked like a step backwards. Even ABC curbed its expectations somewhat for the show.*

Monty addressed this at the time of the switch. "I know our viewers are loyal, but I'm as aware as anybody else of the so-called 'third network' stigma associated with ABC. The ABC brass says we'll be heroes if we even approach our NBC rating, but I want more and that's why I'm going all over the country promoting the switch."

There was another problem with doing Let's Make a Deal *on a new network; it meant getting a new crew. The NBC stagehands would remain at NBC. A team of ABC stagehands now had to be trained for the job, and Monty was surprised to learn that there was tremendous resistance to that.*

MONTY HALL[xxix]

When we first started the show, we taught the NBC people how to do this. Now we sell the show, we move the show from NBC to ABC, we move from Burbank to Hollywood. And we describe the show to the ABC people and they say, "We can't do that show! We can't do it that fast!"

And Stefan Hatos, being the taskmaster with the riding crop, says, "You will learn to do it!"

And he whipped these guys into shape. And when they did it…the stagehands backstage were so proud, they were literally cheering themselves.

So the first year we did it at ABC, we threw a Christmas party at Lakeside Country Club for the entire crew at ABC. All the stagehands, all the technical crew, all the people backstage in the bowels of the earth. We threw them a huge black-tie [party]. These guys never saw a black tie, never saw a tuxedo in their lives….But we wanted to show them that they were the class of the operation and they were the professionals.

We got up and we said to them that night, "This is because you came through for us. We challenged you to come through. You were professional. You were terrific. This is our way of thanking you."

CAROL MERRILL

When we first moved to ABC, and the crew there was still getting used to the show, Joe Behar told the cameramen, "When it doubt, follow Carol, because she knows what she's doing."

That was enormous pressure on me because now, if I make an error and walk to the wrong spot, for the rest of the segment, the cameras will be shooting the wrong things.

STEFAN HATOS[xxx]

Everyone said we couldn't do it, but we discovered that one can do almost anything if he sets his mind to it. The big problem was one of logistics. First there was the problem of where to store the prizes, and then came the problem of what to do with them after they're taken out of storage. Remember that on each show we have from 16 to 24 prizes ranging from a two-ounce package of hosiery or a small watch to a 24-foot mobile home…and remember, too, that these prizes have to be moved sometimes in a matter of seconds. That's why I really hand it to our crew. They're hand-picked, for they simply have to be the best.

**Moving Day! Monty, Carol, and Jay head off to ABC to relaunch *Let's Make a Deal*.
(Author's collection)**

JOE BEHAR[xxxi]

[Stefan Hatos] was very nice. A very stern guy, a stern boss. He wanted everything exactly his way. He was a little anal as far as getting it right and making sure you didn't miss anything. One thing about [Hatos] that was interesting…If anyone on the staff made any little mistakes, he would get on their case and just really yell at them. But if they made a big mistake, a big mistake, he would never say anything. "Eh, don't worry about it." If you made a big one where you felt worse than he did, he wouldn't say anything.

CAROL MERRILL

Stef had a thing that he would say to Joe Behar over and over again. "Reaction shot! Reaction shot! Reaction shot!" To Stef, that was the entire show. If we didn't get a shot of the contestant's face right after the prize was revealed, then the show was pointless, in Stef's eyes.

STEFAN HATOS[xxxii]

Joe really has to be on top of things every second. This show is like an obstacle course. We literally edit and re-write while we're on the air. We have absolutely no idea what the contestant is going to do until he does it.

HANK KOVAL

Stef really had total control of the show. NBC and ABC never offered any input, and Monty really, really trusted him.

MONTY HALL

Our negotiations had been headlined in *Variety* for weeks. When a top program threatens to switch networks, it's a big story in show business circles. We became even more newsworthy after we went on ABC. ABC had six shows opposite us while we were on NBC. They came and they went. They had a 15.5 percent share of the audience when we went on. We doubled that within a week and then shot up to 35.2 percent. NBC lost everything it had gained with us, dropping back into the 15 percent range. First, they tried a soap opera, then Art Linkletter, then a game show, then some other things, but they never recaptured what they dropped when they lost our show. CBS held fast.

But our success went much deeper than that. A popular show pulls up programs that surround it because viewers tend to turn to the channel of a show they want to see and leave it there, especially in the daytime. Even at night there is not as much dial switching as is commonly thought. In our case, we hoisted the ratings of the show preceding and the two following us. The emcee of one of them [Bob Eubanks of *The Newlywed Game*] told me, "Thanks for the ranch you got me."

Let's Make a Deal solidified the network into a virtual daylong tie with NBC and CBS, a situation that holds to this day. *Variety* reported that ABC made so much money that it was in a position to pull up to the two other networks at night, too. Instead of dying, we were more alive than ever and so was ABC.

On January 29, 1969, *Variety* reported:

DEAL THAT SHOOK UP DAYTIME ABC GRAB MAKES CBS THE LEADER

Seldom has a top network suffered from the defection of a single show as has NBC from the loss of Monty Hall's *Let's Make a Deal* daytime strip to ABC. And along Gotham's video row the wisenheimers are claiming that NBC would have saved itself grief aplenty had it made a deal to keep Hall.

As it is, the subsequent ratings skid since Deal lammed the net have shrouded the 30 Rock citadel in gloom. For in the weeks since CBS has forged in front (while ABC has moved right in behind).

Though nighttime prime-time is the glamour area in Nielsen points, more true anguish attached to day¬time numbers...

For acute evidence of daylight billings impact on a web, take ABC where the 1968 profit and loss statement showed an approximate $1.8 million loss due to news operations. What's interesting is that the week-long nighttime deficit was estimated at $8 million but was almost offset by a like profit from the daytime zone, which now is where a net has to make it.

... One of NBC's keystones in its surge up...was *Let's Make a Deal*, which had climbed to a 30 share plateau in its slot and, equally important, was pumping adrenalin through the whole of the net's afternoon ratings. *Hidden Faces*, the serial that replaced *Deal*, has yet to rise above the 12 or 13 share level and, worse, has had a predictably deflationary effect on most of the NBC lineup behind it.

Though CBS is the beneficiary of Hall's move, it appears to be because the NBC slippage has been picked up by ABC. At 2 p.m., for instance, NBC's *Days of Our Lives* soaper still owns the time period but is down to a 32 share, while ABC has moved way up.

The three web stake in daytime billings is figured to reach some $350 million.

Others were enriched, too. For instance, NBC became determined to hang onto everything firm it had. *Hollywood Squares* was holding up its morning lineup, and when they asked for a contract renegotiation, they got a tremendous raise. Later, the show's emcee, Peter Marshall, called me and said, "You're probably the best benefactor I ever had. You have made me a rich man."

People I'd never met thanked me for making them more money because NBC raised them rather than risk losing them. And NBC could have kept us so easily! Well, we live and learn.

HENRY KOVAL

ABC was such a great network to work for. ABC always made it very clear that they were happy to have us on the network and that they wanted us to stay. One of the things that I really liked about ABC was that when they observed a taping, they saw the way that we had to move larger prizes, like cars and boats, in and out of the studio. Somebody said, "There's an easier way to do that." ABC had a special ramp constructed in the studio just for moving cars back and forth.

196 ✠ *Monty Hall: Big Dealer*

Monty in his new home, the trading floor at ABC. (Hall Family Archive)

Five years in a three-channel universe was enough exposure to solidify a reputation for the show and its talented host. Phil Silvers once glowingly said that Monty Hall "conducted a symphony" with his contestants, directing their attention from curtain to tray to table to money clip on each episode with a rhythmic smoothness. General Motors once sent a "motivation research" team to attend a series of tapings and figure out how Monty always seemed to know what each contestant was going to do, in hopes that they could apply it to their dealings with employees.

Stefan Hatos said later, "They were looking for some occult nonsense, but there wasn't any. This show is a Christmas Eve enterprise, you know. The participants are in a game and it's a game they want to win. It's the expectation…We bring no message, nothing. All we've got is 30 minutes of entertainment."

As far as Monty's ability to gauge what each contestant was about to do, the plain truth was he really didn't. It was an illusion generated by a well-run TV show and more importantly, a host who had seen it all. It wasn't that Monty always knew what decision contestants would make. It was that after all this time, no decision surprised him anymore.

Monty said, "About all I've learned is that it takes all kinds. We've had people hang onto $100, afraid to go any further; and we've had people who don't hesitate to trade in a Chevrolet convertible for $4,800, hoping to get the $9,000."

Monty makes a deal with Jimmy Durante and Kaye Ballard in a sketch on *Jimmy Durante Presents The Lennon Sisters.* **(Author's Collection)**

MONTY HALL

As I write this, in our fifth year on ABC and tenth year on television nationally, *Let's Make a Deal* remains at a peak of popularity, with an estimated twelve to fifteen million viewers daily.

And how quickly the five years have gone by! By the time we had to face ABC in negotiations as we had NBC, conditions had changed, and many people had become wiser. We had no difficulty making a new deal with the network. We got a very large increase on our daytime show, a deal for making several pilots for daytime, more reruns, generally making *Let's Make a Deal* the hottest property in daytime. On top of all this, our deal is firm for three years, non-cancelable. You don't see many contracts like this one around. For Monty Hall personally, it was also a good negotiation. I contracted to do one major variety special a year in prime time and two weeks of the late show *Wide World of Entertainment* each year. The network also offered us a chance to develop primetime series of a non-game sort with their funding— all of which makes us most happy clients, and I am sure, as far as the network is concerned, the feeling is mutual.

Nighttime was another story, though we were just as solid there. ABC launched us in February 1969 at nine on Friday nights opposite *The Name of the Game* on CBS and *The Friday Night Movie* on NBC, which were both successful. We started with a 20 percent share and rose to 25 percent. Then we were shifted into the 7:30 slot opposite Don Adams's *Get Smart* on CBS and *High Chapparral* on NBC, and we lifted our network's rating from 18 percent to 28 percent, and *Get Smart,* which CBS had just picked up from NBC, died. So, ABC switched us again, this time to Saturday night at 7:30 against *The Andy Williams Show* and *The Jackie Gleason Show,* and we lifted our slot from 22 percent to 31 percent, and Williams's show went off.

Most of the television critics said Gleason killed off Williams, but a fast study of the situation will show that Gleason's ratings remained the same, while ours went up and Williams's went down, so we did it, even if we didn't get credit for it. Li'l ol' David and his slingshot. ABC switched us once more to Monday nights at 7:30 opposite *The Red Skelton Show* and *Gunsmoke,* and we took the slot from 21 per cent to 28 per cent, and Skelton skidded toward cancellation. The critics said *Gunsmoke* did it, but *Gunsmoke* didn't. In fact, it lost and fell from the first five for the first time in years. We went up while Skelton went down. Again, the situation wasn't seen for what it was.

I do not totally delight in all of this. Some of the shows that lost out were performed by the greatest talents in the business. But the name of the game is ratings, and I am proud of the way our show stood up. No one could admire Don Adams, Andy Williams, or Red Skelton more than I do. All enjoyed long-running success on television—but so has *Let's Make a Deal.*

Our reward for beating the big boys time after time was to be bounced around like a poor relation. Game shows lack prestige, you see, especially at night. In the early part of 1971, the Federal Communications Commission ruled that the networks had to return a half hour of prime time nightly to the local stations. It was an effort to stimulate local programming and provide a new market for the independents, but it has not worked. For the most part local stations filled the period with syndicated shows on tape produced by the prime packagers. But the regulation remains. All networks had to drop three and a half hours a week. ABC decided to give up the first prime period, the 7:30 slot, such as we were occupying. However, we were assured by various ABC executives that they would find another time for us.

A day or two before the new schedules were to be published for the fall, Jimmy Saphier called ABC to double-check and he was told, "How can we keep you off?"

The next day the schedule came out without us. It was a shock. Unproven shows, such as *The Bobby Sherman Show* and *Nanny and the Professor* had been purchased and were on the schedule, but not us.

Monty makes a new deal, taking *Let's Make a Deal* into syndication after losing the nighttime slot on ABC. (Author's collection)

We couldn't believe they would dismiss us so easily, but there it was. We telephoned people. We saw people. Everyone said they were sorry, but we'd been squeezed out. Yes, our ratings were good, but something had to go and in a pinch all the networks had removed most of the game shows because they weren't prestige items. But even after the *Sherman* show and *Nanny* bombed and were canceled, we could not talk our way back on as replacements. We asked for the *Monday Night Football* slot after the football season ended and were refused.

To salve my wounded feelings, Michael Eisner, still in his twenties and the new vice president for daytime programing, offered me eight to ten summer variety shows at $60,000 each. I was hesitant. Few shows make it to the fall lineup off the summer showings, and $60,000 was insufficient to do an hour show right. It would be an opportunity for me to make it as a variety performer, but the show would have been an unfair exchange for a regular nighttime spot and I turned it down.

Stefan and I decided we should syndicate the nighttime show, but ABC owned the rights to it and would have to release us. They refused. We met with Saphier and our attorney, Leo Ziffren. Angrily, we agreed to hit ABC where it would hurt the most. Either the network would restore us to a nighttime slot, or release us for syndication or we would stop producing our daytime shows. We lacked legal grounds, but we felt this was the one way we could force the issue, regardless of the risk. Again, this is the business. Talent is treated roughly and sometimes it must respond in kind. If you win, all is forgiven. If you lose, forget it.

Monty and Jay Stewart on *Let's Make a Deal*. (Hall Family Archive)

I decided to approach Leonard Goldensen, chairman of the board, and a personal friend. I explained the situation to him, and he seemed sympathetic and asked how much time he could have to look into it.

I said, "You can have a week, until next Wednesday."

He said fine. I didn't threaten him with our plan to halt production.

I waited until Wednesday morning without hearing from him. I called him and he was out to lunch. Quitting time in New York came and went.

An hour and twenty-three minutes later, Jim Duffy, president of the network, called and said, "Monty, we have had a meeting and we have something that will make you happy."

It turned out they had agreed to release our show for nighttime syndication. It did make me happy. With this almost eleventh-hour decision, we did not have to test our threat. I feel we would have gone through with it.

The network did ask that its own division, ABC Films, be given the right to syndicate the show. That was fine by us. Most of the ABC affiliated stations that had shown us so successfully before no doubt would buy us now. We were bought by 131 stations, an enormous number for a syndicated show.

We were bought by stations in ninety-two of the one hundred largest cities. Now we are in different time slots in different cities and our ratings vary from city to city, but our average 35 percent share of the audience is the highest of any show in syndication and has made us the number one prime-time access show in the country. Our success in some cities is startling. We have had 62 percent of the audience in New Orleans, 52 percent in Philadelphia, 51 percent in Cleveland and Cincinnati, 48 percent in Atlanta, 46 percent in Salt Lake City. Variety called us "the one unqualified rating success in the field."

We sold ourselves cheap. The various stations that bought the show were raking in huge sums for their own spots. ABC Films charged according to the size of the station's market, and they soon realized we were getting about half of what we were worth. Our rates were doubled for the 1972-73 season. Several stations protested. Our Cleveland outlet, for instance, has been paying roughly $1,000 a week and was asked to pay $2,000. They offered $1,500. In the stalemate, they protested to the Wage and Price Board on the basis of the freeze. They lost their case.

A 1972 Broadcasting *Magazine article covered the annual NATPE convention, a gathering of buyers and sellers who negotiated for syndicated programs. Despite the elevated prices, an ABC Films representative, Jerry Smith, joyfully told the magazine that the company was getting "renewals like crazy" from buyers who visited the company's suite during the convention. The reason, Smith said, was because Monty Hall came along, and he didn't budge from the suite through the entire convention. Everybody who was even slightly considering the show was personally greeted by the star and executive producer. The results showed in the ratings, even in New York City, where the nighttime version averaged about a 30 share despite Monty's complaint* that the station in New York promoted the show so poorly that "they must use the same guy who publicizes the Unknown Soldier and Howard Hughes."

MONTY HALL

Meanwhile, we remain on the network afternoon schedule and ratings are as high as ever. Stefan Hatos and I also developed, packaged, and sold *Split Second* to ABC. Emceed by Tom Kennedy, it has become by far the most successful new show in daytime television and is seemingly assured of a long and prosperous run.

STU BILLETT

I had relocated from New York to Los Angeles in 1969 because television was starting to move from the east coast to the west coast, so everyone who still wanted a job had to make that move. Monty had just taken *Let's Make a Deal* to ABC, which was such a huge thing in TV at the time because nobody believed Monty would actually do that, and because ABC gave him such an amazing contract.

I reached out to Monty, who said, "Come work for me! Stefan Hatos doesn't like working on development. The contract with ABC says I'm entitled to make pilots for three new formats, and I need ideas. Would you like to go to work for me creating ideas for new shows?"

The zonks keep rolling out. (Hall Family Archive)

After building their company on easy-going fare like Your First Impression *and* Let's Make a Deal, *Hatos & Hall put their stamp on Stu Billett's creation, a hard quiz called* Split Second, *hosted by Tom Kennedy.*

STU BILLETT

I was involved in the pitch to ABC for *Split Second*. Stefan Hatos hated that part of running a production company, he never liked going to pitch meetings. So Monty asked me if I would help him with that.

For pitches, the networks would have representatives from both coasts at the meetings, and the executives loved that. They would go someplace in Beverly Hills, have a nice lunch at an upscale place, and have the meeting.

We go to Beverly Hills, we do our pitch, we have lunch, and of course, everyone's in a suit and tie for this. After we finish, we go out to the curb to wait for the valets to bring our cars around. We see a Stutz Bearcat driving up the street. It was such a strange thing to look at, because it was a 1932 model, but you could also tell it was new. Whoever was driving this car had commissioned a new Stutz Bearcat. Midnight blue with whitewall tires. Just a fantastic model.

The car pulls over and the driver gets out. Holy shit. It's Elvis Presley. Monty is busy talking to somebody and I'm going, "Monty…Monty…"

I reached out and hooked Monty's arm to spin him around and make him look. And as Monty spins around, Elvis notices him. And I swear to you, Elvis saw Monty and yelled out "HOLY SHIT, IT'S MONTY HALL!"

Elvis walks right up to Monty and says, "Man, when I tell Priscilla I saw Monty Hall, she'll faint!" He is jumping up and down as he greets Monty, like he's a woman on *Let's Make a Deal*.

Elvis says, "Monty, I'll make a deal with you right now!" and he pulls out this unbelievable-looking gun. It's covered with jewels. Rubies on the handle.

He says, "Monty, take a guess. Which of these did I pay more money for? The gun, or the car? You guess right, and I'll let you keep it."

Everybody is just staring and going out of their minds. But Elvis and Monty hit it off so well, Monty asked about the car and talked about a fundraiser he was doing for some charity, and on the spot, he talked Elvis into donating one of his other cars for this fundraiser.

It was a perfect day. Monty befriended the biggest star in music, Stu Billett had a story to tell for the rest of his life, and ABC executives had a brand new game for their schedule. They bought Split Second. *The series launched in daytime on March 20, 1972.*

Three contestants competed. Tom Kennedy would read a question, usually directing them to "look at the board" next to him to keep track of the info he was asking for. For example, the board might read:

JAPAN

GERMANY

FRANCE.

Kennedy would ask, "How do citizens say 'thank you' in each of these countries?" The contestants hit their buttons, with the order they hit them determining the order in which they could answer. The first contestant could choose any portion of the question and give an answer—"Japan, domo arrigato"—and if correct, the second contestant could only choose from the remaining portions of the question. The third contestant in line might not even be able to choose which portion to answer, only trying to solve whatever was left. The contestants received $5 if all three of them answered correctly, or $10 if only two of them answered correctly. If only one player answered correctly—which the show called a singleton—that player received $25. In round two, the stakes were raised to $10, $25, and $50.

Two of the greatest hosts that game shows ever knew. Monty Hall strolls onto the stage of *Split Second* with Tom Kennedy. (Photo courtesy of Zane Enterprises)

STU BILLETT

Tom Kennedy was a great host. At the very beginning, he had a problem, and I could never get over how he decided to handle it. When we first began doing run-throughs, we found that Tom fumbled with the question cards. He'd read the question, he'd look at the board himself, look at the contestants, and then look back at the question cards to see the answers and see if they were right or wrong. Tom had the worst trouble with losing his place every time he looked away from his cards, so there'd be this little delay when the contestants gave their answers in the run-throughs.

I had worked for Merv Griffin Productions before I moved to LA. I had worked on *Jeopardy!*—the original *Jeopardy!* with Art Fleming on NBC. Art Fleming had a set of lights on his lectern, out of view of the audience. A red light meant "wrong answer." A green light meant "right answer." A yellow light meant "more information is needed." Art would just refer to those lights when a contestant gave a response.

I told that to Tom and said, "We'll put three lights in your lectern. It'll be hidden from the audience, no one will ever know."

Tom said, "I don't want you to do that. If I have a set of lights that tells me what I'm supposed to say, it will make me feel like an automaton."

Instead, Tom came to the studio two hours early and asked to see the question cards for the taping. He sat in the dressing room and committed the answers to memory, like he was studying for a test. I never saw a host do something like that. Every taping, he'd memorize the correct answers, so he wouldn't have to search for his place on the cards.

TOM KENNEDY

When ABC was considering the show, we played some run-through games in the network offices. I did one game and something about it felt off. Monty says to me, "Tom, for the next game, pick up the pace."

I hosted the game faster and everything clicked. That's why I became so diligent about studying for the show. For each taping, I would have the staff send the material to my house and I'd read it. Then when taping day came around, I'd get to the studio early, and an associate producer would come into my dressing room and we'd go over it again.

I'd stand at the lectern during the taping, and I had a stack of question cards an inch and a half thick. I looked like James Lipton on *Inside the Actors' Studio*. All of those cards had the questions divided into three parts and three correct answers. The name of the show, *Split Second,* was the entire point. We wanted the game to move so fast that the contestants had to stay on their toes from start to finish. That's why I felt it was so important for me to study the material and show up prepared. I didn't want to risk making a mistake that disrupted that flow.

The game show hosts of ABC: Bob Eubanks of *The Newlywed Game*, Jim Lange of *The Dating Game*, Allen Ludden of *Password*, Monty Hall of *Let's Make a Deal*, and Tom Kennedy of *Split Second*. (Fred Wostbrock Collection)

The final round was the Countdown Round, in which the players were given goals to meet based on their scores to that point. The contestant with the most money needed to give three more correct answers to win the game. The contestant in second place needed to give four correct answers. The contestant with the least money needed to give five correct answers.

STU BILLETT

I got the idea for the Countdown Round because I had an objection to the way *Jeopardy!* was played. If one contestant does well enough, there's no reason for you to watch the end of the game. If a contestant has a commanding lead, invariably, they'll wager little to nothing in Final Jeopardy to protect their score and win the game. So, on many episodes, there's no reason to even sit through Final Jeopardy.

The Countdown Round was designed so that no matter how much one player dominates the game, it still has a climactic ending. Their performance in the game still means something—they've earned the right to give fewer correct answers than their opponents—but three answers against four answers and five answers? There's a chance that those players who are trailing can pull that off.

The winner of the game was shown five cars. The contestant was given a key, selected at random before the show, picked a car, and put the key in the ignition. If the car started, the contestant won it, plus a cash jackpot. If not, the contestant returned the next day, and if they won a second game, they only had to choose from four cars. If they failed again, another victory in another game meant they would choose from three cars, then two cars. If they won five games in a row, they automatically got a car.

Monty just kept rolling along from one successful venture to another. Friends like Jay Stewart and Carol Merrill were happy to help him. (Hall Family Archives)

STU BILLETT

I have to say this to Monty's credit. He really trusted Tom Kennedy to do the job as host. Here's a man who is a master of ceremonies himself, overseeing production on another show with a different master of ceremonies. That was fine. Monty didn't stand to the sidelines and say "Hmm, I would do it this other way…" He just allowed Tom to host that show his own way.

TOM KENNEDY

At that first run-through, when Monty told me to pick up the pace, that was the first and last note he ever gave me. When you have one host being the boss of another host, that can be a sticky situation. But Monty respected me. We were friends before I was hired, so he knew what I was capable of. I had hosted network game shows before, so he knew what he was getting when he hired me for that job. I hosted *Split Second* for three and a half wonderful years. I never heard a word from Monty about how I did my job. He just trusted me to do it.

MONTY HALL

So, this is success. It took a long time coming. Polls have named Monty Hall the best-liked emcee in television, topping stars I respect enormously. In August of 1973 my star was placed in cement on the Hollywood Walk of Fame, alongside the greats of motion pictures, television, radio, and the music world. Hatos-Hall Productions has hit the top as a packager of game shows, which remain indispensable to the television economy. I have made and am making more money than I ever dreamed possible. It was certainly a struggle and often it still is, but the old fears do not dog me today.

BILL LIBBY

He knows in advance which wallets, boxes, and so forth contain which items, and he guides each bit accordingly. There have been times when no item or the wrong item was revealed, and he had to improvise as he went along. No one noticed because he is so smooth.

Once there was a big buildup for a prize in a box, which when Monty opened it contained nothing at all. The lady contestant could not believe it. Neither could Monty. The box was supposed to contain chicken feathers, but no one believed it, no matter how hard Monty tried to convince everyone.

Another time a contestant turned down a box in favor of a bag. The box supposedly contained a $1,650 watch. As Monty opened it, he said, "And here you could have won, worth *one thousand, six hundred and fifty dollars, a...*" The box was empty.

Swiftly he said, "All right, Blair—Blair's our prop man—where's the watch?"

And he looked in the direction of the curtains as the audience laughed. They cut to a commercial while everyone searched for the watch without finding it. They came back, and Monty said, "Our prop man, Blair, has gone home. He locked the watch up in a safe, and our other prop man doesn't know the combination. But backstage in a safe is a watch worth $1,650—*one thousand, six hundred and fifty dollars!* And at home somewhere is a prop man worth about twenty-five cents at this moment." The audience laughed.

But Blair wasn't to blame. The watch had been stolen. Valuable small items usually are locked in the safe until showtime. Guards are posted to watch them once they are removed and packaged for the show, but someone had stolen this watch right out from under the guard's nose. It never was recovered.

Monty Hall provided the voice of Monty Hall, for Hanna-Barbera's animated sitcom *Wait 'Til Your Father Gets Home.* **(Photo courtesy of Zane Enterprises.)**

MONTY HALL[xxxiii]

I think I embarrassed myself mostly when I was doing a quickie. I ran out of the quickies. We had three or four minutes to fill. Now I'm looking for things to ask for. I see a man in a Navy outfit.

I say, "I'll give $200 if you have a boatswain's whistle."

He didn't have it. Another lady was wearing a beautiful Chinese dress. I said, "I'll give you $200 if you have any Chinese money." She didn't have it.

And talking a mile a minute, I turn around. There's a woman holding a doll in her arms like a baby. She's feeding the doll with a bottle. Because I'm such a great ad-libber I took the bottle away from her and I said, "Show me another nipple and I'll give you $200."

I never heard the end of that one. The crowd started to scream. They screamed for 30 seconds. I turned as red as a beet. Then I confound and compound the issue by saying, "I didn't mean that." They started screaming all over again.

The show goes off the air. I didn't even have time to sign off. Jay Stewart's in the control room and he's signing off and he's breaking up. He couldn't finish a sentence. That's the way the show went off the air. That's one of those cases where your ad-libbing gets you into trouble. Somebody said to me after the show, "What you have done if she did?"

I said, "I'd give her half the farm."

You don't edit. We never edited. You know when we'd edit. You've seen other shows that show bloopers, where a woman faints? We had people faint on our show but I would never, never show that. I'd stop the show immediately, stop the taping immediately, revive the woman, talk to her for a while, make sure she's OK. It was just tension. Then we'd go back to her where I went to her with a question. But you never saw any fainting on *Let's Make a Deal*.

A woman came in wearing a see-through, flimsy harem dress. We did the first part of the deal and went into commercial. The guys in the control room said, "When the lights are on her, you can see Pittsburgh. What are you going to do?" I said, "When we come out, shoot her from the neck up," because you really could see everything.

Disasters could happen even when the contestants wore opaque clothes, even when Monty spoke properly, even when the prizes were there. During the show's first year on NBC, a woman won shares of Fargo Oil stock, valued at about $300. After the program taped, the company that issued the stock certificates made a mistake and sent her shares of stock in a different company; the certificates they gave her were worth $135,000. Remarkably, when the mistake was caught, the woman happily returned the certificates without any trouble.

Let's Make a Deal could be a lot of laughs sometimes. And not always on purpose. (Author's collection)

CAROL MERRILL

Most of the mistakes I remember are things that happened backstage, because that was where I spent most of my time. The doors had a tendency to open late, or sometimes it would be the wrong door that opened. Monty would say "Let's show you what's behind Door #3!" and Door #1 would open.

Monty would handle that masterfully. He'd say something like, "Okay, you asked for Door #3, but now that you've seen Door #1, let me ask, are you sure you want Door #3?" You wouldn't see any trace of confusion or anger on his face when that happened. I honestly think there was something inside him that liked it when there was a mistake. I think he took it as a challenge, and he enjoyed having to think of a new idea.

The crew would play pranks on me during rehearsal. Usually with food because they knew I was a health nut, so there'd be rotten bananas or something on top of the coffee table I was modeling. One day they put a rubber chicken in the refrigerator to surprise me during the rehearsal. Well…then they forgot to take it out, so we taped the episode, and I opened that refrigerator, and there was the rubber chicken. We aired it like that.

I put electric rollers in my hair between tapings to restyle it for the next show we taped that day. A roller got stuck in there one day. We treated it like a live show, and I didn't want to hold anything up, so I just went out there that way, and modeled the entire episode with a roller in my hair.

There was a day where I had to model the fur coat from Dicker & Dicker. We didn't want to wear out the fur coats from overuse because they had to be returned to the shop afterward, so the crew would always put a temporary lining in the coat to protect it from damage. I went to my mark and put the coat on, and the lining got caught between my artificial nail and my real nail, and I couldn't put my arm down. I had to model all these prizes with one arm in the air.

Monty and a contestant react to a Zonk. Not everyone was this horrified. Some contestants were so tickled by the sight of what they won that they happily took their booby prizes home. (Hall Family Archive)

BILL LIBBY

Nevertheless, the cars, boats, and beagle puppies usually are there when their hiding places are revealed. Tires, wheels, and hubcaps have been stripped from cars, however. Some of these cars are especially made for the show and are called "Zonks." One lady took home a Zonk and displayed it in her backyard.

Except for the animals, the contestants must take the prizes they win. They have to pay the taxes on them, too. Producer Stefan Hatos once tried to have the show pay taxes on a needy contestant's prize, but the contestant had to pay a tax on the money given him for his taxes, and it turned out to be an endless cycle.

The show will not buy back prizes or make substitutions. Even the companies that provide prizes are not permitted to repurchase them.

The contestants may sell their prizes to others, of course, or they may keep them. They seldom keep the animals. But one lady who took home a lion cub called up the show a few months later to ask if it would take the lion back because it was eating up her furniture.

A schoolteacher won a heifer worth $1,000 but not worth a nickel to him. Since the show does substitute gifts for animals, he was offered a color television set, which he accepted. However, before it was delivered, friends convinced him he should have gotten a substitute closer in value to the $1,000 value of the heifer. He called up the show to complain, saying he didn't want the set. He wanted a $1,000 value or the heifer. An assistant said he would discuss it with his bosses. When the schoolteacher returned to his apartment that day, there was a truck outside with the heifer in it. The heifer was unloaded and presented to the man with the comment, "You want the steer, you got the steer." He rushed upstairs to call the show to ask if he could have the TV set, after all. He got it.

Could you deal with it if you ended up trading your way to the world's largest can of sardines? (Hall Family Archive)

As much as $28,000 in prizes has been given away in a single show. Of course, everyone can't win big or winning big wouldn't seem big. Whatever they win, the contestants seem happy. Even the losers seem happy. Monty says he has seen ladies make bad deals, perhaps trading a $3,000 car for three young pigs, and hug him. He has had men grab him and throw him straight up in the air. This scares him because he worries about his back, which goes out on him constantly. He goes backstage complaining, "Oh, my back."

Few women miss the chance to kiss him. He says he is the only person in the world who comes home from work with lipstick on his collar and his wife asks him if he had a hard day at the office. This is one of his favorite jokes. Another is that when he comes home without lipstick on his collar his wife is suspicious and asks him just where he has been and what he has been doing.

Requests for tickets come by the thousands from all over the country, and there is now at least a two- year wait. Those who are selected have no guarantee they will get on the trading floor, much less on camera. They dress up in their costumes, and they show up as squirrels or trees or nuts, and they wait in line for hours and a couple of writers walk up and down the line and pick potential contestants by pointing at them and that's it. The rest retire to the audience. Then, on the trading floor, Monty points at someone and he or she suddenly is on camera, a contestant.

A fish, or at least a man dressed as a fish, trades a can of sardines for a car. He jumps a full foot off the carpet, claps his hands excitedly, and reverts in age for a moment from fifty to fifteen. The audience cheers as if it shared in the winning. A can-can dancer calls the cost of five items within pennies, and wins a car. Another contestant goes through the stages of agonizing decision and ends up with a $1,500 ring.

But, wait, it is not the final triumph. At show's end she has another step to go. She is asked whether she will trade her $1,500 ring in for what waits behind one of three curtains. From having watched the show, she knows great prizes wait behind two curtains, the grand prize behind one, but she also knows a "Zonk," a surprise worthless or worth little, waits behind the other. Will she gamble? Will she risk the treasured ring? The audience shouts advice. She looks appealingly to her husband for his advice, but he will give her nothing. He wants no part off such a critical decision. He will help decide every important matter in their life except this one. What will she do? The suspense mounts.

"Yes," she screams. "I'll go for the curtain."

Suddenly she is Bankroll Bernie. She hesitates betting two bucks at a racetrack. Never in her life would she wager a ring worth $1,500, Except now. She picks her curtain. Another contestant picks hers, risking her prizes. Her curtain slides back to reveal a houseful of furniture worth $8,000. More cheers. More tears. Another hug and another kiss. She shakes from the thrill of it all, her face ecstatic. One of the other contestants has swapped a fur coat for a trip around the world and cash for expenses. She shrieks. She hugs her husband. She kisses Monty. She is a working lady. Her husband is a working man. How can they take time for a month-long trip around the world? They have kids. Who will care for the kids? No matter, they will manage. They will go.

A lady after losing, "It's not so bad, not winning. You can't count on winning, you know. You want to win. You hope to win. Watching it at home, we want people to win and we don't even know them. It's all for fun. It's fun to be on and it's fun to watch. You feel sorry for people who lose, but you know some of them have to lose. If you lose, it's all right. It really doesn't matter that much. Ifs not important. It's not the end of the world or anything like that."

Some people took buses, some people hitched rides, and some people made other arrangements to get to the studio for *Let's Make a Deal*. (Hall Family Archive)

A man says, "Greed doesn't enter into it. Everyone wants something for nothing. That's human nature. On this show, if you get on, you've got a chance. But it's the spirit of the show that counts. If we weren't willing to let our hair down and just have fun, we wouldn't be dressed like this, not for anything, not for any prize." He is dressed like a cave man. He holds a club in one hand. In the other he holds tightly to a key to a new camper.

A lady dressed like a frontier woman, who did not get on, says, "I'd have picked the right curtain. I had a feeling about it. I'd have dressed like Tarzan to win that camper. I waited two years to get to the show and then I didn't get on. It's all right. I don't mind. I enjoyed the show. I always enjoy the show. I always watch. I wanted to be on once, though. Just once. I told everybody I was going on. Oh, well, it was fun being here. I guess I'll write for tickets again. I can wait two years. I'm not going anywhere. What do you think I should wear next time?" Smiling hopefully, she walks away into the night.

CHAPTER THIRTEEN

(Author's Collection)

Monty had wanted to break loose and try something other than a game show, and he hadn't been quiet about it either. He had told every reporter and interviewer that ever had a word with him that he wanted to act, and every newspaper profile of Monty Hall for several years made note of the popular emcee's desire to act in a movie.

While sitting in his office one day, Monty got word that famed film producer/director William Castle wanted to speak with him on the phone. Monty, ecstatic that someone in Hollywood heard his pleas, took the call. Castle asked if he could get some tickets to Let's Make a Deal *for family visiting from out of town.*

BILL LIBBY

Don Rickles lay on a couch backstage at the Riviera Hotel in Las Vegas. He said, "I don't know why the hell Monty wants to play our game. We couldn't play his game. I'd die trying to handle his show. And he's liable to get killed doing our shows. When you're the best at something, and he's the best at his thing, the dummy should be satisfied. He's a nice guy. Good talent. But he seems to have suicidal tendencies."

Monty Hall sits by the pool outside the condominium in Palm Springs that his family sometimes uses. It is a clear day and the mountains are a magnificent backdrop. The sun burns down bright and hot. His daughter Sharon is playing in the pool while Marilyn sits reading and watching her, wearing a wide-brimmed straw hat to protect her fair skin from the sun. Monty lies in a lounge chair, grateful for the break in his schedule. He speaks of the television special he is planning.

"I had a commitment to do a special for the network," Monty Hall said. "I wanted to do a variety show with music, but I did not want to be surrounded by superstars. I didn't want anyone to say later that I just stood there and introduced those performers. I wanted to come out of it a new man with a new image as a star who could make it on another stage. But I couldn't figure out how to do it. I discussed it with top producers and writers, but they all suggested things that someone else had done. I wanted to be different. ABC kept asking me if I was ready and when could they expect the show? Finally, they said they were holding a spot for me on June 5—Monday night at eight. I had about decided to let it go rather than do something I wasn't sure of when the William Morris office asked me to speak to Art Fisher and Neal Marshall, two young men who were starting as a production team. Artie had never produced a show before, but he had been acclaimed for his direction of the Sonny and Cher television show, which was successful and imaginative. They worked out an idea I liked and their enormous enthusiasm for the project convinced me to take a chance on them and go ahead with the hour."

Before the taping, Monty was excited about the prospect.

"We've been promised $250,000 to do it," he said, "and I'm prepared to spend every available cent on the show. ABC wants more hour specials, so the first one can be a pilot for a series of hours. Or it can just stand by itself, and we can try other things with the other hours.

"On this one we're going to put me with the people of California in their natural settings. We'll do segments all over the state. We might do a segment in San Francisco's Chinatown, another in a fishing community around Monterrey, or on a real ranch in cowboy country, in an Indian community in the desert or a Mexican town near the border.

Maybe someday? Monty considered film, theater, and other endeavors at the height of the success of *Let's Make a Deal*. (Author's Collection)

"I'll talk with the people about their lives. I'll dance and sing and fish with them. I'll participate in any traditional festivals they may do, and I'll stand aside and let them do the things they do best, too. We'll have some guest stars, a singer maybe and perhaps a singing and dancing group, but no one who will overshadow me. It will be all class with no slapstick stuff. We'll call it *Monty Hall: Of, For and By the People*. I'm tremendously excited about it.

"We have six weeks. I'll be busy with *Let's Make a Deal*, and I have some appearances to make in Chicago and Florida. After that, I'll have three weeks free for taping. For the first three weeks, Fisher and Marshall will have to work things out themselves. But I'll try to stay on top of it.

"I'll judge the show's success by the ratings, the reaction of network executives, the critical response, and my own feelings about it. We have to get a 30 share or better. Of course, that depends on how much the network promotes and advertises it and on the lineup of stations. If it's successful, we'll have a ready-made audience for the next one.

"This is very important" he admitted. "If it's successful, it will open up whole new vistas for me. I've had popular success. Now I want artistic success, too."

In Los Angeles, Artie Fisher is Monty's guest at a Variety Club luncheon that salutes Monty as "Mr. Variety Club, a man who has done more for charitable causes than anyone in Hollywood." Fisher, youthful-looking, his hair resembling a Chico Marx fright wig, wears a brown polka-dot shirt under a brown jacket. He comes across as a sharpie—clever and confident. He talked about his own prospects.

"What does this show mean to me? It means a good deal of money." He laughed. "Since it's my first producer-director deal, it means a chance to impress the important people in this business. When I tell people I'm producing and directing my first network special, they ask me who it's starring? I'd love to say Frank Sinatra or Barbra Streisand. But I have to say Monty Hall. People ask 'What can he do?' I don't know. Yet. I know he does the most successful game show ever. But we're not doing *Let's Make a Deal*.

"I have to find out when he can do. *Let's Make a Deal* stars the people. This special has to star Monty and me, in that order. We'll find his strengths and play to them. I know his weaknesses. But I'll keep that to myself.

"The format will work if we dress it up. Some day we'll take this show to Bar Harbor, Maine; Eagle Pass, Texas; Savannah, Georgia. This time we'll take it to Japanese Deer Park in Buena Park, Olivera Street in downtown L.A....You thought we were going afield. The network only came up with $225,000 instead of $250,000. That cuts out travel.

"We've got Cass Elliott, the Mike Curb Congregation, and Fred Smoot. We'll do some slapstick stuff to liven things up, but it'll be different than *Deal*. This isn't going to be any freak show. We're not going to have any oddball people. We'll have a beautiful show. The camera work will turn up lots of color which we'll splash all over the screen. I got ideas dancing in my mind.

"I did The Monkees Special. That established me. I created a show so bizarre they stood up and took notice. I did it out here. I flew back to New York, and got a call to return to L.A. to do an Andy Williams Special. Did that so well I wound up doing his series for two-and-a-half years. The thing they like about me is that I get unusual ideas and put 'em on the screen. And I'm the fastest in town. I do a lot of homework before I show up for work. We don't waste time shooting. I did the Wow Special, which was a smash. Now it's Sonny and Cher—a director's show. Cher suddenly is a sensation. Well, I handle women well.

A scene from *The Monty Hall Smokin'-Stokin' Fire Brigade*, Monty's special that somehow ended up out of his hands. (Author's Collection)

"Monty Hall is something else. He's scared, and I'm aware of it. I'm not scared, but I'm not in front of the camera. I have to work it so his fear doesn't show on screen. He's a real mensch. He wears a coat and tie. He won't let me dunk him in a mud puddle on camera. He wants to come across with class. All right, I'll work it out. It's my show. The producer and director have to be in charge. They have a list of ten or twelve guys they consider producers in this business. I want to be on that list. It just takes one winner to get on and then you can stay on forever, even with losers. You risk riding a loser while you're looking for that one winner."

Monty went on his trip, but he called up every day to find out what progress Fisher and Marshall were making. They kept telling him he had nothing to worry about. He pressed for details, and again they told him he had nothing to worry about.

Once when he phoned, Neal said, "Don't worry, *The Monty Hall Smokin'-Stokin' Fire Brigade* will be a smash."

Monty was stunned. He said, "What's that?"

Neal said, "That's the new title of your show."

"Why a new title?" Monty asked.

Neal answered, "We're going to put you on the back of a fire engine and we're going to race around and get a lot of attention from people. It'll provide a colorful opening for your show."

Monty didn't like it at all. It didn't make any sense to him. Was he going to be a fireman or was he going to be a man of the people?

He said, "I thought the original fit perfectly."

Neal said, "It had no life to it. This is like the sound of a fire siren. You stop and look. It'll be terrific. Don't worry."

Monty with one of his co-stars from the *Smokin'-Stokin' Fire Brigade* special. (Author's Collection)

Monty was in Jacksonville and was tired from his travels, and he figured if they had this much enthusiasm for a new title, a gimmick, he should share it, not dampen it. He told himself they knew what they were doing.

When he returned home and asked to see the script, he was told that things weren't ready yet. He asked again, from time to time, and kept getting put off. Nothing was ever brought to him for his approval. Neal Marshall wrote some comedy material and it was approved by Art. It called for some cameo appearances and Art booked Dom DeLuise, Jim Backus, Rosey Grier, and Jo Anne Worley. Creative control had passed from the star, Hall, to the producer, Fisher. Hall let it go because he was told only half the show would be scripted—the stuff with Fred Smoot, Cass Elliott, and Mike Curb's Congregation—while the rest would be ad-libbed by Monty.

The first location was Zuma Beach, where Monty would ride a fire truck up and down the Pacific Coast Highway for the opening shot of the show. The aide came for Monty and suggested he wear a brimmed cap to shield himself from the sun. Thinking there was one in a closet, he stepped into the dark to pick it out. Unknown to him, a trapdoor leading to the basement had been left open by a telephone repairman. He stepped into the air, and as he started the plunge, he managed instinctively to throw out an arm and shove himself backward to safety. In a split second he had saved himself from a dangerous eight-foot fall.

Later, at Zuma Beach, he rode the fire engine up and down the highway for hours, hanging on for dear life, scared to death, thinking, "I was saved from that fall because the good Lord meant me to die on the highway."

Then everyone adjourned to the beach, where Monty was to stand and sing with a large group around him. There were five hundred persons in the group, and they ran at him hard, so hard that they rammed into him. The shot was redone.

In the evening, after ten hours of shooting on the beach, the scene that would be the finale of the special was shot. The temperature had dropped from 70 to 45 degrees. Bundled in a borrowed jacket, lying on his back, Hall sang to the accompaniment of a guitar, but his voice cracked on a high note. No singer would do this scene without prerecording the number in a studio. At the end of the take, Hall wanted to do it over.

Fisher yelled from the truck, "It's perfect!"

Hall said, "But I think I can do better."

Marshall said, "It's money in the bank. After all, they don't expect you to be Andy Williams."

The critics later will pick on this flaw in the scene, whereas in fact Hall has a better than average voice. There was no need to sacrifice him in this scene.

They worked with Indians in Westlake. It was 110 degrees, and everyone was practically prostrate with heat exhaustion by the time they got to Monty's shots. His scenes were always last. They had to rush, and that worried him. "Don't worry," Artie said. In Turlock, they were at a rodeo and spent more long hours shooting another fire engine running up and down the coast.

"Can't I talk to one cowboy?" Monty asked.

"There isn't time," Artie replied.

"But the idea is for me to talk to people," Monty said.

"We don't have it set up here. We have an old lady for you to talk to in Watts," Artie answered.

At Japanese Deer Park, Monty was made up in a mobile truck parked outside the main entrance. A Japanese-American woman brought her little girl through the gates. The girl was to be one of the dancers and was in traditional costume.

Another little dancer asked, "Is this a commercial or somethin'?"

An aide answered, "No, it's a Monty Hall Special."

One girl said, "Hey, Mommy, this is a Monty Hall show."

The mother said, "Ah, Monty Hall. Maybe we win lots of money."

Monty, made up and wearing a kimono, sat off to one side, signing autographs for some dancers. Cameras and other equipment were all over the place, Artie Fisher ran here and there giving orders. Someone asked Monty how it was going. He squinted, made a face, and said, "I don't know. By this time, it's impossible to tell. We're really rushed. We're depending on lots of energy but I don't know where it's going. I'm really getting tired. After the beach business they had to rush me by helicopter to the studio to tape two *Let's Make a Deal* shows. The pace is starting to tell. My back is really beginning to bother me."

In his first scene at Japanese Deer Park, he played with a little girl. He sat down next to her and smiled softly at her and began to engage her in conversation. At first, she was shy and silent. Gradually, he drew her out, and she started to giggle. She took his hand. He sang "If I Were a Rich Man" from *Fiddler on the Roof* to her and she was fascinated by it. He kissed her and she kissed him back. (This sequence, lost in the editing, never appeared on screen.)

Monty spent five hours a day talking to television editors across the country in quest of publicity for the show. He suggested that his future lay with programs of this sort, not with *Let's Make a Deal*. As the days began to run out, he called Art and Neal and said he wanted to help with the editing.

"We're doing fine," they told him. "We don't need you. You do your thing. We'll do ours. The show will be sensational."

Four days before the show was to go on the air, he saw the editing. He had been getting more and more uneasy, hanging on to the hope that when the show was cut and pieced together in final form, there would be more continuity than there seemed to be when they were shooting it. Now he knew better.

"It's not good," he said to Art.

"You're wrong," Art said. "It's so good it should be put in a time capsule."

"Maybe," Monty replied. "If it's buried deep enough."

Two days before the show, Monty screened it for Jimmy Saphier and the people at the William Morris Agency. They watched in depressed silence. As it went along, there were good things here and there, and they said something nice about it. But when it was done, they agreed: The first half was terrible, the second half wasn't bad, but it wasn't great either, and by then the whole thing was lost. It wasn't the show he had planned.

Jimmy Saphier said, "Your big mistake is you let other guys take over for you. Bob Hope tells everyone how he wants everything. He supervises his own cutting. That's what you should have done." The William Morris agents agreed.

Monty said, "Now you say it. All the time you saw what was happening, and you didn't say it. Why do you guys always give me good advice too late?"

He went home deeply depressed. It was too late to change anything. He lay in bed with Marilyn and stared at the ceiling and told her how disappointed he was. She tried to console him but there wasn't anything she could say.

On Monday the big ads appeared: HOP ABOARD *THE MONTY HALL SMOKIN'-STOKIN' FIRE BRIGADE!* IT'S A BELL-RINGING ROMP!" But those who read the advance reviews learned that it is not much of a show.

Morton Moss wrote in the L.A. *Herald-Examiner:* "What seems to have been sought by Art Fisher is an air of the spontaneous. You do get a feeling of an entertainment that appears unstructured…it loses shape. The burst of colors…is typical of Fisher, who seeks to turn the screen into a bath of sensuousness. We thought the concept of celebration a good one, but not entirely fulfilled. Certain particularities we liked…"

Monty Hall waited for the show to go on, knowing it would not help him at all. It was, he said, like knowing an accident was going to happen to you when you couldn't do anything about it.

The show went on. The fire engine screamed down the coast, Hall hanging on. A Mexican dance began delightfully, then was destroyed as Smoot moved in to parody a bullfighter. The slapstick intruded. The first half of the show was terrible, and dials must have been switching all over the country. But the show got better. The contrast between the Japanese dancers and the rock dancers was striking. Monty's conversation with an aged lady in Watts was a pure delight. The bonfire scene on the beach for the finale was lovely. The second half, in fact, was pretty good.

The best things were those that were done as Hall had said he wanted them done originally. The worst were those that were added and changed. The bursts of color dazzled, but the special did not show off the host, Monty Hall.

The critics were lukewarm. The ratings were good but not great. Few network executives called Hall to comment on the show. Those who did said, "Well, Monty, there were some good things in it…"

Back to familiar territory after the *Smokin'-Stokin'* special. (Author's Collection)

It was done. Standing in the cool night, Hall said, "I think it could have been saved. Had we replaced six minutes of that dreadful slapstick comedy with six minutes of human comedy. But I talked to more interesting people like that wonderful woman in Watts. Had I insisted on this or that being done. But right from the time I let them change the title and take control from me, the show was lost. I don't blame Art Fisher, He has great talent and got the show he wanted—the movement and color. It just wasn't the show I wanted. It wasn't any good for me. I blame myself. I should have been stronger, tougher, more insistent on my rights as the star and owner. I know what is best for me.

"In recent years, I've let others take over too much. It's worked out with *Let's Make a Deal* because Steve and I have the same concept of the show, because we respect each other's talents, and we have a team that knows it inside out. But the two biggest failures of my life—Vegas and this special—came because I let others run the show and run me. The biggest successes of my life came when I ran my own shows and did what I felt was best for me. Well, I've either got to revert to this or get tougher, or I've got to quit trying these things.

"I think the original concept of the show was good and would have worked for me," Hall said later, "but I just don't know anymore. I know that wasn't the show we did. And I don't want any more of these disappointments. I'm not sure what my next move will be."

He sighed and continued, "Well, I can't kick. Life has treated me well. I lead a good life. I am in a position to do what I want to do. I have a fine family and a warm home. I have a sense of satisfaction about the obstacles I've overcome, the work I've done for others, and the children I've raised with my wife. I suppose these are the important things anyway."

(Author's Collection)

CHAPTER FOURTEEN

Columnist Will Tusher asked Monty Hall what he planned to do for his upcoming Las Vegas stage show. Monty answered, "I'm going to sing like Frank Sinatra. I'm going to dance like Sammy Davis, Jr. I'm going to tell stories like Buddy Hackett. And I'm going to get the hell out of town like Howard Hughes."

BILL LIBBY

"The truth is, I'm not prepared," he admitted. "And I want so much for this to work."

It was around noon and he sat backstage in his little dressing room waiting for the final rehearsals before his opening show that night. He was worried about what he had to do because he had not done it for many years, and in a way, it was more than he had ever done in his life. He looked tired and somehow, he seemed frightened.

It was the spring of 1971. Monty Hall's *Let's Make a Deal* was in its eighth year on television. It had made him a star with a tremendously loyal following. But though it was the most successful game show in broadcasting history, it was still a game show and he was still a game show emcee, and he had reached the point in his life and career where he hungered for more.

Some entertainers, friends and colleagues, needled him at times about being a "game show emcee" who could always buy his way out of a tricky situation by giving away a refrigerator. Many openly admired his skill, such as Red Skelton and Jack Benny, and Jimmy Durante and Don Rickles. They said they couldn't do what he did nearly as well as he did it, and said they watched his show and loved it and admired his work and were fans of his. Hall was grateful, but he wanted to do the things they did, too. He was an entertainer and he wanted recognition as an all-around performer who could succeed singing, dancing, talking, or telling stories.

Now he was about to open in the Congo Room of the Sahara Hotel in Los Vegas. Since the nightclub business has almost disappeared, these big hotel showrooms in this gambling town have become the biggest of the big time for singers and dancers and comics. If you can't make it here, you are not truly a star. And for the first time Hall was trying to make it where his most gifted friends had made it...

He didn't want any part of *Let's Make a Deal* in his act, but his manager, his agent, the writers, and the hotel executives told him he had to have some of it anyway. Reluctantly he agreed to end his Sahara show with some routines from his television program, but he insisted that he do a monologue at the beginning and then sing and dance. To help him he hired a group called The Kids Next Door, a comic named Carl Ballantine, and his *Let's Make a Deal* aide and announcer, Jay Stewart. A month before the show was to begin, he started to learn his songs and routines.

The Sahara contracted him for $80,000 for two weeks, which is a large salary, not as large as a Sammy Davis commands, but larger than the amount received by many who play Vegas regularly. Out of this he had to pay for his supporting acts. The hotel offered additional money and gambling "scrip" for prizes. In return he felt an obligation to repay the house with a hit and a series of sellouts or near sellouts for the fourteen nights and twenty-eight shows he would work.

The Sahara management told him not to worry. Everyone was excited by his appearance, and he was certain to be a smash. He was thrilled to see his name and face up in lights outside the Sahara, on billboards throughout the city, and in newspaper ads. He kept telling himself he was making the right move. He was gambling, but this was a town for gamblers.

"It might be a passport to a new career or an interesting experience," he said. "At worst, it can't hurt me. I have my television show. I'm not dependent on being a hit in a saloon. But I have to admit I'd like it. And I keep thinking it could lead to great things."

He shook his head as if to shake away his worries. He studied his cue cards intensely. He was up against it now. Time was running out. Tonight, he had to go on. "I can do all these things, but I haven't been doing them for a long time. I have to remember the words to my songs. I have to synchronize my dance steps with the other dancers. I have to get the timing down. I have to get it all down."

Outside, Carl Ballantine, who had taken ten years off from the saloons to act on television in *McHale's Navy* and other shows had just finished rehearsing his old act—magic tricks that don't work. The Kids Next Door were onstage working on their routines. Most of them started their careers with The Young Americans. They were young, enormously attractive, and apparently talented. They worked hard on their numbers, starting, stopping, starting all over as their director drove them toward perfection...

They ran through the opening routine in which they introduced the star of the show by coming on carrying *Let's Make a Deal* signs, wearing *Let's Make a Deal* costumes, and singing a *Let's Make a Deal* song: "Just in, from New Orleans...with money jingling in our jeans...Just arrived from North Dakota, and we aim to win our quota..."

They rehearsed and rehearsed while others set up the lighting and microphones in the near-deserted supper club. Outside it was another world, with a hot sun pouring over the people by the pool and bright lights illuminating intent players at the slot machines and crap tables. But there in the casino where there were no windows and no clocks, and it was never night and never day, Monty Hall came out to rehearse his routines with the group. He smiled and made small talk with several of them.

"He's a very nice man," a girl said. "He makes us feel like we're friends. It's not like a star and the supporting cast. How good is he? At this? I don't know. He has a nice personality. He's good-looking. He can sing and dance some. It might work for him. I hope so."

And they went back to work, sweating away the long afternoon on stage in this shadowed place. Hall strutted through a straw-hat-and-cane number with the kids, trying to get his steps right, trying to reach his turn at the right point in the song, trying to get it straight and come out even.

One doesn't realize how hard they work to prepare what must appear to come easily that night. Finally, the kids were released and sent away to rest up for a few hours. You look closely at some of them, and you see their watering eyes are winking, and they are breathing hard. Watching a pretty girl in a skimpy outfit depart, you notice the muscles twitching under the skin of her back, and you see that her eyes have gone hard and cold.

Monty rehearsed on, perfecting his routine with Ballantine. He placed himself in a box and let the "magician" shove swords through it.

"This is a trick, isn't it?" Hall asked.

"I've been doing it for years," Ballantine replied. "Never with a live person, however."

No one laughed. Finally, it was time to knock off. Show time was only a few hours away. Walking slowly, Hall returned to his dressing room.

On the door it said "Johnny Carson." He was the last headliner here, and the management hadn't removed his name. The room was small. The walls were paneled in brown wood. There was a gold rug, a sofa, a few chairs. A bouquet of roses sent by the hotel sat on a table. Before the night was over, Hall had received 131 telegrams of good wishes. The wires said "The best of luck"..."Go for broke"..."Knock 'em dead"..."Be a smash"..."Be a hit"..."Be a smash hit"..."Wishing you another success." Some of them say, "Congratulations," although the show had not yet started. One said, "Imagine ham from a kosher butcher shop."

Monty smiled at some of the messages and shook his head wistfully at others. He handed them to his wife Marilyn and looked at the gold carpet. They brought in a tray of food and he tried to eat, but he couldn't. He picked at it, then pushed it away. Someone came in to say, "Richard Nixon called."

It turned out he had—only it was another Richard Nixon. Monty got up and went into another room to lie down. He lay there in the dark with his eyes open for an hour.

After a while he began to talk. "I don't see why I can't do this," he said. "I know I have the talent. It's just a little rusty. And the audience is accustomed to something else from me. What I do, I do damn well."

He sighed and was silent for a moment. The only sound was the hum of the air conditioning. He started to talk again: "It's tough when you've been away from something for so long. I used to do variety shows in Canada. I haven't had much chance in this country. I'm just rusty. I'll be okay. I'm not nervous, just tired. There's no place I'd rather be. Really. It's very exciting. For someone in show business, headlining a showroom in this town is really something. Only the best play here. Some good ones never make it here. I don't need it," he said, "but I want it."

He grew silent again and did not speak until later when he got up. He went into the outer room where his wife and his manager and his agent and his writer and his choreographer and the producer and the director and others were wedged in and waiting.

He got help dressing and with his makeup. His pants didn't fall quite right, and he kept smoothing his hair and looking at his cue cards. He started to speak the lyrics to one of his songs "There's no place I'd rather be..." Then he began to sing the song. After a few words, he stopped.

"I know it," he said.

"Of course, you do," his wife replied.

His manager said, "Don't worry, you've got it cold."

There was a lot of commotion in the room, and finally it was decided Monty should be left alone for the last half hour so he could compose himself. Only the writer stayed, sitting in a corner, watching, listening, not saying anything.

Monty sat before his make-up mirror and touched up his face. Several the of the bulbs were out. "I wish I wasn't doing any *Let's Make a Deal* out there," he said. "It's my show. It's a great show. It's brought me everything, I love it. But I wanted to get away from it when I worked here. I wanted acceptance on a totally different level. I wanted to do the other things, not this thing.

"The hotel backed out on some of the extra money they were going to give us for the gambling scrip. We'll have to take money out of pocket. Our budget is tight. We have our big prize, a little car, behind one of the curtains tonight. It should last several shows before someone picks it. Then we'll turn to a color television set for a big prize. That should get us halfway through the first week…"

Monty was blindsided by another expense that came up in the preparation stages. It seemed unlikely that anybody would show up wearing a costume, but since the venue reasoned that there simply had to be costumes for a Let's Make a Deal *performance, they shelled out $3,000 for a costume designer to whip up 14 costumes for the show to use every night. Monty was aghast at the quality of the costumes, which he called "foam rubber monstrosities."*

Monty didn't hold back, telling the Las Vegas crew, "If you'd gone down to a taping of the show on any given night, you could have taken fourteen costumes off fourteen people, which probably cost fourteen cents each, and they would have been much better!"

BILL LIBBY

He shook his head. "What the hell, this isn't my real racket. Show business isn't my best thing. My real business is benefits."

He picked up his cue cards and started to study them again, then flipped them away. "I don't know why, but this has awakened so many memories. I keep thinking back to my boyhood. The butcher shop. Delivering meat on a bike in twenty-below cold. I almost became a doctor; did you know that? I went into radio. Then television. It's been a long haul from Winnipeg to Toronto to New York to Los Angeles. And now Las Vegas. Everyone wishes me luck, but they all think I'll need a lot of it. They say, 'My God, what the hell is he going to do on a stage in Vegas?' Not many think I should be doing this. They figure I'll make a fool of myself."

His head hung down, and his hands were clasped as though in prayer. "Well, what the hell," he said. He got up and snapped off the loud speaker and lights and sat back down in the dark and was silent, lost in thought.

A hotel official came in, snapped on the lights again, and said, "Twelve minutes. Good luck." Monty thanked him. The man said, "We've got a full house outside. The dinner show is sold out. Seven hundred and fifty people to see you."

When Monty asked whether all opening nights were not sold out, he was told that not all were. "There must be a convention in the hotel," Monty said.

The man smiled. "There is. But no one forced them to come see you. Don't worry. Just be yourself. That's why they wanted you here."

Monty said, "Well, there's no place I'd rather be."

When his wife came in to kiss him good luck, he put his arms around her and held her close to him for a minute, then let her go. She returned to her seat at one of the long tables near the stage. The room was full. The people had polished off their meals and were drinking their coffee and chattering away waiting for the show to begin.

Marilyn smiled and said, "Last night Monty said, 'This is coming fifteen years too late.' I said it wasn't. I said, 'Maybe five years....'"

The lights in the room went down and the stage lights came up. A voice boomed out, "The Sahara is proud to present the Monty Hall show, starring Monty Hall, the amazing Mr. Ballantine, and The Kids Next Door." The Kids, costumed now and seeming fresh came on: "Just got in from New Orleans…"

Monty entered, smiling and at ease. "A lot of people wonder what the hell is he going to do," he began. There was laughter. "I've been performing since I was five years old," he continued as he went into his monologue.

Some of the stories worked, some didn't. Some got laughter, some only smiles. He began to work a little faster. Still, the routine ran long. Then the Kids came back on and did their stuff. The audience kept breaking into spontaneous applause during each bit and then rewarded them with cheers at the finish. They beamed through their make-up, their eyes gleaming. Then Monty joined them in "Mame," working hard and well.

Marilyn's eyes were riveted on the stage and on her husband. She was almost expressionless. A thin smile tugged at the corners of her lips. Hard lights sparkled in her eyes. She was very intense, worried, reserving judgment. Ballantine did his stuff and the people out front laughed a lot.

Next Monty and Jay Stewart moved among the audience. He sang "The Anniversary Song" to a couple and got a tremendous response. He offered $5 for every lipstick she had. She had two. He gave a man $5 for something else. It was time to offer the big deal located behind one of three curtains at the rear of the stage. A lady guessed the right curtain and won the car. The crowd reacted with applause but no great excitement.

Monty moved into his closing medley, singing songs like "Everything Is Beautiful." He sang attractively and was well received. As the show, closed, the crowd applauded. There was no standing ovation, but everyone seemed pleased. Someone said, "We need more shows like that."

It wasn't a bad show. It didn't lay 'em in the aisles, but it wasn't bad. The monologue needed punching up. The singing and dancing were successful. The show did need a faster pace.

After a quick round of opening night parties full of false smiles and pretense at celebration, the people around Monty began to tear the act apart. The managers and agents and directors and producers and executives crowded around Monty telling him that it hadn't worked as it should have worked and that they had to make some changes fast. He seemed surprised. He kept saying he thought most of the things came out pretty well. But the others insisted that this thing hadn't worked and that thing hadn't worked.

Each one had a different idea, and no one had a final say. Somebody picked up a grease pencil and began slashing stories from the routine. And another picked up the cue card for the songs and began to cut material there. Monty sat back and closed his eyes, and his wife sat off to one side looking down at her hands.

When he went on for the second show, he was doing less of the other things and more of *Let's Make a Deal*. The house was half empty. He worked hard but the show faltered. "The Anniversary Song" had been slashed and was missed. He and Ballantine had trouble with their routine, and a lady picked the curtain that concealed the color television set. When it was finished, the people applauded and left, returning to the roulette and blackjack tables. Monty and his wife received friends in the dressing room and tried to retain a "high." They smiled and accepted congratulations and chatted with visitors, but conversation was forced and uneasy.

Finally, at three in the morning, he and Marilyn walked out through the crowded casino and got into their car and drove quietly to the handsome house that the hotel furnishes to its stars. As he drove down the sparkling strip and turned out into the dark night, his wife huddled close to him. Outside the house, he parked the car and stood under the stars.

"It wasn't too bad, I guess," he said. "But it wasn't what I hoped it would be." Suddenly, he seemed exhausted.

The review in the *Los Angeles Times* by John L. Scott referred to the act as something new in Las Vegas shows, pointing out with surprise that a car had been given away at one show, a color television set at another.

He wrote: "It's difficult to appraise Monty Hall's work except on the basis of his host activities. He's a genial master of ceremonies, glib and personable, but I hesitate to predict a great future for him as a singer and dancer. (As if he cared.)"

The review ran eleven paragraphs. The ninth and tenth paragraphs described Ballantine as a real pro who had the crowd in stitches. The eleventh and last paragraph said: "The Kids

Next Door, a lively group of singers and dancers, provided the youthful accent on the Sahara's bill." It was the only mention they got. Some reviews did not mention them at all.

Most of the reviews said it was a nice show, but not a knockout. *Variety*, the bible of show business, said Hall was personable and sang well and was supported by good acts, but suggested that the people who patronized his shows were not apt to be the high rollers favored by Vegas hotels. Some of the reviews said it was a bad show for Vegas. Ralph Pearl in the Las Vegas *Sun* said Hall was "a personable, charming rascal," but his show was bad and boring and there was nothing more boring to cafe-goers than to watch other cafe-goers win goodies.

The best of the goodies were gone the first night, and the Hall team had to dig deep to produce new superprizes and wound up giving away fives and tens to visitors who were throwing away tens and twenties on a single roll of the dice in this place where money soon means nothing even to a miser. The best of the reviews were forgotten and the worst remembered, and more slashes were made in the show—until Monty Hall wound up doing more of the thing he least wanted to do, *Let's Make a Deal*, and less of what he most wanted to do, singing, dancing, telling stories.

He never had a chance. He wasn't so bad. He was good. If they had let him polish his performance, it would have worked, but he didn't get to try it out at Tahoe or Reno. He got one show in Vegas, at the top, and when it wasn't perfect, they panicked and started to slash away at his act, not one man paring prudently, but several men each hacking out what he didn't like, shoving the headliner back to where they believed he belonged. And Monty Hall let them.

They made him a game show emcee again. Attendance at the shows dipped. It was the off-season, anyway, and he soon was struggling before houses that were less than half full, embarrassed and defected, just waiting for his run to end. He waited through lonely days, waited for his wife's visits, waited for the nights when he could put two more shows to rest. He was thrown into a jungle and torn to pieces. He came close to what he wanted most in life, but this time he never had a chance.

MONTY HALL

Over the years I received offers from time to time to take *Let's Make a Deal* to Vegas. I never was interested. I knew I could take the show on the road and succeed with it everywhere—people are people. But why leave home to go on tour? I couldn't see playing it in the showrooms because I couldn't see people paying $10 to $20 to see our show there when they could get it for free on television six times a week.

Johnny Romero, the Sahara publicity chief, had insisted that with my following I could do a stand-up comedy routine and be a success. But I didn't want to play the lounge. Then he began to talk about doing a show in the main room. Other hotels sent out feelers to see if I'd be interested in trying a show in their main rooms. I began to become interested.

I wanted to prove to everyone, including myself, I was an all-around performer.

Raymond Katz became my manager because he felt he could develop me into such a performer. We agreed that we would try it for a while, and if it didn't work, we would part company. Raymond knew I wanted to break away from the game show emcee rut and move into the variety field, and he felt I could and wanted the opportunity to set it up for me.

Others warned me against it, but I knew they were worried about my making a break from projects in which they were involved and putting a hole in their personal worlds. If they felt I would fail, they weren't so bold as to say it to me. They just said, "Monty, who needs it?" Well, I felt Monty needed it.

Katz signed me for the Sahara. Since it had been a long time since I sang or danced extensively, I knew I needed practice. I worked on my dancing and took singing lessons from a variety of teachers. That was a wild experience in itself. I went to three singing teachers, and I was fortunate to survive! I found there were as many charlatans in voice coaching as in anything else. The first one I went to started me out with long-winded recitations on his philosophy of singing. He likened me to a tree in which the sound started out in the roots, rumbled up through the trunk, spread through the branches, and poured out the top. I couldn't follow him at all. So, he switched to a metaphor in which I was a gun and the bullet was my voice and I pulled the trigger and sent the bullet through the barrel blasting out my mouth. I couldn't follow this either. He kept saying, "Don't you see it? Don't you feel it? Shoot it! Let it go!" I let him go.

I turned to a teacher recommended by Sandy Gallin, Raymond Katz's partner. Gallin explained that the man used unusual methods but had worked wonders with others. I went to his office where the teacher pounced on me and began to pummel me and apply half nelsons and headlocks. He twisted my neck until I screamed. His philosophy was that we don't use most of our vocal capacity because our vocal cords are too involved with our physical movements and bodily tensions, and that to use them to capacity we must somehow separate them from the rest of us. It seemed to me he was trying to tear my head off.

As I left after my first lesson with him, he smiled and said, "I'll probably never see you again." He was right.

The third teacher was less a modernist and more an old-fashioned sort who had me singing scales and learning to project properly. I spent several sessions with him and he was a help. However, he was always expressing delight and amazement at how good I was and what great potential I had. I felt he was spreading it a bit thick. I can carry a tune, I have a pleasant voice, I can sing as well as most non-singing performers—but I am not Andy Williams. My last teacher helped me, but he didn't fool me. At least he didn't kill me.

I taped my numbers and listened to them everywhere I went. I began to rehearse more with an accompanist, Jack Elton, and The Kids Next Door. I began to get better.

I was having trouble with my monologue. I had met with comedy writer Martin Ragaway and spun some amusing true stories, which he enjoyed and incorporated into the first draft of my routine. But the routine was a combination of stories and jokes. The jokes leaned heavily on *Let's Make a Deal*. I had to temper them because I have made it a rule not to demean the participants on the show. I have had a lot of fun with them, but I have never deprived them of dignity. As a result, the jokes were lukewarm and did not blend well with the long stories. Ragaway tried hard, but neither of us could find the right combination.

Ragaway kept saying, "Don't worry. You just take what you want from this draft, and I'll keep bringing you more stuff."

But the more he brought me, the more I worried. He was a skilled specialist, but he was used to working with comedians like Bob Hope, and the rapid-fire joke just did not work for me. I tried some of the material out on benefit audiences, and I got more smiles than laughs. We did part of the show at a temple's annual meeting and received a lukewarm response.

But everyone kept saying, "Don't worry. We're working out the wrinkles. It will work in Vegas."

One of the problems was that I simply did not know what *would* work for me in Vegas. I should have studied other non-singers and dancers who have done well there. I should have been sent to the minors to master my act. I rushed into the hottest spotlight in the industry without proper preparation. As experienced as I was in show business, I was a babe in the woods on the saloon circuit. I paid people who didn't protect me properly. And I didn't insist on doing the right things when it began to go wrong. I wasn't strong enough.

We left for Vegas on the Sunday before the Tuesday we were to open. We spent all day Monday and Tuesday rehearsing the entire show with the entire cast on stage. It wasn't nearly enough. We gave it everything. We worked and sweated almost in a panic. We just didn't have time. I had only one workout with Ballantine. Our routine didn't work at all, but he insisted he was an old pro. and would pull it off when the time came.

I had a lot of workouts with the Kids and they were great. In this, they were the veterans, and I was the beginner, but they were marvelous to me.

Meanwhile, all was bedlam around us. In Vegas, one show closes and the new show opens the next night. In very short order the technicians throw a new setup together, and for a while all seems madness. Then the Sahara backed out on its contribution of scrip to the prize fund. We screamed bloody murder to no avail. With fourteen shows a week, we were reduced to $400 a show in prizes.

Again, we made a tactical error. We should have refused to go on without the big prize budget. How could the biggest giveaway show on television go into the biggest gambling colony in America and offer penny-ante rewards to high-rollers. My gut instinct was that it just could not play that way. Later, my fears were proved right.

By opening night, I was straining to keep myself together. I could see that we had only the skeleton of the show I wanted to do, and that it was a fragile package that could come apart as we unwrapped it in public. I knew we faced the toughest audience a performer can face. The critics would not consider the circumstances of my situation and would review it as a finished act instead of a debut.

I was worried, but I kept telling myself I kept telling myself I just suffering opening night jitters, especially since I was doing something different, and I should respect the optimistic views of those around me that we had something that would work. I figured they knew better than I. I was wrong. Whatever we do, we know better what is right for us than others do.

My wife's spirit sustained me. Without her, it would have been tough to get through that first night. Marilyn is a lot of my strength and I leaned on her a lot as that first show neared. The fears began to build up and a strange sort of loneliness assailed me in which I was driven by memories of all the steps I had taken that had got me to Vegas. I was lucky that I didn't need success there. But I would be lying if I said I didn't want it badly. I felt as though the eyes of all my family and friends and fellow performers were on me.

I went to work before a full house. But there was a Variety Club meeting in town and a convention in the hotel, and an opening night always attracts an audience. So, I didn't kid myself that it meant much. Still, it stimulated me. I thought a lot of things worked well, but I saw that some things did not. I felt strangely let down. I suppose while I had not expected it, I had hoped for more.

After I got through the between-show parties and the false smiles and the expected congratulations and the routine glad hands and backslaps and returned to the dressing room, I was startled to find all the people who had thought our format was perfect now were prepared to pull it apart. Instead of using a surgeon's scalpel, they began to wield axes. No one person was in charge. I should have been, but I wasn't. They grabbed the cue cards and everyone began to cut something. If something wasn't perfect, they didn't try to figure out how to improve it, they just cut it out completely. They chopped some of the best or most promising items. They panicked. I let them pull my show apart. I figured they knew best.

The second show was very different from the first. I led off cold with the monologue, which was cut to five minutes. From start to finish the show was chaos. The house was only about half full and far from fascinated. It was depressing, and I left in a trance.

The reviews were better than I expected, but the bad reviews were the ones we reacted to. My writers axed out more stuff and rearranged further. The monologue was removed completely. Ragaway felt terribly guilty. He had been paid well, and after the first night his material was not used again. After he went back to Los Angeles he kept calling me to offer lines that I could use in the audience or on stage or anywhere, anything that could be considered a contribution. He was a faithful friend.

My *Let's Make a Deal* section, which I hadn't wanted to do in the first place, and which I really hadn't wanted to do under the restrictions of money and prize availability, didn't work out as a giveaway show. So, we resorted to the only thing we could do: we made it into a comedy segment. I knew I was in big trouble when I went up to a corpulent lady in the audience and offered her $50 for any kind of pill, and when she didn't have one, I chided, "You just blew fifty bucks!"

She looked at me and said, "Honey, I just blew $3,000 at the crap tables. What the hell is another fifty bucks! Just give me a kiss and forget about the money!" I had to do a lot of kissing during that two-week engagement.

We had some sellouts or near sellouts, but mostly we drew crowds of, say, 250 for the supper show and 200 for the late show. The high-rollers weren't interested, and the Las Vegas townspeople, our natural audience, couldn't afford it. The visitors support the Vegas shows, not the locals. I'd peek around the curtain, see the tiers of empty tables, and grow more and more depressed. The Sahara people pointed out that it was the off-season and the hotel was only half-full. I was drawing as well as could be expected. Only Tom Jones at Caesar's Palace was pulling big crowds. This was true, but it came as scant consolation.

I'd stand in the wings and Jay Stewart would smile and say, "Well, this tests you as a performer."

I tried to meet the test. I gave the smallest crowds the best I had and the receptions got better and better. The people came to be wonderfully responsive, but there just weren't enough of them.

Later, some of my fellow performers seemed to regard me in a different light simply because I had played there, no matter how successfully or unsuccessfully. It was as though I had become one of them, and I was greeted with new respect. Just playing Vegas was almost enough. Almost.

It was not good enough for me, however. I know now that you do not go into a main showroom in Vegas without a polished show. I do not blame their people for staying away from the show I gave them. If I were them, and I wanted to see a comic, I'd go to see a Buddy Hackett; if I wanted to hear a singer, I'd go to see a Tom Jones. And if I wanted to see a variety show, I'd go to see the Follies or Lido de Paris. I'd go to see a Monty Hall only if I read or heard that he had put together something special and appealing. And Monty Hall hadn't done that. He had an idea that might have worked, but he let others pull it apart.

After the first nights, the shows became an ordeal. Unlike other stars who only work the last half of their shows, which perhaps I should have done, I was on stage much of the time from start to finish, and it was exhausting.

I would go out dinner at two in the morning with Ray Katz, my wife, or friends who were playing Las Vegas, like Danny Thomas and Abbe Lane. There is a strange camaraderie among Vegas performers. When they meet each other backstage or in restaurants, they cling and embrace with surprising intimacy—like survivors of a holocaust. It is a lonely world, and it seems as though they are together in strange, hostile territory while all around them is alien, and they show a desperate need for one another. The same effusive embrace in Las Vegas is just a casual hello in Los Angeles.

Danny Thomas softened my hurt with a pretty good lecture at four in the morning. He asked, "Why are you so low?"

And when I responded that I had only 175 customers at the supper show, he raised an eyebrow and hurled back, "I only had 150. Look, kid, this is my business, and I love it, and there are some times when you are going to have an empty house, and then at others you'll be turning them away. It's all part of the business, and you can't take it personally. For crying out loud, Juliet Prowse had a dozen people the other night, and you wouldn't suggest she give up the business, would you? Stop suffering. Do your best and enjoy it."

All this was good advice from a veteran star; but he had earned his spurs in the nightclub business, and I had just been thrown off my first horse and found it tough to climb back on. During the days I loafed around the house, conserving my energy, waiting for the nights, dreading them and, like a prisoner, scratching the dates off the calendar.

Strangely, in light of my feelings about the experience in Vegas, other hotels want me back. I still feel I can succeed there, but I won't go until I can present something properly prepared and foolproof. Recently, Joe Delaney, Las Vegas television host and critic, asked me whether I was coming back.

When I said no, he responded, "Nonsense, you will be back. The people love you."

MAURICE HALPARIN

Monty is one child in a million. It has been a struggle for him in show business, but he never quit. He always had ham in him, always was in every school play, always was headed in this direction. I was afraid that it would be too tough, but he was tough, too, and never quit. I am proud of my son who struggled to become such a success.

The Las Vegas experience was harsher in Monty's mind than in reality. He lamented to one newspaper writer that he had performed for "a lot of white tablecloths in a half-filled room," but the writer looked into it and found that Monty significantly outdrew a number of the marquee stars in the strip during those weeks. While the finished product hadn't quite worked to Monty's liking, he recognized that he had something there, and for a few months, The Monty Hall Show *toured the country as a featured attraction at state fairs.*

CHAPTER FIFTEEN

(Author's Collection)

Monty once battled some health issues that required him to go in for X-rays. As he sat in his office one afternoon, he got a call from a nurse.

"Your X-rays are back," she said, but then suddenly added, "The doctor's wife wants to know if she can get four tickets to Let's Make a Deal.*"*

Monty patiently guaranteed four tickets for the doctor's wife. The X-rays showed no signs of trouble.

BILL LIBBY

In Monty Hall's office on Sunset Boulevard hangs a sign quoting a magazine story. It reads: "You can learn more about America by watching one half-hour of *Let's Make a Deal* than you can from watching Walter Cronkite for an entire month."

STEFAN HATOS

I don't talk to Monty about his excursions into other fields of entertainment. If he wants to try Vegas or TV specials, that's up to him. He can sing and dance a little. I don't know how far he can go with it. I think he has his limits. But he may go further than I think.

I don't want him putting down our show, though, which he seems to do when he talks of leaving it. Until the time he really does leave, he shouldn't mention the subject. I've pointed this out to him. I think he agrees with me.

If he leaves, it will hurt the show. He's not irreplaceable—no one is. But it would take just the right talent to replace him, and I'm not sure we can find him or get him. Monty is so closely identified with this show after all this time it would be bound to sag right after he went. In the beginning it could have worked with someone else—and in the end it might, too. But the network isn't so sure. No one can be.

I couldn't care less what the critics write or what some people say. We have a clean show, an exciting show, and it entertains people. If it is not high art, it reaches thousands of times the number of people high art reaches. I don't know what the point is if you don't reach people.

I think it is safe to say that Monty and I share equally in everything connected with *Let's Make a Deal*. I came up with the title, but we developed the show together. I think the format is as foolproof as a game show format can be. It is incredibly consistent. It played perfectly the first time, and it plays exactly the same today.

I put the show on the floor, and Monty plays it. We have a large staff working for us. I decide which stunts will be used each show, which prizes will be at stake, and how the show should run. I parcel out the assignments to our writers and merchandizing people. They whip up the details and I formalize them into a final script. Monty takes it and makes it work. He is everything a top emcee should be—handsome, glib, personable, quick-witted. He is very smooth and does not wear out his welcome. He loves people and is able to have fun *with* them without making fun *of* them. It is a very tough show for an emcee to operate, and he performs skillfully: But he has a foolproof vehicle.

Over the years, however, Monty has made it his own show. Publicly it has become his show. But I have an ego, too. Privately, I feel it's my show. I feel I make it go as much as he does.

Monty plays a dentist on *That Girl*, with star Marlo Thomas. (Author's Collection)

I have fought fights alongside him—and I have had fights with him. We always agreed on what we wanted from the networks and stood shoulder-to-shoulder in every confrontation. But we have beefs. What business partners don't? I don't know if our disagreements will ever drive us apart. It could happen. We have contributed to each other's success, but we see many things from different viewpoints. He is talent, I am production, and there are natural conflicts.

He has a large ego. It's what makes him tick as talent. Most performers must have this sort of confidence. He is a hypochondriac. We all know it and accept it—he has to be babied. His back bothers him—or his stomach. He hates to work. We had one hell of a row when I was working eighty hours a week and he wanted to stop rehearsing his shows. But when he works, he works beautifully. He walks out there into the audience, and when the red light goes on on that camera, he comes to life.

He may have lost some enthusiasm for the program. It doesn't show yet, I don't think, but it could hurt. I suppose it's to be expected. We do more shows than anyone—237 daytime shows and 39 nighttime shows a year. That's a lot even though we limit taping to three nights most weeks. It's a rut, and Monty's tired of it.

But what do any of us do in any job? We do the same things. We sell shows or we sell insurance or we sell real estate. Monty should realize that if it's not this show, it's going to be some other show. I'll be damned if I know why the comic wants to play Hamlet. And I'll be damned if I know why the best game show emcee in the business sees himself as Sammy Davis. Hell, a man should be satisfied to be the best at anything. It's helped make us both rich.

Why is a variety show or a talk show any better than what we do? I've been in this business a while. I'm an old pro. I measure the importance of programs by their returns. I have no desire to do arty stuff no one wants to watch. If something flops at the box office, it's no good. If it brings in business, ifs good. I could handle high drama. I'd rather run a good game show at twice the ratings. It's not that easy, you know. For every one that succeeds, a hundred fail. It may look easy, but it's not. It's harder to come up with a game show that will work for ten years than it is to create a super-duper variety show that is lucky to last a season or two.

Still dealing after all these years. Monty, Carol, and Jay get started on a new season of *Let's Make a Deal.* **(Author's Collection)**

I like the life game shows have brought me. I wasn't born into money any more than Monty was, but I learned faster how to spend it. He's still conservative with cash, not for charities, but for himself. I figure money was made to be used. My wife and I have three daughters and a nice home in Encino, and we have what we want and go where we want and go first class. Monty is more careful about things.

In business we're close. I don't have to worry about offending Monty, and he doesn't have to worry about offending me, because we say what we think and we play straight with each other. We don't men have a contract between us.

We don't agree on a lot of things, but we know how to disagree together, which is important. He had a hard fight on the way up, and I admire him for making it. I like him personally. Our office *is* sort of a fun place. There's no backbiting. We're riding the crest of a great wave. If Monty wants to do something else, he can be my guest. I can walk away from this, too. But personally, I feel this has been a nice thing. It's kept me out of pool halls for ten years, anyway.

Day after day, sharing the spotlight with Monty was announcer Jay Stewart. A journeyman broadcaster who made his way from Terre Haute, Indiana to Cincinnati, then took a gamble and moved to Los Angeles, Jay was one of those remarkable people who could say "I've done it all" with a straight face. He announced concerts at the Hollywood Palladium, hosted his own show on CBS's radio network, acted as pitchman for commercials, worked as an associate producer for Ralph Edwards, and slowly moved into announcing for TV game shows.

Jay became a fixture on Let's Make a Deal *for the simple reason that Monty only had two arms; and with a handheld microphone, only one free arm. No announcer on TV worked harder on a single program than Jay Stewart. When Monty needed to tempt a contestant with something hidden under a box, Jay hauled that box across the studio to wherever Monty needed him. When Monty did one of the show's most popular deals, one in which contestants selected keys on a cash register and tried to avoid the one that brought up the NO SALE readout, with a car at stake—Jay set up the cash register. He had to carry a sturdy tray loaded with canned hams and small appliances for price-guessing games, or gingerly carry an arrangement of a glass bowl and raw eggs for another popular deal. Most impressively, Jay had to stealthily sneak away from the festivities, without arousing suspicion, to do a wardrobe change while reading his prize copy into the microphone so he could be part of the surprise when the Zonk was revealed.*

When the curtain would swing open and reveal the hilarious Zonk that a contestant was saddled with, the surprise wasn't a six-foot-high rocking horse. It was Jay, in a Buster Brown outfit, perched atop the horse and mugging for the camera like an obnoxious little kid. In a burned-out kitchen filled with rusty, dilapidated appliances, Jay would stand surrounded by smoke, with soot smeared across his "What happened?" facial expression. If it was a camel, Jay would don a keffiyeh and the audience would howl in delight at "Jay of Arabia" weaving back and forth unsteadily on the uncooperative creature's back. As Monty marveled time and again at how the losers seemed to laugh and have a good time, enough credit could never be given to Jay Stewart, who threw himself wholeheartedly into the clownish antics and took the sting out of getting Zonked for countless contestants who made the wrong deal.

HENRY KOVAL

Jay was terrific on the show. He'd wear the spoiled little brat costume and really get into these characters. We loved him.

Jay Stewart gets into character for another Zonk. (Hall Family Archive)

JAY STEWART[xxxiv]

Monty is the best in the business. But the only thing I couldn't do was to get him to call me Jay Stewart on the air. He'd always say, "Now here's Jay to tell you all about it."

I would remind him that I always called him Monty Hall, but no matter how hard he tried, he never remembered. Monty would say that he knew me too well to call me Jay Stewart. "When I go home at night and say hello to my wife, I don't call her Marilyn Hall."

I've been the announcer on *Let's Make a Deal* since it started. A lot of us have been with it from the beginning. If Monty leaves, it will be tough to replace him. I think I could handle it, but I probably wouldn't get a shot at it.

The prospect scares us. In show business, you know better than to count on long runs, but after ten years most of us have been spoiled. We're no longer used to hocking for work. We've all gotten raises over the years and we're used to more money than we'd make if we were hired for a new show that wasn't assured of success. The new contract makes us all feel good; mighty good.

Some staff people were uptight about Monty's hints that he might leave. They told him he shouldn't try Vegas or specials because he might get hurt, but they're not thinking of him; they're thinking of themselves, and they didn't want him to find something which might take him away. It's a touchy situation.

Monty is marvelous to work with. He has chutzpah, which is one way of saying gall and guts. I don't know about the other things he wants to do, but I know he has varied talents and could probably be successful with many things—if he found the right ones. Anyway, he's got what I call screw-you money. He can do what he wants to do. He can afford to take chances. He could retire tomorrow.

NAT LIGERMAN

I was running a laundromat at Sixth Avenue and Eleventh Street in New York City when Monty Hall came into my life. When I came out of the Army, I thought I might have a future in radio. On the GI Bill, I went to the Columbia School of Broadcasting.

I went to a TV school. No one thought I had any talent. So, I got a laundromat in the Village. But I had ideas. Ideas are a dime a dozen. Who knows what's good? I sent in a lot of ideas for shows. Most of them were sent right back. A few were considered and came close. And I did get shows on. The idea for *Dough Re Mi* was mine. NBC bought it. I had no representation. I didn't know what the hell I was doing. A guy there offered me $50 a week royalty for it. I said it didn't sound like much. He said, "You take it or we'll do it anyway." I took it. I got screwed. You want a list of the screwings I got before I met Monty?

I begged to be given a job, any job, when Monty went west. He took a chance on me. I've watched Monty get rich. And I've done all right. I've seen him work in pain, surviving on Percodan. I'll tell you, he's a mensch. I mean a real gentleman. He hasn't changed in all the years I've known him. Only gotten wealthier—and even that hasn't changed him much. He lives about the same as he always did.

I'm not sure I want him to leave the show. I'm still paying off a car. Sure, it worries me. What will I do if he leaves the show and the show leaves the air? Write *The Godfather?* It's already been written. I could write for other shows. Maybe. But I like this show. After ten years, it's like a treasured old overcoat. Lose it and you freeze to death.

The devil made Monty zonk Geraldine! Monty and Sandy Duncan guest-star on *The Flip Wilson Show*. (Author's Collection)

DENNIS JAMES, friend and fellow game show host

I don't want to break out of my bag. If I'm doing a game I enjoy, it's great. I don't mind being called a game show emcee. I think Monty minds a little. He shouldn't, but he does.

He kept a lot of people alive. There is not a man in this town who has done more for charities than this man.

Monty is tops as a game show man, and he's the greatest dinner emcee I've ever known. I think he's getting into a rat race with very keen competition, so keen I wouldn't want any part of it. But Monty wants to play Hamlet—and he might make one hell of a Hamlet. He's beaten the odds before…

MORT WERNER

It's hard to say why I hired Monty Hall. Why did I hire Johnny Carson? It's a gut reaction. I put Monty to work on *Monitor,* and we kept him working after that.

You have to give ideas a chance to work. Maybe some of our people weren't sold on *Let's Make a Deal* after a run-through, but the idea just seemed to fit Monty Hall. I said, "So we blow fifty grand on a pilot, let's get something to see." The pilot showed we had a hit on our hands. Of course, you think every show you put on is going to be a hit, and not many are. This one was.

The experts agreed, nobody could do it quite like Monty Hall. (Author's Collection)

Some parts of our association with Hall weren't so pleasant. We put on *Hollywood Squares* instead of *Deal* because we felt *Squares* was more of an adult show that fit a nighttime, prime-time audience better. It is a hit in nighttime syndication now, but it doesn't have prime-time opposition, and syndication selling is different from network programing. On the networks, ratings aren't the only measuring stick. You want balance and program flow and content that can catch the best sponsor.

Which is not to say I wasn't sorry when we lost *Deal*. I'm only glad I wasn't responsible. As head of programing, my job was to put shows on the air and try to keep them there. Contract negotiations are handled by others. Possibly our people were overconfident and didn't pursue the renewal aggressively enough, but I can't say for sure. Whatever the snags were, they were unfortunate for us. As I observed it, Monty conducted himself with dignity and honesty and was open and aboveboard about everything...

On a personal basis, I judge him as a very bright, kind individual, quite aware there are other people in the world beside himself.

ED VANE

I was an executive with NBC when we bought *Let's Make a Deal* from Monty Hall and Stefan Hatos, and I was an executive with ABC when they switched the show to that network.

The first I saw of the show was the pilot. It was sensational. I know some of the fellows felt it couldn't be maintained, but we decided to take a chance. You always take a chance anyway. If you can't take a chance on a sensational pilot, what can you take a chance on? We took a chance on Monty. He'd kicked around for years without a big break, but he'd done enough by then to prove he was a pro. He turned out to be more. There are maybe four or five great emcees in the business. He is one of them.

He and his show made a lot of money for NBC. It attracted and held a wide audience. It not only drew top ratings, but pulled its surrounding shows up by the bootstraps. Our daytime picture became as bright as CBS's. ABC wasn't even in the picture. He and his show made millions for NBC and they were not even remotely rewarded in kind.

ABC felt it needed *Deal* desperately to become competitive. Maybe NBC underestimated the unique importance of his show. We didn't at ABC. The daytime is when you make your money, and we felt Monty's show could make our daytime.

Many millions were at stake, more than the public realizes, and they were very delicate negotiations. Throughout them, Monty operated with total candor with both sides. He is an honorable man who told the two sides what he wanted with complete honesty and did nothing devious. At the zero hour we celebrated a great victory. He and his show turned our daytime fortunes around dramatically. He hoisted the shows on both sides of him. He about matched CBS and destroyed the NBC replacements in his own time slot. Overall, he thrust us up into a three-way battle for daytime dominance for the first time. And he has held his place.

The decision to take him off nighttime was not made hastily. We had to take off three and a half hours of shows. His ratings were good, but we felt they wouldn't go higher than 30 percent. We had to gamble on shows we felt might reach 35 or more. On nighttime you need that. It's true that many of the shows we put on flopped, but they were shows with potential. It's hard to predict which shows will catch fire. Often, we've been right. We were wrong on these shows, and we had to go back to the drawing board and develop other shows that had super potential.

We want to keep Monty on *Let's Make a Deal,* day and night, for a long time to come. Frankly, we fear the show will fail without him. I know he's been interested in doing other things for a long time. I'm not sure why. He's the best at his business. Does Willie Mays complain that all he is is a great baseball player? Is Willie looking to make it as an airline pilot? Monty's aspirations to break into musical comedy or some such thing may be too much for him. His aspirations may outstrip his ability. However, it is possible he has unexploited talent. We want to keep him happy and give him every opportunity. Possibly he could be more valuable to us in another slot.

Special guest star Monty Hall makes a deal with Jack Klugman and Tony Randall on *The Odd Couple*. (Author's Collection)

MICHAEL EISNER, network executive

I couldn't speak to a person dressed like a duck without laughing in his face. Monty has a sincerity and sense of sympathy that enables him to dignify nervous people in costume.

I have no idea if he has other talents. I suspect he does. He feels he can be big as host of a talk show or variety show. We are as interested in finding out as Monty is. So far, however, the evidence is not exactly in his favor. His special was not great, but not bad. The numbers surprised me some. Our show in that time slot the week before got a 19 percent share. Monty got a 23 percent share against *Laugh-In's* 28 percent and *Gunsmoke's* 36 percent. That's all right for the first time out, but the show could have been better.

We want to keep Monty and *Let's make a Deal.* We have tried and will continue to try to make him happy in other areas, too. He's a very smart, aggressive man and drives a hard bargain.

In any event, we are grateful for what he has done for us. The shift of his show resulted in a gain to ABC that must be measured not in millions but in the hundreds of millions of dollars. I wonder if the general public can comprehend the impact that this man and his partner Stefan Hatos and their show have had on the television industry.

STU BILLETT (2019)

I couldn't imagine that Monty ever really wanted to walk away from *Let's Make a Deal*. I can't remember ever hearing him talk about it in the office. But for the years he spent trying to get that show on the air, I can't imagine him seriously deciding, "Okay, now I want to get away from it."

He was hosting the daytime and nighttime version, plus the rehearsals; that was three days a week he was giving to that show, and when you're doing as many other things as Monty did at the same time, three days a week for that one thing is a lot of time.

If you're going to the World Series every year, you don't replace your pitcher because you're tired of seeing him on the mound. You keep that pitcher on the team year after year after year until he gives up six runs in the third inning. Monty had to know that *Let's Make a Deal* was the same thing. That show did so much good for him that he'd be crazy to leave it behind. Hosting the daytime and the nighttime versions may have been time-consuming, but for all the money he raised for charity, he had to know that *Let's Make a Deal* was giving him a platform that allowed him to raise that much money.

MARILYN HALL

I am Monty's biggest fan. I laugh at stories I've heard for twenty-seven years as though it's the first time they've been told. Not because I'm conditioned to laugh, but because I thoroughly enjoy the man as a performer. The impact of his personality is always fresh, always new to me. Since I know him so well, when he gets into trouble with his craft, I go through agonies for him.

Vegas was a nightmare. I took a tranquilizer before the show. Monty's one failing is his trust in people and letting them make decisions for him. His stamina and fortitude constantly amaze me, because he is not a robust man. His energy is not physical but comes from some secret well of determination inspired by some driving force that says, "There are people out there who have come to see a performance, and I cannot fail them." He can't say no, and consequently he takes on so many commitments and obligations that I wonder whether he will survive; but he comes through a winner, and I sigh with relief over another crisis passed. He has a kind of divine inspirational confidence that the timing will be there, the fast repartee, the give and take—and it is, without fail. It is true that I hung back for many years as a performer in my own right. But life has brought us so much, I can't complain. And Monty, more than life, brought it to us. He fought for it.

Monty's no chicken. He kept pursuing new opportunities even as he continued hosting *Let's Make a Deal*. (Author's Collection)

ROBERT HALL (2019)

Marilyn was an amazing woman, and she was the perfect wife for a man in show business. Monty was hypersensitive. All television emcees were and are like that. Because you only have that job as long as your ratings are good. Even when you're at the very top, nobody can promise you you'll still have that job in three months. So Monty could really agonize about that. She gave him a lot of stability and reassurance.

JOANNA HALL GLEASON

I can remember living in Canada when Dad was in New York and in New York when he was in California. He called long distance every night and talked to us, and we exchanged tapes. Even when we were apart, he was with us. We're a very close family, intensely loyal to one another, and while Dad had to be away from us a lot all these years, he always made his feelings felt. He is a very good man. By nature, he is a straight, almost puritanical person who believes in home, family, God, and hard work, and he has always instilled a feeling for these things in us. When I think of my parents' marriage, I think of warmth and togetherness and understanding.

I wasn't aware for a while of who he was and what he did. But I did, of course, become aware. When I was young and I'd meet other youngsters and they'd find out who I was, or, rather, who my father was, it would color their attitude toward me, and I didn't like that. Now I relax, enjoy it, and let it pass. I had been the one to make it an issue, becoming defensive or feeling no identity of my own. But it was all part of my adjusting to life, and my life now is so apart from my parents that there is no competition—only love and mutual pride.

Of course his family was proud. Monty made winners and losers alike laugh and smile for half an hour, and it kept a roof over his children's heads.
(Author's Collection)

I started performing in high school. I love it. I love to act and sing, and the stage attracts me enormously. My life will be theater. Now I feel that if Dad's name or his friends can help me get a foot in the door, I would be foolish not to take advantage of it. Theater is a business, and when you are given a good business offer, you accept. In the end, it is my work that will be judged.

It used to really hurt when people slammed *Let's Make a Deal*, or when friends would ask why my father didn't do something better. I always stick up for it and for him. I think it's an entertaining show, and it does just what it wants to do. Dad could do more. I admire him enormously for his courage in trying other things. I have great faith in him and his talent, and I root for him terribly hard. I feel his disappointments very personally. I don't worry about him in terms of success or failure, though. I worry about the stiff pace he keeps.

RICHARD HALL (1973)

I remember when I was very young and Dad replaced Warren Hull on *Strike It Rich*. A friend told me he had seen my daddy on his television. I was surprised. I thought my dad was only on my TV. I thought everyone saw their dads on their own TV's. It took a while before I realized he was set apart as a TV star, a celebrity. And it took even longer before I understood what sort of life it was.

I was driving somewhere with my dad and we heard on the radio that Walter Alston, manager of the Los Angeles Dodgers, had just signed a one-year contract. "One year!" I said. "He's the best in the business and they give him only one year!" And then Dad said that his contract was up every thirteen weeks. Of course, that's not the case now, but it was then. For the first time I realized the relentless insecurity and pressures he felt and appreciated what he had accomplished.

I used to hate it when I'd be introduced as Monty Hall's son. People immediately liked me because of my father. I immediately disliked them because of this. I resented it, and still do. These people have no idea of me. It's affected my feelings toward my father and complicated my search for my own identity. As a teenager I had this almost fanatical drive to be so successful my father would be introduced as Richard Hall's father. I don't feel this much anymore.

I don't think I'm emotionally closer to one parent than the other. I want to write, which is more like my mother. But I want to write different things than my mother does. I want to be a serious journalist. I don't want to write entertainment. I really don't think I'm too much like either of them.

They feel I never wanted to be a performer. I'll tell you a secret: I wanted it more than anything in life for a long time. I envied my father and sister their talents. Their personalities overpowered me. I didn't try out for drama or variety in high school because I couldn't see trying to live up to my father and trying to follow in the footsteps of a sister who had been the star of the school shows. I knew I wasn't good enough. I wish I was, but I'm not, so that's it, and I gave up on it long ago.

Because of his heavy schedule, my father missed a lot of my growing up. We always talked about going fishing together and never did it. I guess we missed some father-and-son things we might have done together, and I felt bad about it. But I had him on weekends, and we'd play touch football and swim. He was always interested in my hobbies. I had a coin collection, and he helped me. I was aware that Dad cared.

I am still dependent on them financially. But I do have some independence of them. I came home this summer to be with my hometown honey. I saw my parents, too, of course, but I was mostly with her. We had this understanding that they would pay for my tuition and room and books, but that I would earn my own expenses. However, when I went back and was poverty-stricken, there was never any question that they would take care of it. They just sent me the money so I could live decently. There was no point in my starving. Things like this are beautiful between us.

I was very disappointed in Yale. I found a lot of snobs there. They were only concerned with having a good time and later becoming successful. To them success was measured only in money. They thought because I had a similar background I should think as they do—but I don't. I want to help make this a better world for people who are not successful and rich and comfortable. I don't expect to have any great power to right wrong, but I hope I can at least exert some influence for good.

I argue with my father about politics a lot, but we are really not that far apart. He is a liberal; I am an ultra-liberal. He was a Muskie Democrat; I was a McGovern Democrat. But he never put me down for my views; and I honestly think I have influenced him some. I was surprised when he contributed money to the McGovern campaign. His prominence gives him certain power, and I don't think he has used this power enough politically. He has used his power for good in other ways, though, and I'm proud of him for that. He's given of himself to needy causes much more than almost anyone I've ever known, I do respect him. He is a man of ideals and this is rare.

If people bait me about *Let's Make a Deal,* I defend it. And if they put him down, I defend him— very strongly. At Yale, a professor started to say sarcastic things. I suppose he thought I would have agreed with him. I told him to shove it. When there was a sarcastic article in the Columbia University Newspaper, I wrote a very strong letter to them supporting my father and his show. I simply won't stand for a superficial, sarcastic sort of criticism. If someone doesn't like the show or his performance, that's fine, but if they just say what they think they're supposed to say about such shows and their emcees, I get angry—and in one way or another I tell them to shove their superficial opinions.

Joanne and I worry about Dad. He has emotional toughness, but not professional toughness. He's all alone out there trying to do something no one else thinks he should, I don't think he's realistic about his talents. If he would surround himself with proper support in the right setting, he would come off fine, but he plunges right in unprepared. He worries too much about what his fellow performers think about him. He's over-anxious to prove himself on an elevated level. I hope he gets what he wants out of it.

Critics may have sneered at the daily costume party, but these folks had too much fun to care. (Author's Collection)

SHARON HALL (1973)

What do I think of *Let's Make a Deal*? I'm bored with it. It's been on as long as I am old. It's OK. OK, it's good. I'm not excited by it. I don't watch the program all the time. I've seen it. When I was two or three, it confused me when Daddy was here in the house and on TV, too. That was fun watching him with him. Now I'm seven and I'm used to him being on TV. By the time I'm eight I'll be tired of it. I'm not tired of it yet. He's not just a daddy to me. He's a daddy on TV. And I like it. And the other kids like me because of it. It bothers me a little. I'm me. Ever since I began camping when I was four years old, the kids would ask me for his autograph every day. Now the kids are used to me.

I miss him when he's away working. I want to see him more. Watching him on TV isn't the same as being with him. Is he a good daddy? Yes. One thing, I tell him to phone me before I go to sleep when he's away and he always calls me. I'd rather he'd come home. He hollers when he gets mad. He doesn't scream his head off. He doesn't get mad at much. He's a pretty good daddy. He lets me do what I want. Mommy is always saying don't do this and don't do that. But she's a pretty good mommy, too. Am I spoiled? I don't feel spoiled. My mom forgets to give me my allowance all the time. I can't have all the things I want.

Lots of kids at school, their daddies are on TV, too. Maxine Komack. Her daddy's Jimmy Komack. And Patrick Cassidy. Well, it's not really Cassidy. His mom is Shirley Jones. And his daddy was Jack Cassidy. Only I don't think he's living at home anymore. It gets very confusing in a lot of my friends' homes with all the different daddies. I'm glad I've just had one daddy and one mommy all the time.

What do I think about my daddy's work? I think it's a hard life. Not scary. Hard work. I don't know anything else about it. Would I care if he gave up *Let's Make a Deal?* No. I'd make him start another show. I always want him to have a show on TV. I'd like to be a performer. But not on TV. I'd like to be on the stage like Joanne. I'd like to act. I don't know what I want to be. But I want to be like my sister. I think she's going to be a star. She lets me comb her hair.

I've been around performer people. I met Mama Cass when I was on the special. I just sat there around the bonfire while my daddy sang to me. When I saw myself on television, I thought I looked yucky. and my marshmallow never got roasted. I was nervous at first. Then I felt comfortable. But I didn't do anything. I liked my daddy on it. I like to hear him sing. I'll let my hair grow so I can be a performer, too…My brother? I like him. He plays hide-and-seek with me. I like my whole family. I like my life. It could be better. I don't like it when we go to a show like the ice show and a great big line forms to get my father's autograph and I can't see. It bothers me. I wish people would leave us alone more. I don't know why they make such a fuss over him. He's just my daddy.

ROBERT HALL (1973)

My brother went through hell to get where he is, and he deserves all the credit in the world. I have no envy of him or his success. I have my own success.

I guess it's a disease of his profession, but as successful as he is, he seems insecure. Which is why he is trying these other things, always wanting to nail down another piece of security. He worries about himself. If he has a weakness, it's that he is hyper-critical. He criticizes me, my wife. He sees things, and if he doesn't like what he sees, he has to have his say. I say, "Monty, old boy, you may be God at the studio, but you are just a rich relative here."

I think he has been too tough on our father. Mom was superhuman. You can't compare parents. We all do the best we can. Our father fought for survival, and it made him short-tempered, but he never hurt a soul and always did his best for us.

He is basically a beautiful man, my brother. He is generous to his family. He gives to others. His charity work is incomparable. And he is a success in his profession.

So much excitement!...(Hall Family Archive)

MAURICE HALPARIN (1973)

I wish my son would quit. He's got enough money to sit on. What does he need the knocks for? If he's in it for the green stuff, he'll just give it away. He's got guts. He's got it in his head he can do other things. And he could. But what does Monty need it for? Why does he drive himself so? So the critics can spit on him?

No one could ask for a greater son. Wealth and affluence did not change him. Just gave him the chance to do more good for others. Tears come to my eyes when I think of my family. You should have such a family. Such a pride as I have.

When they moved us here, it was so wonderful. We used to pinch each other to make sure we weren't dreaming. And then my wife died. What a loss. Without her, life was terrible. Monty invited me to live with him, but I like it here. This is my home. He sees that I have every luxury. I am married again now, and things are running smoothly. We have a lot to thank him for.

...Sometimes it just wore Monty out. (Hall Family Archive)

CHAPTER SIXTEEN

(Author's Collection)

BILL LIBBY

"What time is it?" seven-year-old Sharon Hall was asked.

"It's five minutes to *Let's Make a Deal*," she replied.

A child of television, she tells time by shows. Channel Seven was turned on. The shows are taped weeks in advance, but Monty seldom gets to see them when they come on. That evening, however, he was at his beach home in Malibu, a triple-tiered condominium facing the pounding Pacific.

He sat in a soft chair watching the show. "I shouldn't have worn that suit," he said.

Marilyn replied, "It looks fine."

"I don't like it," retorted Sharon. Hall made a face.

A man won and jumped high in the air. "There, don't tell me the men don't react as much as the women," Hall said. "Look at him, he's crying. Can you believe that?"

Like any viewer Monty rooted for the contestants. But he kept noticing little things. "I shouldn't have turned my back there," he said. "And I should have done more with that gal."

A man won some furniture. "He seems happy," Monty said. Later, the man risked the furniture and wound up with a year's supply of popcorn. Monty said sadly, "Poor Joe looks heartbroken." A lady won a fur coat, screamed with joy, and kissed Monty. "Well, she's happy, anyway," Monty said.

"It was a good show," Marilyn observed. Monty shrugged.

Sharon asked, "Can I go on the beach now?"

Monty walked to the balcony and stood there, looking out over the ocean. "Twenty-three hundred shows," he said.

MONTY HALL

I'm not the star of the show. The contestants are. When I watch the show, I can't help watching myself to see if I'm the way I should be. But otherwise I watch the expressions on the people's faces. Their reactions make this show. They become performers on the show.

Norman Brokaw, the William Morris agent, called it a "happening." That's as good a description of it as any. Most critics rap the show, but they don't really represent the public. And they miss the point of the professionals, which is to please viewers and draw the largest possible audience to which a sponsor may sell his product. I don't know what is wrong with pleasing the audience. Isn't that what any entertainer tries to do? And I'm not sure why a Bob Hope standing up there telling his writers' jokes and acting in comic skits is performing on a higher plane than we are, wringing varied reactions from excited and very real people. The show should be judged for what it is, not what it isn't. It should be measured against its ambitions and its competition. It is the sheerest sort of snobbery to suggest that the millions who watch us are idiots.

I am proud of how I do the show and of the recognition I get. Signed to do a show with Jimmy Durante, I entered the studio when he was twenty steps up on stage. He came bounding down, this aging great, and threw his arms around me, saying, "I just love this guy.

I just love this guy." What a thrill that was! And then I answered a knock at my dressing room door and found Jimmy Stewart standing there. He said, "I just wanted to let you know that my wife and I are great fans of yours and your show."

Monty may have insisted that the contestants were the stars, but there was no doubt about who gave *Let's Make a Deal* its soul. (Author's Collection)

At Chasen's Restaurant one night, someone said, "Jack Benny's been trying to get your attention." Startled, I looked up. There at a table fifteen feet away was Benny.

He shouted up at me, "My wife is crazy about you."

I walked over and spoke to Jack, whom I'd never met, and he introduced me to Mary, and she said, "I adore you," and pulled me down and gave me a great big kiss.

I'd heard Red Skelton stopped whatever he was doing to watch my show. At a luncheon, his wife repeated this to me, then Red himself confirmed it, saying, "It's an exciting show and you do an exciting job."

At a Friar's Club luncheon, Phil Silvers asked the show business people there if they realized I did a daily half hour without a script. "He's fantastic," said Silvers.

And at a dinner, the great Metropolitan Opera singer Richard Tucker told me, "I'm thrilled to meet you. I watch your show all the time."

Well, I am in awe of such people, and their plaudits mean more to me than all the raps of all the critics. As do the compliments paid me by all sorts of people wherever I go.

Let's Make a Deal is a tough show to do. But I am quick and I can talk. I think the real reason for my success is I sincerely like people. People like to be liked. I have a knack for relaxing them. Most people want recognition. When a celebrity treats them as if they were important, it matters to them. Few can be one of the beautiful people. But with a smile, a handshake, a hug, you can give them a dignity and an importance that they seldom get in everyday life, and I enjoy giving this to them.

The hazards of hosting. (Hall Family Archive)

I think it is the genuine excitement of the people who are on our show that makes it go. And I do not believe it stems strictly from the value of the prizes to be won. The reaction of wealthy people to the winning of a prize is the same as that of poor people. And the reaction is almost the same to small prizes as to large prizes. And even losers do not seem too disappointed. The "Zonks" seem to amuse them. The prizes vary, but the fun is always the same.

I watch the contestants like a hawk when they win big. A little old Italian lady gave me a belt that bruised a rib. I said, "I always rated Rocky Marciano the greatest Italian boxer until now."

One seventy-year-old grandmother from Nebraska hugged me, lifted me straight up, and threw me over her shoulder like a sack of wheat. I dangled there helplessly while the show stalled, but the audience loved it. I was scared to death. One big guy picked me up and threw me straight up in the air, and when I came down I tore a cartilage in my knee. Another fellow hooked me with a fishing pole. The women's kisses are sweet. Three men have kissed me, too. I couldn't get out of the way fast enough. One was an elderly man who was simply exuberant. Another was a European, where such is a custom. But the third was terribly suspect.

> One reporter, Harold Heffernan, interviewed Hall in 1967 and expressed surprise at what he called "ragged-looking dents" covering Hall's skin. It came with the job.

MONTY HALL[xxxv]

[Contestants] demonstrate their gratitude in the only way females know best. They rush in to kiss the Santa Claus figure—and that's me! I've been kissed on the mouth, the eyes, the shoulder, the shin, the hand, the chest—anywhere they can reach. And those ladies who can't reach my face to buss it have been known to dig their fingernails into my arms with such avidity that I go home looking like I'd tried to come between a couple of fighting kittens.

ROBERT HALL (2019)

Monty would sleep in his dressing room during the taping breaks at *Let's Make a Deal* because the show wore him out.

> A woman elatedly raised her arms to hug Monty, but had her fists clenched; he took a shot to each jaw. An overjoyed man scooped Monty up by the legs, jumped up and down, and released him. Monty wasn't ready for the landing and limped for a week. Another lucky winner jumped up and down while standing too close to Monty's bent arm, and accidentally shoved his microphone into his teeth, making Monty's dentist a rich man that week. A particularly strong woman once grabbed him around his knees and hoisted him over her shoulder. Still another bumped into him hard enough that he tumbled down the studio steps. Monty amassed a steady collection of cuts and bruises, as well as five dislocated shoulders from any number of happy winners with terrible aim. He had been unintentionally poked and pierced by wayward pins holding together ladies' costumes umpteen times. Monty maintained that he never picked anyone based on their costumes because the show moved too fast for him to really stop and study them; as a result, he had selected a number of contestants dressed as football players over the years, and without fail, he'd suffer an unintentional knock from the helmet or the pads. It wasn't

just winners that Monty had to look out for, either. One woman was annoyed that Monty didn't pick her for a deal and whacked him with her umbrella. She thought better of it and apologized afterward, and Monty was quick to forgive.

MONTY HALL[xxxvi]

Everybody, but everybody, gets excited. I had three women contestants on once, one of them quite blasé, and when the other two won something and threw their arms around me, yelled and killed me, she muttered, "Where do you get these crazy contestants from?"

Then, when she did almost exactly the same thing, I just looked at her and said politely, "Well, that's where I get the people from."

Part of the magic of Let's Make a Deal was that it was real. That might sound like an obvious statement, but you were seeing contestants' genuine reactions: anxiety when Monty told them what decision they had to make, relief when the box was concealing a TV set and a vacuum cleaner, a distressed hand on the forehead when they wound up with a rusted garbage can. Monty reciprocated the honesty, with Let's Make a Deal being done live-to-tape. Each episode was done in a single take, unless there was a major technical gaffe that would prevent the show from actually being completed. Monty didn't stop tape for a hurt knee or a knock to the jaw or a jab from a pin; he limped, rubbed his cheek, and just kept going, sometimes making a fist to stop the bleeding from a cut as he proceeded with the next deal.

Another show, another smooch. (Hall Family Archive)

Monty and Stefan Hatos were so committed to keeping the show real that they laid out unusual instructions to the stagehands. Although the program was preceded by a rehearsal, the entire crew was instructed to do whatever Monty said as host, even if they knew it was wrong. If they knew Monty was supposed to reveal what was concealed in the box, and he said, "Open the curtain," they'd open the curtain. It may have ruined the next part of the deal, but Monty would work around his own mistake and ad-lib a new dilemma for the contestants for consider.

The command went both ways. Monty would just keep going in the event that the crew made a mistake. One day, he asked a woman if she wanted to trade the prize she already had for what was behind the curtain. The contestant and the entire audience gave Monty puzzled looks that he couldn't understand right away.

The contestant replied, "You mean, do I want that car?" Monty turned around. The crew had opened the curtain too soon. There was a new car, sitting in plain sight. Monty laughed, nodded his head, and said the only thing he really could say. "Yes, that's exactly what I'm asking. Would you like that car?" She said yes.

MONTY HALL

It has been a consistently entertaining and popular show. Morton Moss in the Los Angeles *Herald-Examiner* wrote, "Prizes aside, it lives off the vitality of its emcee." Well, I don't expect to win an Oscar for acting, but I do want to be appreciated as an emcee. There are fewer top men qualified to host game shows on television in this country than there are performers able to handle the roles in every other kind of show.

When I leave *Let's Make a Deal*, it will be a sad day. But I will leave it, sooner or later. Before long, I will have done 3,000 shows. A person just cannot do the same show forever, especially one with a tough schedule. I get tired. I feel dead. But when the lights go up, I come alive again. I don't look forward to doing it the way I once did, yet when I get to it, it's still great. I may go on with *Deal*. But ten or fifteen years is a long time to be doing the same show. It flatters me to say no one else could do it, but I prefer to feel it eventually will carry on successfully without me.

Let's Make a Deal is unique in that it has been staffed by the same people for the whole ten years of its existence. They have been paid well, and we have provided them with pension and profit-sharing plans and other benefits. Stefan Hatos and I not only created and sold the show, but have stayed with it as executive producer and emcee, respectively.

Stefan Hatos is a smart, tough man. He has been an almost-perfect partner. We have complemented each other perfectly. He was strongest where I was weakest, and I was strongest where he was weakest. We have had our disagreements, especially in the early years, but there has been no behind-the-back stuff, and we still work together wonderfully well. We have different personalities and lifestyles, but we have enjoyed considerable success and made a lot of money together. He is a proud man, and I know he resents it when interviews with me appear and don't mention him. I have never, absolutely never, discussed our shows without crediting Stefan, but writers usually leave him out.

Stefan does not like the thought of my leaving *Let's Make a Deal*. He does not want to disrupt a smooth team performance, and I don't blame him. But I must make my own life, too. Stefan is content where he is. I am not. I am a good emcee, but that is only one of the things I can do well. There is much of me that does not show. I am not putting down an emcee's role or the show by saying I want to do other things. I have to protect myself by proving myself in other roles while I can. I can command other opportunities only while I'm on top.

Look, it's a brutal business. It is run by ratings. We brag about them when they are good and rap them when they are bad, but we live and die by them. And it doesn't matter who you are or what you do. The ratings are based on a small sample, and a few people in Oklahoma can knock a star right out of the sky.

One of Monty's more serious-minded specials for ABC. Actor Jack Klugman took a test to see if he had a gambling addiction, while Monty spoke to a panel of experts about the harm that the addiction can do. Monty explored a wide range of territory in his ABC special programs. (Author's Collection)

At the zenith of Let's Make a Deal, Monty received an offer to host a daytime talk show, something akin to the crowd-pleasing chat and music program presented by Mike Douglas at that time. He was torn between the sure thing of remaining with his hit game show, or moving into helming a talk show—something he admitted was a dream job, but as a rookie in the field, surrounded by giants like Johnny Carson and Merv Griffin, it would have been a bigger gamble than any curtain or box he could ever offer.

It was, he admitted later, the first time he felt trapped by his own show. He said no to the talk show offer, afraid to walk away from Let's Make a Deal. It wasn't exactly the work he wanted to be known for...but the problem, for Monty, was that it was making him wealthier than he could have imagined.

MONTY HALL

If I don't make my move now, when can I? I have compromised in the past. I remember going to Grant Tinker, at that time an executive at NBC (and the husband of Mary Tyler Moore), to ask his advice about a talk show.

"Why leave a hit for something uncertain?" he asked me. "It doesn't matter whether it is a game show or a talk show, a hit is a hit and a miss is a miss, and if you have a hit, you stick with it. It doesn't matter whether it is daytime, nighttime, anytime; if you are winning, you go with it as long as it lasts."

I didn't make a move. I wanted the other show in the worst way. But I didn't have the courage to give up a secure thing to take a chance.

I have been a guest on many shows—*The Dean Martin Show, That Girl, The Flip Wilson Show, The Odd Couple,* and others—and have done well. But for every show I have taken, I have had to turn down ten others because my *Let's Make a Deal* schedule would not permit it. I want time to do these things and more—a variety show, perhaps, and especially a talk show.

RICHARD HALL (2019)

When my dad was writing the book he began talking a lot about wanting to star in his own variety show, but if you look at TV as a whole, that was about the time when variety shows started to die off.

MONTY HALL

I am no fool. I know Vegas didn't work. I can't be kidded that it was better than it was. But there were facts in that failure that went beyond Monty Hall alone. I wasn't tough enough to see that everything was done the way I wanted it done. The same is true of the television special in 1972. It wasn't what I had planned or hoped for, but there were some good things in it—and it could have been all good if I'd been tough enough to insist on having things my way. As always, there are discouraging defeats in life and in a fellow's career, but they don't have to defeat him. I'm not the kind of guy to give up in the face of disappointment.

ROBERT HALL (2019)

I don't want people to think that Monty hated *Let's Make a Deal*. That's not true at all. He loved that show. He just didn't love it to a level that he was willing to let it be the only thing anybody knew him for.

Ed Asner and Cloris Leachman belt out a tune with Monty. A variety show was one of Monty's not-so-secret wishes for his career. (Author's Collection)

CHAPTER SEVENTEEN

(Author's Collection)

"Monty Hall is something else again. He is—Bob Hope, Jerry Lewis, George Jessel, Danny Kaye, and Debbie Reynolds notwithstanding—the busiest and most productive philanthropist in show business today. Monty Hall has been on his do-good-for-others trips for over 30 years now. He has covered upwards of half a million miles."—TV Guide, July 23, 1973

MONTY HALL[xxxvii]

Anyone as volatile and active as I am feels a lull much more deeply than an ordinary person. I have peaks and therefore I have valleys, too—they go with the territory. Action! Activity! [Those are] the answer to the valleys.

> *What did he mean by "action" and "activity"? Monty and Marilyn took a vacation in Hawaii during the run of* Let's Make a Deal. *Since good relations with network affiliates could be so important, Monty guest-hosted a two-hour morning program on the ABC affiliate while he was there. He stuck around afterward to record some promos for the station to use. He also learned that there would be a breakfast meeting of advertising agencies, and since, of course, commercials were so valuable to a TV show, Monty gave a speech at the breakfast. He visited with the staff and students of a school for children with learning disabilities. And he agreed to serve as master of ceremonies for a Variety Club luncheon. That was Monty's idea of a vacation.*

BILL LIBBY

On a trip to Hawaii, Monty and Marilyn Hall visited the Variety Club's school for retarded children. Surrounded by students, they stood talking to the school's director, Mrs. Rose Lee. Suddenly from one corner of the room came a young boy's voice. "Mon-ty Hall… Mon-ty Hall… Mon-ty Hall," the boy said, slowly, over and over again.

He had been standing facing into a corner with his back to them when they entered, but then he had turned around to sneak a peek at the visitors. His eyes widened when he saw Monty and he kept repeating, "Mon-ty Hall…Mon-ty Hall."

A hush settled over the room. "This is an autistic child," Mrs. Lee explained. "He has not communicated with anybody. His mother brings him here every morning and leaves him in the hope that we can help him, but we have not been able to break through to him. He seems removed from all reality. He stands in the corner by himself. At lunch he even takes his tray of food into the corner. He doesn't play with any of the children. We haven't been able to get him to say one word to anyone. Until now." As she speaks, she starts to cry.

At this point, the boy's excitement rose. "Mon-ty Hall…Mon-ty Hall…Mon-ty Hall," he said faster and faster. Monty bent down, embraced the boy, and began to cry. The other youngsters seemed touched, too, and tears filled their eyes.

Later, Mrs. Lee thanked the Halls and asked them if they knew how much their visit meant. Monty, embarrassed, smiled and said, "It's my privilege," and he and his wife left, deeply moved by the experience. One is inclined to contrast the contestants on

Monty Hall's show with the people who benefit from his charities. The contestants reach out eagerly, laughing, not really needing, but wanting. The others reach out regretfully, sometimes weeping, often not wanting charity, but needing help.

They are the people of Monty Hall's two worlds. He is a man who has given much of himself to others. It has had its rewards, he says, though it has not come without sacrifice and disappointment and even, he admits, some regret.

SHARON HALL (2019)

I came along for that hospital visit. I was only eight but I'll always remember it. Everyone in the room was sobbing because this child had never said a word. I think it was the first time that I realized that my father was special to more people than just me. I really saw the effect that his fame had on people.

Another weekend, another telethon. Monty goes to St. Louis to benefit the local Variety Club chapter. (Garage Sale Finds blog)

Marilyn Hall once teased her husband by saying, "It's a good thing you weren't born a girl. You can't say no."

Philanthropy would always be a more deeply personal effort than a signature on a check for Monty Hall. The telethons, auctions, golf tournaments, banquets, and awards ceremonies ran him so ragged that he finally told one reporter, "I just can't physically do it."

TOM KENNEDY

When you become famous, the charities come after you. Charities need attention or else they can't raise money. They need to attach themselves to people who already have attention on them. And Monty was so highly qualified. He was glib, he was personable, and he just couldn't bring himself to say no.

But he would always try. In time, viewers would notice how often they saw Monty's name in the newspaper for a telethon or some other fundraiser he was involved in. When one viewer wrote a letter questioning how a man could divide his energy between so many different causes, instead of just focusing on one or two, Monty related a story that he thought perhaps explained his obsession with helping as many causes as possible.

In World War II, Monty's uncle, who had twelve children, was notified that three of his sons were missing in action. Young Monty tried to console his uncle by reminding him that his other nine children were still with him and close by.

Monty's uncle appreciated the effort, but told his nephew, "When you have 12 children, you do not divide your heart into 12 pieces. Each of them is your whole heart."

Despite the physical exhaustion, he found himself repeatedly making the journey to one benefit or another, overwhelmed by the sense of obligation that he felt. Not just obligation to his deal with Max Freed, but obligation to help anybody. Charities needed money, and Monty was so skillful in his approach to raising money that it didn't feel right to him to say no to any cause that needed him. How much might they be losing out on if Monty wasn't there to lend a hand? In time, he had turned fundraising into a science, one that he was happy to expound on.

MONTY HALL[xxxviii]

There are four different fundraising techniques. You can use intimidation, but this is difficult to do and I don't like it too much. You can use an emotional appeal. This works with a group, but not on an individual basis. The group-fever captivates people. This is a good way. There's also the appeal to common sense. You point out that a contribution is tax deductible.

Monty preferred the common-sense appeal.

MONTY HALL[xxxix]

It's the person-to-person method. It's a tough method. You can lose both friend and sale. It can only be used by people who are not afraid to put themselves on the firing line. You have to know the person you're dealing with and show how life has been good to both of you over the years. I do this by letter individually. I remind the individual of specific blessings and that we have a way now of showing our gratitude. I've had dramatic results with this method.

Monty threw everything he had into a show that could last 12 hours or more in cities across the country. (Garage Sale Finds blog)

Nothing dissuaded Monty's efforts. Even when the common-sense approach succeeded with a donor who had a lot to give, Monty noticed that a successful sales pitch could breed resentment.

MONTY HALL[xl]

No one will thank you for taking money from them. They'll even give you a hard time. At least three times a week, I say, 'Who needs this!' I do it because it has to be done.

Someone who devoted such a level of thought, energy, and time to raising funds could have simply decided that the effort more than fulfilled the obligation to give. Monty, on the other hand, concluded any fundraising effort by pulling out his checkbook and giving a chunk of his own money to the cause. When you got right down to it, effort was great, but it would never be valuable enough to a worthy cause. You couldn't pay a bill by saying, "Monty worked really hard to raise money for us." So just offering to help was never good enough. In Monty's eyes, dollars were the only things that truly counted for fundraising. He had to give of himself.

MONTY HALL[xli]

You do not measure your own capacity to give against your neighbor's ability to give. You measure it solely against your own ability to give.

Monty thought back to a destitute childhood, where a cash box sat in the kitchen even as his own family struggled to get by. And yet the Halparin family still gave. As an adult, Monty had so much more. He knew that this only meant he had so much more to give.

MONTY HALL

I am a star. Others can judge for themselves how much of a star I am, but I know I am enough of a star in the entertainment industry to be a celebrity and instantly recognizable to many people.

One of the privileges stardom produces is the opportunity to help others. I am a salable commodity. My presence as toastmaster at a dinner, emcee of a variety show, or host of a telethon builds up the audience and increases the returns. There are other personalities whose name and presence could mean as much, but many of them do not do as much charitable work as I believe they should. Some lend their names, but do not serve on committees or donate money. My participation means a lot. I am in demand a great deal, and I respond—so much so that I am stamped as a soft touch and sought out constantly.

Some performers, such as Danny Thomas with St. Jude's Hospital and Jerry Lewis with the Muscular Dystrophy Fund, concentrate on one worthy cause. I give a great deal of time to as many as I can manage to help. I average fifty major charity performances a year, all around the country and in Canada. I receive invitations to approximately 350 of these affairs every year. I cannot begin to guess how much money I have raised for charity, but it runs into the many millions of dollars.

I have stated that a concomitant of success is responsibility and obligation. Those of us who have made it have the responsibility to make sure we put something back into society, and we have the obligation not only of giving of our time and talents, but of our money as well. The caring for the sick and handicapped, the building of hospitals and communities, are not to be left only to the doctors and lawyers, builders and oil tycoons, but entertainers as well. We are also citizens. Taking this position, I am often at odds with my fellow performers. I have told them that doing one benefit is not a commitment. I urge them to sit on committees, give money, help build, whatever it is. For this and my other speeches, I am sometimes labeled with derision a "do-gooder." I am surprised that a do-gooder in our society today is a dirty word. Maybe it shows the extent to which cynicism has taken over.

I am not ashamed of what I do, and I don't want any medals or honors, although I have accepted some. From the Variety Club, I have run the gamut of winning the Heart Award in Toronto in 1953 to a similar award in Los Angeles in 1971. I have been honored by countless numbers of organizations whose plaques adorn my walls. But I turn down ten for every one I accept, especially those labeled "Man of the Year." The "Man of the Year" award is a running gag among those of us in show business. What usually happens is that an organization decides to have a dinner, gets a plaque, fills in the legend on the plaque for the recipient who is being honored, but leaves off the recipient's name until they get somebody to accept. It is more a build-up for the gate than it is the respect paid the recipient. I myself have been the toastmaster at a score of these Man of the Year dinners where the presentation of this honor almost made me retch, especially when I knew that the recipient was somebody who hadn't done a damn thing to earn it.

Then there are those performers who receive huge fees for doing so-called charity events, whether they be fund-raising dinners, speeches, or telethons. I do not accept a penny other than expenses. I did so on only one occasion, years ago, at the insistence of the host because everyone else was being paid; and I immediately donated mine back to charity. I have two fees—one is very expensive, for television and commercial appearances; and the other is gratis, for charitable and worthwhile causes. But by having such standards, one can run into some terribly frustrating experiences. I was called to a charity event in Canada. When I said I would be pleased and would waive the $3,500 fee, the woman caller was delighted. Since I had five days free, I requested round-trip fare and hotel for my wife and myself for five days. The woman wrote me, saying that they would pay for the plane but only two days at the hotel because that was the length of their bazaar. I was furious. If I had accepted the $3,500 fee, it would have cost them thousands more than my request. Since my mother belonged to this organization, I grabbed the phone, called her long distance, and before she had time to say hello, screamed all my frustration and anger at her. And what do you think she replied: "Good for them! You can afford it more than they can!" Never underestimate the power of a woman, especially a club woman, especially my mother. Naturally, I went. (P. S. We stayed four days, and the organization paid for all four nights at the hotel.)

Working for charities can be lonely and thankless. Often, I have traveled thousands of miles to do a show, to be met at the airport not by the chairman, but by a flunky; booked into a hotel room without air conditioning; and left to my own devices for twenty-four hours until my appearance. Sometimes the audience is nowhere near as large as promised when you accepted the invitation, and you realize that you have been had. Little surprises are always in store for you. You arrange for one performance, and you find that you have been booked for three, and so on. Still, I continue to make these appearances because, in the final analysis, the result is more important than one's ego and comfort.

Monty could say he had a big ego, but millions could say he also had a big heart. (Garage Sale Finds blog)

RICHARD HALL (2019)

My dad used the word "ego" a lot when the book was originally written, so I feel like I need to add context. My dad wrote this book at a stage in his life when *Let's Make a Deal* was at its zenith, and he really wanted to do other things at that time, and he was in the middle of negotiating with ABC to do those other things. So the word "ego" pops up because my dad was telling this story at a very specific moment in his life.

In the 1970s, the Age of Aquarius had come and gone, and people became a lot more self-examining and self-critical. People began throwing around the word "ego" a lot.

If there's a way to describe my father that stands the test of time and isn't stuck in 1973 terminology, I think it's that my father had a presence to him. If you were in a room and my father walked in, no matter how crowded it was, you knew when my father was in a room. What my dad called "ego" at the time, I'd just call "a presence."

SHARON HALL (2019)

He had high self-esteem. I don't know if that's the same as ego, but he held himself and his talents in high regard. I work in the entertainment industry and I know people who work very, very hard. And that attitude about yourself can sometimes come from doing all that hard work. You come to feel that you're owed something, and it's not always monetary. It's that cylinder that needs to be filled up, and the only way to fill it was with recognition.

ROBERT HALL (2019)

I would agree with the word "ego." We talked about this once. He said, "You HAVE to have a big ego in my business. You have to think you're the best."

In show business, you're selling yourself, whatever you're doing. You want people to believe you're the best actor, the best singer, the best master of ceremonies. And like any product, how do you convince people to buy you if you don't think you're the best? So yes, in that sense, Monty had an ego.

But people get a certain image in mind when they hear the word "ego" so let me elaborate. My brother would never say "Do you know who I am?" as a means of getting his way. He didn't have that kind of ego. But yeah, he had an ego.

CAROL MERRILL

He wasn't that much of an egotist. When he interacted with the traders on *Let's Make a Deal*, he was always very warm and very giving. He was always happy to make them the star of the deal, and I liked that about him. He didn't use the contestants to bounce off of. He didn't use the contestants as his own means of looking like a star. An egomaniac would have done that. The way Monty treated the contestants was endearing.

At the beginning of *Let's Make a Deal*, we would get calls asking for Monty and me to make personal appearances. I was shy and I let it be known that I would, but that I wasn't chomping at the bit to do it. So Monty did these appearances without me. Well, that meant all of the limelight was on him. And he was in command of the event. And I think he liked that. When I gradually realized that people really did want to see and hear me, I said I was more willing to do the personal appearances, but then I ended up never getting booked for them. I think Monty just really came to enjoy working alone. So I missed my window of opportunity.

MONTY HALL

I also admit that my motivation is not altogether purely philanthropic. These appearances enable me to exercise talents I do not get to use as emcee of *Let's Make a Deal*. I might write a satirical piece or a mature monologue. I pride myself on being able to go into a town, read the local newspapers, familiarize myself with the names of important people, and deliver a highly personalized monologue that evening. This pleases me, and it pleases me further when I gain a measure of respect from my show-business confreres.

ROBERT HALL (2019)

Monty wanted to know that the charities appreciated what he did. He didn't demand recognition to an extreme degree. If he did a fundraiser, he wouldn't send out a press release announcing that he did a fundraiser, and he wouldn't ask a gossip columnist to mention that he had done a fundraiser.

MONTY HALL

However, I have reached the point where I think I am doing too much, giving too much. I can't easily say no and it's gotten out of hand. I know I am being taken advantage of, but I don't know how to get out of it. I have neglected my wife, my children, and my work. I'm going to cut down, but I'm not sure how or where, because I'm caught up in it.

My charitable activities expanded with my membership in The Variety Club, the international show business organization that aids underprivileged and handicapped children around the world. I joined the organization in Toronto in 1948. Our aim was to raise funds to set up a vocational guidance school for handicapped kids. Land was donated by the province of Ontario, and we were left to finance construction and operation of the school. We needed more than $200,000 to get going, and we launched many moneymaking projects.

I organized a series of Sunday night movie shows all around the area. In those days, movie theaters were closed on Sundays in compliance with Canadian blue laws, but we got permission to stage our shows. The films were first-run and were given to us free. We put together a vaudeville show to play with the movies, and we worked all the small towns around Toronto. Everyone from ushers to performers donated their time and effort. I emceed the show and performed in it. At the intermissions we asked for additional contributions. Often a show made $600, $800, even $1000, and we did them for years.

Most of the money came from an annual baseball game. Jack Kent Cooke, now the owner of the Los Angeles Lakers and Kings, then the owner of the Toronto Maple Leafs, donated the use of the park for the night, and we did raise a considerable amount of money. This, plus our out-of-town appearances and other donations, finally resulted in the construction of one of the greatest vocational guidance and residence schools for handicapped children in the world, Variety Village. I will never forget the dedication of this school and the pride that we all felt on that day.

In East Los Angeles, where many Mexican-Americans are struggling, the Variety Boys Club has three thousand members who swim and play and learn arts and crafts. In a wealthier section of Los Angeles, we support a children's heart clinic at UCLA. We support pediatric research at Cedars-Sinai Hospital. We have bought dozens of "Sunshine Coaches," vans with special seating and ramps that are donated to organizations to transport handicapped youngsters to hospitals, to places where they receive treatments, to parks, to ball games, and so forth.

I've worked with many other organizations that do wonderful work. I once visited the Southern California Adolescent Psychiatric Center at Los Angeles County Hospital. Noting how excited these troubled teenagers seemed to be by my appearance, Dr. Ruth Sinay asked me to stay for lunch. We had sandwiches and lemonade. Then each child took me to his room, and proudly showed me his furnishings and belongings. For hours I talked to them, kidded with them, teased them, hugged them. They seemed like normal, joyous youngsters.

One struck me especially because she was as beautiful as any teen-aged girl I've ever seen. She looked as if she could step out of this institution and into a studio and play "Gidget." I mentioned this to Dr. Sinay.

She sighed and said, "Yes, but she is one of our worst patients. She has tried to commit suicide on more than one occasion. Her body has been slashed with knife and razor wounds."

As I was leaving, Dr. Sinay said: "You've done more with these kids in two hours than I've managed to do with them in the last two months."

I was ripped right through with two contrasting emotions. On the one hand, my heart ached for these youngsters. On the other hand, we had just shared two hours of sheer delight. Driving back to my office, my car never touched the ground. It was a warming experience. We do have the power to do so much, and there is so much more we can do.

I have had a hundred such experiences, over hundreds of visits to the children's wards of hospitals, where I have tried to cheer up and make contact with the emotionally disturbed, mentally retarded, and seriously or incurably sick or crippled youngsters. Their faces etch themselves on your brain forever. You do not have to be an especially sensitive person to be moved by these visits.

Celebrities have a curious power, and I don't believe we should turn our backs on it. One time the city of Wichita declared *Let's Make a Deal* day. I appeared at luncheons, did radio, television, and newspaper interviews, and was hosted by the city's mayor and the governor of Kansas. Shortly before we were to meet with the mayor, my host was chauffeuring me around. He mentioned that my biggest fan in town was a man with incurable cancer.

I said, "Let's go visit him."

My host said, "That's what I was hoping you'd say." We went to the hospital.

This man clearly knew his days were numbered. But he played his role to the hilt. He talked about his family, about how he was going to get well, how he was going to go out to California to be on my show and wear one of those crazy costumes. We laughed and talked and pretended life for him was not what it was. But when we parted we shook hands, and in his eyes, and I'm sure in mine, there was an honest admission of the realities. It is difficult to describe the feelings that sweep over me at times like this. I feel good and I feel bad. I know I am doing no more than the Bob Hopes and Martha Rayes and countless other performers. Because of our interest these unfortunate people know they have value, that others care. It is not much to do, but if we give them one more laugh, or even a smile, it is something.

My secretary, Jerita Ingle, has been with me for twelve years. She screens my mail: the requests for tickets, pictures, or money—and there are many of those—or the crank correspondence. She tries to protect me from people who would pester me, but she knows I want to see the personal mail. So, she brings it all to me, sometimes with a tear in her eyes and the comment, "I didn't want to show you this one."

Maybe the letter is from a mother whose daughter is dying of leukemia. As the child lies in bed she watches *Let's Make a Deal* every day and loves Monty Hall. Could I possibly send the child an autographed photo with perhaps a short note? I send a using whatever information the mother has given me—the name of her dog, the school she went to, her favored friend, and so forth—to make it as personal as possible. I say that when the child gets better I want her to come out to see the show as my guest and visit me. But these children seldom get better.

Perhaps they answer my letters. I reply, sending a souvenir, something, anything. And one day I'll get a letter from a mother telling me that the child read and reread my letters and propped my picture up beside her bed and talked to it and watched our show until the day she died. The mother will thank me on behalf of the family for the happiness I provided this child. Then Jerita and I can only look at each other and try to restrain our emotions. The mother has lost a child and is thanking me.

I am Jewish and have worked hard to raise funds for Israel and for the United Jewish Appeal, but I have also represented almost every religion and many nationalities the world over. One week I emceed a Communion Breakfast for Cardinal McIntyre, was honored by the Armenian Society of Southern California, and received the Mitzvah Award from the Sisterhoods of America. Another week, I made appearances in Los Angeles, New York, Miami, Chicago, and Montreal. I have worked so many charity affairs at the Beverly Hilton, the Century Plaza, and a few other hotels that the staffs and I are on a first-name basis.

One comment I can make about the variety of groups I perform for and a generalization I can easily make, whether they are Italian, Armenian, Irish or Jewish: the women all embrace you the same way, they kiss you the same way, and they look at you with the same love. The men have a warm smile and a hearty handshake that doesn't differ from black to white, senator to sanitation worker. And conversely, no one group has a monopoly on driving you crazy.

I have also found that If you find time to talk to one group in one community, ten other groups from ten other communities are immediately writing or telephoning to demand that you honor them with an appearance, too, and are insulted if you do not. They also are disappointed if you do not make a contribution to their cause or at least shower the group with color television sets, washing machines, and other paraphernalia.

On *Let's Make a Deal* we pay for the expensive prizes. The rest of it is given to us only to be handed out on the show with plugs for the products. I do not get cut-rate prices or outright gifts from any company. I buy my cars at dealers and my TV sets at discount stores. The public doesn't seem to understand this, however. Heads of charitable organizations seem to think all we have to do is pick up the phone and order a few hundred free cars or cameras and have them delivered immediately.

I once spoke at a memorial luncheon for my mother in Palm Springs. Afterward the president asked if I could get them a color television set wholesale for their bazaar. I said I was sorry but I could not; I had no such connections; I had nothing to do with the prizes we gave away on our show. The president would not take no for an answer. A few days later she wrote to ask if I had found a color TV for them.

I wrote back politely saying I was sorry I couldn't help. A few days after that she called to ask me if I had located the set for them. I was losing patience fast, but again I said I couldn't help. She called again.

I exclaimed in exasperation that I had a color television set in my office. I said, "Look, if you can have someone over within an hour to pick it up, you can have it."

She thanked me triumphantly. Sure enough, within an hour someone showed up at my door to haul away the set. A few days later, the president of a Desert Hot Springs group called to say she'd heard of my gift to the Palm Springs group and asked if I could get a color TV for them!

I spend most of my time on the other side of television sets, anyway. Often it is spent hosting telethons, a very special sort of charitable endeavor. I'm usually on the air twelve to eighteen hours at a stretch. Most telethons originate in New York or Los Angeles and are broadcast on as many stations across the country as will carry them. Most of the pledges are telephoned in and the organizers must follow up with letters and telephone calls to those who are slow in mailing the amounts pledged. The results are inconsistent. As a rule, if you receive more than 70 percent of the sums pledged, you are satisfied. It is a fact, however, that some telethons have netted more than pledged. Some who can't or don't try to get through on the telephone stall contribute.

Among the most successful telethons is Jerry Lewis's annual pitch for muscular dystrophy funds, which has raised millions. Others don't do nearly as well. A telethon is not like any other television show, and putting one together is tricky. It must be broadcast from a single center with a single emcee front and center. The audience must be given a sense of structure and continuity. People do not watch telethons for five or ten minutes and then send in money. They watch for a long time, often for many hours. They become almost mesmerized and after a while they begin to identify your cause. Their reserve resistance is slowly, carefully rubbed away until they are moved to contribute.

It is important to attain some success from the start. As the figures on the tote board mount, others are inspired to jump on the bandwagon. Pleas based on building up low totals seldom work. No one wants to go with a loser. The success of the Lewis telethon starts with the success of his past telethons. They have been winners. There is always a healthy total from the previous year to be topped. The early returns usually are large and bring more in turn as the telethon progresses.

In the summer of 1972 I appeared on a telethon for the Democratic National Committee. It was broadcast from different centers with a variety of emcees and got looser and looser until it fell apart. As the show shifted between Miami and Los Angeles, people were cut off in mid-speech, mid-song, and mid-dance. There were too many entertainers, and viewers were more aware of the multitude of talent than the money that was needed. I emceed the first two-and-a-half hours and was pleased. when critic Cecil Smith of the Los Angeles *Times* commented that I projected an image of class. A lot of other classy citizens were available to follow me, but the producers turned instead to members of the younger set, and it is doubtful if their long hair, tie-dyed shirts, and blue jeans were right for the more mature, moneyed audience they were trying to reach.

I was disappointed, though not surprised by the results. The Democratic Party was more than $9 million in debt. The telethon raised less than $5 million, a poor total for a show with an unusually large and strong national network of 175 stations and a produced that generally attracts large donations from wealthy men. The show cost approximately $1,500,000 to put on, so $3.5 million was all that was left—provided that much was sent in—to lower the debt.

Although I am not affiliated with any political party because of my Canadian citizenship, I still feel that I want to make a contribution to the political process in the United States; and helping to preserve a viable two-party system through the telethon was my contribution.

In the spring of 1972 I did an Easter Seals telethon in Las Vegas. It must have had the classiest cast in telethon history: Jack Benny, Bob Newhart, Alan King, Robert Goulet, Debbie Reynolds, Bobby Darin, and many others. Sergio Franchi, who had been out on the desert camping with his son, drove 500 miles in a jeep to appear. Then he gave $5,000 himself.

The show was telecast from the enormous convention hall in the Sahara Hotel. It was beset with problems. The local Las Vegas station we were using had burned down and could provide only rudimentary equipment. Our mikes often were not working. We were seen in New Orleans, but not Los Angeles, where no station would give us time. Still, we raised nearly a million dollars.

I worked terribly hard, as I do on all telethons. After a week of taping my own shows, I flew to Vegas from Los Angeles late the night before the show, checked into the suite provided me by the organizer, and early the next morning, went to rehearsals. Most of the stars do not rehearse in advance for such shows, but the orchestra must practice its music, the cameramen must know what to shoot, and a schedule has to he plotted. In mid-afternoon, I took a nap. I had dinner, shaved, and was dressed by seven p.m. The show started at eight. I was on from then until four in the morning. I returned to the show at ten a.m. and stayed on it until it ended at four in the afternoon.

You don't feel tired while you are working on a telethon. Performing carries you along and keeps you going. You hit a peak and maintain it. In a place like Las Vegas, there is a large live audience out front stimulating you. You eventually become dazed, however, and must rely on instinct and experience to hold things together.

When you are finally through, it seems as though you have been working for a week. And an enormous sense of exhaustion settles over you. But if the show has been successful, you feel an enormous sense of satisfaction, too—that is, if it isn't taken away from you. At this telethon, Mr. Easter Seals, the gentleman from the Midwest who was national chairman to the cause, flew in to make an appearance during the last hour of the telecast, shook my hand, then flew away again.

It happens too often. As with other charity shows, the front men take the credit, while the emcee and the others who work as hard as people in this business can work to make a success of a show are fast forgotten at the finish without even a private expression of gratitude, an offer of dinner, or a ride to the airport to ease our weariness. Men like Dennis James are called upon to work many telethons because they do them beautifully and succeed with them. There are only a few such experts, yet Dennis had many a lean period between telethons, his expertise suddenly forgotten.

I worked a local telethon in Nashville, Tennessee. The chairman was a Mrs. Hoity-Toity. The show was on for about twenty hours, and I was on for about sixteen. I never saw Mrs. Hoity-Toity until that last hour when all the Big Wheels arrive on camera to accept credit for the cause. I never saw her again.

This show raised $270,000—a lot for a local show, and the best this one had ever done. When it ended at six o'clock, with a great, spirited rush of music, I was exhausted, though exhilarated. The show was broadcast from a sports arena, and a trailer backstage served as a sort of dressing room. I went to the trailer to stretch out for a minute, leaving word of where I had gone. I fell asleep. When I woke up, it was silent and dark. Everyone seemed to be gone. I had worked sixteen hours for their cause, and not a single one of the sponsors had hung around long enough to thank me or see if there was anything they could do for me. The stillness was broken by a solitary figure who poked his head into my trailer.

"Are you still there?" he asked.

"Where the heck do you think I'd be!" I replied, "and where is everybody?"

Sheepishly, he explained, "I think they've all gone to the country club for a celebration dinner. They must have figured you had gone back to Hollywood."

"By the way," he continued, "what are you doing for dinner?"

I looked at him pleadingly. "I'm having it with you if you're free." And we did.

A few years ago, when the Wichita State University football team was wiped out in a charter-airplane crash, I organized a special national telecast to raise funds for the families of the victims. I put together a plan for an all-star show to be broadcast from campus with all of the proceeds coming from the sale of seats and from contributions we would seek from the TV audience.

I called my manager, Ray Katz, and told him what I wanted to do. He wanted to help. We placed a call to Martin Umansky at KAKE, our ABC affiliate. He told us that, by coincidence, they were in the process of placing a call to me because they felt I would be willing to help. Swiftly, we agreed on a plan. I would emcee the show in the school's firehouse and set it up with the help of Ray Katz, who would line up the talent. Stars and even technicians would be flown into Wichita. No one would be paid anything. A date was set.

A committee was formed in Wichita to help organize things there. One of its members, a former writer long removed from the Hollywood scene, apparently said, "The show idea is okay, but who the hell is Monty Hall? I can get you Jerry Lewis."

And someone or another apparently said, "Oh, wow, Jerry Lewis—well, wouldn't that be something!"

The next thing I knew I received a call from someone at Wichita State asking me if I would share the spotlight with Jerry Lewis. I asked how Jerry Lewis had got into the act. I was told that someone there could get Jerry Lewis, and, of course, he was such a big name that it would probably boost the show's impact considerably. I suggested that what he really wanted was for me to step aside. He admitted this was so. I said that was fine with me. I wished him well and hung up.

A few days later I got another call from the same official. He said the deal to get Lewis had fallen through. They were in trouble and would appreciate it if I took over again. I suppose I should have told him where to go. But the cause was worthy, and I agreed to resume. Maybe I should have displayed some ego. In any event, I put off my own work in order to work on this special show.

Then the plane carrying the Marshall University football team went down. This second tragedy was so close to the first that we felt we had to include them in any fund-raising project The Wichita State officials agreed, but the Marshall people were not so sure at first. It was right after their youngsters and coaches had been lost and they felt a show might be in bad taste. They did not seem to trust Hollywood people in general. But we were concerned that it would seem strange to the public if the show was done for the families of the ill-fated players of one school and not the other. Eventually, Marshall agreed.

We rounded up stars such as Bill Cosby, Lou Rawls, George Gobel, Leif Erickson, Marilyn Maye, Phil Ford and Mimi Hines, The Young Americans, and Kate Smith. Lear Jet put planes at our disposal, and we flew in Hollywood musicians and engineers. Conditions in the fieldhouse were not up to professional standards. Final rehearsals were chaotic. Late in the afternoon, we lost all electricity and had to resume by candlelight. As showtime neared that night, the power had not been restored and it began to appear that there would be no telecast. All was madness. At ten minutes to eight, forty minutes before showtime, power was restored. The Wichita Power Company had erected giant poles and brought power in from miles away. Just like the popular song, the "Wichita Lineman" had come through. The show, lasting two and a half hours, was a smash. Bill Carruthers, who directed, kept his cool through all the problems and did an amazing job. Mind you, he did all of this without benefit of a camera rehearsal. As we say in the business, "He winged it," and he didn't miss a shot.

The fieldhouse was packed. At $10 a ticket, those 10,000 or so seats raised $100,000. The show was carried on an astonishing 202 stations. Most carried it live, but some carried a cut version later. These stations produced hundreds of thousands of dollars. Carroll Rosenbloom, then owner of the Baltimore Colts and now the owner of the Los Angeles Rams, contributed $100,000. It all came to more than $700,000, which went into a scholarship fund for the children of the players and coaches of the two teams.

Sadly, there were some unfortunate postscripts to this story. Ohio State football coach Woody Hayes telephoned a personal letter from President Nixon, congratulating us on what we had done. Later, I thought it might be nice to have a copy of the letter, and I wrote to the White House for one. Sometime later, while playing golf at the Hillcrest Country Club, I was paged to take a telephone call from the White House.

When I got on the phone, a lady who described herself as an assistant to the President said, "In answer to your letter, Mr. Nixon does not believe in signing the same letter twice."

I asked, "What does that mean?"

She said, "It means we'll send you a copy of the letter he sent to Mr. Hayes, but it will not be signed."

I was stunned. It seemed sort of silly to me, but she did not agree. Nor, apparently, was the situation worth a new signed letter. I was sent the unsigned letter. It is not my proudest possession.

Reflecting on the episode, I thought it strange that the President, who will call to congratulate winners of golf matches and football games, will not write a note of congratulations to one who does what I did. It seems strange that the White House would even go to the expense of a long-distance call simply to tell me the President would not sign a letter I was being sent.

I never received even an unsigned letter from anyone at Marshall. As far as I know, the money had not been distributed because the two schools were squabbling over which was to get what share. The whole thing is incredible, but there you are. It is experiences like these that sometimes take the edge off, but still I continue them. I would like more time to live a normal life with my family and to work creatively at my profession. But it is not easy to turn from endeavors that have produced so many satisfactions. And I remember. It is not as if I were not given help when I needed it.

RICHARD HALL (2019)

The anger about Nixon's letter might make someone say, "Well, what's the big deal? A signed letter isn't such a big thing."

Well, that's just it, a signed letter isn't such a big thing. So, the idea that Nixon couldn't be bothered with it really annoyed my dad. You can't take three seconds out of the day to put your name on that? You're not even writing the letter, you're not even dictating the letter. It's already written, they're making a copy. Nixon was only asked to sign it and he said no. And that really irked my dad.

Anything has its frustrations when you devote as much time and energy as Monty devoted to charity work, but it wasn't just obligation that motivated him. He genuinely loved charitable work. In many ways, he found it more satisfying than working in television.

MONTY HALL[xlii]

I belong to at least 100 committees. When you have a job, you're basically satisfying yourself, but when you're doing charitable work, you're doing something for someone else. You don't have to wait for the ratings—you know instantly in your heart how you did. Community work is open to everyone. No one can fire you and every contribution is acceptable.

(Author's Collection)

CHAPTER EIGHTEEN

Late in Rose Halparin's life, she looked at the fates of her two sons and worried to herself. Robert Hall could never be considered a disappointment. He was a prominent lawyer in Toronto, known for devoting his time and checkbook to numerous causes. But still, he didn't sign autographs. His face wasn't on any magazine covers. 40 million people per week didn't watch him argue a case in court.

Rose talked to Robert one day and asked him to be honest...did he resent being the brother of the famous Monty Hall? Robert smiled and promised his mother that he didn't mind a bit.

ROBERT HALL (1983)[xliii]

If they stuck his picture up on the walls of post offices like a criminal, I'd resent his notoriety. But I can honestly say there's just one word that expresses how I feel about the respect he's earned as a fund raiser for worthy causes. That word is kvell—Yiddish for the pride I take in being the kid brother of a renowned humanitarian.

MONTY HALL

As I began to rise in show business, as my brother began to rise in his legal practice, we began to be able to help our parents. First, we contributed to a fund that would allow them to feel secure. Then we backed my father in a move of his butcher shop to a better part of town. It went well for a while, then competition crowded them. We sold out and invested in a pair of drive-in restaurants for him to run in Toronto. Proudly, he said, "I've traded my butcher's apron for a briefcase." However, we had bought a bad business, and in time we had to sell it.

By then our parents were in their late sixties and it was time they retired. So, in 1968 we moved them into a condominium in Palm Springs. I turned a new car over to them. When they reached their new home, tears were in their eyes. They were like Mr. and Mrs. Rockefeller. They called it, "The Garden of Eden." Sadly, paradise paled. My mother became ill and returned to Toronto for surgery.

But Rose didn't leave for surgery right away. This was, after all, the mother who wouldn't let Monty go to the bathroom when he became nervous before his first stage performance. She had told her son on that night that he had to go out there and perform, because he had made that commitment. No matter how sick, she held herself to the same standard.

MONTY HALL[xliv]

The last speech she made…I retired them to Palm Springs…but she was going to going to fly back to the hospital in Toronto, where my brother was.

And she says to my father, "I have an engagement. I promised the Desert Hot Springs Jewish Community that I would speak to them."

And my father took her, and she made her last speech. My father described it this way: she came out to the car afterward, she was white as a ghost. She was so sick. She had cancer. Got on the airplane, and she went to the hospital in Toronto…but even to her last, she kept her obligation.

Rose Halperin's health began failing while her son was at the peak of his career. In a way, that seemed to be fortuitous. Good news, Monty reasoned, could help her spirit.

MONTY HALL

I flew there to bring her two pieces of news that I thought would cheer her. The first was an invitation to be the guest of honor at a large charity banquet in Winnipeg. Because the cause was close to her heart, she had always told me that when I was invited to speak at this dinner, I would have "made" it. She already knew that I was going to appear there in October. Then I went on to describe the offer of my first special on ABC. Attempting to take her mind off her illness, I tried to involve her in the various formats I was considering. She sat, looking out the window, as I ran out of things to say about the special. The room grew silent.

After the longest time, my mother began to speak. "I want it to be the best you have ever done."

Quickly I broke in, "You mean the special."

Without turning her head, still gazing out the window, she replied, "No, October... October."

In July 1970, my mother died at the age of sixty-nine. Her death was a blow to all of us. Tributes to Rose Halparin poured in from everywhere. She was beloved by many, but especially by her family. My wife has meant as much to me as a woman can mean to a man, but I must admit my mother was the most unforgettable person I've known, and even today I feel her loss daily.

Monty didn't learn until much later in life that on several times, Rose's skills as a speaker, a fund raiser, and a labor negotiator had led to numerous job offers that would have meant double or even triple what Maurice made at the butcher shop. She declined every job.

MONTY HALL[xlv]

I've often thought of how opportunities for women have expanded in recent years and how welcome and wonderful that is. I just feel sorry that many of those changes came too late to benefit my mother. Had she been born a generation later, she might have found a proper stage for her talents.

However, her final legacy to her family indicates that Mother herself had no regrets for the path she chose through the years. When she died, she left a very brief will, for she had few possessions. In that last testament, she made some simple bequeaths, then addressed herself to my father in words that have made me think not only of all the years she spent working side by side with him in the butcher shop, but also of my great grandfather feeding my blind great-grandmother at every meal and my grandfather, the patriarch, holding hands with his aged life partner in the parlor.

"And now to my husband...Remember that I love you. I have always loved you."

That was the summation of her life—her commitment to my father and to their marriage vows. Her constancy was love, love for her husband and children. Love, that thing that binds couples together, the centripetal force of families, the glue of the universe. That was the value she took from the past and handed on to the future, the value that sank so deeply into my own heart, and which has contributed so much to the years that my wife Marilyn and I have shared.

"Remember that I love you..." That was what my mother was saying by her selflessness all her life, a message spoken over and over again, not just to my father and my rother and me, but to families everywhere, now and forever.

Some years later, while receiving an award from the Na'amat Pioneer Women during their annual Adopt-a-Child dinner, Monty spoke reverently of his mother, and told the assembly, "The Jewish woman, as far as I'm concerned, is the greatest human being on this earth."

MONTY HALL[xlvi]

The main thing I learned from my family is that you have to work together. When my father was down, my mother pulled him up by his bootstraps. When he was ill, she went to work. She was so powerful that people wanted her to come into businesses…anything she wanted. And she wouldn't take it.

She said, "No, my husband has to be the breadwinner. If I took the job, it would diminish him. He's gone through such terrible times himself. His ego has been so destroyed by his father, his brother, the business…that I could not do this to him."

Maurice Halparin adjusted to life without Rose with help from his family. He took his grandson Richard with him to the Santa Anita racetrack on weekends, a ritual that Monty found comically different from walking his grandfather to shul for the Sabbath. Monty also smiled at a change that his father made in his twilight years. Years earlier, when he was told he had to change his name from Halparin for broadcasting, Monty accepted the order but dreaded how his family might react. He was surprised when they took it well. His kid brother Robert even adopted the name Hall when he reached adulthood, again to no consternation. Maurice, who was retired and living what probably felt like 10 million miles away from the miserable butcher shop where he had toiled his life away and living in the comfortable Palm Springs community where his son had bought him a house, began going by the name Maurice Hall.

MONTY HALL

My father was as though cast adrift. Eleven months later, he remarried. Five months after that, they were divorced. More than a year after that, he married a third time. But I think this one was not so much from desperation, and it may endure. His new wife is a lady he has known on and off since he was very young. He is a man who cannot bear to be alone, and perhaps she can be a companion to him and give to him and take from him and it will be good for both of them.

A few months after his divorce, he suffered a heart attack. I don't think he had been ill for forty years and he recovered remarkably. He tends to set too fast a pace. He has his cronies and his card games and his part-time volunteer work at the hospital. He has had hard times and he has managed to survive.

I have resented his rough treatment of me in the past, but I have come to know him better in recent years and I respect him. He is a remarkably resilient man.

SHARON HALL (2019)

My grandfather always struck me as a Damon Runyon character. He loved his whiskey, and horses, and telling a great yarn. He was a simple but fantastic person.

My dad owned a Cadillac, and then he got a new one from doing *Let's Make a Deal* and he gave his old Cadillac to his father. My grandfather loved that car. He drove the car from Palm Springs to Winnipeg every year.

MONTY HALL

I am close to my brother, although we are parted by many miles. We slept in the same bed for many years. He grew up as Monty's brother, in my shadow. But he overcame this and became his own man, earning himself an outstanding reputation in Canada. We disagree on some things, but with respect. I am proud of my brother.

I think my feelings for my wife must have shown through throughout this book. Marriage is not an easy matter. But it has not been hard for us. We got married young and got through a lot of tough times together and stress seemed to strengthen us. I suspect we have had fewer disagreements and more real love between us than most couples. We suit each other, so we have been fortunate. We celebrated our silver wedding anniversary in September of 1972.

Our oldest child, Joanne, who, for professional purposes, has changed her name to Joanna, has graduated with honors in Theater Arts from Occidental College and has begun to seek a career on stage on her own. She is singularly attractive, a good actress and a good singer, has won awards and received some marvelous notices in various local productions. She has a shot at stardom. She doesn't like to be called Monty Hall's daughter, but I'd like the day to come when I am called Joanna Hall's father. I am proud of her and close to her.

I am equally proud of my son. Richard has overcome a bad back problem which has plagued him since youth. He wants to be a journalist and has shown a talent for it. He is very much a mod young man, long hair and all. He is very much his own man. We argue politics. Like many young men today, he is impatient with the state of things. He has stirred up some sparks in high school and at Yale, but a guidance counsellor once told me, "You don't have to worry about this young man."

Once, when we met at Sardi's on Broadway, he arrived looking like a hippie while I had on a conservative suit. I held out my hand, but he went right past me and embraced me and kissed me on the lips. I will never forget it. I will not worry about him. He will do all right.

Sharon came along late in 1964. She was a surprise, but a marvelous one. She took away the free life we thought we'd be entering by then and gave us the best life we could ever have had. She is another Joanne, only more so. She is the most natural little person I've ever known. She's a great mimic and a born actress. When she was five, she and the twins next door got together and worked up a sketch on Cinderella. After rehearsing it for hours, they came into the den where I was watching a football game on television.

"Daddy," she asked, "the twins and I have an act for television. We'd like to put it on *Let's Make a Deal*. Can we?"

"No!" I roared, "and leave me alone!"

They left, and after a caucus they came back and confronted me again. "Daddy, are you sure we can't go on *Let's Make a Deal?*"

"No!" I replied emphatically.

"Okay then," she answered, "we're going to take it to Art Linkletter." She has been a blessing.

Monty, a decade into the job that he could never fully leave behind.
(Author's Collection)

CAROL MERRILL

I became pregnant with my daughter during the show. Marilyn had given birth to Sharon only two and a half years earlier, so I think it was still fresh on Monty's head and he was sensitive to it.

You need to understand why this meant a lot to me. During the 1960s, people didn't think it was attractive for a pregnant woman to be in front of the camera. But it was never once suggested to me that I take time off. Neither Monty nor Stefan ever brought up that idea.

At the same time, as luck would have it, tent dresses were in, so when I started getting bigger, the head of wardrobe gave me these A-framed outfits to wear. Joe Behar really worked with me too. He gave me a note one day and just told me "Try to stand straight forward as much as you can, I want to avoid shooting you in profile."

The entire staff really was supportive and helpful, and in fact, I was fairly late into my pregnancy before we began getting letters from viewers wondering about it. I didn't take any time off until it actually became physically difficult for me to handle doing the show. And the timing on it was perfect because the tapings that year were scheduled so we could all take a two-month hiatus, and the hiatus just happened to line up with my due date. The entire staff was wonderful to me.

MONTY HALL

I have been a scrounger. I always would pick up any work I could get. I worked around the clock if necessary. I always got by financially. But success changes you. After *Let's Make a Deal* was a big success, our company got *Chain Letter* on the air, too. I was emceeing the first and producing the second and it was just too much. The show had troubles. I went out to Malibu and when they started to call me with their troubles, I said, for the first time in my life, "I don't care."

And when they offered us only a part-time renewal, I said, "Just cancel the show. I am not going to commit suicide for a few weeks. If not this show, there'll be another show. Life is too short and I want to enjoy it." It was a turning point for me.

I will go on with *Let's Make a Deal* as long as it is made attractive for me to do so. I love it, but I have been doing it a long time and I want to do other things that attract me as they come up. I am not afraid to fail. I am sure I will in time succeed. It is not a matter of money. It is a matter of pride. I am a performer. There is more to me than the public has yet seen.

CAROL MERRILL

There was never a time when I got sick of being "Carol Merrill of *Let's Make a Deal*." I was proud of it.

Of course, that may have had to do with me not being as recognizable as Monty. On the show, I wore short-hair wigs. I learned that Stefan Hatos liked short hair. His wife had short hair. I wanted to make my boss happy, so I kept my hair long, but I would cram all of it underneath this short-hair wigs. I was married to a hairdresser at the time, and he custom-made all of my wigs for me so they fit really well.

Well, since I only wore the wigs on the show, people didn't recognize me in public. Every once in a while, people would stare at me, and I could tell they were thinking, "I know her from somewhere…" but nobody ever approached me on the sidewalk. So I think that was the difference. I could put the show away every week when the taping was done. Monty couldn't do that.

Jay Stewart and Monty see what it takes to make a contestant give back whatever's in the box. (Author's Collection)

MONTY HALL

I have made, and am making, a lot of money. I have made some investments, some good, some bad. I will continue to make major contributions to charity, but I will, if I can, cut down on my charitable works because I have reached the point where I want more time for myself and my wife and my youngest child and my two older children as they may need me. It is time my family came first.

We have lived in the same home in Beverly Hills for eleven years. It is a nice house and we are happy with it. We could afford something grander, but we don't feel the need for it. Then there's the condominium, provided for my father in Palm Springs, which we use sometimes. And we have gone in with friends on another one on Malibu Beach, which we use sparingly.

We don't enjoy the social swirl in Hollywood. It all gets gossipy. Once I appeared at a Cardinal McIntyre Communion Breakfast and was photographed with the four Lennon Sisters and the Cardinal. I happened to be standing next to Peggy Lennon. A TV-movie magazine cropped us out and ran the picture with a hint that we were a new twosome about town. Who needs that?

Marilyn and I like to go out to concerts and to the theater, and to good restaurants, but the fans keep looking at us and coming at me for autographs and it's difficult to relax, so we usually just stay home or go to someone else's home and relax with our best friends, some of whom are in the business and many of whom are not.

I still serve as toastmaster at banquets. In the summer of 1972 when I emceed the B'nai B'rith "Man of the Year" tribute to Gordon Stulberg, the president of 20th-Century Fox, I introduced him with a biblical parody I'd worked out myself. It received tremendous favorable recognition from both the audience and my peers. I enjoy that sort of challenge.

Some appearances are satisfying. Some are not. At a "Salute to Israel," a flag standard was knocked into my face, cut me, and nearly took out my eye. I said, "I'd give blood for Israel, but this is ridiculous." They laughed, I bled.

But there is always the challenge of coming up with the right speech for the right audience at the right time. So, whether it's Jacksonville, Phoenix, Vancouver, Albany, Montreal, you tailor your speech to the audience; and your success is measured in applause and laughter. And don't kid yourself—applause and laughter still mean more to a performer than money. And there have been some great reactions to my work.

Perhaps the most unforgettable came in Israel. My wife and I like to travel, we are able to, and we have enjoyed many marvelous moments with many marvelous people. One that will never be forgotten was when we attended a dinner party at the home of the noted Israeli prosecutor, Gideon Hausner, who took us around and introduced us to a stunning list of celebrated guests.

One, who turned out to be an Israeli delegate to the United Nations, asked, "Mr. Hall, from American television? What do you do on television?"

And I was immediately embarrassed in front of all these highly-educated, accomplished persons to say that I was emcee of an audience participation game show. Hesitating, I said, "Well, I am what you would call la this country a *compere*," which was, roughly, the European name for a master of ceremonies.

"Ah," said the man, "a *compere*." And the others gathered around and nodded.

And then the man asked, "And what type of program do you moderate?"

They all looked at me expectantly. I found myself wishing I could really say I was Lawrence Spivak and my program was *Meet the Press* and I brought on important persons to be interviewed by journalists. But I could not say that, could I?

Stammering, I said, "Well, I am not a moderator exactly. I am more a master of ceremonies. And it is an…audience participation show."

And the man said, "Audience participation? What does that mean?" How could I explain it to him?

Struggling, I said, "Well, we have a show in which I perform in the middle of an arena of people…"

I realized I was trying to make it sound as if I'm working the state senate floor. I said, "They get an opportunity to win prizes and then they get further opportunities to trade them in for unknown prizes, which may be better or worse."

And as I was struggling, the man said, "Wait, do they dress in costumes?"

Surprised, I said, "Yes. Yes, they do."

And he said, "Oh, my, why, when I am in New York for United Nations sessions and I am in my hotel room I always look to see if that show is on because it is so diverting and you, whom I recognize now, are marvelous and it always gives me much pleasure and much enjoyment. I am what you might call a fan."

And this was where Monty Hall and Bill Libby left the story when they published Emcee Monty Hall *in 1973. Monty's efforts to promote the book were brutally honest. He lamented that the original publisher forced him to whittle down his manuscript as much as possible, and even after Monty reduced it to the minimum he thought he could tolerate, editors still removed fifty pages, and used an outdated photo of him on the cover to boot. He said that if it wasn't for the fact that Libby would be hurt financially by the move, he would have bowed out of releasing it altogether.*

"If I had to do it over again, I wouldn't have written the book," he lamented in 1974. "My life isn't over yet. Dictating all those memories into a tape recorder was like lying on a psychiatrist's couch reliving all the deep hurts and unhappiness."

He went on a book tour to promote it, but found that unfulfilling. He was dismayed to find that many of the bookstores where he appeared weren't even carrying the book he was there to sell.

But Monty conceded that the book accomplished some of what he intended for it to accomplish. When his father learned of his son's impending autobiography, all he said to his son was to "tell it as it is." Maurice had no ill will about what Monty wrote; he probably expected it.

What surprised him, though, was the way it brought him closer to his sister-in-law.

Monty touts the original release of his autobiography in a 1973 segment. (Author's Collection)

MONTY HALL[xlvii]

We've been enemies since she married my brother. But she read the book and called me to say that she never really understood all I had gone through until she did read it. For that, at least, I consider the book a success.

PART 2: CITIZEN MONTY HALL

(Author's Collection)

CHAPTER NINETEEN

Life is *Let's Make a Deal*. The program is split-second decisions. It's costumes. It's greed. It's heartbreaking. It's spectacular. It's put down by critics. It's enormously middle class. It will go on forever. It's the most honest thing on television. It's the best fashion parade there ever was or ever will be. – *The Los Angeles Times*, 1973

Though Monty's autobiography suggested a man, and a show, on the verge of transition, Let's Make a Deal and Monty Hall just kept right on going the way they always had after the release.

MONTY HALL[xlviii]
My show is like Ol' Man River; it just keeps rollin' along. Over the years it has become a warm, intimate type show that can be tuned in at any home. It is for all the family. And it is more than just prizes. It is people enjoying themselves and that is good.

On April 27th of 1973, the year that Monty Hall's autobiography first hit the bookstore shelves, *Let's Make a Deal* aired its 2,500th episode, commemorating the milestone with the rare sound of Carol Merrill's voice. Merrill was hired to be a model, and in her own words, "Models don't talk."

It never bothered her that Monty never bantered with her on the air. But after a decade on the job, a small trickle of letters came in from viewers wanting to hear her talk. In the era of Women's Liberation, a handful were letters from viewers who took offense to Merrill's quiet performance. The bulk, though, were just fans who were curious.

CAROL MERRILL

Monty was consistently asked about me when he made personal appearances. We always got mail from viewers who wanted to hear from me. the show's writers came up with this idea and they wrote a script for a segment. I was nervous about doing it. I had never received any formal training for anything like that. Stephanie Powers, the actress, was a friend of mine. She coached me on how to do it, and she got me calmed down and comfortable. The segment went great.

Monty asked me to join him on the trading floor and said viewers wanted me to talk. Monty said he had a list of questions to ask me. The first one was "How do you change your wardrobe so quickly?"

I answered, and I just kept talking, and talking, and talking, and talking, and the show fades to black and we have a commercial break. We fade in back from the commercial break, and I'm still talking. The audience loved it. It really got some laughs.

Jay, Monty, and Carol celebrate a milestone broadcast on ABC. Carol had a lot to say that day. (Author's Collection)

Let's Make a Deal *and its host were both firmly embedded in the nation's collective mind. If two baseball teams traded talented players, sportswriters would describe it as "a deal that would make Monty Hall smile." If a politician got caught using his office to perform favors for friends, the reports might say "he got caught playing* Let's Make a Deal *with the taxpayers' money." Comedian George Carlin acted out an episode of the show for a routine on his album* FM & AM.

Monty's name found its way into Johnny Carson's monologue more and more often. "For Halloween, Monty will put on a moose suit and everyone in the audience will dress normally."

Choose whatever word you wanted—phenomenon, institution, hit—all those words and more applied as the show closing in on a decade.

Monty started learning how to balance his obligations to his family and to charity a little more carefully. As part of Monty's ongoing effort to do other things in television that weren't Let's Make a Deal, *he acted in an episode of ABC's anthology series* Love American Style. *The segment, titled "Love and the Man of the Year," was penned by Monty's wife Marilyn, who wrote a funny but very pointed story about an entertainer whose wife was frustrated with him because he committed himself to so many charity functions that he was neglecting his family.*

RICHARD HALL (2019)

My mom really made that episode happen. She was so talented in her own right. It was a mark against her to try to pitch something in any form of entertainment, because people would say, "Oh, it's Monty Hall's wife, what does she want?" In other words, the perception would be that she got something she wanted because of someone's sense of obligation.

But she was so sharp, and so witty. She made her own inroads, and quite a few of them.

Monty got the message of the episode, although he still had trouble saying "no." Monty recalled sensing the frustration that Marilyn felt as she watched her husband head to the airport for a flight to Philadelphia, where he was committed to host the Variety Club Telethon.

MONTY HALL[xlix]

Just before I left, she said, "How about a moratorium for six months? Just say no to every request, spend some time with your family."

SHARON HALL (2019)

You can't even say that saying no was something my father was uncomfortable doing, because that doesn't capture it. It was more like, he didn't metabolically know how to say no. It really made my mother angry, but the thing is, Mom had the same affliction. She had trouble telling people no, too.

But Variety Club was important to him because they did work with children in need. My father had been in that scalding accident, he had the double pneumonia, he grew up poor. When my dad was in his 20s, he developed Crohn's Disease and he had it for the rest of his life. And he just soldiered through it and kept going. There'd be these periods in his life where he was just in constant pain. Dad loved working with Variety Club because he really saw a lot of himself in those children.

Monty with some of his favorite people: kids. (Author's Collection)

When Monty took an extended vacation in 1972, he took Marilyn to New York…although on the way, he emceed a benefit for families of POWs. While in New York, Monty went to some business meetings at ABC's offices in New York and gave a batch of interviews to the local media to promote Let's Make a Deal. Then it was off to Yale to visit their son Richard, and up north to Toronto for a Halparin family reunion. Then to Oklahoma to visit Marilyn's mother and sister, then back to Wichita, Kansas, to honor a promise Monty made that he'd visit the city on the one-

year anniversary of the plane crash that killed 25 football players, then back to Las Vegas to serve as master of ceremonies for the State Fair Managers Convention. He tried to limit himself to 100 charity events per year, out of typically 500 or so invitations, and that seemed to give him the balance he was seeking between his family and his causes.

MONTY HALL[1]

I think I have made it as a man, even if I haven't fulfilled all my early dreams. I have my family, my charities, my lifestyle. I'm proud of all that.

Monty continued giving thought to walking away from Let's Make a Deal. *Virtually every other game show in production was taping five episodes a day as standard operating procedure, but because of the complexity of the deals and the rehearsals that they commanded, Monty couldn't handle more than two episodes a day. While other game show hosts only needed to be at the studio once a week, Monty had to put in three particularly exhausting days at his show, added onto the obligations of running the production company. None of that had changed since he had put it into writing for his autobiography. And yet, he couldn't leave.*

MONTY HALL[ii]

My big break came for me as an emcee. And if you follow the opportunity and if you're accepted in one particular field, common sense dictates that's the field to pursue. An emcee operates on personality. It's the toughest commodity to find. So when you do break through and become a success, you can make a long career of it.

In 1972, Stefan Hatos-Monty Hall Productions looked to be on the verge of becoming a busy entity. With two solid hits on ABC, Let's Make a Deal *and* Split Second, *Hatos and Hall were pitching three more series: another game show, titled* Anything Can Happen; *a game show parody called* It Pays to be Ignorant, *adapted from a classic radio show; and* Inquiry, *a talk show to be hosted by famed attorney Melvin Belli. The possibility of overseeing five shows at once made Monty realize he might not be able to give so much energy and attention to hosting three tapings a week of* Let's Make a Deal, *so the search began in earnest for a replacement.*

Geoff Edwards was a top disc jockey on Los Angeles radio who had some success with Lucky Pair, *a game show on local Los Angeles TV. Edwards was surprised to receive a call asking him to guest host, little realizing at the time that Monty had grand plans for him. In a 1972 interview, Monty told reporter George Maksian that he would only host* Let's Make a Deal *for one more year, and after that, he would remain onboard only as a producer; Geoff Edwards would take over* full time as host. When Monty was briefly sidelined by illness one day in the early 1970s, Geoff got to step in as guest host.

GEOFF EDWARDS[lii]

[*Let's Make a Deal*] is the hardest game show there is to do. I don't know why they asked me.

So I said, 'Okay.' I practiced at home, I had the script, I had my kids being contestants. I went and I did the show. The first one went pretty well. The second one; I had a lady, and…what happens on *Let's Make a Deal* is, no matter what you say, the people on the floor are going to do it. I said, 'Do you want this or that?' [The contestant] said, 'That.' I said, 'Well, let's take a look at that!' I take a look at the floor manager, who went 'Aaaaah!' What I had done was I left myself in a place where I had given away the end of the deal.

So I said, 'Well, I'll tell you what you can have. You can have that, or you can have what's in my pocket.' What was in my pocket was an empty hand sweating. Monty got well really fast.

"Just when I think I'm out, they keep pulling me back!" Monty gave his notice and even named a successor, but ABC wouldn't make a deal without Monty at the mic.
(Author's Collection)

ABC vetoed Geoff Edwards, as well as every other name Monty pitched as his own replacement. TV show ratings aren't precise enough to tell you exactly why viewers are tuning in, and there was no way to predict what might happen to viewership if Monty walked away. The future of the show might be at stake.

Although its colorful doors, lavish prizes, screaming contestants, lovely model, cheerful organ-driven soundtrack, boisterous announcer, and handsome smiling host may have made Let's Make a Deal seem like the archetypal TV game show, it was, in truth, a very different creation, in that it required the host to develop a relationship with the contestants.

As an example, let's take a look at episode #116 of the nighttime syndicated version, an episode about which there is absolutely nothing out of the ordinary, but provides a good sense of why Monty was so crucial to his own show.

Monty opens the episode by picking a nervous redhead dressed as a cowgirl. He looks at her nametag, sees the name "Marilyn George," and laments that he doesn't know if he's talking to Marilyn or George. Not a knee-slapper, but it puts a smile on her face. He notices her costume includes a rope so he whips out a cowboy movie cliché, warning her, "You're gonna swing!"

Then he notices the badge on her chest, switches to a flirty tone, and asks, "Swinging sheriff, huh?"

She starts to hand Monty the badge—it's the white elephant that she brought for trading—but Monty pushes the badge away for the moment, saying "You can pin me later…and then we'll be engaged."

This entire exchange took about 15 seconds, but in that 15 seconds, he got four small laughs out of her. Suddenly she's relaxed and she's made friends with Monty Hall. So now, when he hands her $300 and offers a curtain if she gives up the money, her reaction to the offer is telling. She doesn't even look at the curtain. She looks at Monty. Surely her new friend Monty isn't leading her astray with a Zonk…but what if he is? The tension of the moment came from a relationship that's existed for all of one minute.

The next deal is for a married couple dressed as farmers. Monty kids them about the sloppy handwriting and too-long-to-read message on their cardboard sign, but then abruptly switches to a compliment about how good their costumes look, before making another conversational turn, channeling Mister Rogers as he tells the couple it doesn't matter what they're wearing. He just wants to make a deal with them.

Later in the show, he picks a contestant who's dressed as a mailman. Monty looks him up and down as he stands up, and instantly surmises that the quality of the "costume" is too good, so the contestant must actually be a mailman. He hands the mailman $500 and offers him a curtain, unless he wants to keep the money. Monty offers him a choice of a box or "one-fourth of your weekly salary…$400." *The universal feeling that I'm not being paid enough for this job has been tapped into and for a moment, it's a dilemma for the contestant looking at the bills in Monty's hand.*

Imagine being the executive who had to approve Monty Hall's plan to quit the show. Can you find a host who can riff so easily that he can make a woman laugh four times in a matter of seconds? Can that host make a stranger instantly accept that they're friends? Can that stranger take a game of blind luck and make a player feel like something's up? Like they need to take a moment to think about what they're doing? Can that host twist the knife as the contestants second-guess themselves into a lather?

Besides, Geoff Edwards was right; hosting Let's Make a Deal *was a deceptively difficult job. Three or four deals on every episode, each with four or five built-in variables that altered every other part. Monty could handle it because it was his own creation. He was in tune with it. But plenty of people at ABC and even Monty's own employees at Hatos-Hall dreaded the prospect of searching for another host that could handle it.*

"The Wind Cries…Monty?" This big winner is so happy he might feel like he's in a purple haze. (Author's Collection)

BOB BODEN

In some ways, "master of ceremonies" is an outdated term, but it's a perfect description of what Monty did on *Let's Make a Deal*. He didn't just read the cue card and keep the show moving along according to the outline. Monty created bits, reacted to moments, and made the contestants the stars. Monty knew that the people standing next to him were the real stars of the show. They created this entertainment spectacle, and Monty adjusted everything he did to the moment.

STU BILLETT

Monty was interesting in that he didn't see what he himself brought to that show. You ever seen a guy on the boardwalk doing games of Three Card Monte? Monty had that quality. You're handing somebody $500 and trying to convince them that they should spend it on a box without knowing what's inside. Monty had that quality.

It was so strange; when Monty would hire people to guest-host for him, or when he'd look for people to replace him, someone to pass the torch to, he never sought out people who had that quality. They were always nice guys who could carry on friendly conversations with the contestants. That's great, but they didn't have that extra something that Monty had. Monty didn't realize he needed people who could sell the contestants on things.

MONTY HALL[liii]

It's a very demanding show. Physically, I'm constantly dodging people lunging, grabbing at me. Emotionally, thinking without a script for 30 minutes takes a lot out of you. Some people have to be prodded to get reactions, sometimes I can let the camera do the work.

RICHARD HALL (2019)

I don't know what my dad could have done, if not *Let's Make a Deal*. I think developing game shows was his greatest talent. He got other shows on the air besides *Deal*. He had some ideas stolen from him too. But I don't think my dad really had a specific thing in mind when he said he wanted to quit *Let's Make a Deal*. I think he just saw the world outside of that show and he was curious. I think he just wanted to see if he could handle a stage show or a road show. He was looking for new challenges, he just didn't know what those challenges might be.

The only thing I can say with certainty is that my dad never wanted to be an executive. He was never offered, but we had this conversation once. He only wanted to work as a performer or a packager for TV shows. My dad believed that in entertainment, there were creative people, and there were decision makers. He didn't believe decision makers were creative and he didn't think creative people should make the decisions. They were different people, and never the twain shall meet. My dad never wanted to move into that area.

The big moment…the big deal…did one of these couples pick the right door? (Author's Collection)

The next time Monty's contract came up for renewal, ABC gave him more specials and more opportunities to try acting and singing; however, the contract renewal came only on the condition that Monty and nobody else would host Let's Make a Deal, a condition that Monty finally, reluctantly, accepted. During negotiations, Monty did manage to shoot down one of ABC's demands; the network wanted a Saturday morning children's version of Let's Make a Deal, which they called off once Monty pointed out that a show where children gambled just might receive some backlash. Of the three new shows Hatos-Hall pitched, only It Pays to be Ignorant came to fruition, airing for one season in syndication.

Being locked into Let's Make a Deal wasn't so terrible, though. It still gave Monty the high profile that kept him in demand for telethons, golf tournaments, and banquets across the country, and his philanthropic itinerary stayed full on the days that he wasn't in the studio. Besides, after years of making deals, Monty found that interacting with strangers couldn't possibly be easier. When he went to a banquet in Iowa or Ohio or anywhere else, people tended to say the same things, and Monty had the perfect line for everything now.

"Hey Monty, let's make a deal!" some wise guy would invariably shout.

Monty would reply, "Okay, I'll give you what I have in my pockets for what you have in yours!"

Monty had delivered the line a million times, but the wise guy would let out a laugh and run off to tell his wife what Monty Hall just said to him. If a woman yelled "Let's make a deal!," Monty would flirtily ask, in a hammy voice, "What did you have in mind?"

By far, the most common question Monty got when he was encountered by fans on the street was "Do you have to wear a costume for the show?" He'd give the fan a smile and a wink and say, "No, what you're wearing will do just fine."

Just about the only time Monty was caught speechless was an evening when he was out with some executives. A small group of ladies of the evening were working their corner, and one walked right up to him and said, "Hey, Monty, let's make a deal."

"They feel like they know me." Monty was never shy about accepting a hug from a contestant or a stranger on the street. (Author's Collection)

RICHARD HALL (2019)

My dad was always very gracious to fans. Always signed autographs, always posed for pictures. And when he talked about his fans and the way he treated them, he had a very old-fashioned way of phrasing it, but he'd say, "Without these people, there'd be no roof over our heads or food in our stomachs. They're paying the bills. We owe them."

SHARON HALL (2019)

I'm a little bit claustrophobic and I avoid people sometimes, and it's a direct response to what I saw when I was a kid. I hated the way crowds would gather around my dad and I hated seeing people reach out and grab him.

My dad would tell me, "Sharon, when you're on TV, you're in people's living rooms and their bedrooms. That's why people reach out like that when they see me. They feel like they know me."

RICHARD HALL (2019)

I won't name any names in this story, but I once worked on a TV show with a professional athlete, and his wife was famous in her own right. His wife could not stand it when they were recognized in public. She was very rude to fans and she insisted that they say no when someone asked them for autographs, or asked them for photos. She felt that fans should always keep their distance and that they weren't owed anything. She went on a tangent about this once and I could tell from his face that he felt conflicted about it.

One night we were talking. He knew that I was the son of a famous father, and he asked me, "How does your dad deal with his fans?"

I think I picked a nicer way of saying it, but the gist of my answer was, "Pretty much the opposite of the way you handle it."

I don't know if it's entirely because of that conversation with me, but I've since heard from other people that have dealt with this man that he was incredibly polite when somebody recognized him. But that was just how my dad felt about the people who watched *Let's Make a Deal*. He felt he owed them.

One night we were out on Hollywood Boulevard, and some tourists are getting ready to take a picture at one of the landmarks. They recognize my dad so they ask if they can get a photo with him, so he stops and poses for a photo with them. Well, since they were about to take a photo anyway, my dad just asks, "Do you want me to take that photo for the two of you?"

They hand my dad the camera…and he drops it on the ground and it cracks. And he just stares at it. He was just in shock. The fans were great about it. "Don't worry, we're sure we can salvage the film, it's okay!" But my dad felt so bad about it! I don't know why that memory jumps to mind, but when I think about my dad meeting fans, that's the one interaction that stands out.

ROBERT HALL (2019)

We took a vacation in Rome once. You wouldn't expect Monty to be recognized in Rome, but there happened to be a group of about 15 American college students, all girls, and they recognized Monty and just swarmed him. I was amazed at how Monty reacted to it. He had a conversation with each of those 15 students. He wanted to know where they went to college, what they were studying, what their career goals were. He didn't respond with "Uh-huh, uh-huh." It was a back-and-forth discussion with each one. 15 conversations, and then he signed an autograph for each of them.

Monty pays off a pair of smart traders. (Author's Collection)

LLOYD SCHWARTZ, family friend

Monty was a good friend of my father, Sherwood Schwartz. We actually put his name into an episode of *The Brady Bunch*. Cindy was on a quiz show and we named the host Monty Marshall.

I remember we were going through an airport once and somebody walks up to Monty and says "Hey Monty! I'll take Door #3!" Monty throws his head back and lets out the biggest laugh.

How many times a day do you think Monty heard that line? Everybody who said it must have thought they were the first one. But Monty always acted like they were the first one. He reacted like he had never heard anyone say it before. That's my memory of Monty. He was just so gracious to that fan.

Let's Make a Deal was put together by a veteran crew at this point, and so much of the show was routine. Mickey Garrett, an advertising executive, had stumbled into a job as a "Zonk finder" and would spend his days scouring Los Angeles for funny props to use on the show. His triumphs included a bed of nails, airplane wreckage, a live vulture, a six-foot ashtray, and a 10-foot hairbrush.

The writers, meanwhile, sat in the office discussing the deals they had already designed and debated how to tinker with them so the next episode would be different.

Downstairs, the security guards at ABC, although it took some time, had grown accustomed to the sight of the network complex's parking lot being treated like a giant dressing room. The costumes had become so intricate by this point that many contestant-hopefuls came to the studio with things that couldn't safely be worn while driving, and employees just learned to live with pulling into the parking lot and weaving past a woman struggling into a horse costume and wrapping a lavish wreath of roses around her neck. One unlucky group of friends, who told Monty the story after the show, drove to the studio wearing matching prisoner costumes. They loaded into one car to drive to the studio, but the driver made an illegal u-turn and got spotted by a cop who pulled them over.

The cop examined them carefully, thought for a moment, and then calmly asked if they were going to Let's Make a Deal. The friends insisted they were, and the cop let them off with a warning so they wouldn't be late for the taping.

You didn't have to wear a costume, but it was just part of the fun when you did!
(Author's Collection)

MONTY HALL[liv]

The psychology department of Yale University came to study our contestants and find out what motivates people to get dressed up in those crazy costumes and go down to a game show, thinking that when they came there they'd strip the layers away and find a bunch of idiots.

Well, they were surprised and they came back with their mouths wide open, saying there were seven doctors on the show and the district attorney of Orange County, who was dressed as an orange.

They said people why they did it and people said, "Why not?" The obvious answer was that they were having a hell of a good time.

It's worth noting at this point that the ubiquitous costumes had led to a misperception among viewers and critics that the dressing up for the show was mandatory. It absolutely wasn't. People could come without costumes. The writers picked people who weren't wearing costumes. Monty picked people who didn't wear costumes. When costumes first showed up among the Let's Make a Deal *hopefuls, the magic of it was that they had chosen to wear them. The staff determined that the costumes were fun strictly because people wanted to wear them, and never enforced a rule requiring one. As Monty thought about it though, he concluded that the people who wore costumes had a psychological edge when the time came to make themselves known to the writers.*

MONTY HALL[lv]

You don't have to dress but I think people have a lot more fun when they do. What we found is the people who came down dressed for the show, and they all did eventually, had so much fun preparing—finding what they would wear, getting dressed up in some kind of costume, joining their friends and coming to the studio…that by the time they got there, they'd had more fun that they'd had in months. Then the whole thing turned into a happening for them. So I would suggest to the people if they want to get into the spirit of it, get dressed up, come on down, and look the other people who are just as outlandish.

As the line formed, the staff rehearsed the program. Monty, after so many years of perfecting his role on the show, usually sat that part out.

JOE BEHAR[lvi]

They were such sticklers for rehearsal. We would rehearse every bit of that show…with stand-ins. And we did it all. Not just checking it out. We really would play the game when we rehearsed it. Monty was so smart, and knew how to do it so well, that eventually he decided he was not going to come and rehearse anymore, because he could do it. So Stefan Hatos would do Monty's part. And Monty had an assistant, Hank Koval, who would brief Monty when he came in about the deals. And the deals were all variations of stuff we had done before, so it was okay for him not to do the rehearsals. But we would rehearse everything, because [Stefan] never wanted to edit that show. So you had to be on your toes with that show.

Stefan Hatos takes the microphone; Monty's business partner usually played the role of host for the rehearsals. (Hall Family Archive)

HENRY KOVAL

Monty seldom rehearsed because he liked the audience to see him "fresh." And if he already went out there and conducted the deals with stand-ins acting as contestants in a rehearsal, he felt he lost that freshness. Eventually, it got to a point where he'd just show up, go to his dressing room, go through the script, chat with a cue card person, and that was about it for him.

The same batch of writers went out before each taping to handpick 36 audience members to take a seat on the coveted trading floor. After so many years of looking at costumes, they had picked up on the hints that audience members conveyed unintentionally. They tried to weed out anybody who struck them as having professional acting training. They liked wild, enthusiastic people, but certain costumes were tip-offs that the wearer was a "kook." The enthusiasm had to be genuine, too. One writer made a habit of standing extremely close to the people he was considering; he was standing close enough to examine their eyes and get a whiff of their breath, looking for warning signs that the enthusiasm was, shall we say, chemically induced.

Monty arrived to rehearse a mix of new and old deals—maybe today, they'd play the game with dollar bills hidden in envelopes, or the contestants would have to play a memory game and recall which grocery item was hidden under each box, or try to select the raw egg hidden among the row of hard-boiled eggs. He'd head backstage to change into his suit, in one come the audience to fill the seats on the trading floor, and out would come Jay Stewart to warm them up, whip them into a frenzy, and give a few minimal instructions to the folks on the trading floor, telling them little more than "You be good to Monty and he'll be good to you!"

Then Monty would take to the stage and start pointing his magic index finger, declaring "You!" and eliciting the usual scream of excitement. Monty's criteria for selecting a certain contestant to make a certain deal wasn't something that he widely shared, aside from one detail—people who sat in the aisle frequently tried to get his attention by waving their hands directly in his face. He couldn't stand that. Whatever other needs Monty had in mind for this deal or that, hand-wavers in the aisle never, ever got picked.

Monty empties his pocket for a winner. (Hall Family Archive)

HENRY KOVAL

During the show, I stood to the side of the stage, and my job was to make sure that Monty only had whatever he needed for the next deal. Imagine Monty telling a contestant "You can have what's in my pocket..." and he reaches for his wad of bills, but he accidentally pulls out a set of keys that he needs for another deal. That would be bad. So after each deal, Monty walked off-stage, emptied his pockets, and then I sorted everything and handed him things for the next deal, so Monty never had more than he needed.

I also told Monty what area of the trading floor to go to when it was time for him to pick a contestant. There was a logistical reason for doing that. We wanted to make sure there was no obstructed view of anything. We considered where the cameras and the technical equipment would be if we had prizes behind curtain #1, or curtain #2, or curtain #3. If, for example, there were prizes behind curtain #3, we would ask Monty to pick contestants sitting near curtain #1 because that way there'd be nothing obstructing their view of curtain #3 and we'd get that reaction shot when they saw what they just won. They wouldn't be confused about how they did.

Meanwhile, Jay Stewart was a human pinball, bouncing from curtain to tray to announcer booth as needed for the entire night, and dealing with whatever disasters came up at the stops along the way. One night, a kitten was supposed to be inside the box on Jay's tray. The kitten fought its way out and scampered off, with Jay weaving through the audience seats to chase it down. Another night, Jay was dressed as Santa Claus, in a sleigh harnessed to a single donkey. No sooner had the curtain opened than the donkey took off, dragging Jay and the sleigh behind him. None of this was any worry to Jay. It came with the job that he signed up for, and he recognized the endless supply of fun stories it gave him.

JAY STEWART[lvii]

Once, we had a rhinoceros as one of the Zonks, but he didn't want to go onstage. You just don't up and move a rhinoceros. He was supposed to be behind one of the curtains, so we had to stop taping until we could persuade him to get in place.

A woman brought a panda bear to trade and set it in the aisle. My tray was loaded and I couldn't see the stuffed animal, so I tripped over it.

Then we had this chimp we had used for a lot of different Zonks. But one evening something frightened him and when the curtain opened, instead of being behind it, he was hanging from the rafters.

Once, I was supposed to be a cowboy. The curtain opened before I could get on the set and I had to make a fast decision, so I ran out and leaped onto the covered wagon we had there. That same situation happened with our cradle. I was getting dressed in a baby gown and the curtain opened before I could get behind it. At first, I thought I would run and jump into the cradle, but then I realized I would probably hit my head or the cradle would overturn, so I just pretended to sleepwalk onto the set.

CAROL MERRILL

We had a goat for one Zonk. I was born on a farm and I don't know how I forgot this. You are not supposed to touch a goat's horn. Why did I do that? And the goat turned right around and butted me on the leg. I thought I'd pass out from the pain.

We had problems with turkeys and donkeys because they liked to make a lot of noise. Monty would ask "Do you want the $500 or do you want what's in the box on the display floor?" I'd be standing next to that box and suddenly there'd be a very loud "Gobble gobble gobble!" from behind it. The contestant knew they should probably hang onto that $500.

Carol with a baby goat. This one gave her an easier time than the adult goat that butted her leg. (Hall Family Archive)

There was also the day when Carol Merrill was standing behind the curtain with a live elephant harnessed to a rope. The elephant broke free from the rope and when stamping through the exit doors and out onto Prospect Avenue in Hollywood. The Zonks could be a real hassle sometimes, but since they were such an intrinsic part of the show's identity, the staff learned to put up with whatever headaches the Zonks ended up creating for them.

STEFAN HATOS[lviii]

One woman won a camel—a one-humped camel. Now it happens that a camel is worth close to $3,000, which is why the woman decided to keep it. She figured she'd sell it and pocket the money. I pointed out to her that there were no used camel lots in the neighborhood. There's no Blue Book on used camel prices.

She took the camel home and tied it in her backyard. She ran newspaper ads. She called all the zoos. Two months later, the camel buyers were still holding out. The zoos were overstocked on the item. Meanwhile, the camel ate her backyard, fence and all, and left a ton and a half of camel dung for a bonus.

Finally, she called and begged us to take it back. We couldn't. The Standards and Practices people would throw us in leg irons if we took back a prize. We helped her locate a zoo that took it off her hands for $50. That's $50 that she had to pay.

We used to rent an old-fashioned, horse-drawn milk wagon from a dairy museum, and we'd used it as a Zonk several times through the years and we never figured there was any risk that somebody would want to take it home. Well, we got Zonked.

On one show, a minister won the milk wagon. He ran a children's camp in the mountains and he thought it would be great fun to have a milk wagon to take the kids on rides. The museum wouldn't sell.

Just another day at the office. But the show was obligated to honor the prize since they had shown the milk wagon on TV and announced it as the minister's prize, so Stefan Hatos got on the phone and scoured America for a similar milk wagon. He found one in Tucson, Arizona, had it remodeled to match the one shown on TV, and then delivered it to the minister's camp. Final cost to the show: $3,800.

With two shows in the can at the end of the taping, Monty headed home, strolling in at 10:00 pm and finding a hot dinner, courtesy of Marilyn, who had already cooked breakfast for the kids at 7:00 am. The gesture was particularly special, in Monty's eyes, because he knew that during the 15 hours in between, she had been doing some writing, running an antique shop, and pursuing her master's degree in classes at UCLA. Still feeling a performer's high as he walked through the door, he'd unwind by doing a crossword puzzle and reading a book until he dozed off.

The show was in a happy rut; ABC, which fully expected to see ratings go down when the show jumped from NBC, happily reported in 1971 that the show was actually outperforming its final months on NBC three years prior. ABC commanded a tidy sum for commercial advertisements on the show, while expenses for Let's Make a Deal *came to $12,000 per episode, compared to $100,000 for an average 30-minute episode of a scripted drama or comedy. At a time when the TV landscape was packed with game shows,* Let's Make a Deal *was TV's third most-popular game. And since the contestants were different every day, Monty certainly didn't feel complacent as he walked out onto the set. Moment to moment, he was meeting a new person and having a new conversation.*

In 1973, Monty's search for respect finally bore fruit, as his name was added to the Hollywood Walk of Fame. Monty's name was immortalized in terrazzo and brass on the 6800 block of Hollywood Boulevard. Monty noticed the star's location was right at the corner of the block and jokingly asked Mayor Tom Bradley not to widen the street any further, because his star would be the first one removed.

900 guests attended a luncheon emceed by Sammy Davis, Jr. One of the keynote speakers, Stefan Hatos, remarked, "Who would have guessed that three doors and a rubber chicken could produce all this?"

"Who would have guessed that three doors and a rubber chicken could produce all this?" –Stefan Hatos (Author's Collection)

MONTY HALL[lix]

You know, it was inconceivable to me when I was growing up in that butcher shop in Canada, and I didn't know where my next meal was coming from, and the greatest thing I could look forward to was a game of football at the corner lot before my father called me back to the store, let alone go to college, let alone ever get into broadcasting, was to have my star placed in the Hollywood Walk of Fame.

I'm next to Joanne Woodward. You gotta realize all the years I've been walking up and down the street looking at other stars in cement. Famous people like Clark Gable and Ronald Colman, you know. To think I'd ever be placed in cement, next to them…That was quite an occasion, a reflective occasion, not one where I sat back and puffed out my chest, but where I thought of where it had all begun and where it had led to.

Time and success hadn't made critics any kinder, though. Monty lamented at one point that in the 1970s, only Richard Nixon was maligned by the press more often than him. Periodically, newspaper writers would tune in and then write a column to assure us that, yes, they did in fact still hate Let's Make a Deal. *Mindless, demeaning, tacky, blah, blah, blah…*

MONTY HALL[lx]

I don't ask critics to like my show—just to be fair. It's only entertainment—not the university of the air. Accept it for what it is—fun, excitement, participation. Greed is always something the other guy engages in. It just depends on whose ax is being gored.

Nobody loves me but the public. Wherever I go, my fans embrace me because I come into their homes as an honest man. They see me for what I am—a natural human being, executing my job with affection, warmth, humor, wit and talent. They accept me. They want to be entertained—and they are. After all, they have switches and can turn off their sets.

I have a theory about the people who put down my show, especially critics. When they write a column, they think they elevate themselves by standing on top of a game show. They'd much rather be reviewing George C. Scott, thus accruing prestige to themselves within their own peer groups.

The nicest audience on television. (Author's Collection)

The critics, apparently under the impression that there was a prize for being the writer who hated the show the most, still complained of greed, but as the years wore on, attacks on Let's Make a Deal *grew increasingly sociopathic, directly assaulting the contestants themselves. These weren't professional performers. These were average people who had never set foot in front of a TV camera, but writer after writer aimed their noses high as they lashed out at the people who shared the spotlight with Monty.*

"One fat lady wore a supergirl outfit," sneered a writer for The Los Angeles Times. "... another fat lady whose placard warned, 'Monty Hall, if you don't trade with me, I'll tell your mummy,' and neither last nor least, a bony woman in a Latin outfit that would have made Carmen Miranda look like a nun."

Monty, on the other hand, looked at the sea of crazy costumes and only saw, in his words, "sheer, uninhibited happiness."

MONTY HALL[lxi]

That's what makes the show so beautiful. Our audience is the nicest of any game show I know of.

When they come to ABC Television Center, they don't know if they'll be picked, although they have dressed for it. This means that those who do appear on the show haven't had time to worry. Their reactions are purely spontaneous.

I really respect the audiences we get on *Deal*. They are emotionally involved in the show, but not selfishly. I've actually seen traders break down and cry with happiness when someone they thought was deserving won a marvelous prize. Everybody's happy.

The critics and their contempt for the audience—Eww! They scream and jump up and down! Eww! They wear silly costumes!—was a little funny to Monty. The behavior they detested so much wasn't restricted just to the lowly commoners who played Monty's games. Monty was once serving as master of ceremonies for a lavish benefit that included a drawing for door prizes, worth about ten dollars apiece. Monty looked at the audience, all wearing ostentatious $5,000 evening gowns and tuxedos that they could never, ever wear in public, stood up and screamed when their numbers were called.

Rosalind Russell, sharing the stage with Monty, covered the microphone and whispered, "They're just like your contestants, and if they call my number, watch me act just the same."

People were the same all over, which was why Monty was so relentless in defending the audience that writers so haughtily scorned. It also irked him to no end when he'd see provably wrong information in a critic's review of his program; while any performer would make themselves crazy responding to every unfavorable review, Monty made it a point to contact any writer who said something blatantly wrong while unleashing their poison pens on him. A writer for The Wall Street Journal called Monty "a short man in a double-knit suit," so Monty wrote him a letter clarifying that he was 5'11" and that not one of his 300 suits was a double-knit. Another writer taunted Monty by saying that he "had probably never set foot in a newsroom," which prompted another letter from Monty, detailing his experience in

Not just another game show, and not just another game show host.
(Author's Collection)

MONTY HALL[lxii]

My knowledge of broadcasting far supersedes what I do. I've done it all. What happened is, I became successful. I started packaging shows and *Let's Make a Deal* became the first one I owned and performed in, which became a runaway hit. It was like owning Secretariat, a tremendous horse, and I was the jockey and away we went together to the Kentucky Derby and there was no way I was going to let go…

I'm proud of my performances. And then you pick up a newspaper. It's been the biggest bone in my throat. When a critic hates my show, they'll hate me. They even follow me into my public life. I'll do a telethon and they hate me for raising half a million dollars. If I had a kid on my lap, they'll make some oblique, terrible reference. They just want to pursue me down the road screaming after me…

I'm very proud of what I do with my life. But it bothers me that people are so hung up on disliking something, they'll go out of their way and be cruel.

One reporter, on a quest to figure out why anybody would ever watch something like a game show, reached out to psychologists in search of answers. What he got were some amazingly cynical and grim theories about human behavior. The "experts" likened Monty to a sugar daddy and the contestants as prostitutes, reasoning that the costumes were a way of showing Monty that they would be anything he liked in exchange for whatever he offered.

What's wrong with wanting to go to a giant costume party and win some cash and prizes for it? (Hall Family Archive)

DR. SHELDON ZIGELBAUM, head of the New Center for Psychotherapy[1]

Monty Hall makes the women appear ludicrous, absurd. That show is one of several in which the game is used only as a cover. What we're really seeing is how easy it is to get people to degrade themselves. How far are you willing to go in self-denigration to get the prize. It's a form of sadism, a subtle form of sadism. Contestants who have gone through every single form of degradation on the show may get nothing, while someone else wins the prize, gets the reward.

It reminds me of the old movie *The Blue Angel*, in which the professor loves the nightclub singer, and at the end, after this process, he's dressed up as a chicken on the stage. In the movie, however, he's aware of his degradation. That's the point. That is not true on these shows. In [*Let's Make a Deal*], there are the sadists, the masochists, and the onlookers. It's reminiscent of public flogging, perhaps our modern-day resolution of it.

DR. JEAN ROSENBAUM, author and psychiatrist[2]

The two primary fantasies of people are sex and money. Americans, by going through psychoanalysis, have partly resolved their sexual hang-ups, but not their money hang-ups.

At the peak of Monty's exasperation, reporter Dick Adler gave him a chance to address the most repetitive criticisms one at a time and say his piece about each of them.

---

1 Stoehr, Chris. "The Decline of Game Shows." Austin American Statesman. 4 Mar. 1979.
2 Ibid.

MONTY HALL[lxiii]

[On accusations that the show celebrates greed] I'd be a fool to say that there has never been a greedy contestant on a game show. But I think there's an important distinction between greed and gambling. If gamblers can be called greedy, then each and every one of us is greedy. I can't imagine a game show becoming successful by parading greedy, avaricious contestants before the cameras. The viewing audience would quickly be turned off, and would turn the programs off.

[On contestants accused of being freaks and weirdos] Researchers who have studied our audiences say that they represent a true cross-section of America. We get doctors, teachers, social workers, psychologists, all sorts of professionals. I went to a very exclusive costume party at a Beverly Hills country club not long ago, and a judge said to me, "Monty, this is your audience." Every time I go to a gathering somebody inevitably collars me, talks about "all those crazy people," and then winds up by asking how he or she can get on the show. I used to get angry. Now I just smile and nod.

[On accusations that his show glorifies American consumerism] It can't be, because everywhere I go, they have a version of *Let's Make a Deal*—Japan, Spain, Sweden, everywhere!

[On complaints that the show gives away luxury items instead of a meaningful prize like a scholarship] We couldn't guarantee anybody getting into college, and they'd probably want the cash instead anyway. As to our other luxury prizes, we have tended to go much more for economy cars recently.

[On complaints that there were too many game shows] It's true—there are too many game shows on television. There are too many cop shows, too, but what can one producer do? My partner, Stefan Hatos, and I have tried other kinds of shows…and we lost a fortune on them. We're doing a prime-time access pilot now, which we'll try next season—a variety show introducing new talent. But nobody can force stations to try new shows. Game shows are popular and cheap, so they get made and sold.

At the height of his success, it must have struck Monty that all of this was due to the generosity of Max Freed, and now he found himself cursed to the same fate as his benefactor: wealthy and famous, hobnobbing with society's elite at lavish functions night in and night out, and despised by total strangers for the way he attained that wealth and fame, with no regard given for all the good he had done with it.

SHARON HALL (2019)

I don't think my father made that connection between himself and Max. My parents were rather guileless people. They were like characters out of a Jimmy Stewart movie. I think the fact that it took so long for them to achieve that success helped them in a lot of ways. My father was 42 when *Let's Make a Deal* went on the air, so he had a lot of years of hard work in his past by the time he finally hit it big. My parents had tuxedos and ball gowns in the closet, but my dad was still Monty from Winnipeg.

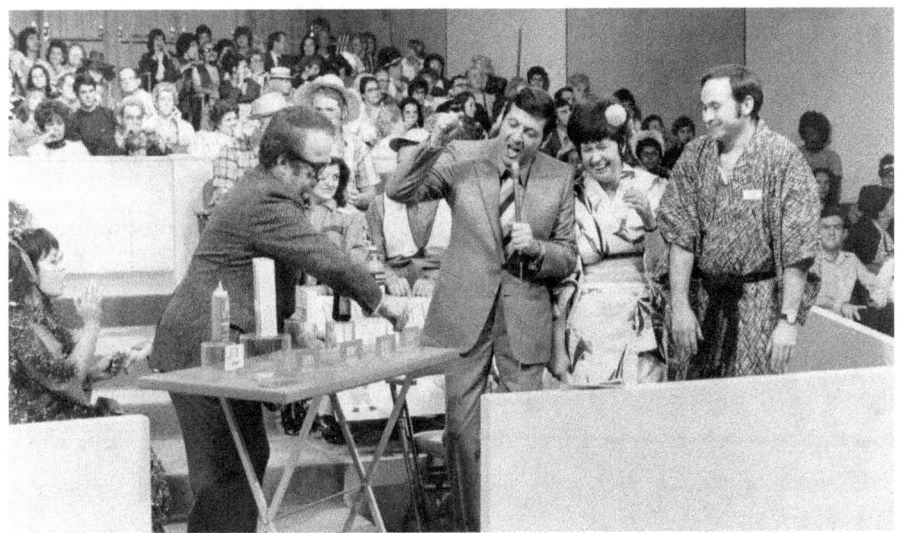

At heart, he was just Monty from Winnipeg. (Author's Collection)

The endurance of the show, and the continuing flow of venom rushing toward it, caught the attention of John Schott, a photographer and filmmaker. In 1974, he reached out to Hatos-Hall Productions, seeking to make a documentary about Let's Make a Deal. *The film, bearing the stylized title* $DEAL$, *opens with a quote from* Variety *Television editor Les Brown: "People are the merchandise, not the shows. The shows are merely the bait. The consumer, whom the custodians of the medium are pledged to serve, is in fact served up."*

JOHN SCHOTT

I was living in New York and working with my filmmaking partner, EJ Vaughn. We had completed a film called *America's Pop Collector*. We were both young art historians and interested in cinema verité, which was a new filmmaking movement at that time. Prior to the 1970s, documentaries had to have narrators. That's the way they were all done. But technology was evolving. Filmmaking equipment got smaller and more portable. A filmmaker, a cameraman, and a sound man could walk around together. Cinema verité was the concept that you could just show the footage you shot, and if it was edited cohesively, the story could tell itself, instead of needing narration to tie things together. So, we had just done a cinema verité film about the art world and we decided to do a comparable film about popular culture. In this case, that was television.

We thought *Let's Make a Deal* was an interesting case study in what television was at that time, and the spectator's relationship to it. We thought it would be fun to do a behind-the-scenes look at a game show. At that point, *Let's Make a Deal* was the very best-known of them. We were intrigued because it elicited such different reactions from people. Among some audiences it was an enormously popular show, but at the same time, there was so much criticism towards it. It was a game show and the feeling was that the contestants were exploited, but then there was the argument that it was a willing playfulness.

We called Stefan Hatos and asked if he'd be interested in taking a meeting with us. He said yes. We flew out from New York and came to his office. He said, "I have ten minutes to talk with you boys."

We panicked because we had flown across the country to discuss making a film. As it turned out, that was just his introduction, and we ended up having a really nice, long conversation with him. We presented the idea of doing a non-narrated documentary that just covered the events of a day at the show. He talked to Monty about it and they agreed to do it.

We had no expectations. We went in with the idea that if you film something with detail, a point of view will emerge. One of the things we found we liked about cinema verité was that it could embrace ambivalence. We didn't show anything that was "good" or "bad." We presented it without judgment. It was observational cinema. Viewers could draw their own conclusions. We didn't go into it with a journalistic point of view.

We shot for about three weeks. We had permission to go everywhere behind the scenes. Into the writers' meetings, even. Monty wore an electronic mic that allowed him to move around apart from us, but we could still hear him and our equipment would record the audio. Once we had all the footage, we edited it together and that was the movie.

You ought to be in pictures. John Schott and his crew saw an interesting story in the making of *Let's Make a Deal*. (Author's Collection)

In its finished form, the film shows the blunt end of the business. Two ABC network executives freely discuss the show's success is targeting the lucrative 18-34 housewife market; "the buyers," the executives casually classify them. Monty is shown recording a message for a new sponsor where he refers to the show's viewers as customers. An ABC page notes that due to the recent economic downturn, a number of people are making return visits to tapings, hoping that next time would be their time to finally win something.

JOHN SCHOTT

The making of a game show allows you to explore sociology, which you couldn't do if you were doing the making of a scripted fictional television show. An audience has at least a basic understanding of how a comedy or a drama on TV is made already. We were interested in a show that had a social process. So, one of the things that we did was follow the contestants as best as we could from beginning to end.

    Monty was very guarded in the beginning because he was concerned that this movie was going to be, as I call it, thesis journalism. Something where we came in knowing the story we were going to tell and the slant we were going to give it, and we were going to shoot and edit footage in a way that confirmed the story that we wanted to tell. But after continuing conversations with us, I think he came away with a sense that we would be true to what we observed and that we didn't bring a point of view. An audience could come forward and make a judgment based on what we were doing. Now granted, we chose *Let's Make a Deal* because it had a controversial quality to it, but we undertook it in a good spirit. I think they felt like they were in a position where, if the filmmaking unrolled and they started to feel uncomfortable with where they thought it was going, they could simply say "That's enough, guys."

What surprised me was how good-hearted it all was. The people in the audience are like a lot of contestants on other shows, or interested in television in any case. They're all excited, as though they're going to a birthday party or some kind of dress-up party in which they've done all these crazy things. They're excited and nervous about whether they'll be able to get on the show. There's a sense of keeping them waiting and what's going to happen. So, there's a theatricality to the way they approach the show and that produces a kind of excitement on their part. Contestants got so crazy and over-the-top emotionally, but I thought that what you saw behind it was the way that it was orchestrated structurally. Keeping people in line, picking them in a way that made them feel special, bringing them inside, having a warm-up with a comedian, encouraging them and telling them it's okay to laugh out loud.

The audience was quite a cross-section. There were upper-middle-class people in the audience that day. They weren't in want of anything, but they wanted to come and dress up and be a little silly and have fun at a TV show. I never felt that the contestants were manipulated or disrespected. They were willing participants. The approach to the whole process from Monty, who struck me as a total gentleman at all times….I felt he was aware that he had talents that exceeded the role he was in, but he had a dignity and showed kindness to people.

Monty was never really defensive, but he was never really confessional either during the film. Neither warm nor distant, but he certainly wasn't forthcoming. He didn't have anything that he wanted to say the camera. He didn't feel the need to make the movie about him, or talk about his career or where he came from, which I found to be very professional of him.

Here's my perception of Monty. I think so many people in Hollywood fall into a slot. The trap of it is that they become so successful that they can't walk away. It's exciting to every performer when the lights come on, the applause takes place, you feel the show going on around you, and you respond to that 100%. But after you've done each show, and certainly after you've done hundreds and hundreds of them, you think about what else you might do.

The illusions of television. What looked like a daily party was the result of several dozen people's efforts coming together, as documented in the film *Deal*. (Author's Collection)

Interspersed were shots of very normal people working in a very normal-looking office complex; a man sitting at a typewriter and trying to figure out how to keep the plugs for Rice-a-Roni, Leggs Pantyhose, and Creamettes (the quick-cooking macaroni) from exceeding 60 seconds; a team of writers trying to invent fresh spins on deals they've already done before. Monty and Jay Stewart joke around with the staff. The taping ends, and everyone just says goodnight to each other and leaves the ABC complex; another hard day's work ended.

JOHN SCHOTT

It was a workmanlike process that was very well-honed. We never felt that they were putting on a façade for the cameras. The show ran so smoothly while we were there that they couldn't have been faking this for our benefit. Everybody knew when people would show up, what time the audience would be brought in, how to move everyone around between tapings, what was supposed to be placed where, when Jay needed to go out and warm up the audience.

Although Monty never spoke publicly about his opinion of the film, Schott had pledged not to release it without the approval of he or Stefan Hatos. Schott delivered the final edit to the office for a private screening. Both men watched quietly, then gave Schott the go-ahead to release the film without making any changes. Schott, though he wasn't and would never be a fan of the show, found himself on Let's Make a Deal's *side whenever he encountered criticism of the show in the future.*

JOHN SCHOTT[lxiv]

We went to Hollywood thinking we'd find real demons, [but the show is] still relatively innocent.

Shying away from it has more to do with how you feel about yourself, not what you're seeing. If you're saying you don't like those people, you're saying you don't like lower middle-class people.

Class warfare among the critics? Filmmaker John Schott hypothesized that a person's attitude about *Let's Make a Deal* reflected their attitude about the middle class. (Author's Collection)

MONTY HALL[lxv]

I'd like to tell you something else about *Let's Make a Deal*. Until *Let's Make a Deal* came on the air, all contestants on all game shows were nice, lily-white young people. *Let's Make a Deal* used black people, brown people, yellow people, old people, young people, fat people, skinny people…That's what America looks like! They're different colors, different sizes, different ages, different shapes. Everybody makes a good contestant.

I got a letter once from [a viewer]… A person wrote in and said, "I watched the show the other day, and Monty Hall walked by a black person to make a deal with a white person."

…NBC asked, "How are you going to answer this?"

We had more black people than any other show in history. I was offended by that remark. But rather than quoting how many black people we had used on the show—I don't believe in quotas—I wrote a letter and I said, "This is America. I believe in equal opportunity for everybody. And a black person has the same ability and the same right to be passed by as a white person."

The NBC lawyers thought that was the most brilliant answer they ever heard. And it was true. You have the same right to be ignored as a white person…If you go back and look at my tapes, you will see an inordinate amount of minorities used on the show.

The trials and tribulations of the Las Vegas show and Monty Hall's Smokin'-Stokin' Fire Brigade *notwithstanding, Monty still sought, and received, opportunities to expand his horizons. ABC, which struggled as badly as CBS at gaining a foothold against Johnny Carson and developing a late night franchise, would reinvent their after-prime-time schedule every few years, and a handful of network executives believed in Monty enough to at least get his name in the discussion. When Joey Bishop was turfed in 1969, Monty was considered as a replacement. A few years later, ABC considered reviving a prime time variety show,* Hollywood Palace, *as a late night series, to be hosted by Monty. It was an opportunity he savored. Not just for the change of pace after nearly a decade of dealing, but because of the elevation in status it could mean for him.*

MONTY HALL[lxvi]

I was a comedian, singer, and actor before I became an emcee. I was also a producer, director, and writer for my own shows back in my radio and television days in Canada. Las Vegas isn't the right vehicle for me. But I think I'm right for a late night talk show because I can communicate with anyone at any time. And I can entertain. I can't sing like Andy Williams or act like George C. Scott. But I can put it all together and make myself the complete television entertainer.

I'm a contented man, except I want people to think of me as a member of the entertainment community. I would also like to have the respect of my peers in show business, especially from comedians. I want to be a rounded entertainer as well as a rounded human being.

Charles Nelson Reilly, Jonelle Allen, Monty, Florence Henderson, and a friend, in *Monty Hall at Sea World*. (Author's Collection)

Monty was well into the planning/daydreaming stages of developing his late night talk show—he was adamant that the set would have neither a couch nor a desk—but ABC eventually decided against it. They did sign Monty for more specials. Monty was given a great deal of control over the subject matter and the nature of the show, and presented a smorgasbord of programming for the network.

No more Fire Brigade *fiascos; Monty made the kind of specials he wanted to make*. Monty Hall at Sea World *featured Jonelle Allen, Florence Henderson, Charles Nelson Reilly, Bobby Sherman, the Carl Jablonski Dancers, the Oak Hurst High School Marching Band, 12 Hawaiian dancers, a group of Japanese pearl divers, Shamu the Killer Whale, performing seals, dolphins, penguins, and walruses.*

Once the show was edited and finished, Monty gathered some friends at his house for a screening and discovered, to his relief, that he was completely happy with how it turned out. And in a shocking change of pace, so were critics. For the first time in his career, Monty was getting a pat on the back in print.

For another special, Monty ventured back to Las Vegas, this time to conduct an in-depth interview with Liberace. The experience left him with a story that he told at charity functions for years.

MONTY HALL[lxvii]

After a recent fund-raising dinner in Fresno, California, I had to depart immediately for Las Vegas to tape an interview there with Liberace for a late night TV special. As there were no scheduled flights, I chartered a small private plane.

Taking off my pilot said, "Lean back and relax, Mr. Hall, we'll be in Las Vegas in about an hour."

An hour and a half later, I casually asked him, "Shouldn't we be fastening our seatbelts for the landing?"

He looked at me and said, "I hate to tell you this, Mr. Hall, but we're lost. My radio went dead a half-hour ago, and since then we've strayed from the flight path and I can't spot a familiar landmark."

We finally did land in Las Vegas two hours late, but safe. Yet for the remainder of that chilling flight, my mind kept flashing to newspaper headlines. "MONTY HALL MAKES LAST DEAL." "IT'S CURTAINS FOR MONTY HALL: CURTAIN NUMBER 1, CURTAIN NUMBER 2, AND CURTAIN NUMBER 3."

And that wasn't the only time that travel could be hazardous to his health. Monty ventured to England for a ceremony where he was officially named president of Variety Club International. A few days later, it was off to Rome for an audience with the Pope. Almost.

MONTY HALL[lxviii]

There was a big strike by all kinds of workers and we never did see the Pope. We went to Florence first and there was a strike there. We couldn't eat at the hotel and we had to go out prowling for food and wound up at some little side street place.

[On the flight back from Rome] the pilot told us over the intercom that there was more luggage aboard than passengers. Someone decided that maybe a bomb was planted on the plane. But they would not let us leave the plane while they searched for a possible bomb!

John Wayne, Frank Sinatra, and Monty in preparations for one of the All Star Party Specials. (Author's Collection)

Monty's role as president led to a new way to bring together his television career and his philanthropy with a series of successful prime time specials for Variety Club.

MONTY HALL[lxix]

CBS came to us and said, "We have an idea. We will have a salute to an outstanding star. And we'll have a studio filled with a hundred celebrities or more. We'll have a tremendous show, a tribute to the star. And during the show, we will donate money to a hospital where Variety Club has one of its chapters, and we'll make the donation in that star's name."

Over the years, the All Star Party specials would honor superstars like John Wayne, Jimmy Stewart, Ingrid Bergman, Carol Burnett, Ronald Reagan, and Clint Eastwood, with Variety Club reaping the greatest benefits from the tributes. Monty kept doing specials as part of his contract with ABC, covering some extremely eclectic ground. One special was an in-depth look at sex in the '70s, featuring interviews with pornographers, psychiatrists, and a nun; for another special, Monty interviewed members of Gamblers Anonymous, and actor Jack Klugman subjected himself to a test to determine if he had a gambling addiction; Another special delved into the history of comedy, with Monty performing an old vaudeville routine, "Slowly I Turned" (a/k/a the Niagara Falls routine) with Jack Carter. He even gave a nod to the work that paid the bills with a ninety-minute special about game shows, featuring special guests Mark Goodson, Bob Barker, Ralph Edwards, and Betty White.

Goodson's involvement was indicative of the strange relationship that he and Monty maintained. Goodson had swiped an idea of Monty's, presented the guise of disliking it to get rid of him, and then developed the concept into a blockbuster called Password, *without paying Monty a penny for the idea.*

When Monty hung up a shingle for his own production company and launched Let's Make a Deal, *Goodson was one of his most vocal admirers.*

Monty Hall surprises Bill Bixby by revealing that he just made a deal with an audience member and gave away his wallet. Host Steve Allen looks on in this segment from Goodson-Todman's *I've Got a Secret.* **(Author's Collection)**

MARK GOODSON[lxx]

I had been one of those who had said that a game of pure luck would not succeed. Monty is brilliant the way he does it… the tension he has built up. He makes those people feel that what they are deciding is decidable on the basis of judgment they have to make when indeed it's not. I mean the fact is they could probably do just as well by flipping a coin every time. But he creates tension, and there is also that marvelous thing of vicariously sharing the win with someone else.

In 1972, Mark Goodson-Bill Todman Productions, which had enjoyed nine years of success during the '50s and '60s with an auction-inspired game called The Price is Right starring Bill Cullen, began making plans to launch The New Price is Right, *a dramatically refurbished version of the show*. Bill Cullen had already been asked and declined the chance to host a new series. In search of the ideal host, Bill Todman stumbled on Let's Make a Deal *during a day when Dennis James was pitch-hitting for Monty*, which led to James being hired to host the version for syndication.

This led to a surprising arrangement between Hatos-Hall and Goodson-Todman. Hatos-Hall allowed Goodson-Todman to make a sales pitch film for local stations to consider The New Price is Right *that included extensive footage of Dennis James hosting* Let's Make a Deal. *In exchange, Goodson-Todman booked Monty Hall as a special guest star on their own* I've Got a Secret *for a segment in which Monty made deals with the celebrity panel, effectively allowing ten minutes of their own show to serve as an advertisement for Monty's work*.

When The New Price is Right *was launched, Monty was appalled to see the new format for the show was a series of smaller games within a larger game, including contestants picked from the audience, and most egregiously, a set consisting of three large doors. Nothing came of the anger; Monty probably remembered his urge to file suit over* Password, *only to be convinced by NBC that it was in everyone's best interest to maintain peace among the production companies. With* Let's Make a Deal *and* Password *both thriving on ABC in 1972, Monty seemed resigned to let Mark Goodson get away with a little bit more*.

MONTY HALL[lxxi]

Well, we've had people poach on us, taken some of our ideas. I won't name them. I don't want to get into a fist fight with some of these guys, but they did. ...They still show up at the networks with ideas and someone will say to me, they came to me and it was a steal right out of *Let's Make a Deal*. You can't stop that. The best you can do is copyright your name and *Let's Make a Deal* and hope for the best.

In 1974, Monty saw his history with Mark Goodson come full circle when ABC suggested a "Summer Festival" of special daytime programs. The Goodson-Todman staff came up with a marvelous idea for a special week of Password *in which host Allen Ludden would play the game for charity with a rotating group of celebrity partners. With Allen having to abandon the host's podium, Monty Hall was called in to guest host, overseeing the very game show that he maintained Goodson had stolen from him*.

Monty joins Carol Burnett and host Allen Ludden on *Password*. Although Monty was hurt by being left out of the show that he maintained he had created, he made numerous appearances as a player and even as a guest host during *Password*'s years on ABC. (Author's Collection)

(Author's Collection)

CHAPTER TWENTY

HENRY KOVAL

There's a story I love telling about Monty. Marilyn had taken her car into the shop. The shop called one morning and said the car was ready.

So Monty says "Don't worry, I'll go pick up the car."

Marilyn says, "Good idea."

They don't discuss this at all. They both just agree without thinking about it, and Monty goes off to pick up the car.

Monty drives to the auto shop, parks his car in the parking lot, and goes in to pick up Marilyn's car. He looks back and realizes he drove another car here. So now he has the car he drove there in, and the car he's picking up from the shop, and he has to get them both home.

Monty drives Marilyn's car for a few blocks. Then he walks back to the auto shop and drives his own car and pulls up one block ahead of Marilyn's car. Then he goes back to Marilyn's car and drives it a few more blocks. Then he walks back to his car and pulls it up. He just keeps going back and forth between the two cars until he's gotten both of them home.

He gets home and tells Marilyn, "I forgot to take my Stupid Pills this morning."

Monty Hall always said he had little interest in running for high office, but in 1975, he was bestowed an honorary position by the Hollywood Chamber of Commerce. The man who arrived in California as mayor of Video Village *was named the honorary Mayor of Hollywood. Preceded in office by luminaries like Betty White, Art Linkletter, Charlton Heston, and Lawrence Welk, Monty would hold the office for five years.*

MONTY HALL[lxxii]

You had to go and officiate every star in cement. You had to go and cut every ribbon for every store that came up. That wasn't so bad. The Christmas parade was the terror of my life. Every year of my life, in an open convertible, in the front of the parade, the honorary mayor of Hollywood, with a million people lining the streets, yelling, "Monty! Monty! Make a deal! Monty! Monty! Make a deal! Let's make a deal! Door number one!" through the whole parade.

One year, my daughter Sharon sat in the back seat. When it was over, she said "Daddy, I don't ever want to do this again."

I said, "You know what? Neither do I."

In 1975, American television achieved "peak game show," with a total of 25 game shows dotting the television schedules of all three networks and most local TV stations through syndication. The logical assumption would be that anyone in the business of game shows would be delighted by this development, but this wasn't exactly the case. Monty Hall merely had great ideas for game shows and struck gold with those ideas; it was just how he made his living.

Monty and Stefan Hatos. Even though they agreed there were too many games on the air, it was hard to complain when they were on top. (Author's Collection)

MONTY HALL[lxxiii]

I feel there are too many game shows on the air. I'd like to see a better balance, actually. But the networks seem to think that only the soaps and game shows are successful. But there are other types of shows, such as the old Arthur Godfrey and Garry Moore shows. They were good, entertaining programs. The public liked them. I've been trying to get the networks interested in different types of shows, but nobody is buying it.

Monty was the first to admit that the television industry's aversion to risk had benefited him handsomely. The second to admit that was Stefan Hatos. In 1975, reporter Dick Kleiner examined the prime access time rule that went into effect in 1971; the rule that required networks to hold off their prime time schedules until 8:00 p.m. Eastern so that local stations could introduce prime time shows of their own creations. The FCC publicly claimed that the implementation of the rule had been successful, but privately, numerous members of the FCC lamented that the rule was violated by nearly every station in the country and not realistically enforceable. Kleiner's article specifically cited Stefan Hatos-Monty Hall Productions as arguably the most enriched beneficiaries from the policy. Let's Make a Deal *filled hundreds of holes in station schedules across the country.*

STEFAN HATOS[lxxiv]

In syndication [during 1974], we took in close to $7 million. Nobody is getting that kind of dough from nighttime network programs…I think we'll continue the way we are for three or four more years. The FCC is very slow at changing anything. There are still some folks trying to get the rule knocked out of the box for next season. I don't think there's a chance that will happen.

Game shows are instant profit today. The only problem is that you are classified as a second-class citizen. Everybody looks down at game shows. But they are gold mines. I don't think there has been a more successful commercial venture in the history of television than *Let's Make a Deal.*

MONTY HALL[lxxv]

There are too many game shows on television, too many medical shows, too many police shows. They're all the same. I can watch the first few minutes of *Kojak* or *Columbo* and tell you what's going to happen for the rest of the show.

I'm not saying *Let's Make a Deal* is a paragon of entertainment, but we do try to make it the best in is field. Frankly, I'm not crazy about game shows myself. More than half of them have no right to be on the air. They're nothing more than a lot of flashing lights. There should be a greater choice of programs on television.

In the glut of game shows saturating American TV in the 1970s, there were a few trends that Monty found disquieting and disheartening. First and foremost was that, on humor-driven games like The Hollywood Squares *and* Match Game, *the content was becoming increasingly edgy. Some would even say "crass." Producer/packager Chuck Barris, best known at the time for his naughty hits* The Dating Game *and* The Newlywed Game, *cheerfully took credit for this development, calling himself "The King of Slob Culture," a moniker that left Monty horrorstruck.*

Don't you dare call it "slob culture." *Let's Make a Deal* **was just good, clean fun. (Author's Collection)**

MONTY HALL[lxxvi]

Chuck Barris started this whole trend with *Newlywed Game*. When you ask two newlyweds, "What's the first thing you do when you climb into bed?" or "What's the first part of your body that you wash when you step into the shower?," then you know the questions are being deliberately framed to embarrass the couple.

He's fouling his own nest when he makes statements like ["king of slob culture"]. I resented it because I regard a show like *Let's Make a Deal* as perfectly valid light entertainment, no better or worse than a prime time action show like *Kojak*. And I know judges and doctors and professors who get some laughs out of my shows. Would they be considered members of the slob culture?

The second thing bothering Monty was that the games, in his eyes, seemed very derivative of each other.

Host Dick Enberg (center), with guests Dick Gautier and Linda Kaye Henning on *Three for the Money*, Hatos-Hall's short-lived hard quizzer from 1975. (Author's Collection)

MONTY HALL[lxxvii]

Television producers are the biggest bunch of copycats anywhere. This is what I have always riled against.

When we came on TV eleven years ago, we were the first game show to put ourselves in the audience. The audience became a highly-charged arena because none knew who was going to be selected as a contestant. The selection on the air had an emotional impact on people. After all, they had waited a long time for tickets and they were selected outside to sit down front in the theater and only when the show began were they selected. It became a highly nervous show.

Now there is a tendency on some game shows to have the studio audience scream and jump up and down and they are not even participating. That bothers me, because ours was always an honest reaction. You must know how I feel when I see a dishonest reaction—one that is goaded, promoted and excited and which has nothing to do with the contestants on stage.

The camera turns on them and I assume they are told to act in a frenzied manner, because they say, "This is the way *Let's Make a Deal* does it, so let's do it ourselves." The other shows are more contrived in their efforts to simulate us.

Also irking Monty was the oversimplification that was trending in TV game shows. Hard quizzers were out. NBC's original Jeopardy! *with Art Fleming bit the dust in early 1975. ABC cancelled Hatos-Hall's hard quiz* Split Second *a few months later—a cancellation that Monty said hurt him a lot; "I loved that show." A handful of Q&A games remained, but the subject matter didn't exactly strain anyone's gray matter.*

Monty sought to fill the gap by developing a tough new quiz show called Three for the Money.

MONTY HALL[lxxviii]

The pilot was a hard quiz show. NBC loved it. But then they tested it on audiences, and they decided it was too hard. They said we should make it simpler so the people at home would think they were just as bright as the contestants.

I don't understand this. You might think people are becoming less intelligent, yet daytime viewers are able to handle soap operas that deal with very mature subjects, like incest and infidelity.

With the simplified subject matter preferred by NBC, Monty got Three for the Money *on the air*. It was cancelled eight weeks later.

The copycat issue that Monty took umbrage with was about to become more of a problem than he anticipated. This had really begun in the 1972-73 season, when CBS revamped their daytime line-up with game shows that altered the genre in striking ways. The sets for CBS games were larger, brighter, flashier, and livelier. The music was synthesized and slick. The payouts were bigger than ever. Game shows had kept their prize budgets conspicuously modest for over a decade after the quiz scandals, but once CBS introduced The $10,000 Pyramid, *the purse strings got looser all over*. The Hollywood Squares *offered an $18,000 bonus to contestants who could win five consecutive matches*. Chuck Barris introduced a prime access time offering, The New Treasure Hunt, *with a $25,000 cash prize*. On NBC's Jackpot, *the stakes could go as high as $50,000*.

ABC jumped on the big bucks bandwagon, because why wouldn't they? The network actually snapped up The $10,000 Pyramid *when it was abruptly cancelled by CBS*. ABC also enhanced the payouts on the game shows it already had on the air and introduced a few new games with five-figure paydays possible.

It was a sound business decision, but the size of the stakes made a few network executives nervous. One, speaking anonymously, reached out to reporter Tom Tiede to express his concerns about the sumptuous giveaways.

"We worry about some of these people—not just about them physically, but emotionally. Some of them are so wound up by the time they get on the air, anything could happen. I don't know of any case where a loser has hit a host, but it could happen. I've seen some of these people after they lose a big prize and they are just desolate. One minute, they are jumping up and down in anticipation, the next minute they are desolated by defeat. There is some risk here, I think.

"It's queer, really, what people will do for a new refrigerator. Some of the people connected with our quiz shows have been propositioned by women wanting a chance. It gives you pause. Is a refrigerator really that important?"

The emotional state of the contestants didn't worry Monty as much. He was still convinced that the contestants really weren't in it for the big haul. Monty's concern was that a colossal giveaway would give viewers an expectation for every episode that the show simply couldn't accommodate. A company once offered Monty a single $35,000 yacht to offer as a prize, and Monty declined it because they didn't have a $35,000 prize to give away every single day. what do you do to live up to the excitement of that single day that you gave away the yacht?

How much is enough? *Let's Make a Deal* never offered a Maserati or a Lamborghini. They didn't need to. (Author's Collection)

MONTY HALL[lxxix]

I could get the same reaction for a $5,500 boat and trailer. What's the point of having to top yourself every week? It's the manner in which it's done. I can extract more excitement per square nickel by slowly peeling off five $100 bills than some other show gets by giving away a house.

STEFAN HATOS[lxxx]

I think it's strange when people ask me what's the most valuable prize we've ever given away. I have to tell them I don't know, honestly, for we just don't pay that much attention to monetary value. If we did, we'd just out-prize ourselves, and I refuse to do that. There's always the worry of what you're going to do next week to top the week before, so why do it? I think the only taboo we have on the show is real estate. We don't ever give real estate away because we think it imposes too many limitations on the contestants.

But in the fall of 1975, the mail from viewers suggesting a bigger haul because they were seeing it everywhere else was getting a little harder to ignore. After ten years on the air, the show was due for a facelift anyway; a new set, a new music package, a trippy new animated opening in which Monty, perched on a flying dollar bill, zoomed past the doors…and a few changes to the nighttime version.

The first change to the nighttime version came about because of a change happening to the nighttime version of another game show. The Hollywood Squares *had started offering one episode per week for prime access time in 1971 at the same time as* Let's Make a Deal. *Shortly after the nighttime version debuted, the daytime version's ratings trickled away slightly. It was still a mega-hit, but the impact on the daytime ratings was significant enough that it made other packagers wary about launching nighttime versions of other game shows. ABC had even denied Hatos-Hall Productions permission to shop around a nighttime version of* Split Second *because they were concerned that a nighttime version would kill off the daytime show.*

But in 1974, Heatter-Quigley Productions surprisingly expanded the nighttime version and started offering stations two episodes per week. After looking at a season's worth of ratings data, ABC's Owned & Operated Stations (O&Os) insisted that Let's Make a Deal *add a second nighttime episode each week, too. Hatos & Hall were both adamantly against the proposal, but because O&Os were the stations that aired* Let's Make a Deal *in the largest television markets, saying no to the demand was far too big a risk, and Hatos-Hall reluctantly produced two nighttime episodes per week, starting in the fall of 1975.*

To drum up some interest in the expanding nighttime version, Deal *now had a celebrity guest on the trading floor. Monty made deals with stars like Milton Berle, Bill Macy, Nanette Fabray, and Nipsey Russell, all of whom played as proxies for home viewers selected at random.*

Actor Bill Macy (*Maude*) competes against a contestant in the Big Deal of the Day on the nighttime *Let's Make a Deal.* (Hall Family Archive)

Monty, who was always surprisingly honest when promoting anything, acknowledged to one interviewer that the addition of the celebrity guest was "bad for the studio audience." After a few weeks, the ratings were in for the nighttime episodes with celebrity guests; not only did it fail to generate any new interest in the show, but ratings were actually down for those episodes.

There were a few basic problems with having celebrities play Let's Make a Deal: #1, even knowing it was on behalf of someone else, watching the rich and famous win prizes isn't much fun. #2, the satisfying reaction of a contestant winning a big prize was lost in the celebrity segments because the person winning the prize wasn't actually there. #3, amidst a sea of hopeful audience members in costumes, the celebrities wore nice suits and dresses, making it look as if the very show they were appearing on was beneath them. The celebrity experiment ended after eight episodes.

Another change was significantly better received. The Big Deal of the Day was now followed by The Super Deal. A contestant who won the Big Deal of the Day was offered a shot at $20,000 in exchange for forfeiting the Big Deal. If they did so, they'd be shown three mini-doors, all hiding cash prizes, as low as $1,000 or as high as $20,000. If they picked the $20,000 door, they won the money and the Big Deal was returned to them. A successful contestant could come away from the Super Deal with about $30,000 worth of loot.

A change to the daytime version proved to be the unexpected undoing of the show. In September 1975, The Price is Right commemorated their third anniversary on CBS with a special week of one-hour episodes. The stunt worked so well that two months later, the one-hour format became permanent, giving ABC and NBC a new Jones to keep up with. NBC briefly tried hour-long Hollywood Squares and hour-long Wheel of Fortune, without much luck.

On the other hand, ABC looked like they might have a victory in this battle. They had a game somewhat similar to The Price is Right that looked perfect for a week of one-hour shows. The network announced in November 1975 that for one week at the end of that month, Let's Make a Deal would be an hour-long show.

As it happened, two months earlier, Monty had shrugged off the idea of ever doing a one-hour version of any game show, telling a reporter that the idea of doing so was draining, and that a 21-year-old kid with more energy could try a one-hour version of Let's Make a Deal if Monty ever walked away from the job.

What changed Monty's mind only two months later? Well…nothing, really. ABC foisted the hour-long episodes onto him as a direct order. To Monty's aggravation, they only gave him two weeks' notice. With time to brainstorm and workshop ideas, the Goodson-Todman staff had altered The Price is Right in a way that gave the hour-long format for that show more of a reason for existing. Their show was now a mini-tournament between six players, whittled down to two with a new addition called the Showcase Showdown, where the spin of a wheel determined who would go to the Showcase at the end of the hour. The Showcase Showdown was also different enough from everything else seen in the hour that it felt like a change of pace, a breather to take between the bombardment of bids and price-guessing games during the rest of the hour.

With only two weeks until taping, ABC hadn't given Monty and his staff a chance to flesh out any ideas for what to do other than deal after deal after deal. Hour-long Let's Make a Deal was just more Let's Make a Deal.

A raw deal. Monty was unhappy with having one-hour episodes thrust upon him by ABC executives. (Author's Collection)

HENRY KOVAL

Nobody was happy with the expanded episodes. Three acts and a Big Deal were enough for one day. Doing more than that was just too much.

MONTY HALL[lxxxi]

I never liked [the one-hour episodes]. Not that we weren't capable of doing an hour. I felt we were expanding the show just for the sake of expanding it. We didn't have enough time to prepare to do them right.

I told ABC, what if you don't stay with an hour? Then, the next week, we come right back with our regular format. How do we do that without looking like we're pulling back?

ABC, which had such big expectations for the special week, was furious when the ratings came in and found that the audience was actually lower for the hour-long episodes. Rather than dismiss it as an experiment that didn't work, ABC made a move that Monty perceived as a punishment.

The network moved it into a new time slot, noon eastern. With more and more network affiliates electing to air local newscasts at noon, the noon timeslot was becoming toxic for any show unlucky to occupy it. Let's Make a Deal had survived time slot switches before, but not this one. Less than nine months after the hour-long programs, Let's Make a Deal was cancelled, airing its 3,125th and final daytime episode on July 9, 1976. The series ended its ABC run with a smile—the final episode included clips from the pilot episode shot for NBC 13 years earlier, plus a special tribute to Jay Stewart, Carol Merrill, and 12 members of the production staff, all of whom had been with the show since the December 16, 1963 taping.

Behind the scenes, Monty was hurt. Yes, the show had enjoyed more than 12 years on the air, but he felt he deserved, and his show deserved, a better fate than it had met in that final year.

MONTY HALL[lxxxii]

[ABC] changed our time period…from 1:30 p.m., where it was every day, to 12 Noon, which was station-option time, and many stations carried their own show in that period. So instead of having 100% coverage, we went back to eighty percent coverage.

This gentleman, who was head of the network, said, "Well, you've gone down twenty percent. We're gonna cancel you."

I flew to New York with my attorney and called for a meeting with the network. I said, "How can you make an argument that we've gone down twenty percent in our ratings when you took twenty percent of our audience away from us? Of course we lose twenty percent! What's the justification for that?"

All the people around the room are sitting, hiding their heads in shame. Then they started arguments of another sort. "Uh, well, we gave you a deal to make a pilot of a comedy show, and then you sold it to NBC!"—which I did, I owned it…. It was called *The Prime of Life*.

I said, "Gentlemen, you had first call on that show. That's in my contract. You turned it down! Then I sold it to NBC."

Heads hang in shame again. Every argument they brought up, I turned it on them. When we came out of the room, my lawyer said to me, "Well, you won every battle, but you lost the war. You weren't going to win."

I said, "I knew I wasn't going to win when I got here, but I needed my satisfaction."

This gentleman says in embarrassment, "Well, we paid you a lot of money…"

I said, "Well, you came from the other network to this network. I hope they paid a lot of money to bring you here too."

He says to me, "Well, *Let's Make a Deal* has had its run now. Why don't you make three pilots of three new ideas of yours, and we'll select one of them to replace you in the fall."

I go back to Los Angeles, I make three pilots, I go off to London for an international meeting of the Variety Club. I pick up *Variety*. I read it on the plane, I see the fall schedule, I'm not on it. He didn't pick one of the three shows.

So I came back and I called his assistant. I said, "What happened?"

He said, "He didn't even look at the pilots."

These are the heartbreaks of the business. These things do happen…It's a betrayal of trust. And betrayal happens in this business.

Fare thee well. Monty signs off from the ABC version of *Let's Make a Deal* in 1976. (Hall Family Archive)

(Author's Collection)

CHAPTER TWENTY-ONE

After 12 years on the air with Let's Make a Deal, *Monty found it difficult to find time for mourning the end of the daytime version. When the ABC series met its demise, Monty was in the middle of preparing* Monty Hall's Variety Hour, *a network summer special that he hoped would lead to a full-time series. Monty was joined by comedians Andy Kaufman and Gallagher, singer Minnie Ripperton, mime team Shields & Yarnell, and actors Ed Asner & Cloris Leachman. Monty himself sang and had a panel discussion with a group of kids.*

Monty also wasn't all that broken up about the demise of daytime Deal *because he didn't see it as an ending. The stations carrying the nighttime version had signed up for the 1976-77 season, so he still had a few months of deal-making ahead of him. And because he had already squeezed over a decade out of the format, with strong ratings for most of that run, Monty figured that "cancellation" wasn't an apt term. It was more likely just going to be a long break.*

MONTY HALL[lxxxiii]
We'll rest it for a year, and then bring it back with a new set, a new look, and some new variations on the game. Plus a new host—after punishing myself for twelve and a half years, I'm ready to bow out.

Convinced that the twice-a-week offering for the nighttime show had done more harm than good, Monty scaled back to once a week, offering stations only 32 episodes for the entire season. To convince them that less was more, Monty did something he had been resisting for a few years: he went back to Las Vegas. The iconic three doors and curtains would be placed in the showroom of the Las Vegas Hilton for every episode of the 1976-77 season.

That meant having to uproot and entire set for a four-hour truck drive, working out contracts for a showroom in Las Vegas, re-selling another season into a bloated marketplace—there were only so many 7:30 pm time slots to fill on so many TV stations in a five-channel landscape—of a show that hadn't really recovered from a 1975-76 season that did a surprising amount of damage to the franchise. It was diminishing returns. Monty felt like the need for more, more, more, was slowly choking away at TV game shows.

The final *Deal*, taped in Las Vegas, must have called for a really big bottle of champagne at the wrap party. (Hall Family Archive)

MONTY HALL[lxxxiv]

What we had for these fourteen years was good, plain fun. The audience was all cranked up for a contestant who maybe was trying to win $300. They were all made to feel the spirit of the game. Today's new shows are flashing lights and gadgetry. There's nothing in the body of the show to intrigue.

What they've got is giveaways to the tune of $25,000, $50,000, and $128,000. Money is the message. What happened to the cleverness of the game? I'd love someone to just hold up his hand and say "Enough is enough. Go back to where you were and be clever with your shows."

CAROL MERRILL

We taped 32 episodes in Las Vegas. What I'll always remember about that season was my dressing room. I loved it. It was so enormous I could have played tennis in it.

Normally in that era, a syndicated show would tape episodes, mail them out to local stations along with a list of other stations that aired the show. The local station would air the show and mail it to the next station on the list—a process known in the TV business as "bicycling." This meant that a show finished taping the season months before there was enough ratings info to judge whether or not a show would be renewed for another season, or if it was even worth the effort of trying to sell it. Monty, sensing the show was winding down anyway, simply decided to beat everyone to the punch and shut down his own show. He made it known that the December 29, 1976 taping of Let's Make a Deal *would be the last…for now.*

MONTY HALL[lxxxv]

The last few years, it was very, very tough to do the show. It became very repetitive. I found it difficult to find new ways of expressing the same things. How many different ways can you ad-lib around a chicken or a soup can or a crazy sign? One day when we were doing the show in Las Vegas, I heard myself doing an ad-lib I had used not once, not twice, but three or four times before.

I came offstage and told my staff, "Today's the day I have to stop."

I had promised myself when I got to that point, I would call it quits.

CAROL MERRILL

You know what's funny? I don't remember being told that the show was cancelled. I don't remember anyone breaking the news to me when the ABC version was cancelled.

I don't remember anyone telling me when the nighttime show was ending. You'd think that would be so upsetting that I'd remember it forever. I can't remember ever being told.

At the time we taped those last episodes, I felt fine. I didn't really feel any emotion. It was just another day, another show. A few years later, I was a guest on *Donahue*. The subject was "Second Bananas," I was there with Ed McMahon and Willard Scott. Phil Donahue asked me how I felt when I learned the show was ending, and all of a sudden, the emotion hit me and my voice started quivering. After all those years, that was the moment that it really hit me that the show was over. It was just out of nowhere.

HENRY KOVAL

I really loved those years. Nobody was ever stabbed in the back at *Let's Make a Deal*. We were a family, and we loved each other a lot.

The final episode didn't have any explicit acknowledgment that it was the final episode—the bicycling method meant that episodes usually didn't air in the same order from one station to another, so it wouldn't have made sense to mention it—but the show managed to subtly acknowledge that this episode was different from all the others by giving Zonks the night off. The deals were all set up so that there was no way to lose.

The staff had a small party and Monty gave quotes to the press that he'd regret quickly, because most of them made it sound like the show was going away forever and that Monty was retiring to Hawaii and leaving show business. The truth was, Monty was already looking ahead to pitching a new version of the show, and that he was looking forward to having a blank schedule for a few months upcoming; he had been fantasizing about being on a beach with Marilyn and telling her on a lark that they should stay an extra week.

Monty, that night, felt a sense of closure. In a realm where jobs are on the line every thirteen weeks, he created something that lasted for thirteen years. He had made himself wealthy, and done so in such a visible, iconic fashion that he had a reputation that he could borrow from indefinitely for future work, future fortune, and future fundraising.

Jay Stewart, on the other hand, fell apart.

JAY STEWART[lxxxvi]

When [*Let's Make a Deal*] went off, it was worse than getting a divorce—it was really just like a death in the family. We had all been so close that I was simply at a loss.

I was worried. There was my salary. After fourteen and a half years, it had gone up a lot, and I knew that whatever job I got next, it would have to be much lower.

**The best years of his life. Jay Stewart had a hard time saying goodbye.
(Hall Family Archive)**

Jay had once done some math and figured out that he spent more time with Monty than he had spent with his own family. Without Let's Make a Deal, *Jay reflected later, he felt that something was wrong with his life. He asked his wife for a separation.*

JAY STEWART[lxxxvii]

The first month, I enjoyed it—the second month I was miserable. The third month, we started talking about it. And the fourth month, we got together again and things have never been better between us.

But even with things patched up between the Stewarts, Jay still felt depressed and searched for some repair to make. Jay went to a church, poured his heart out to an associate pastor, and found a sense of peace when he was done. He declared himself a born-again Christian, and although he wanted to keep his religion private and didn't wish to preach about what he had been through, he felt that the experience had been a breakthrough for him, and his devotion to his church, and the guidance he felt he received from it, somewhat mirrored his friend Monty's dedication to Judaism.

In time, Jay found work again. He was able to do voiceovers for TV commercials, something that had actually been off-limits to him for years because of Let's Make a Deal; a car company brought Jay in to record commercials for them, but then chose never to use them because they felt Jay's voice was too recognizable from Let's Make a Deal, a show on which he had often read fawning prize copy for multiple competitors, and so Jay's presence in a commercial was considered a conflict of interest. With the show no longer on the air, advertisers started calling again, giving Jay and his wife money to live on while his Let's Make a Deal money could sit in the bank.

Monty, on the other hand, was so busy that, going into 1977, he had to put off the vacation to the beach he'd been dreaming about, because he had committed to three Variety Club Telethons—Los Angeles in January, Philadelphia in February, and St. Louis in March.

BOB BODEN

I was actually a cue card boy for a Variety Club telethon that Monty hosted. Didn't interact with him a lot, but he was so nice to everyone around him—the talent, the crew, the staff. Every interaction I had or that I witnessed with him was first-class, menschy, respectful. He was a class act from morning until night. I never saw him be arbitrary or raise his voice with anyone. I never saw him mistreat anybody at any level. He had a great heart, he cared about people, and he understood the right way to manage people was to respect them and trust them. When you show people respect and trust, they give you the support you need for your role.

ROBERT HALL (2019)

Monty's devotion to charitable causes was amazing. He never charged massive fees for anything he did on behalf of a charity, and there aren't that many celebrities that can say that, sadly. Charities will sometimes boast that their fundraiser will include an appearance by some big star and what they aren't telling you is they paid $50,000 for that star to show up. Monty only charged expenses. If the charity could cover his airfare and his hotel room, he'd be there.

Monty also started 1977 as executive producer of a prime-time sitcom. Originally a pilot titled The Prime of Life starring William Windom, the show was recast and retitled. The McLean Stevenson Show would go on the air in December 1976. Stevenson had left M*A*S*H in 1975 after three seasons, with his character, Colonel Henry Blake, written out via a helicopter crash. Stevenson, a quick-witted deadpan humorist who had become a favorite guest of Johnny Carson, seemingly had unlimited career prospects. The McLean Stevenson Show had a murky *premise*—Stevenson was the owner of a hardware store who lived with his wife, mother-in-law, two grown children, and three grandchildren (Stevenson was a rather youthful-looking 49 at the time the series started).

Mark Evanier, who co-wrote the first aired episode, later wrote on his blog, "Even before this one went on the air, the network was unhappy with it, the producers were unhappy with it...and Mr. Stevenson was wishing he really had been in that helicopter that got shot down on the way home from Korea.

"Several episodes were taped and everyone involved knew the thing wasn't working so new producers and writers were brought in...But then they all had different ideas about how to fix the show anyway. One that I heard and liked was that they should ditch the whole premise of the home life of a guy who ran a hardware store and just videotape the meetings where McLean and Monty yelled at each other over which of them knew more about comedy."

Long before an episode was on the air, viewers could sense that something wasn't right. On May 21, 1976, McLean Stevenson was a guest on The Tonight Show Starring Johnny Carson. Johnny introduced him as the star of a new series that "will begin rehearsals on May 29, and will premiere when they decide to air it. There's apparently no date set for it."

Stevenson told Carson that rehearsals weren't starting until July 21 and that "between now and July 21, we hope to figure out what the show's about." Carson needled Stevenson, saying it felt like the show had been in development for years.

MONTY HALL[lxxxviii]

McLean Stevenson was very hard to work with. And he was hard to work with on *M*A*S*H*, Larry Gelbart told me. I used William Windom in the pilot...John McMahon at NBC called me and said, "Monty, we have a contract with McLean Stevenson. You use McLean Stevenson, you got a deal." It was sad for me to call William Windom and tell him, "I gotta sell the show, Will. And you can have friendship and admiration, but I gotta sell the show. So, I gotta take McLean Stevenson." Which turned out to be a big mistake. McLean changed every script. McLean changed every person, every character in the pilot, fired them all. And he wanted all the laughs. The secret of sitcoms is you have to have an ensemble. Ensemble. *Cheers. Taxi. Seinfeld.* Jerry Seinfeld made umpteen zillion dollars because he let the other three people be stars. McLean didn't want anybody else to have a laugh. You cannot be successful with 30 minutes of you.

Monty was also annoyed because he wanted to use his daughter, Joanna, for a role on the show, and despite being the executive producer, he was overruled, told repeatedly that she was wrong for the part.

Critics hated the show, although they seemed relieved that Monty Hall was in charge of it because it made writing their review so easy. "The executive producer...is game show impresario Monty Hall, in his first comedy effort. That should tell you something," one grumbled. Another writer speculated that a guest star in a future episode would be a man dressed as a rutabaga...then presumably stepped away from his typewriter to smile at himself in the mirror for coming up with such a brilliant bon mot. The McLean Stevenson Show *ended after only ten episodes aired. Monty moved on from the fiasco and spent part of the next two years trying to do something for himself. He satisfied his need to try dramatic acting by playing the role of an Air Force general in a TV movie. With the grueling schedule of* Let's Make a Deal *no longer interfering with Monty's evenings, he finally made himself available for a summer stock production, playing the role of Harrison Floy in* High Button Shoes *at Melody Top Theater in Milwaukee. The chance to act in a musical excited Monty so much that he turned down an offer from the Sahara Hotel & Casino in Las Vegas at the same time.*

MONTY HALL[lxxxix]

[It was] the one and only movie I made for television. *The Courage and the Passion.* How do you like that? A guy who never got higher than sergeant in the army and I played a general. It was a pilot made for Vince Edwards and Don Meredith, and myself. *High Button Shoes* was great because I did musical comedy...and I lost 20 pounds. It had eighteen scenes and I was in sixteen of them, running around, up and down the stairs, up and down the stairs, and I was in great shape. I enjoyed it but...you can't do all things. Television was still where you made your living.

Almost unrecognizable under the straw hat and glasses, that's Monty, fourth from right, taking a bow at the end of *High Button Shoes*.

For someone who had been itching to act on television for so long, Monty could be surprisingly picky about what roles he would take. A favorite plot of prime-time sitcoms was "Characters appear on game shows," and Monty repeatedly rejected every offer he got to play the game show host.

MONTY HALL[xc]

If I could tell you how many shows I've turned down playing Monty Hall…

"Is there a part for me? You're calling me. What is the role?"

"Well the role is of a game show MC."

I said, "Forget it."

I did a few as myself, but actually that was "Monty Hall's coming on the show," "Monty Hall's going to be here today," that kind of thing.

For what it's worth, Monty was also offered a wider variety of parts on TV shows. Surprisingly, Monty could be just as picky about those other parts, particularly if it was a role so undefined that the casting director really just needed to find any actor. Monty would reject any part if he sensed that it didn't really matter who played it.

MONTY HALL[xci]

It makes no sense for me to play a cowboy, or a sea captain. They wanted me to play one of the short roles on *Rich Man, Poor Man* but I turned that down, too. They were the kind of roles no one would rush to get, so why should I?

The Courage and the Passion *was an ambitious pilot that was supposed to lead to a weekly series called* Joshua Tree, *about the cadets and their leaders at an Air Force base. Had it come to fruition, it actually may have become a classic example of "Be careful what you wish for" for Monty. Monty Hall, who had itched to be taken seriously as a potential actor, who was finally getting his break in a high-profile project…and he hated it.*

MONTY HALL[xcii]

Movie acting didn't live up to my expectations. We were out in the desert standing around in the heat and sand, waiting and waiting. Then we'd do the same scene over 35 times. [Movies are] a director's medium. Movies don't allow much creativity for a performer. I discovered I like to perform for live audiences.

Being on stage was only slightly more gratifying. Monty was happy when he got that instant feedback from the audience right in front of him. And although there were weeks and weeks of rehearsal, you certainly didn't stand around and wait like you did on a movie set. There was instant gratification every night. But Monty came to the sobering realization that he was happy only when he was on that stage. His fantasies of life as a stage actor never considered what it would be like when he wasn't actually performing.

MONTY HALL[xciii]

I was really disappointed. No matter how well received you are, no matter how great the applause at the end of the performance, it still means living in a motel room on the road.

SHARON HALL (2019)

I think it was just physically hard on him. He was in his late fifties when he did his first production, and they performed the show in a large tent.

Monty was still trying to make a name for himself as a talk show host. A syndicated show hosted by Lorenzo Music (best known at the time for voicing the unseen doorman, Carlton, on Rhoda) *was abruptly cancelled, and Monty was offered the chance to host the remaining episodes to see if he could generate new interest in it. Monty declined the offer, feeling it was a no-win proposition. Four different television syndicates approached him in 1977 about hosting a talk show. It was another shot at a dream job, but always risk-averse, Monty asked the syndicates to reach out to local stations first and see if a Monty Hall talk show was something they would consider, and assemble a list of stations that said they'd at least be interested, if not fully committed to the idea. All four syndicates obliged, and all four syndicates delivered lists of stations that Monty found lacking. Dinah Shore, Mike Douglas, Merv Griffin, and Phil Donahue were occupying some valuable real estate on TV station schedules, and the stations weren't budging their schedules to risk a new offering from Monty Hall. Monty also conceded that the last four specials he had done under his ABC contract had done poor-to-lukewarm ratings, and he could understand the reluctance at the time. Monty was even willing to go so far as to promise that he wouldn't be the center of attention on the new show, he'd be, in his words, "a go-between" for the audience and the talent featured. But the promise didn't matter. The syndicates struggled to find interest in major cities that would be key for generating high ratings, and he simply decided it wasn't worth the risk to his reputation to host a talk show, as much as he wanted to, that would only last a few months before withering away. Monty again found himself declining his dream talk show. It was a decision that haunted him. He later called it the biggest mistake he ever made.*

Monty chats with actor Dennis Weaver. A full-time talk show gig never came to pass for Monty, and it was one of his great regrets. (Author's Collection)

ROBERT HALL (2019)

When Monty said he wanted to be a talk show host, a lot of people at the time probably assume he meant something like Johnny Carson. Monty didn't want to be Johnny. He liked Johnny. They knew each other. But that's not what Monty was going for. Monty had traveled the world, and his work with charity had introduced him to so many people. And Monty loved talking to people. He was interested in talking to foreigners, talking to politicians.

CAROL MERRILL

Monty wanted to sing and dance. I never saw that as a forte for him. But he would have been an outstanding talk show host. He had a delightful personality and a lot of charm, and I think a talk show would have been a great forum for him.

At the same time, he and Stefan Hatos were collaborating again. They had tried getting Let's Make a Deal *off the ground with a new host; from the day Monty shut down production on the syndicated version in Las Vegas, he had promised that the show would relaunch in the 1977-78 season with a new host. That proved easier said than done, for the same problem that reared itself before—networks and syndicates wanted Monty Hall. Buyers just weren't interested in* Let's

Make a Deal *with a player to be named, so Hatos-Hall Productions gave up on that plan. They did, however, give the buyers what they wanted by packaging episodes of the nighttime version and offering them for five-day-a-week reruns.*

What was Monty's next career move in 1977?
It's Anybody's Guess. **(Author's Collection)**

Stefan and Monty had devised another game show format that involved two contestants competing against each other in a game that involved five people pulled from a studio audience. NBC said they would buy the show, but only if Monty hosted. Monty had said numerous times at the end of Let's Make a Deal's run that he would never host another game show, but he quickly realized there were a few advantages to going back on the job. It would satisfy, as he called it, "the performer's urge." And although he wanted to get away from the hosting end of the game show business, he thought that putting himself in front of the camera as the master of ceremonies for another hit game would make him more lucrative to those stations resisting the talk show. Another hit would mean that station managers wouldn't look at Let's Make a Deal as a fluke. If Monty had another popular game show, he reasoned, station managers would assume that audiences gravitated toward anything he hosted. So, for now, Monty decided, another game show was fine.

It's Anybody's Guess *was, in a way, Monty Hall's answer to two recent hits from Goodson-*

Todman, Match Game *and* Family Feud. *Five audience members would be called to the stage at the start of the show and stood across the stage from two contestants who would compete against each other. Monty would ask a question, like "What's the first thing a guy does when he and his girlfriend park the car?" The contestants would be shown a secret answer, like "Turn on the radio," and had to predict whether or not any of the five audience members would give that answer. The show debuted on NBC in the summer of 1977.*

Without naming a competitor, Monty promoted the show with the promise that watching five audience members trying to match an answer would be a more entertaining show than watching celebrity panelists try to match an answer. Monty reasoned that putting witty celebrities on a stage and then watching them give witty answers could be fun, but that it lacked surprise. Of course they were giving funny answers! Monty felt it would be more fun to use a panel comprised of average people, because there was no anticipating how clever, or not clever, they might be, so when one of them came up with a smart answer, it would be more exciting.

Monty hosts the short-lived *It's Anybody's Guess.* **(Author's Collection)**

The show lent itself to surprising answers, as Monty anticipated. On one of the first shows taped, Monty's question was "Name a U.S. President that most people today know nothing about." The secret answer was Millard Fillmore. One of the audience members guessed Jimmy Carter, the incumbent commander-in-chief.

"He's been on television more than I have!" Monty blurted out in shock.

Another day, the question was "Name a celebrity that you think wears a toupee." The secret answer was Howard Cosell. An audience member looked the host right in the eye and answered "Monty Hall." Monty offered the audience member a rare chance to run his fingers through Monty's hair just to prove it was the real deal.

It's Anybody's Guess *was cancelled in the fall of 1977, with Monty later saying he found the show to be a confining fit for him.* "Uncomfortable," *he called it.*

STU BILLETT

I can tell you what he found confining about it. It wasn't a hit! When you host a new show, and you tape a few weeks of it, and you get the first week's ratings data, and you see the show's a bomb, suddenly, you start to feel pretty darn uncomfortable in that show. If *It's Anybody's Guess* had been a success, I'm sure Monty would never have said it was uncomfortable for him.

For the first time, things got quiet at Hatos-Hall Productions. The company stayed afloat by selling a Deal *reruns. But it seemed as though the band was breaking up.*

Carol Merrill more or less retired from modeling and opened a restaurant. Jay Stewart had signed on with a home gym company to be their national spokesman. The contract came with $10,000 worth of gym equipment for Jay to set up in his house and use regularly, to turn himself into a walking advertisement. Jay, combining the daily workout regimen with a liquid protein diet, dropped about sixty pounds, but he also dropped $30,000 building a new room onto his house to hold the equipment. Stu Billett, meanwhile, had developed a series for Hatos-Hall Productions in 1975 that they found intriguing, but after negotiations with the networks proved to be a non-starter, Hatos-Hall let their option on the format lapse, and Stu Billett resigned to try his fortunes elsewhere.

STU BILLETT

In 1975, Monty got a phone call from John Masterson, who had created a show called *Bride and Groom* some years earlier, and it had been very popular. John said he had an idea, and Monty had put me in charge of developing shows, so he told John, "See Stu Billett."

John came in for a meeting with me. That year, 1975, California had made it legal for cameras to be in a courtroom. John suggested we go to court houses, put cameras in the courtrooms, let the tape machines run, and then we just pick out the most interesting cases and air that. It would cost next to nothing to produce and he thought it would get big ratings.

I told Monty, "Let's make a deal with this guy to hold it for six months."

To get a sense of how much usable material there would be for a show like this, I decided to go to court every day for three weeks. I went to a courthouse and just observed cases. And like most people, my only real exposure to a court up to that point was what I saw on TV shows.

I sat in that courtroom for that first day…oh my god, that was the most boring day I've ever had in my life. I noticed the judge physically holding his eyelids open to stay awake during the hearings. The other problem, in terms of making for an interesting TV show, is "guilty beyond a reasonable doubt." What that term means, as far as the trial is concerned, is that a defense attorney spends an hour zeroing in on minute details and picking them apart one by one. It can be very complicated and very confusing at times. He'd use terminology that wasn't familiar to the average person. I couldn't figure out how to make this an interesting TV show that the audience could process in a 30-minute time slot.

Occasionally, something interesting would happen, but after about two weeks, I began to think this wasn't a workable concept for a TV show. Then I saw a door in the courthouse. "Small Claims Court."

What I learned immediately from sitting in there is that most small claims cases are very open and shut. Often, the defendant doesn't even show up. Just as often, a defendant will say, "No, I didn't pay this guy, because I didn't like him. Screw him." Well, you owe people money even if you don't like them, so as soon as a defendant says that, judge's gavel comes down and that case is finished.

I'll tell you the case that changed everything for me. This little old Jewish guy was the plaintiff. The defendant was a very well-dressed, slick-talking, swinging black kid. The defendant was selling eyeglasses on the street, with sequins on them. He had a permit to do that. The plaintiff asked if he could buy a pair for his wife. The defendant told him, "One pair is $10, or I can give you three for $25."

The plaintiff says, "I buy a pair for my wife, one for my sister Sybil, one for the lady in the apartment downstairs from us. I put the glasses in the bag I had with me, I went to the subway, and then I took a bus home. Then I called Sybil, and I called my downstairs neighbor and said I had presents for them. They come upstairs and I pull out the glasses, and there are no sprinkles on them"—I'll never forget that, all through the hearing, he kept calling the sequins "sprinkles." "There's no sprinkles on the glasses! The sprinkles are all gone!"

The defendant refused to give him a refund. The plaintiff showed him the inside of the bag, all the sequins had come off the glasses and gone to the bottom of the bag. The defendant still wouldn't give him a refund.

The defendant says, "Let me explain, my honor."

"Not MY honor, say 'YOUR honor.'"

"Your honor, let me explain. I made the deal with this guy, and I started wrapping them individually in separate bags. The guy said, 'No, no, I don't want three bags.' I tried to explain why I was wrapping them in three separate bags. He said he wouldn't pay for them unless I put them in the bag he already had. The customer's always right, so I put them in the one bag, and he went off. Now, your honor, would you please look at the plaintiff's hands?"

"Why should I look at his hands?"

"Just look at them."

The plaintiff holds up his arms, and his hands are flopping and flying all over the place. He had a nerve disorder, he couldn't hold the bag steadily. So he spent an hour walking around with this bag, with the glasses rattling in there, and his hands shook so bad that it knocked all the sequins off.

I just instantly realized, if we stay with small claims court, this show could work. I did the math in my head and figured, if we do two cases an episode, that's ten cases a week. 39 weeks is 390 cases. There's no way 390 cases will all be gold, you want to shoot enough that you can afford to throw out the boring ones, so I figured we needed 500 cases to shoot one season. I did the research and found out that in LA County, there were 75,000 cases pending for small claims court. This show was going to work.

I received incredible support when I began telling people in the legal system what I wanted to do.

A woman in San Francisco said, "People come here and they have no idea what the hell they're supposed to do. They don't know how to conduct themselves, how to present their cases...If there was a show on TV every day where people could see Small Claims Court, it would make this so much easier for us!"

I put together a presentation for the show. I was going to call it *Small Claims Court*. A number of systems at that time used the term "The People's Court" for their small claims courts, but I didn't want to use that as a title, because communists use "the people's" in a lot of their terminology, and I didn't want people to see a promo for *The People's Court* and yell, "What kind of damn commie show is this?"

Stefan and Monty gave me their blessing to pitch it on their behalf. They really were not involved in the discussions with the networks. The three networks not only said no, they used terms like "piece of shit," and told me it would ruin my career. An executive at NBC said, "This will tear down jurisprudence in America."

I wanted to go into syndication, five days a week, but Monty and Stefan wanted nothing to do with daily syndication. In those days, daily syndication was seen as bargain basement, lowest-of-the-low programming, and Monty and Steve felt they were above that and it would reflect poorly on the company if they did original programming for daily syndication.

Monty and Dinah Shore. Monty still wanted to be considered as an all-around performer, but show business thought of him as a master of ceremonies. (Author's Collection)

After *It's Anybody's Guess* was cancelled, I began looking at my options. I loved working for Monty and Stefan. Never had an unkind word. We had a great relationship. But it was to a point where the networks knew me as well as they knew Monty and Stefan, and I just decided it was time to see if I could make a go of Stu Billett Productions. Monty and Stefan let their right to *Small Claims Court* lapse, so I took that with me. I ended up joining forces with Ralph Edwards, who loved the word "People." He used it to describe his shows, like *This is Your Life*. He called them "people shows." He sold it in five-day-a-week syndication, because he didn't think of it as being beneath him. And we made a lot of money.

I don't know if that was a sore spot with Monty. To be very clear, everything I did was on the level and ethical. Hatos-Hall had a chance to put that show on the air. They had so many years to do it. They didn't. I was within my right to take it somewhere else after that, and so I did. I think Monty was fine with it—it's easier to move on from something like that when you've already made a fortune from the things you got on the air, so I'm sure deep down it didn't bother Monty at all. We never talked about it, though. But Monty Hall's name could have been on *The People's Court*.

Monty, meanwhile, signed a contract with CBS offering his services as a performer—and only as a performer. After years of toiling behind the scenes to mount talk shows, situation comedies, and game show formats as a producer, Monty was now contracted to offer only Monty Hall and nothing more. It was a juicy contract too, because there was low pressure. Because he hadn't signed as a producer, there was no pressure to create or reinvent anything. He was paid each week by the network whether he performed or not (though to the network's chagrin, it was usually "or not"—they hadn't found a spot for him yet). Best of all for Monty, the contract came with a pledge from the network that he only had to work during daytime hours. He would never be asked by CBS to tape a show after dark. Monty wanted to make sure those hours were open so he could attend fundraisers.

MONTY HALL[xciv]

Because if you're a member of that society, you've got to participate in that society. You've gotta work, you've gotta give, and if you have talent on top of that, you've gotta perform.

The CBS contract didn't bear fruit for some time. But when CBS called Monty and said they were finally ready to utilize his services, the able host probably wished he hadn't picked up the phone. Of all jobs, he had been asked to host a new game show for Mark Goodson-Bill Todman Productions, a company with which Monty had endured a strange relationship with for so many years. They had been competitors. Monty felt that one of their most famous successes had been an idea that they stole from him. Yet the Goodson-Todman staff cheerfully invited Monty again and again to appear on their programs as a way to promote his own endeavors, and Goodson himself had never been anything but complimentary toward Monty when asked about him by interviewers.

The All-New Beat the Clock, **one of Monty's least-liked gigs. (Author's Collection)**

The 1970s had been an extraordinary decade for Goodson-Todman, which raked in big audiences and big revenue with what was, at the time, an unconventional business model: taking formats that had already succeeded, reinvent them thoroughly, and put them back on the air. The Match Game, *a fairly quiet team game from the 1960s, was* transformed into a raucous comedy game with a star-packed panel. The Price is Right, *a straightforward show in which contestants placed bids on prizes in a format that looked like little more than an auction, became a sprawling series of games-within-a-game.* Goodson-Todman was now turning its attention to one of its earliest TV hits, Beat the Clock. *The original TV incarnation premiered in 1950 with host Bud Collyer and enjoyed 11 years on CBS and ABC. It was a zany game in which married couples were given a task to complete before the time on the clock expired. The stunts typically involved props like fragile cups & saucers, gobs and gobs of Reddi-Whip, or imaginative custom-made items like a human-sized grocery bag for the challenges that the players had to meet and beat. The show returned in 1969 in first-run syndication with Jack Narz, and then Gene Wood at the helm, and lasted another five years.*

In 1979, CBS was still paying Monty for his talents as an on-air performer without ever finding a job for him. CBS, in search of a return on investment, called Mark Goodson-Bill Todman Productions and asked for a revival of Beat the Clock, *virtually guaranteeing that the show would go into production so long as the company agreed to let Monty host. Monty, under contract to CBS, couldn't refuse the job, though he certainly wished he could. The show's former host, Jack Narz, was hired to be the show's announcer, as well as working behind the scenes as a producer.*

DAVID NARZ, stunt coordinator for *Beat the Clock* **and son of Jack Narz**
I was at CBS Television City one day doing a walk-on part on *Archie Bunker's Place*. And during a break, my dad walks into the studio and says "Goodson-Todman and CBS are bringing back *Beat the Clock* and I'm going to be involved. Do you want a job?"

I worked with Mark Bowerman in what they called "stunt factory." We'd think up ideas for the show and then get out the tools and attach cups to the tops of helmets or whatever the idea needed, and test it.

My dad and Monty had an interesting past and Monty would acknowledge it with an inside joke sometimes. He'd talk with interviewers about his career and say, "Thank God for Jack's wife." And sometimes he'd say that to the audience during tapings of *Beat the Clock*. He'd say "Folks, how about it for our announcer, Jack Narz? Thank God for Jack's wife." And he'd never explain what he meant by that.

My dad was the first host of *Video Village*. And he quit the show because he was trying to patch up his marriage to my mother at the time, which led to Monty being hired for *Video Village*, which was his first big success on television.

Goodson-Todman was still workshopping the format when the series was announced, and as a result, early publicity didn't match the finished product at all. The format initially touted *in press releases was that three teams of three players, all of whom had something in common (all stewardesses, all blondes, all poker players, etc.) would compete in a series of stunts for an entire week, with each day's episode ending with something called the Record Breaking Stunt. Once the show made it on the air, it was a daily competition between two couples, with money awarded for each clock beaten. The score determined the number of discs each couple was given for the Bonus Shuffle, a tabletop shuffleboard marked with cash awards; the object was to have one of your discs settle on a larger cash amount than your opponents, while also trying to knock your opponents' discs off the board. The winner of the Bonus Shuffle played a Bonus Stunt that could pay off between $3,000–$10,000 (depending on where the discs had landed). Overseeing all of the action was Monty Hall. And Monty hated it.*

MONTY HALL[xcv]
I hated it with all my heart. The people were asked to do stupid stunts and so on. I just didn't care for it. I'm so glad it wasn't successful.

DAVID NARZ
We had a lot of stunts that involved food, like bagels or eggs. And I remember Monty looking around during the stopdowns and grumbling, "This is so wasteful." Or he'd look at things that had to be custom-built for the game and he'd say, "What a waste of money."

Monty's performance on the show was rather snarky. Monty would say things like "Well, when you blew on the straw, it landed on that part of the stage, how are you supposed to do anything with that?" Or he'd say, "I knew when I saw this in rehearsal that you wouldn't be able to do it."

Beat the Clock *with Monty Hall premiered on CBS on September 17, 1979. It bombed so hard that after only seven weeks, it was relaunched as* The All-New All-Star Beat the Clock. *The audience was divided into red and green sections, with teams of celebrities competing against each other, and the prize money being split among the members of their designated section of the audience. Not only did this not win over viewers, but the show had a shockingly difficult time filling the seats in the audience for tapings. Even with the prospect of winning money just for sitting and watching, people just didn't want to sit through* The All-New All-Star Beat the Clock. *It left the airwaves on February 1, 1980.*

DAVID NARZ

Monty really didn't like the show, and I think the audience picked up on that. And as the show struggled in the ratings, I remember my dad being really frustrated and saying, "Let ME host it!" Because my dad had already hosted it for three years and he just loved it. He was so into it. But CBS had this contract with Monty, and Monty was pretty much bound to be the host of the show.

Also, the game as we presented it was unwieldy. We had the stunts. It was *Beat the Clock*, of course we had the stunts. And then all of a sudden on every episode, we bring out this shuffleboard table and we play a game of shuffleboard to determine the winners of the game. It was completely detached from everything else on the show. It didn't make sense.

And then they tried relaunching it with celebrities playing the game. Celebrities are like any other people—some of them are comfortable doing silly stunts. Some of them aren't. And the ones who aren't end up doing the show because they need a gig, they need exposure. So, we had some weeks where we already had a host who wasn't that fond of the show, playing the game with some celebrities who didn't want to be there.

I remember a taping of *All-Star Beat the Clock* where the celebrities were behind the curtain waiting to be introduced. One of them was an actress that I won't identify. But she was there because her agent booked her on the show. And I remember she just looked at me and said, "Tell me who I need to talk to and what I have to do with him in order to get out of doing this show."

Monty Hall assessed his career in 1980, what he had done and what he wanted to do. And as 1980 went on, Monty was shocked to realize that the job that made him the happiest was a job that he had spent years trying to escape. When a Canadian production company reached out to him later that year about mounting a new version of Let's Make a Deal *with himself returning as host, Monty surprised even himself by jumping at the opportunity.*

MONTY HALL[xcvi]

After 13 years and 3,800 shows, I was exhausted from the long hours and physical demands of the show. I was also determined to do other things in show business that I had wanted to do. So, I tried some other things and discovered that none of them really satisfied me.

I toured in a musical comedy—and discovered I didn't like being constantly on the road and away from my family. I acted in…a movie made for television. And I was bored sitting around doing nothing most of the day. I hosted two other game shows and felt very uncomfortable on both. None of those ventures provided me with the kind of action and opportunity to ad-lib that I so enjoy.

I finally realized that I had never stopped loving *Let's Make a Deal*. As the host, I am unrestricted in creating situations and dialogue. Three years ago, I was too exhausted to think straight. Now, I'm rested, relaxed, and happy to be on the trading floor again.

(Author's Collection)

CHAPTER TWENTY-TWO

MONTY HALL[xcvii]
We're syndicated and going on the air in 75 stations in the United States and Canada. We're taping the show in a beautiful mountain studio in Vancouver. The show is just like it was in Hollywood, the contestants are just as uninhibited up there as they were down here. It's great to be doing *Let's Make a Deal* again.

IAN MACLELLAN, former president of Catalena Productions
I had started with industrial films, sales & marketing films, and motivational films with people like Douglas Edwards and Norman Vincent Peale. And then in 1977 or 1978, a TV station in Edmonton, Alberta approached us because they were quite successful in what they were doing, and they wanted to mount a TV show with a comic named Stan Kann, who did a lot of talk shows in the 1960s and 1970s, where he did bits about his newest inventions. Also, as a hobby, he had a large collection of vacuum cleaners, and he became popular for these surprisingly entertaining segments where he talked at length about the history of the vacuum cleaners that he owned. We got the show mounted and distributed, and it did quite well, and the business started to grow.

Catalena Productions operated a complex called Panorama Studios, built right on the side of Hollyburn Mountain in Vancouver. Because it had been built with feature films in mind, it was sprawling facility that could accommodate an enormous studio audience, much like Deal *had during its first years at NBC. Catalena reached out to Stefan Hatos-Monty Hall Productions to produce a single 200-episode season of* Let's Make a Deal, *with an option at the end of that season to do three more.*

IAN MACLELLAN

Monty was thrilled about doing the new show. He was very excited about it. There was never any discussion of another host. Monty wanted to do it himself. I mean, anybody who's a TV performer wants a TV show. If you're not on the air, you're nothing. You're out of business.

For our end of things, a new version of *Let's Make a Deal* seemed like a brilliant idea. First of all, there was no need to shoot a pilot. They had tapes of thousands of episodes and executives knew the show. There was nothing to demonstrate. So, a pilot was an expense that we could skip. Second, we already had a distributor lined up to help us there. We didn't need to worry about that.

Third, Monty was from Canada, and that was well-known throughout Canada. He was a favorite son, so we knew it would be a success throughout Canada. And if we did a season in Canada and got good ratings, we could easily go to stations in the USA for season two and say, "Here's a show that was already a success for more than a decade in America, and the new version is already a success in Canada." And then we'd have a success in two countries.

I only oversaw the company. I let the staffs run the shows themselves. Stefan Hatos, I'll never forget. If George C. Scott hadn't played General Patton, Stefan Hatos could have won that Oscar. Stefan was an old military veteran and a commander. He ran that show.

There's a quote that I'll always remember from him: "I only want to hear one voice, that's my voice, and everybody listens to it!"

You didn't cross Stefan Hatos.

Carol Merrill and Jay Stewart were not involved in the Canadian version of Deal. Monty never gave either of them a reason, and Carol Merrill, for her part, was worried about some transgression she had committed without realizing it. It wasn't until years later that she learned about Canadian Content rules, which are regulations for shows that are aired in the United States but are produced in Canada. One of the regulations is that you need a certain number of Canadian-born performers as your on-air talent. Monty's Canadian, of course, so it was okay for him to host the show. But it's likely that he was asked to replace Americans Stewart and Merrill with native talent.

Catalena Productions found Monty a Canadian announcer named Chuck Chandler to take over the tray-carrying duties. Two models, Julie Hall (no relation) and Maggie Brown, stood in for Carol Merrill.

Stefan Hatos was the man in charge behind the scenes. (Hall Family Archive)

MARK MAXWELL-SMITH, game show producer

I was in Canada on business and I was watching TV in the hotel. I turned on that Canadian version of *Let's Make a Deal*. I spotted something that Monty was doing. I guess the crew was still getting used to doing the show, and I noticed Monty was working stage directions into things he said. They were clearly instructions for the cameramen and for the people moving the prizes into place, but he was phrasing them so that it came off as him just having a chat with the contestants and the audience. I thought that was genius.

Although Let's Make a Deal *proceeded business-as-usual on taping days, Monty and Stefan Hatos were slowly starting to realize that something was wrong in Catalena. The company's outreach to Hatos-Hall Productions had been part of an ambitious effort to brand the company as "the Hollywood of the North." They had been reaching out to American producers and performers about coming to Canada to launch shows that would be sold in both countries. It seemed too good to be true for the American business partners who came on board. Increased revenues from doing business concurrently in two countries; an amazing studio complex that had everything you needed and more to produce the show; and the Canadian dollar at the time could potentially shave about 20% off the expenses of the shows, with Catalena Productions partnering with the production company for each show to share those expenses, as well as the subsequent profits. In*

1980, Catalena was able to start production on three new shows: Deal, *another game show called* Pitfall, *and an extravagant variety show,* This is Tom Jones.

But ambition turned to panic as production costs for all three shows began to add up. This is Tom Jones *was contracted for 24 episodes, but the first 12 episodes amassed expenses totaling $4 million and only bringing in about $3 million in revenue.*

IAN MACLELLAN

There was another thing that went wrong for us right as the shows were starting production. Canada was going through a recession. A really bad one. And when you start off with lines of credit and an 8% interest rate, and in less than a year it jumps to a 22% interest rate, it creates a very difficult situation. It put the squeeze on us and it had to be wound down. We finished production on the shows, we got them distributed, so the stations that committed to them could air them, but after that, we were done.

New announcer Chuck Chandler helps Monty with the dealing on the new Canadian version of the old favorite series. (Author's collection)

As the 1980–81 season went along, Hatos-Hall Productions began seeing less and less of the money they were contracted for. And then no money at all. The company was also horrified to learn that several contestants hadn't received any of their prizes yet, well after their episodes had aired. For years, most game shows operated under a policy of paying off contestants with a deadline of 90 days after their game aired.

Not only were contestants getting nothing; in some cases, they were coming out of the experience at a loss. *A married couple won a trip to Mexico and $500 worth of luggage. They got their prizes, but they were surprised a few weeks later when Catalena Productions reached out to them about paying the $50 duty on the luggage. They did so under the impression that they'd be reimbursed.*

Unfortunately for them, Hatos-Hall Productions, unaware that contestants had been billed for their prizes, was, at the same time, confronting Catalena Productions about the money the company were owed. On August 31, 1981, Stefan Hatos-Monty Hall Productions filed a claim under the Bankruptcy Act in Canada.

The other game show, Pitfall, *subsequently shut down production, and that show's host, Alex Trebek, framed his bounced paycheck as a memento from the experience. Tom Jones' show didn't bother taping the remaining 12 episodes of its commitment. An ad was taken out in the* Los Angeles Times *offering a 35-foot color television mobile trailer unit, four cameras, three video tape recording units, an intercom system, complete remote production equipment, a diesel generator, lights, microphones, seats, and cables. Bankruptcy proceedings revealed that Hatos-Hall was owed about $210,000.*

IAN MCLELLAN

Believe it or not, there was good news in all of this. By the time we shut down, we had produced 454 episodes of different shows. And what that did was, it created an infrastructure. When I say "infrastructure," I mean crews. It doesn't matter if you have access to great producers and actors and writers. You can't make television shows without people who know how to do the technical end; the lighting, the audio, the cameras.

The result of that was people began looking at Vancouver as a viable location for film and television production. Even though we had gone out of business, it was now known that Vancouver had experienced technicians who could do those kinds of productions. And interest in Vancouver really expanded.

Unfortunately, we were the pioneers in Vancouver TV production, and the old saying really applies: "Pioneers get arrows in the back, the settlers get to eat the crops."

Meanwhile, in California, Monty had to deal with some pressing business when he was unexpectedly notified that he might become Secretary of State in the event of an emergency. March Fong Eu, California's incumbent Secretary of State since 1974, was asked to submit to state senators a list of six possible successors to her office in the event that she died unexpectedly. Monty was surprised to learn that the state senate had received his name for consideration and approved him. He hastily drafted a letter explaining that he was still technically a Canadian citizen and he couldn't take the oath of office.

ROBERT HALL (2019)

My brother eventually got his American citizenship. He waited a long time to do it, but when he finally did it, it was because he felt uncomfortable discussing political issues with people. How do you hold up your end of the debate if you're not directly involved in it? How do you discuss one side of a Republican vs. Democrat issue? He became an American citizen because he felt that gave him more of a right to talk about those issues.

Political office wouldn't have interested Monty, though. He found satisfaction in a public service of another sort. Hahnemann University Hospital in Philadelphia named their children's wing after him to honor the help that they had received from the Variety Club. Monty railed against such honors bestowed on people who had only signed a check or agreed to let their name be attached to it. Monty had really gone to work for Variety Club, and he was happy to be recognized for the effort. Monty gladly added that honor to the Monty Hall wings at UCLA Medical Center and Johns Hopkins Hospital.

In the early 1980s, America was gripped in a recession and Monty was thrilled, though really not surprised, by the results. Although lavish black-tie gala dinners might have struck outsiders as needlessly extravagant, Monty felt that they delivered results that could never be matched by dollars dropped into jars.

MONTY HALL

What's happening just proves my theory that when the economic pinch comes, the privileged class spends more lavishly than ever. You get the feeling there are a lot of people who want to spend—when they can spend big. Organizations like the Salvation Army that depend on the masses are supposed to be feeling the pinch. But charities that are staging fancy, black-tie events are doing spectacularly.

Monty's setback with the revival of Let's Make a Deal *coincided with Marilyn relaunching her own career with gusto. Once she and Monty started their family, Marilyn left acting behind and focused on raising her children. She and Monty never collaborated on any major projects together—early in their relationship, they had tried writing scripts together, but found that creatively, they didn't mesh well. As the children got older, Marilyn began taking small steps forward, like her episode of* Love American Style, *and taking to her typewriter to punch out song lyrics for Johnny Nash, scripts for public television documentaries, and book reviews for* The Los Angeles Times.

MARILYN HALL[xcix]

I am caught in the middle of two generations; one being passive, an adjunct to my husband. The other is being my own person. Women need to examine their role in society. In the '50s, women only acted on screen. Today they have a lot more power, although men give only lip service to the word "equality." Making pictures today is still more difficult for women that it is for men, although we have made progress.

One morning in the fall of 1980, Marilyn heard a report on TV that a new biopic, A Woman Called Golda, *was starting production.*

MARILYN HALL[c]

I put down my cup and said that they weren't going to do it without me because the people who were going to produce it didn't know anything Jewish or about Israel.

It was a persuasive enough argument that Marilyn got the job. She came into the film with an ambition: she wanted Ingrid Bergman to play Golda Meir. At the time Marilyn joined the project, Bergman hadn't made a film in over two years, and in fact, she had already said "no" to A Woman Named Golda *multiple times.*

As it happened, Marilyn and Monty were visiting London for…what else…a convention for Variety Club International, and she learned that Ingrid Bergman would be in attendance. While Monty spent the evening focused as ever on fundraising, Marilyn fervently pursued Ingrid Bergman, pointing out that she and Meir both had very public battles with cancer, both had made career sacrifices for their family. On a personal level, Marilyn reasoned, Bergman simply had to take the role. Bergman abruptly ended the conversation with a line that Marilyn took to be a blow-off, but the following day, Bergman surprised her with a phone call. She wanted the part. A Woman Named Golda, *produced by Marilyn Hall, was Bergman's final acting role. Paramount released the film in syndication as a four-hour TV movie; it won three Emmys, including a posthumous award for Bergman.*

Marilyn set up her own company, Hallet Street Productions (named for the street where her husband grew up) and unleashed an impressive string of TV movies, including Nadia *(Nadia Comenici's life story),* Do You Remember Love? *(Joanna Woodward as an Alzheimer's Disease patient; it won another Emmy and a Peabody Award), and a production of* The Ginger Tree *for* Masterpiece Theater. *When Monty was asked how he felt about his wife's burgeoning career, he cheerfully said that he had seen his own name in the newspaper enough times, and he was happy to see the rest of the Hall family getting the attention they deserved.*

In the early 1980s, the computer was slowly begin to take over, and many companies saw its potential equally as a toy and a way to boost business. Monty lent his face to an unusual business venture called Touch-n-Save. Push-button kiosks would be installed in supermarkets. The buttons activated one of several videotapes of Monty, looking into the customer and offering to "make a deal" with them. The buttons on the kiosk allowed customers to select one of 1500 items ranging from appliances to sporting goods, marked down as low as 40% below retail, if the customer was willing to wait a few days and have it shipped to their home instead of just getting it at the store. It was a prehistoric Amazon, with Monty Hall's smiling face beaming from the screen. The face was so synonymous with the word "Deal" that the Touch-N-Save manufacturers reasoned customers would expect a good one just from the sight of that familiar man.

A similarly iconic game show host, Bob Barker, had enjoyed tremendous success with The Bob Barker Fun & Games Show, *a touring game show held in arenas across the country during his days off from taping* The Price is Right. *People paid for tickets to come in and get a glimpse of a famous TV star, with a chance at being pulled on stage to play games. Monty had even stepped in to guest-host a* Fun & Games *performance while Barker was tending to his wife Dorothy Jo, who was fighting a losing battle with lung cancer.*

When The Bob Barker Fun & Games Show *drew a massive crowd to Riverfront Coliseum in Cincinnati, a local radio station took notice and decided to stage a touring game show of their own. The station manager reached out to Monty Hall and suggested a touring version of* Let's Make a Deal. *The event went well, although there were enough technical difficulties during the night to tip Monty off that his creation wasn't designed for a national tour. He was accustomed to working with a stage crew that was accustomed to him. Stagehands for the live show seemed unsure of what to do when Monty asked for curtains to be opened, and the models hired for the evening were out of position several times. And that was with rehearsals. Perfect execution would take a lot of work, and every city on a live tour would involve a new crew. Monty also realized that the format of the show might have to change from state to state—an Ohio lottery law was in effect at the time regulating games of chance, so for the live production, all of the deals had to be modified in some way so that they could be considered games of skill and bypass that law. Monty accepted his payday for doing the show in Cincinnati, went back to Los Angeles, and forgot about ever doing a* Let's Make a Deal *road show.*

On July 25, 1982, Maurice Hall, a/k/a Maurice Halparin died at the age of 82. As a child, Monty had endured a tumultuous relationship with his father. Maurice watched his older son become an accomplished broadcaster, star, and one of the most prolific philanthropists on the continent. Maurice had also watched his son Robert become a prominent lawyer in Canada, follow in Monty's footsteps, and become an international president of Variety Club. Late in life, Maurice would fondly take stock of what his two boys were doing, career-wise and for their charitable interests, smile, and joke, "Who are the Kennedys anyhow?"

As he got older, Monty would walk more than a few miles in his father's shoes. He would look back at moments in his childhood with adult eyes and see them in new ways. And with those new perspectives came understanding.

MONTY HALL[ci]

The struggle that my parents went through left an indelible mark on me. I worked in the butcher shop, I saw how hard my father worked. And despite the fact that Saturday night I had to work through the night because we opened after sundown, right through delivering parcels in 40-degrees-below-zero on a bicycle all over the city…when I observed what my father went through, I forgave him for his temper, his outbursts. I understood what his frustrations were, and how strong my mother was to keep him focused and balanced. He was so destroyed by his father and brother…They diminished him. But she kept him going. What an example that was. But as I grow older…I have more of an empathetic feeling for him. Because he never stopped working hard. He worked as hard as he could to keep that family afloat. He suffered the blows but kept going.

And my admiration for him was more than this society gave him. In society, he was Rose's husband. Secondary character. He was a butcher. Secondary citizen. But I knew what he was. And I remembered a line from *Death of a Salesman*. When the wife says "Attention must be paid to this man! Attention must be paid to this man!"

When I saw that play, my heart jumped, because that was exactly what I was thinking about my father. You cannot pigeonhole him as a secondary citizen. He did everything he could for his family. Attention must be paid.

Though Monty had fallen back in love with Let's Make a Deal, *he recognized the demise of the latest incarnation of the show as a chance to do something different and tried his hand at stand-up comedy, for one night only, when he guest-hosted* An Evening at the Improv. *The program provides a glimpse of two different Monty Halls coming together: the Monty Hall of the 1970s, who was itching to prove himself as something greater than a game show host, a "complete entertainer," of sorts; and the Monty Hall of the 1980s, the man who made peace with being America's Top Trader, TV's Big Dealer. Monty did stand-up comedy all right, but totally infused with references to* Let's Make a Deal, *a show of acceptance that he knew he was never going to escape from the shadow of his own creation.*

MONTY HALL[cii]

I've been doing stand-up comedy for years, although not on the TV tube. For many years, I've been emceeing banquets, roasts and the like, and in those assignments, a good part of what I do is stand-up comedy. And I have been writing my own comedy material for such occasions.

That episode of Evening at the Improv *opens with Monty emerging from a limousine and seeing that the improv has altered its entrance to three numbered doors. He flirts with the model stationed at #2, peeks behind her curtain, and goes inside. He's welcomed onstage by Improv owner Budd Friedman, dressed as a banana.*

Monty takes it in good humor, making a joke himself about all the bird costumes he saw over the years before saying a quick word of defense about himself and his show—"It was silly, it wasn't the golden age of television, it wasn't Studio One, *but it was a lot of fun for a lot of years and people enjoyed it"—then cheerfully launching into a version of* Let's Make a Deal *with a Don Rickles-inspired spin on it. He offered money for anyone in the comedy club who had a set of glasses with a funny nose, excitedly thought he found a winner, then looked disappointed to realize that's what the audience member actually looked like. He found a man who had the right kind of glasses and the wrong kind of nose, offering to punch him in the face until he qualified for the prize.*

Monty's performance had an ulterior motive to it though, when he actually did begin playing a game with them. He told jokes and encouraged audience members to guess the punch lines. What he didn't explain at the moment was that he was testing his next game show idea. The Weight Watchers Clubs 20 years ago had given way to The Improv as Monty's personal workshop.

Monty had created a game show called The Joke's On Us *and was in the process of pitching it in the U.S. and Canada. While it would never make it on the air in America, it found a home in Canada during the 1983-84 season in syndication. Monty played host to two contestants and an eclectic group of rotating celebrity panelists—Leslie Nielsen, Fred Travalena, Murray Langston (*The Gong Show's *Unknown Comic) and even "Maytag Repairman" Jesse White. One panelists would read a set-up to a joke, the rest would read a variety of punch lines, with the contestants scoring by correctly guessing which one was the original punch line for the joke.*

ROBERT HALL (2019)

Monty began going back to Canada in the 1980s for TV work, but it was more of a coincidence than anything he set out to do. He was happy in America. You must understand, Canada was very slow to expand when television first became popular. There was the CBC and absolutely nothing else. In time, we got two more networks. Other things came along. But for years, if you were a Canadian and you had any sort of real talent, you got out of here and went to America. And Monty set up his production company and established himself in the US.

In America, Monty found that his success with Let's Make a Deal *didn't easily translate to business as a producer. In 1972, Hatos-Hall had introduced the hard quiz* Split Second *on ABC and enjoyed over three years on the air with host Tom Kennedy, proving that the company could do something more than* Let's Make a Deal. *But in the ensuing years, a steady mound of tapes began accumulating of game show pilots like* The Waiting Game, Talking Pictures, *and* Carnival, *which the networks had all looked at and decided "Thanks, but no thanks."* The Joke's On Us *met the same fate when Monty Hall tried to sell it in the U.S. The enormous success of* Let's Make a Deal *had only generated interest in* Let's Make a Deal.

In the early 1980s, Monty had developed an idea that he had come to fall in love with. He called it Monty Hall For The People. *Monty classified it as "a human interest show." He'd welcome guests with problems, and put each guest in contact with somebody who had the means to help. Any kind of help—as Monty laid out in his proposal, the guests could include a child transplant patient or an aspiring singer.*

MONTY HALL[ciii]

I would call on all my resources. This comes from a lifetime of humanitarianism and show business. I know everybody. I can call the White House. I mean, how many shows have I done with Ronald Reagan? I can call senators, governors. I know stars. I know Sammy Davis, Jr. [Test audiences] all loved me. It came back that everyone loves Monty Hall. So give me the benefit of the show, let me try it.

SHARON HALL (2019)

My father had what we called the Rolodex of Doom. Today I guess he would have had the iPhone of Doom. My parents knew everybody, and they would never hesitate to do favors for people. Favors are a currency in Hollywood, and some people are precious about making connections. My parents loved to do favors, and loved to package people and put them together. And they would get 2 a.m. phone calls from someone saying, "I have a relative who's in trouble," and they'd explain the problem, and Dad would give them a phone number. Mom & Dad were always ready to leverage their fame to help somebody.

Monty went to the National Association of Television Program Executives [NATPE], the annual convention where buyers from local TV stations explored booths occupied by writers, producers, and stars of shows being offered for syndication the following year and considered which programs to buy. Monty pitched his shows to executives and station managers all week. No buyers.

MONTY HALL[civ]

People want to see me give away refrigerators. They don't want to see me get someone an audition with Herb Alpert of A&M Records. It was such a rejection.

The concept had a two-fold purpose. First, it fulfilled Monty's M.O., aiding people however he could. Second, although he had made peace with being "Monty Hall from Let's Make a Deal,*" he had said to numerous reporters that he didn't want* Let's Make a Deal *engraved on his tombstone, and it bothered him to think it would be the only thing mentioned in most of his obituaries. Monty, who was still hosting six telethons a year and honoring commitments for charities for 100 out of every 365 nights, was hoping that if he had a daily show where he did good deeds for people in need, there was a chance that* Monty Hall For The People *would be successful enough that he'd be remembered as "Monty Hall, the nice man who helped people."*

MONTY HALL[cv]

It's a step beyond *People's Court*. It's not the shallowness of a hairdresser dying your hair the wrong color. This is a living soap opera. I want it to be completely honest. I don't expect it to be fantasy or dreams come true. I just want to help people, to be a catalyst.

When you have a successful game show, what can you put on your tombstone—that you had a hit show? The weeds will cover that in a hurry. But when you've done what I've done, you can leave a legacy.

The fact that he was Monty Hall gave him enough clout that he could get meetings with virtually any executive in television. The fact that he was Monty Hall meant that most of those meetings went up in smoke when the executives asked, "How about doing a new version of Let's Make a Deal *instead?"*

A new version of *Let's Make a Deal?* Just do it, Monty decided. (Author's Collection)

MONTY HALL[cvi]

It's guilt by association. Instead of saying, "Look how he orchestrates all those excitable people without a script; no one else could possibly do that," they say, "Oh, he's the one with the dancing rabbits and people in tin cans." The vehicle itself has tarnished the performer to an extent.

While Monty could be frustrated by the lack of interest in a new idea, he wasn't shocked. After all, Let's Make a Deal *had once been a new idea too.*

MONTY HALL[cvii]

It's very difficult for the king of the game shows to be taken seriously in another series. I was an actor for years. I sang, I danced, I did 1,000 Army shows. I had four one-hour TV specials. I played Vegas. I've paid my dues. But when you get so big doing one thing, it's very difficult for the buyer—the networks—to take you seriously in anything else.

[*Let's Make a Deal*] was innovative and different because it was the first game show without pre-selected contestants. Doing the show in the audience spontaneously gave it a whole new dimension. But it took us a year and a half to sell it.

It wasn't just network executives who had him confined to that little box on Jay's Tray. Early in 1984, Monty was walking through a hotel lobby, getting ready to host another telethon, when a woman approached him and asked, "Are you Monty Hall?"

"Yes I am."

She smiled and proudly told him, "I've got a hard-boiled egg in my pocketbook."

In a 1984 TV Guide *story, Monty revealed that NBC had made him an offer to mount a new version of* Let's Make a Deal *but that the negotiations fell apart for virtually the same reason that they had in 1968. Monty asked if the network's offer could include some chances to host holiday parades and maybe some prime time specials. NBC said no thanks. Monty, now 63, recognized that it was now or never if he was ever going to become known as anything other than TV's big dealer. And NBC ultimately opted for "Never."*

But as Monty's bank book could affirm, there was a blessing wrapped in only having "one big thing" attached to his identity. In 1984, the syndicated TV buyers were on the hunt for game shows. Family Feud, *the show that replaced* Deal *on ABC back in 1976, had become almost too successful for its own good. It introduced a five-night-a-week syndicated version that was so dominant that other game shows were dropping left and right; nothing could compete with* Family Feud *so networks and syndicates were just giving up.* Feud *stood tall in a genre that was going stagnant.*

Suddenly in 1983, an NBC daytime game, Wheel of Fortune, *introduced a nighttime version. Expectations were low—daytime* Wheel *had never been a huge hit—but for whatever reason, viewers flocked to the nighttime version, and* Family Feud *crumbled. It wasn't just the dominance over* Feud *that caught the business' attention.* M*A*S*H *was a show so beloved that its final episode, aired in February 1983, had been viewed by 121 million people. In the fall of 1983, reruns of* M*A*S*H *were expected to be a hot property; 172 of the nation's 210 TV markets were airing the reruns that season. The shock could be felt throughout the industry when the nighttime* Wheel of Fortune, *seen in only 59 markets, was soundly defeating it. Local stations* *that had given up in the wake of* Feud's *success were now clamoring to get back into game shows. And station managers would probably see low risk in picking a show with a proven track record, right?*

Monty joined up with the distribution firm Telepictures and made their intentions known at NATPE. By the end of the convention, more than 30 stations had already made commitments to air Let's Make a Deal, *including stations in the key cities of Los Angeles, New York, and Chicago. Monty was back in business. It wasn't* For the People, *but as Monty reminded himself time and again,* Let's Make a Deal *afforded him more than enough of a fortune and free time to allow him to keep his philanthropy going full-speed. He even had it put in writing that he would never have to spend more than three days in the studio in any given week.*

Charity was more important than ever for Monty. Inside the performer was still the teenager who aspired to be a doctor and couldn't do it. Being denied the opportunity to help people in one field had created a void that he worked his entire life to fill. Monty could never shake the feeling that no matter how many checks he wrote, hospitals he built, fundraisers he emceed, or nights of sleep he denied himself for telethons, he somehow hadn't done enough. He was constantly searching for assurance that he was doing the right thing—that using a harmless TV show to build his fortune and then giving to those who needed it more had been the right path.

MONTY HALL[cviii]

I often talk with doctors, because I spend my whole life with doctors now in my charity work. I sometimes say, 'Do you think I made the right decision?"

And they look at me and say "You've helped millions of people, you've built hospitals, you've built camps for the handicapped. Why would you have any regrets?"

Best friends Dennis James and Monty Hall. Both men were talented hosts-in-demand for game shows and telethons, both solidly committed to favorite causes; Dennis to United Cerebral Palsy and Monty to Variety Club. (Author's Collection)

RICHARD HALL (2019)

My dad really didn't regret anything, ever. Once he was denied entry due to the quotas system, he went into radio and never looked back. I will say, he rebuilt his relationship with the University of Manitoba because they eventually did away with the quotas, and because he was successful without the medical degree. But I truly don't think my dad really looked back for even a second once he got into radio. My dad loved show business. He loved making people feel good. He loved being the ringmaster, which is what an emcee is. He loved performing, he loved music. He just enjoyed it so much and he was good at it.

The all-newness of The All-New Let's Make a Deal *included two new models, Karen LaPierre and Melanie Vincz, and a new announcer, Brian Cummings.*

KAREN LAPIERRE, model

I had been a professional ice skater. I dropped out of high school in tenth grade to join

Ice Capades and I was with them for four years, and then I skated for a year in Las Vegas, and then I moved to California. I was volunteering at a fundraiser for Make-A-Wish at the Long Beach Arena. I had been Miss California USA in 1979, so I had this beautiful gown, and I figured since it was a fundraiser I should dress up. Someone asked me to sit in a particular seat at the event, and all they told me was that the seat belonged to somebody else, and they just needed me to sit there so no one else would take it. I didn't find out until the event started that I was in Monty Hall's seat. He was the emcee of the event and I was sitting in his seat for dinner. I didn't find out until much later that the really nice lady I had been talking to for the entire time was his wife Marilyn.

Monty's back for one more tour of duty on the trading floor. (Author's Collection)

My mom and I had a nail salon and tanning salon in Long Beach called Hands & Tans, so I gave Marilyn a business card before I left. I still didn't know she was Monty's wife. But we hit it off so well that I told her, "Call me up and I'll give you a free manicure."

The next day, the phone rings at Hands & Tans. I didn't even have an agent. I had been rejected by agencies because they said they had too many brunettes. It was a staffer at Hatos-Hall Productions asking me to come in for an audition, and I immediately think, "Oh, this is a prank call from one of my friends, because they know I was at an event with Monty Hall last night."

Well, then the staffer begins giving me really detailed information about the audition and the plans for the show, and it got so specific that I started to realize, "Oh, this is real!"

She began talking to me about what they wanted, and they said something that I thought would be a strike against me, they said they wanted somebody "smaller than Monty." I'm 5'11" in my bare feet. So I thought, "Okay, I'm wrong for this." But I went anyway.

They asked me to bring a current headshot. I took a Polaroid. I should not have made it as far as I did in this audition. They wanted professional models. But I was a figure skater, so I had long beautiful arms from doing certain moves. Also, I look back and my state of mind, I think, was "Too stupid to be scared." I was calmer than a lot of people in the room. And in a lot of ways, I'm average, but I'm a good canvas. If a make-up artist works with me, they can do really great things with my face. My hair is the same way, you can do a lot of things with my hair and make it work. But that works to my advantage. I'm not so beautiful that I'm too good for the room.

These other women at the audition are showing each other their portfolios. Some of them have these very professional books made of all their work, and all I have is a freaking Polaroid, and I was laughing on the inside because I just did not fit in at all.

They gave each of us a script of advertising copy. They said when we went in, someone in the room would read that copy, and we had to model the items in the room. I was the last one to go in and the staffer I had talked to on the phone met me face-to-face and told me that Marilyn Hall recommended me, and that was the first time I put it all together and realized how I got this audition.

Monty was in there and I lost sight of why I was there. I just immediately gushed, "Thank you! Thank you! I'm such a fan of the show! When I was a little girl I used to stand next to the TV and pretend I was Carol Merrill! This has been such an experience for me! One day I'll have grandchildren and I'll tell them I auditioned for *Let's Make a Deal*!"

And since I had been a fan of the show, I just suddenly started asking them about the history of it, and Monty told me the whole story. I asked about when the original pilot was shot, and they gave me the date and I said, "Oh, I was four months old!" And Monty and the writers just about fell on the floor when I said that. They were laughing so hard. I just remember right away picking up this vibe that everybody I was talking to had been working together for years and they were all a family. I liked the way I felt when I talked to them.

Bob Synes, who was a producer for the show, said, "Well honey, if you want to tell your grandchildren about the audition, you'd better start the audition then!"

They begin reading the prize copy, and that's when I realize I didn't really pay attention to it when they handed it to me. And nothing in there looks like a prize on a game show. But the first prize in the copy is a TV set, and there's a huge box on the floor, so I figure out how they're doing this. I walk over to the box and model it while they're talking about the TV. I look over and nearby I see this old, baggy, cable-knit sweater on a hook and I think to myself, "That's the fur coat from Dicker & Dicker of Beverly Hills." I watched *Let's Make a Deal* when I was a kid. I watched Carol. I knew what I was doing here. I put on that cable-knit sweater and snuggled up in it, and I nuzzled my chin against the collar, did a twirl.

Monty asked me on the spot if I could come to NBC Studios the following week for an audition on the set. I screamed and I kissed him.

The suspense of making a deal could drive some contestants bananas. (Author's Collection)

BRIAN CUMMINGS, announcer

Daws Butler taught me how to do voiceovers. Daws Butler was the voice of Yogi Bear and a lot of other Hanna-Barbera characters, and he agreed to listen to my demo tape. He said, "You really had some good stuff in there." In my mind, I related that to a quote from the naturalist, Euell Gibbons. He said once, "Some people see humus"—which is the polite word for crap—"but I see a rose."

When I got to Los Angeles, my fantasy was to be a comedian, I wanted to be an on-camera funny guy. I joined an improv group called Off The Wall. One of the writers of *M*A*S*H* was in our group. Peter Noone of Herman's Hermits was in our group, so we did musical improv. Robin Williams had been in the class, but it didn't work out because one of the rules of improv is that you go along with what the other actors are doing in a scene. Once Robin started talking in a scene, though, he'd go so long and he'd do so much that there wasn't anything for the other performers to do except nod and say "Yeah, uh-huh."

As for why I became the announcer for *Let's Make a Deal*...I think it goes back to when I was a kid and my dad motivated me by saying, "You can do anything!"

In my childlike mind, I misinterpreted this and took it to mean, "You can do everything!"

I was hosting a show for Continental Airlines called *Brian's Songs*. At the same time, cartoon studios were all doing a lot more output so it created a lot of work for me. One day, I'm sitting on a couch in LA Studios. It's the summer of 1984, and I remember it was while the Olympics were going on.

Chuck Riley, who was one of the all-time great deep-voice performers, says to me, "Hey, I know someone who's looking for you. I have a friend at Hatos-Hall Productions and they need an announcer. You interested? Call your agent."

I called my agent. I was actually on the way to a venue to do some work for a regular client who hired me to do some stuff during the Olympic events. But the agent says, "Hatos and Hall want to see you NOW."

I go to the office, and I meet with Stefan Hatos and Monty Hall. They gave me some prize copy to read. One of the things that helped me is that I had learned how to sight-read. I got hired for so much voiceover work that I didn't always have time to study scripts. I became really adept at delivering my lines even though I was seeing them for the first time. And they didn't want any of those prize plugs to go longer than ten seconds, so they really liked that about me. I left, and again I had this gig for a client at the Olympics that day. But fifteen minutes later, my agent calls. "Hatos and Hall want you back at the studio. You got the job. The first episode tapes tonight."

I don't know what happened. Nobody told me if they had another announcer who dropped out, or what. But I had my audition, my job interview, I got hired, and taped the first episode, all in the same day. But the great thing was how encouraging the *Deal* staff was when they got to know me. They found out about my improv background, they found out that Daws Butler had trained me and that I had this experience doing cartoon voices, and they said, "If you want to do that stuff, go ahead!"

I went home and got what I called my improv trunk, which was full of costumes, and brought it back to the studio. And Monty was great about that too. There was no trace of, "Hey, pal, this is my show!" Absolutely not. He was all about sharing the spotlight. He even told the technical crew to mic me for the Zonks, in case I wanted to do something.

A robotic contestant with the very human Big Dealer. (Author's Collection)

The All-New Let's Make a Deal *launched in the fall of 1984, on a vivid new set in NBC Burbank. They taped down the hall from Johnny Carson, who liked to joke about walking past a man in a zucchini costume as he prepared to do* The Tonight Show. *The show added a new daily feature called "Door #4." The feature came into being because of a request of Telepictures, which wanted to be able to market* The All-New Let's Make a Deal *as something truly current. In 1984, the best way to look current was to shove a computer into some aspect of the show. Telepictures asked the staff to create a daily segment that made use of a computer.*

Door #4 involved a device called a People Picker, which shuffled the numbers 1-36 on an electronic readout in view of the audience. At the press of a button, the readout would freeze on a specific number, and the contestant sitting in that seat on the trading floor was given $1,000 immediately and given the choice of keeping the check or trading it for the amount of money hidden behind Door #4. The door could be hiding amounts as low as $200 or as high as $5,000.

BRIAN CUMMINGS

Stefan Hatos hated Door #4. When Telepictures had told him the new version had to use a computer, Stefan told them, "Well…people know you can rig a computer. Nobody believes in a computer."

We deep-sixed the original version right away because Stefan thought the segments looked fake. The computer picked a number that people couldn't be sure was a legitimate pick, and then if a contestant chose the door and it was a low amount of money, some viewer at home would say "Oh, see, they set it up that way." And if it was a big amount of money, viewer at home says, "Oh, they wanted her to win a lot of money."

Stefan says, "I don't like what we're doing here. It's not believable."

At great expense, Stefan has a giant wheel built for the show, which I thought was funny because anybody who's ever been to a carnival knows wheels can be rigged.

Picking the wrong door could be a drag. (Author's Collection)

The contestant chosen by the People Picker now had a choice of keeping their $1,000 or giving it up for a spin of the Door #4 wheel, which could lead to a payoff of $5,000, a car, or a t-shirt bearing the slogan I WAS ZONKED BY MONTY HALL.

BRIAN CUMMINGS

Stefan Hatos was an interesting guy. They had a lot of deals where they'd surprise contestants with hidden money. Monty would reveal "Here's a hundred-dollar bill…and another hundred-dollar bill…" and on the original show, quite often, there'd be a big surprise at the end. "And here's a THOUSAND-DOLLAR BILL!"

Well, it's 1984, so the problem was the U.S. had stopped making thousand-dollar bills. But Stefan Hatos had a friend in the banking business, and Stefan arranged for the show to receive a single thousand-dollar bill. They kept it sealed up in plastic, and they'd bring it out whenever they wanted to use it for a deal. And since it was the only thousand-dollar bill we had and it was hard to replace, the show took extra-good care of it. They'd get it back from the contestant with paperwork signed promising that the contestant would get a check. And then they'd take it backstage after the segment, and the make-up artist would set the thousand dollar bill on an ironing board, lay wax paper on top of it, and iron the bill, so it was just hot enough that a little wax would seep into the bill which kept it crisp and new-looking, and then it would be sealed back up and put into a special box and locked away. All that work because Stefan Hatos liked the big reveal for a thousand-dollar bill.

KAREN LAPIERRE

There's a lot of learning by doing when you work on a game show. The first taping I did, nobody told me that there was an easier way to do what I was doing. When Monty says, "Or you can have what's behind the curtain!" I know I'm on camera and I stretch my arm to model the curtain. Contestant makes their decision, and whatever it is, I know that the curtain is going to swing open and then I have to back up and get into place to model whatever's back there.

I walked backward for the entire taping because I figured you weren't supposed to have your back to the camera, so I was moving around nervously and worrying that I was going to crash into something. The director took me aside after the first episode and said, "You know, you're not on camera after we open the curtain. As soon as it opens, I cut to a close-up of the contestants for a camera shot. So just remember, as soon as the curtain opens, you're not on camera anymore."

So after that, the curtain would open and as soon as it did, I'd turn my back to the camera and the audience and run the 10 or 11 steps to get into place for when it got back to me.

BRIAN CUMMINGS

One taping, I had a really ugly checkered coat and a dog chew. I don't smoke, so for improv, if I wanted my character to smoke a cigar, I'd use these dog chews that looked like cigars from a distance. Nobody told me before I did that that these dog chews are made with beef juice in them so when it's in your mouth long enough, you start to feel this little trickle going down your tongue. Eww.

But I had the ugly jacket, I had the cigar, and I had a stuffed cow, and I was going to do a bit where I was the cow's agent. "Hey, kid, listen, *Let's Make a Deal* is back on the air, so get ready, you're gonna be in command for the Zonks and we'll go all the way to the top!"

The NBC studio technician had been with the network for three million years, and he didn't turn the microphone up. The curtain opens and I do my bit, and no one can hear me.

Stefan Hatos, backstage, says, "No one can hear you! Kill the bit, it's done."

I turned to Stef and said, "But it's really funny!"

He says, "Hey kid, if the stuffed cow wasn't funny, nothing you do is gonna make it funny!"

Monty was always cool about it. I wasn't sure if I was doing too much and tried to defer to him. I said to him once, "You know, you're the star of the show."

He said, "Hey, if you make the show better, it makes me look good." Monty was in favor of anything that enhanced the show.

Monty didn't like to stop tape for anything and he wanted to treat it as a live show. We did a deal once where I had keys attached to a piece of cardboard, and the cardboard was mounted on a tray, and I was supposed to bring it down and place it next to Monty as he's talking to the contestants. The stagehands forgot to tape the card to the tray, so as soon as I set the tray down, the cardboard flops over and the keys scatter everywhere.

And Monty smiles at me and says "Hey, I'm not going to pick them up! I'm the star of the show!" So we play this out with me on my hands and knees, crawling around and picking up the keys as Monty just keeps talking to the contestants. And if you ever watch the reruns, you'll see that; they never cut it out.

KAREN LAPIERRE

We taped at NBC's studio complex, and we shared a make-up room with *The Tonight Show Starring Johnny Carson*. I adored Ed McMahon. I'm very, very good at making friends with people quickly, so when I was in the make-up room, Johnny's guests for the night would come in with their management, and I could talk them into coming over to our set when they were done with Johnny, to give the audience a thrill. I kept track for a while. I got at least sixty people to come over. And the *Let's Make a Deal* audience would go wild for them because they weren't expecting to see a movie star or a famous singer that night.

There was just one problem—one of the writers told me, "Karen, it's great that you do this, but you need to tell Monty ahead of time." Monty would blurt out "Who is that?" sometimes because he didn't know who these people were. I brought Eddie Van Halen into the studio once and Monty didn't have a clue who he was. So that became a thing I had to start doing. I'd need to pull Monty aside during a taping break and say "I'm about to bring Jennifer O'Neill into the studio."

One night I crossed paths with Mick Jagger in the NBC studio complex. I tried really, really hard to talk him into actually being on the show as a surprise during a Zonk. Didn't quite pull it off. He came into the studio, he took a bow, but I couldn't convince him to be on the show.

BRIAN CUMMINGS

I was so busy that my agent started booking me in the cracks during my day. There were times when we'd have a one-hour break between rehearsals and taping, and during that break, I'd leave the studio complex, go to another studio, record my lines for this other booking, and then drive back to tape *Let's Make a Deal*. In fact, Telepictures began booking me to do other things, so I got even more work because of *Let's Make a Deal*.

The secret of *Let's Make a Deal* was that the spontaneity was controlled. I interviewed a man once who recorded a spoken-word album of interactive magic tricks. I asked him how you can pre-record magic tricks and have them work. He said, "It's probability. These tricks work because if you tell a person to do X, that will lead to Y."

As it turns out, that's exactly how *Let's Make a Deal* operated. Everybody there had a sense of human nature. "If we do X, then the contestant will do Y." The contestants were completely free to do whatever they wanted. But the people running that show understood people so well and set up those deals to get those reactions and get those moments. Monty was a master. He knew how to set up those moments, how to play them off. And he was just at a point where he could do that show blindfolded.

It was interesting working on the show and seeing it on the inside after watching it as a kid. I remember the production staff was griping one day because they wanted to do His & Hers Garbage Cans as a Zonk, one painted pink and one painted blue. And because of the regulations with the unions in Los Angeles, there was paperwork involved, they had to turn in so many forms and cover so many fees, and by the time these two garbage cans were ready for the show, it cost them something like $4,000.

That thrilling moment when a contestant realizes he doesn't know what Monty is up to. (Author's Collection)

KAREN LAPIERRE

I had been an athlete, so I was very coachable. One of the things they hammered into me early on was that I wasn't there for me. We had sponsors who had supplied prizes, or had supplied grocery items for the games. Some of them paid money for their prizes to be featured, and they wanted to feel like this 10-second promotion was worth their money. So on close-ups of grocery items, I'd hold the box next to my face and then look at the logo, which draws attention away from my face and directly to that logo. For appliances and furniture, there'd be a card attached with the logo on it and I made sure to run my hand across the logo. I was there to sell a product.

Monty noticed that I took direction well and everyone liked me. For some reason, a bunch of different companies all at once approached Monty about doing *Let's Make a Deal*-themed commercials, and Monty always included me when he signed for a commercial. We appeared together in ads for Coca-Cola, Toyota, and MTV.

Monty completely changed my life. He was really into a self-help book, *Think and Grow Rich* by Napoleon Hill, and he shared it with me. It ended up meaning a lot to me. Years later he told me about the book *The Millionaire Next Door*. But we grew so close that

I began to think of him as family. I got engaged during the run of *Deal*, but my dad was going through a lot of health problems. We didn't know if he'd make it to the wedding. I went to Monty during a taping and I asked him, "If something happens to my dad, will you walk me down the aisle?"

Monty cried when I asked him that. And he said yes. And then I cried.

Elation! (Author's Collection)

BRIAN CUMMINGS

I got to a point where my cartoon business was just booming. *Wuzzles*, *Snorks*, and then I got word that *GI Joe* was just starting. And I was doing voiceovers and promos. And *Let's Make a Deal* taped three days a week and required rehearsals. It took so much time to do *Let's Make a Deal* that it reached point that I had to think about what I needed to do and what was best for me. Once we finished that season of *Deal*, I gave my notice and left the show. And Stefan and Monty could not have been more understanding. They were so gracious about it and it was an amicable departure. That whole season of working on the show was a great experience.

DEAN GOSS

I was doing mornings at K-EARTH radio in Los Angeles. Game shows came about through dumb luck. I was asked to co-host the Jerry Lewis Telethon local inserts on KTLA-TV on Labor Day. That was fun. The following morning, I get a call from an agent, Jim Mahoney, at Creative Artists Agency, CAA.

Jim says, "I saw you doing the telethon segments. You have a great look, you have a great voice. Have you ever considered doing game shows?" Well, I went to college and majored in TV & Radio, but how do you do game shows? The Bob Barker School of Game Shows? The next day, I went down to CAA and chatted with him, and I said "Sign me up!"

Before long, he has me in an office auditioning for Stefan Hatos and Monty Hall. Brian Cummings was giving it up because he was really busy with his voiceover career. *Let's Make a Deal* was time-consuming, so Brian literally didn't have time to do the show anymore.

Stef Hatos, Monty Hall, and a representative from Telepictures were there. They had me read the prize copy for the Big Deal of the Day. They were all very nice. But I never expected to get the job. I just thought, "Okay, onto the next audition."

But the next day, I left for a cruise. I got a ship-to-shore call, which involves a 40-minute wait for the connection to be made, and I'm dreading this call because why would anybody be spending 40 minutes waiting to talk to me on the phone. I'm thinking it's my sister-in-law, who's watching the kids, calling me to tell me something is wrong with the baby. It turns out to be my agent, letting me know I got the job.

It had ultimately come down to two candidates, and after some debate, Stefan Hatos and Monty Hall selected Dean Goss. The candidate that they rejected, who had grown frustrated with his struggle to find steady work in Los Angeles, decided to seek his fortune elsewhere and moved to New York City. In 1986, Phil Hartman joined the cast of Saturday Night Live.

DEAN GOSS

I grew up watching *Let's Make a Deal*. It was fun working on the show and learning the ins and outs of it. One of the things that surprised me was that Monty knew exactly where he was going to go before each deal started. They had the people on the trading floor, but there was always a break before each deal, and somebody would pull Monty aside and say, "This is the deal with the chewing gum and the curtain. You need three people, you're going to pick #5, #14, and #28." And those were the seats that Monty went to when he said, "I need three people for this deal!"

And by the way, because they did the show that way, something happened one day that caused Stefan Hatos to nearly go crazy, for the only time I can recall. Monty was told, you know, "Pick #17." So, he picks contestant #17. It's an African-American man. And he's offered a prize hiding behind the curtain, and the curtain opens up, and it's a tanning machine.

The audience comes unglued. The contestant had a great sense of humor about it, luckily, and he tells Monty, "I don't need it."

And Stefan Hatos flipped out backstage on one of the writers. "Why would you pick him? You knew this was the tanning machine segment!"

Announcer Dean Goss with Monty on *Let's Make a Deal*.
(Photo courtesy of Dean Goss)

KAREN LAPIERRE

Now, here was the big secret about contestant-picking for *Let's Make a Deal*. Anybody who showed up dressed as a hockey player got picked. Monty loved hockey. He could instantly strike up a conversation with anybody wearing a jersey, and the writers picking the contestants knew that. So if you came to the studio wearing a hockey uniform, you got picked for the trading floor, and the writers would tell Monty during the breaks to look for your seat number. He was going to make a deal with you.

DEAN GOSS

I was surprised by how busy the show was, and how much went into it. There's donkeys, there's cars, there's lengthy rehearsals, so we could only tape three episodes in a day instead of five. Monty was never there for the rehearsals though. He never had to be. Monty was the most intelligent game show host I've ever seen, by far. I was awed by him.

Monty was amazing. He was so sharp and so smart. Alan Gilbert was a writer for the show and he was Monty's stand-in during rehearsals. And when Monty came in, Alan would tell him, "Okay, at the start of the show, you'll hand one contestant a wad of money. Dean will come out with the tray, you offer that, then we'll go to the curtain…" and so on. Monty had it. You tell him once, he's got it. Didn't need cue cards. There was always a cue card person to do math, just in case Monty needed to do something with numbers, but Monty would always figure it out in his head before the cue card person wrote it down, so we almost never needed the cue card man.

I announced *Let's Make a Deal*, as Jay Stewart did, from a hidden booth offstage. The reason we did it that way was because they didn't want the audience to figure anything out from seeing me. The announcer is usually behind the curtain for whatever sight gag they do in the Zonks. If my announcing booth was in plain sight, and the audience saw me standing there, it would tip them off that there must be a good prize back there. And if they saw me walking away, they'd know there was a Zonk coming. So I was kept out of sight of the audience as much as possible.

I'd have a headset on. In the left earpiece, I'm hearing the director. In the right earpiece, I'm hearing my own voice. As I'm reading the prize copy, I'm changing into a costume, and then I'd take my handheld microphone, and I'm reading copy for the washer-dryer behind Door #1, I'm walking over to Door #3 and climbing on top of a donkey. And then when it was time to reveal me, a stagehand would take the microphone and the script away from me and the door would fly open to show the donkey and me.

I was doing mornings at K-EARTH, I was on the air from 5:30 a.m. to 10:00 a.m. each day. And then I'd go to the studio complex. Rehearsal from 11:00 a.m. to 3:00 p.m. And then we'd tape three episodes, rotating the audience after each episode, with the writers picking people for the trading floor each time, so there was a wait between each episode, so the third episode was finished usually at 11:00 p.m. *Deal* taped on Tuesday, Wednesday, and Thursday, so I had three long days in a row every week.

I was exhausted one day, and it was a deal where I was manning the tray next to Monty, and there was a box on top, and I had to lift the box to reveal the prize hidden underneath. We did these deals every taping. Monty had this habit of tapping the top of the box whenever it was time for me to lift it. And neither of us realized that this was creating a "Pavlov's Dog" condition in me.

Remember, we rehearsed the deals. I knew how these were supposed to play out. I knew when I was supposed to lift the box. But I was dead tired, so I wasn't listening. Monty was talking to the contestant and he says, "Do you want what's under the box?" and as he asks, he taps the box. And on total instinct, I see him tap the box, and I just lift it up right then and there and reveal the prize hidden under the box.

I panic and cover it back up immediately, and at that point, the audience cracks up because they see the mistake I've made. And then Monty had a great reaction when he sees me cover it back up. He says, "We all saw it, Dean!"

So Monty plays out the deal, and it's fallen apart completely, and obviously, the contestant picks the box because I gave away the prize hidden underneath it. And Monty gets another laugh from that, he says, "Congratulations, you won the prize with help from your Cousin Dean!"

I was thinking, "He's going to kill me after the show. I'm going to get fired. I'm never going to get another game show job."

The staff was amazing about it. Everyone backstage was telling me, "Don't worry about it. These things happen. Even Monty makes mistakes on the deals."

I apologized profusely afterward. I felt so terrible. I even told Monty to dock my pay for that episode to make up for it. And he shakes his head. "No, no, no. Don't worry about it. We're a family here. We're having fun. In fact, we don't mind those kinds of mistakes, because a mistake like that proves to the audience that we do this show live to tape. The show isn't manufactured, what we're giving the audience is the show exactly as it happened, and they know that when they see a mistake."

Monty keeps making deals, even as he privately began to feel somebody else should take the job. (Author's Collection)

KAREN LAPIERRE

We had a set piece that we called "the carousel" that we'd use to show off multiple prizes at once. It was a platform with a floor on top and a thin wall along the middle. Two stagehands with ropes would stand on each side of it, and when they pulled their ropes, the floor would spin and reveal the other side of the wall. So you'd see a set of luggage and Dean would say, "And you'll be taking that luggage on your trip..." and the carousel would spin and the other side of the wall would have a sign on it that said PARIS. At the bottom of the carousel is a pair of cleats that keeps it anchored in place. There was a day when the stagehands forgot to put the cleats in, so when the guys pulled the ropes, it jerked the whole carousel from Door #2 to Door #3. And I had to jump off or else I'd fall off. It aired like that. Re-shooting was out of the question. Monty wanted it to look like a live broadcast.

We had a woman who was so nervous and so excited that when Monty pointed and said "I'll make a deal with YOU!" she didn't budge. She stayed in her seat.

Monty said, "It's okay, you can stand up."

And she shakes her head and says, "Oh no...oh no, I just can't."

She was so nervous that when Monty picked her, she peed herself.

There was a guy dressed as an ape once. Big, big man from Louisiana, built like a cornerback. He wins a car, and the next thing I know, I'm being swooped up. I'm 5'11". A man had never lifted me. But he just picked me up and swung me around. And I just went with it. Because it was live-to-tape and I knew it was going to air no matter what I did. So I just went with it.

The crew liked to play pranks. Sometimes they'd stick alcohol in the refrigerator we were giving away, so I'd be modeling it, and I'd start to open the door and I'd look in there and see a case of Budweiser so I'd have to shut it quickly before the camera caught it. We had a giant stuffed rabbit one day and an inflatable carrot. As a joke, one of the guys on the crew stuck the carrot between the rabbit's legs. We were backstage and I just chuckled at it. But then we start taping the show and that curtain swings open and that carrot is still there, I had to dash over and pull that carrot out before the audience realized what they were seeing.

By the end of 1986, Monty had hosted well over 4,000 episodes of Let's Make a Deal. *And while he felt that he needed to remain attached to it when he mounted the* All-New *incarnation two years earlier, by early 1986, he felt that the show was in position to exist without him.*

At the same time, Jeopardy!, *which had also premiered in syndication in 1984, was paired up with* Wheel of Fortune *in most television markets to form the most dominant one-two punch in syndication. This sent packagers again scrambling for some competition. A Canadian TV executive, Jerry Appleton, had recalled being a fan of* Split Second *on ABC and thought that might do the trick. Monty agreed to an arrangement much like he had made with Catalena some years earlier; he came to Toronto to host the new version of the show, which would be syndicated in both Canada and the U.S. This would require leaving* Let's Make a Deal *after completing the second season, but again, Monty was ready to do that anyway. And he even had a replacement in mind.*

KAREN LAPIERRE

I think one of Monty's reasons for bringing *Let's Make a Deal* back over and over was to keep people employed. He brought the show back in 1984, with me, and even though it did a lot of good for me, there's a part of me that thinks he shouldn't have brought it back. He certainly didn't need to for any reason personally.

You know what Monty hated more than anything in the world? "AAAAAAHHHHHHHHHHHHHH!" He hated women screaming in his ear. And he'd been hearing it for 20 years. Monty loved *Let's Make a Deal*. He was proud of *Let's Make a Deal*. But after so many women scream in your ear, you begin to feel like you're not up to doing it anymore.

DEAN GOSS

Monty came to me and wanted me to take over the show. He said "We're going to let you host two segments in the middle of the show. I'll say something like, 'Hey, listen, I need to make a telephone call, so Dean, take over the show for a bit.' And then I'd come onstage and host two segments of the show.

The reason they did that was because they had to show me to Telepictures, the distributor of the show. It almost happened but it didn't, because the buyers felt that the show was "too much Monty Hall." They liked what I did. They were impressed with me. I know I impressed Monty because if I didn't, he wouldn't have bothered showing Telepictures the tape of those two segments.

But the feeling was that *Let's Make a Deal* was Monty Hall and Monty Hall was *Let's Make a Deal* and they couldn't be separated.

But because Monty had already committed to Split Second, *he was firmly out for the 1986-87 season of* The All-New Let's Make a Deal. *Telepictures took the show to NATPE in the spring of 1986, making it clear that Monty would not be hosting the next season, and as feared, nobody wanted the show unless Monty was hosting. The show probably could have enjoyed a longer run if Monty remained, but too many pieces fell into different places for that to happen. The All-New Let's Make a Deal shut down after only two seasons.*

HENRY KOVAL

I retired when Monty pulled the plug on *Let's Make a Deal*. He would occasionally call me to ask for help with something like a state fair show or a charity function, but I never had another job after *Let's Make a Deal* ended. Monty and Stefan wanted to set up a really nice retirement package for themselves when the show moved to ABC in 1968, but they couldn't go to the network and demand it for just two people. They had to ask for the same retirement package for everyone. So, Stefan and Monty had already been paying me very well for all those years, and then in 1986, when the syndicated show ended, I got to take advantage of this package that ABC offered. I never worked another day in my life.

There were two mementos I kept from the show. One was our cash register. We had an old-fashioned cash register—the kind where you'd press a key and a tag would pop up in the little window—and we used it for my favorite recurring deal on the show. There were 15 keys on the register. 13 of them would ring up tags worth $50 or $100. Two of them said NO SALE. If you racked up $500 before hitting a NO SALE key, you won a car. It was a fantastic segment every time we did it because the odds were so ridiculously loaded in the contestants' favor, but the suspense was incredible because the next key just might be one of the NO SALE keys. I loved that deal. And the cash register is still in my garage.

The other memento is my Zonk photo albums. I took photos of every Zonk because they were so fun and so imaginative that I wanted to make sure we preserved them somehow.

Monty, by now, was 65 years old, but hadn't even entertained the thought of slowing down, and neither had the people who wanted to do business with him.

CHAPTER TWENTY-THREE

(Author's Collection)

STU BILLETT

Monty went up to Canada in 1986 to do the new version of *Split Second*. I wasn't involved in the new show because I was busy with *The People's Court*, but Monty paid me royalties. The new *Split Second* failed.

I hate to say this, because I know how it's going to sound. And I loved Monty, and I loved his family. I still love his family. But sometimes, Monty's ego could be the only thing bigger than his brain.

This Canadian production group approaches him and says, "We'll do a new *Split Second*, because it's such a great show, and it was a hit before. And Monty, if you come up to Canada and host it for one season, it'll be a big hit in Canada, because you're such a star in Canada. And then we'll sell that big hit in more markets all through America. Boom. You'll have a hit show in two countries. It'll be huge."

Now, a lot of this is what I've heard—again, I wasn't there. On the original show, here's how a question looked and sounded. Tom Kennedy would say "Look at the board!" and the camera would pan quickly from Tom to a shot of the three options on the board. And Tom would say, "TRIGGER! CHAMPION! TRAVELER! These are the names of three famous horses. Name the three men who rode those horses." And we'd cut to the three contestants ringing in and giving their answers. If you watch the original *Split Second*, Tom is seldom on camera. *Jeopardy!* with Alex Trebek was taking off in 1986 and it's the same thing, you actually don't see Alex very much during the show.

Monty wanted to be on camera more than that. He said, "No looking at the board, here's how we'll stage this."

And they had Monty stand next to a monitor that would reveal the choices, and it would always be a camera shot of Monty standing next to the monitor, then reading the entire question, then the monitor revealing the three options.

So now the way it plays out is, Monty says, "Okay, contestants, I'm about to show you the names of three famous horses. Ring in, pick one, and tell me the famous man who rode that horse. Look at these horses…" And then the choices are revealed. And before the viewer even has a chance to read all three names and take in the question, all three contestants have already rung in and started giving their answers.

Monty wanted to be on camera more, which caused them to change the way the questions were presented. And the new way of presenting the questions made the show harder for viewers to play along with. And to make that problem worse, they taped the show very far in advance. They had nearly the entire season finished before the first episode aired. By the time they figured out the problem, it was too late to repair it.

As the 1980s wound down, Monty searched for another hit. He hosted multiple pilots for a concept called I Predict. *Paul Anka tried his hand at creating a game show format, called* Betcha, *and tapped Monty to host that pilot.* Queen for a Day, *the tearjerker show from the 1950s in which housewives aired their sorrows, with the audience voting on which hard-luck story deserved the prizes the most, mounted a new version with Monty has host, but the show looked woefully anachronistic in 1988 and was off the air in a matter of weeks. On the plus side, Monty landed a lucrative gig serving as the commercial spokesman for Bonanza steakhouses in a series of commercials where he touted all the great deals you could get on a steak dinner, as his way of atoning for all the Zonks he had given over the years to people who just wanted a good deal.*

RICHARD HALL (2019)

My dad and I did Oldsmobile commercials together! We shot the first one, and then it ended up being a hit. Oldsmobile apparently found that people were really responding to this ad, so we did four more. We shot one in Florida, one in Atlanta, one in Hawaii…they actually rented a 747 to use in the background for one of these commercials. I love showing them to people now. It was the '80s. I had a mustache, which was a terrible idea, and it gets a laugh.

Shooting wrapped on filming for one and my dad just smiled at me and said, "Look at this. One day's work…just one day's work. They just cut each of us a check for $20,000. Pretty nice, isn't it?"

Yeah, it was pretty nice. But my dad just loved the work. Once you're on the inside of show business, you have to really, really love it to stay. He never got sick of it.

BOB BODEN

I was an executive at CBS in the late 1980s and I saw Monty quite often. He hosted pilots like *I Predict* for us. He also came into the offices to pitch new show ideas for us.

In a business meeting, Monty would be very articulate, as you can imagine. Monty had this tendency to become the host of the meeting, just as if he was the host of a show. He owned the room, all eyes were on him. Any time he spoke, people listened. You understood everything that he meant. He presented his ideas very clearly. It was a privilege to be in a room with him, because you knew when he came in with an idea, it had been well thought out, it was developed, it was smart. If you gave him suggestions or notes, he would take it graciously, and he would either think about it or respond to it.

There was no ego to speak of. Monty had this track record of success, but he would never say, "I've got this worked out, you have to like it." He was collaborative, he would always respect the development process, both as producer and as talent. I think that helped him. Because he had been both a producer and a talent, he had a unique understanding of the role of the host, even if he was pitching something that he wasn't hosting.

No game show host had a better sidekick. Jay helps Monty with a deal in the 1960s. (Author's Collection)

Opportunity still knocked for Monty, but sadly, not for Jay Stewart.

In an August 1977 newspaper profile, Jay Stewart optimistically vowed that he would never retire. "I'm happiest when I'm working every day, and I'm just going to keep on going!"

There was no reason to think that he wouldn't, or couldn't. Jay Stewart was as perfect an announcer as had ever introduced a brand-new car. His uniquely brassy voice wasn't anything akin to the golden-throated baritones typically associated with announcing, but Jay used his distinctive voice better than anyone else, delivering his prize copy at lightning fast speed, yet somehow with every word pronounced crisply and coherently, with an enthusiasm in his delivery that made you instantly crave a bowl of Rice-a-Roni or want to relax in a new La-Z-Boy recliner.

In his off-hours, Jay was constantly buying gifts. Never for birthdays or anniversaries—friends and co-workers would be surprised by flowers, engraved pens and lighters, or two-dollar bills, with an accompanying note from Jay just letting the recipient know that he was thinking about them.

But Jay had problems with chronic back pain in the years following the end of Deal. *In 1981, one of his daughters took her own life. Jay was so distraught that he left show business for nearly two years to cope with the shock. In 1983, he went back to work, getting hired to announce for a new game show,* Sale of the Century. *By 1987, even a casual viewer could notice something amiss in Jay's performance. He slurred his speech badly, and producers found it increasingly practical to have him pre-record as much of his announcing copy as possible, so* that they could be sure they had a usable audio track to work with when the show taped. Jay had turned to alcohol to cope with his physical and personal pain. In time, he was relieved of his duties on Sale of the Century. He attempted to mount a new career as an agent representing voiceover talent at the Don Pitts Agency, but Pitts later recalled that Stewart's reputation served as a roadblock. Producers receiving messages from Stewart thought he was calling seeking work for himself, not clients, and because his reputation from Sale preceded him, they didn't return his calls.

On Sunday, September 17, 1989, Jay Stewart took his own life. He was 71.

A happier time in the life of Jay Stewart. (Author's Collection)

JOHN SCHOTT

When we filmed him for the documentary *Deal,* Jay was such a warm, open guy. He invited the entire crew to The Magic Castle and bought us all a very nice dinner, which wasn't cheap. It was a lovely night. He was a guy who really wore his heart on his sleeve. He was very reflective about the work that he did, and he was very emotionally vulnerable.

RICHARD HALL (2019)

I didn't know much about Jay as a kid except that he was my dad's funny sidekick. I remember the way he acted was very, very much the same as what you saw on television. We understand more about depression now and we hear more about how people have "on" and "off" modes, and I recognize now that when I was seeing Jay Stewart, I was seeing him when he was "on." I never saw the other side of him. My dad had seen it, though, and even though Jay had demons, my dad was extremely loyal to him. It made him furious that Jay was unemployed later in life.

BOB BODEN

Jay announced for some of the pilots we shot at CBS in the 1980s. He was jovial, jolly, always smiling….I had lunch with him on his 71st birthday, in September 1989. That lunch was one of the most fun hours I had ever spent in the game show business. Jay told so many stories, and I listened in awe of this legend sitting across the table from me. I was on such a high after that lunch after having spent an hour with him.

A few days later, he sent my boss, Michael Brockman, a letter, telling him that he'd had lunch with me and really enjoyed it, and he would like to be hired as my assistant. He asked Michael if he would consider that. Michael got that letter on a Friday. Michael forwarded the letter to me through the interoffice mail system, with a note attached saying "Please reach out to Jay."

I got the letter on Monday morning. Unfortunately, on Sunday, Jay had taken his life. I didn't know that yet. I found out and I was shocked beyond belief. I broke the news to Michael, and he was also truly taken by this horrible news.

As it turned out, Jay was very unhappy. Despite his public persona, despite his business face, he was a troubled man.

At the funeral, I approached his widow and introduced myself. She said, "He loved you so much. Last week, when he came home from lunch with you, he was on Cloud Nine. He really wanted to work with you."

I told her, "I wish I had intercepted that letter a day earlier. I had no idea how bad things were."

She said, "Nobody knew."

There can be ageism in this business and it can be hard for a 71-year-old man to find any job. I understand where he was coming from when he wrote that letter. There was no other opportunity for him to work for me because I already had an assistant. But if I had called him on Friday, I could have said, "I can't make this work, but is there anything else I can do for you?" It's presumptuous maybe, because I don't know I could have had influence on his mental state at that point, but maybe if I could have called him Friday, the course of history may have been altered.

In 1988, Jay Stewart got a last-minute call to fill in as announcer on the CBS game show *Blackout*. This photo was taken on that day, the last time that Jay Stewart ever announced a game show. (Zane Enterprises)

Monty really was offended at how Jay's career went after *Let's Make a Deal*. Jay was called the announcer of that show, but that role on that show spanned so many things—the zonks, carrying props around, bantering with Monty—that Monty, as an on-air talent, viewed Jay as an equal. He felt that he and Jay shared that show. After *Let's Make a Deal*, Jay announced other game shows, but the other shows he was on just had him announcing the opening, signing off at the end, reading the prize copy when it was called for, and never showed him on camera. He had done so much on *Deal* and then the next shows he did all just used him as a voice and nothing else. Monty thought that was a slap in the face to Jay. He felt Jay deserved more prominent roles on the shows he did.

HENRY KOVAL

I had lunch with Jay a week before he died. He seemed depressed. When he was with *Let's Make a Deal,* he was a sidekick, but Monty treated him like an equal, featured him prominently, showcased him in the publicity for the show, and really used Jay like he was a co-star. Jay never worked on another show that treated him like that, and it was a blow to his ego. I can't say enough about what a talented man he was.

CAROL MERRILL

When my daughter Hillary was a toddler, I brought her to the studio sometimes. Jay loved to play with her during rehearsal breaks. When Hillary wasn't paying attention, Jay would dash to his booth, and he'd call "Hillllllllllaaarrrryyyyyy..." in this booming voice. She'd look around so confused, wondering where the strange voice was coming from.

Jay and I saw a lot of each other. At ABC, I had a plastic collapsible three-sided dressing room set up backstage and it was right next to Jay's announcer booth, so we were constantly bumping into each other getting into position for whatever was about to get revealed. And I enjoyed being around Jay. I got to know his wife Phyllis well. I called him on his birthday a few days before he died, and we had a long chat. It was clear he was unhappy about being an agent. I didn't realize how unhappy he was.

I feel it's important to talk about Jay's suicide. Jay had such a good life. He was so happy doing his work. I can't imagine that he wanted to do anything other than what he was doing. He loved wearing the silly costumes for Zonks. He and Stefan were close so Jay was in a position where he could have said no to anything he didn't like, and he never said "no" to anything. He had a wife that he adored. People need to understand that when someone is successful, that doesn't just automatically mean that everything is okay.

MONTY HALL[cix]

Jay Stewart was a great friend. Jay Stewart can't find work...he gets a job with *Sale of the*

Century as the announcer, and I don't know what happened, but he gets the call at home. "Don't come into work today." That's the way they fired him. "Don't come into work."

He came to me and he was crying. I told him, "I don't have a show on the air right now. I don't know what I could do for you. But I'll try."

He came to me and said, "I'm going to be an agent!"…He knocks on doors for several months. He and his wife went to Sunday brunch at a friend's house. He excuses himself, goes down to his car, opens the trunk, takes out a gun, and kills himself. He left a note: *I can't stand the pain any longer.*

I blasted the business. Here's a man, one of the great announcers in our town, and there came a time in his life when he went to CBS and when he walked down the halls, nobody said hello to him. Nobody knew him. He was yesterday's news. No respect. There was no room for Jay Stewart anymore. What happened to the 35 years that he put into this business? We owed him that. And we buried him.

The cynical edge of the television business had long been a sticking point for Monty, from the day he had first overheard his name mentioned as one of the same old names suggested for every show, without ever having been hired for one. But as the 1980s ended, the cynicism became more brazen. Monty found himself booked for fewer and fewer telethons, because fewer and fewer were on the air. Telethons never got particularly good ratings—they disrupted regular programming, and viewers were prone to change the channel when they saw that the show they wanted wasn't on. But those viewers might watch for two or three minutes first, and the telethon's goal was to convince the viewer to pledge a few dollars before they changed the channels. In terms of money raised, telethons were enormous successes. In terms of sheer ratings, though, they had always underperformed, and station managers, who had in the past been willing to sacrifice a day or two of solid ratings in the name of goodwill, were more concerned about the bottom line. One by one, the annual telethons disappeared. Monty Hall For The People, *an intended daily parade of simple acts of kindness, couldn't find a buyer. It was becoming more difficult to find humanity off or on the air.*

MONTY HALL[α]

Putting [*Monty Hall For The People*] on TV was just an extension of my life. It's stuff that warms my heart and makes me feel good.

Monty at a fundraiser with friends Joanie & Norm Crosby. (Author's Collection)

I was astounded to find the station managers coming up to me and saying, "Well, we don't believe in stuff like this…give them a refrigerator."

That kind of comment just soured me. As a matter of fact, I left the convention after the second day. I never tried to sell the show again. I just put it away and forgot about it.

If you take a look at shows on the air today, it's not for the good of the people…It's all these other talk show people…with all the dirty laundry being hung out to dry.

BOB BODEN
Monty knew I was Jewish. I don't think I could ever be as Jewish as he was, though. Monty's values were rooted in Jewish values…respect and kindness regardless of who a person is, where they come from, or what they come from. And I think those values showed themselves in his production style, too. There was an inclusiveness to his staff and the way he oversaw them.

Every Jewish kid learns the word "Tzedakah" in Hebrew school. Many Hebrew schools teach the kids to bring in a coin every week, and it goes in a tin can with a slot in the top. Monty gave far more to the world than he took, ultimately.

RABBI SHARON BROUS

Tzedakah is a Hebrew word. It means "justice." People often use it to refer to charity, though. "How much tzedakah are you going to give this year?" The word is used interchangeably because the point is, when you're asking about charity, what you're really asking is "What are you doing to make the world more just?"

Judaism teaches that people have a legal right to food, clothing, and shelter, and that it is unjust for a more fortunate person to deprive. The belief is closely tied to the principle of Tikkun Olam (Hebrew for "world repair"), which has become synonymous with social justice. It was invoked as early as the 3rd Century A.D. in rabbinical teachings to refer to safeguards provided for those at a disadvantage. In more modern texts, it's defined as "when the world shall be perfected under the reign of the Almighty." It's considered the guiding principle of philanthropy, and though Monty was all too happy to help with Jewish causes like Hadassah and American Jewish World Service, Jews are encouraged to participate in all communities, not strictly Jewish communities— to work for the greater good in society.

Dennis & Mickie James, Monty & Marilyn Hall, and Sid & Florence Caesar at another benefit. Monty couldn't say no to one. (Author's Collection)

RABBI SHARON BROUS

Tikkun Olam is the belief that the world is shattered, and that humanity is capable of putting it back together. There are acts of healing and ways of connecting people. Monty believed in that. If you look at every Jewish organization in Los Angeles, Monty had some connection to each of them, often through donations or fundraising.

> As Monty had grown more successful, he had an urge to give more, an urge that fed on itself more than on any outside force. When Monty first penned his autobiography, he had fumed about not getting a signed copy of Richard Nixon's thank-you letter, feeling underappreciated.
>
> Monty, older and wiser in the years after the book was published, no longer felt an appetite for plaudits. When Monty accepted an award from the Na'amet Pioneer Women in Toronto in 1986, a reporter noted that Monty seemed slightly embarrassed as he accepted the plaque. He admitted to the audience that he had now amassed 300 such plaques from various charities, to the point that it became a quandary for him. How do you accept a request from a charity, knowing it's going to include a public display of recognition, after receiving so standing ovations from so many causes that even the most cynical observers could be forgiven for assuming it was the only reason you did it? But in that case, what do you do? Say "no" to the charity? Deprive them of a special appearance by Monty Hall in person, knowing that such a selling point was sure to drive a few extra dollars their way?
>
> A scant two weeks after the Na'amet Pioneer Women's event, Monty received the surprising news that the city of Winnipeg was naming a street after him. A Winnipeg resident named Tillie Goren learned that Monty was a native and that he had just lived around the corner. Goren spearheaded a movement to rename her street Monty Hall Street but per city law, the three-quarters of residents on O'Meara Street who signed a petition in favor of the change weren't enough to move forward.
>
> Then Goren learned about a new housing development near Winnipeg's Seven Oaks Hospital. The development was to be named Seven Oaks Drive, but Goren met with City Council members and argued that because of Monty's role in founding the Manitoba chapter of Variety Club, it was only fitting to honor him with a street located near a hospital. City Council agreed, and by the time construction was finished, the new street was officially named Monty Hall Drive.

RICHARD HALL (2019)

My dad never entertained the thought of moving back to Canada. Even when he was doing more and more Canadian TV in the '80s, he was just visiting. But he loved to visit. He was a "favorite son" and that came with a lot of attention. And my dad liked that attention.

Two great MCs, two great humanitarians: Monty Hall and Wink Martindale, raising money for a cause in the late 1980s. (Author's Collection)

Charity work tended to beget charity work for Monty, who found himself unable to turn off lingering thoughts of what was happening around him. Once, during a visit to Atlanta for a telethon, Monty paid a visit to a home that Variety Club had established in the city for mentally and physically disabled children. Monty ventured to London for what he had only intended to be a vacation…one to get away from, among other things, charity work. He and Marilyn had wanted to visit Oxford University to do some studying, and trek through the English countryside.

But after a few days in the city, Monty became curious about a similar home that Variety Club oversaw on the island of Jersey in the English Channel, so he dropped in for a visit.

MONTY HALL[cxi]

And I thought that the juxtaposition of these two visits within a couple of days on two sides of the ocean proves that children can be afflicted regardless of their geographical location, heritage, race, or color...Children throughout the world are afflicted with the same parents, with the same hurts and same problems...and our hearts go out to them.

And Monty's continued work with children led him to wonder what would become of them when they grew up...an issue that Monty felt that even the most dedicated charities and philanthropists were guilty of overlooking.

MONTY HALL[cxii]

The question arises, "What happens after childhood?" It is easy to arouse emotions for a child who needs help, but when the child grows into maturity, the world has a way of turning away, as if to say, "I helped you when you were small, adorable and helpless, but now I'm embarrassed that you didn't go away."

They must say, "I believe in your ability to progress and to contribute. I am willing to do everything I can to give you the tools to reach your own potential, to work with your minds, your hands, and your hearts. I will give you a home, not an institution."

KAREN LAPIERRE

I would help Monty with charity events after *Let's Make a Deal* ended. And you don't do the work for the sake of saying you did some work for charity. You do it because we're called as people to help each other. It makes me crazy knowing that when people vote on initiatives and propositions, they vote based on how it's going to affect them personally. Ask yourself how it's going to affect the community. If my money can help someone else, I'm in favor of that.

And by the way, just something to say about Marilyn. She was an incredible woman. You know how they say, "Behind every good man is a good woman"? That was Marilyn. And whenever Monty talked about his wife, you knew he was prouder of her accomplishments than he was of his own.

SHARON HALL (2019)

My father was not a person who liked or needed to acquire things. He was never extravagant with what he got for himself. I tried to encourage him, especially in his later years, to spend more money on my mother, who had been looking forward to that.

I think anybody who grew up during the Great Depression had the same issues with money that my father had. It's that knowledge that everything could be wiped out.

RABBI SHARON BROUS

Monty's daughter Sharon once told me a story about her parents that I loved, because it says so much about their values. When Sharon was a teenager, she had a boyfriend. He lived in Beverly Hills, too, so he came from money. He gave her a gold bracelet once. Sharon showed it to her parents, and they were furious. They really scolded her for accepting it and told her to give it back to him.

Sharon says, "But Mom, he loves me!"

Marilyn tells her, "If he loves you, let him write you a poem! That bracelet is a gold handcuff!"

That's really how they raised their kids. People are more important than things, the inside is more important than the outside. All of Monty & Marilyn's kids grew up to be incredible people. Monty and Marilyn taught them that no matter how much fame or fortune we have, we are all defined by what we give back. None of those kids was ever taken in by the trappings of celebrity.

KAREN LAPIERRE

Monty and Marilyn lived frugally. Not cheap, but frugally. They could afford to eat out at a five-star restaurant every night, but they didn't. They stayed home and cooked more often. And that was because they saw money in terms of what could be done with it. Monty worked for all these causes and saw all the work they did, and he would make little sacrifices in his own life just so he could write a check for a few dollars more when they reached out to him.

It wasn't an attitude borne from standing on the outside and looking in on the problems of others. Monty's family heritage traced back to a man named Dudi, who had been given a home, and later received tools to reach his potential because of a banker's belief in his ability to contribute. Monty saw the so-called "charity cases" of society and thought they deserved opportunities like the ones his grandfather got—all provided to him by Jewish aid organizations.

Memories of Dudi strengthened each year at the holidays. Joanna, Richard, Sharon, were now grown, with families and careers of their own, but Monty and Marilyn asked them to come to their house for seder every year at Passover. Dudi had been the family historian, a mantle that Monty had claimed over the years. Monty could give a geography lesson about the small villages of his ancestors, tell stories from their lives, and give meticulous explanations of how everyone was related in the massive family tree. He had spent seder in his grandfather's home, a tradition that he now wanted to pass down.

Monty joked frequently with friends and colleagues about his Jewish heritage. For years, his colorful but tasteful array of trendy suits landed him on several best-dressed lists, even during the 1970s when societal lapses in judgment put Monty in plaid as often as any other television performer. A friend once asked Monty if he felt conflicted about wearing a custom-made wardrobe while encouraging people to give all they could for charity, Monty quipped that his personal mantra was "Think Yiddish, dress British." When he got plastic surgery, Monty kidded about a stereotype, telling people that the procedure was "cutting off my nose to spite my race."

He was even the punchline to a joke made in the most inner circles of show business. "How do you throw a fundraiser in LA? Two Jews and Monty Hall."

But beneath the wisecracks were a deeply informed faith that guided Monty's actions, his priorities, and his sense of self.

RICHARD HALL (2019)

My dad spent his childhood sharing a house with a grandfather who had fled pogroms. When he reached adulthood, word came back from Europe about the Holocaust, and there was a direct line connecting those events in history. And then he saw the creation of the state of Israel. My dad was impacted by these events in Jewish history. They all affected him.

SHARON HALL (2019)

Living a Jewish life was the part of that faith that was important to him. He wasn't a big "God person" at all. But living the tenants of Jewish life—community, charity, family—were important things to him.

RICHARD HALL (2019)

Our mom & dad were both Jewish but not devout. And that's how Sharon and I turned out too. My dad was Jewish but not at the synagogue every Saturday. The Jewish faith was important to him as a set of guidelines. That's what mattered to him. To my dad, "being Jewish" had to do with how you treated people, took care of your family, and looked out for your fellow man. He had his bar mitzvah when he was 13, but he had a second bar mitzvah when he was in his seventies. It was a way to celebrate how he felt he had grown and evolved since the first bar mitzvah.

HENRY KOVAL

Monty and I were sitting in a bar one night. And Monty's eating a sandwich, and he begins quoting scripture to me and tying it into some of the charity commitments he has coming up. That really surprised me. But it was a glimpse into what mattered to him.

RABBI SHARON BROUS

Monty was just the ultimate mensch. He oozed love. He had an incredible sense of generosity. I think the expression "There but by the grace of God go I" shaped his view of the world. He remembered the way he was treated when he was in need, the way his family was treated when they were in need. He came from nothing, he was given a path to success, and then he spent his life creating those kinds of paths for other people.

My organization did a fundraiser at the Friars Club one year, and he was the emcee, which was so perfect. He was hilarious. It was very meaningful to have Monty at the helm of that event, and he was happy to do it. He really showed up for people, for causes, for organizations. He passed that down, too. He taught all of his kids, "This is what it means to be a Jew and to be a human being."

WHAT IS A JEW?
by Monty Hall
(Originally read at "Night of Glamour," a 1981 benefit for United Jewish Appeal)

A Jew is a corned beef sandwich, a shrug of the shoulders, Sandy Koufax, Hadassah, Heifetz, Haim Solomon, and a schoolteacher from Milwaukee who became a prime minister named Golda Mier.

A Jew is Bible scholar Maimonides, Mendelssohn, and Milton Berle. A seder, lox and bagels, and Albert Einstein.

A Jew is a Hungarian refugee brought to the USA by the Jewish Agency, given a job by the Jewish Vocational Service, looked after by the Jewish Family Child Service, treated at Cedars-Sinai, give a loan by the Jewish Free Loan Society…and is now Chancellor of the Los Angeles City Colleges.

He is also a refugee from Germany who became the great symbol of mediation and peace between nations—Henry Kissinger.

A Jew is Friday night at Baba's house, fresh challah, sweet honey, and chrain that clears your sinuses.

He is Moses parting the water, and Mark Spitz knifing through it.

A Jew is the Rothschilds, Kirk Douglas, cabbage rolls, King David, Disraeli, Cordoza, Bradeis, Dr. Jonas Salk…and a poor boy from a butcher shop in Winnipeg who now speaks from pulpits all over the world, name of Monty Hall.

This is all part of the mosaic—sweet, bitter, sad, happy, laughing, singing, crying, praying—and above all—loving.

It's a compote with a million different tastes. Try it. You'll like it.

CHAPTER TWENTY-FOUR

(Author's Collection)

Time heals all wounds, including the relationship between Monty Hall and NBC. Monty had acrimoniously departed the network and taken Let's Make a Deal *with him after a perceived lack of respect and a very measurable lack of money during contract renegotiations. In the 20 years that followed, Monty's relationship with the network was on-again, off-again. They bought* 3 for the Money *from Hatos-Hall but imposed their will on the content of the show and, in Monty's view, ruined the game. They bought* The Prime of Life, *Monty's sitcom, but* thrust him into a relationship with the star they wanted, McLean Stevenson, and in Monty's eyes, they had ruined that endeavor too. But in 1990, the relationship went to "on-again" in a way that quietly amused Monty. NBC, the network that decided in 1968 that *Let's Make a Deal* wasn't worth Monty's asking price, was now coming to Monty and asking for a new version of the show.

MONTY HALL[cxiii]

The reason they did was because of Dick Clark. Dick Clark had a great relationship with NBC. And he called me one day and said, "I'd like to partner with you on the show, and I can get the show back on NBC." I said, "Go to it." And just like that, we get an order.

RON GREENBERG, co-executive producer

I was working for Dick Clark at the time. I had very briefly worked on *Let's Make a Deal* when it first went on the air. And when I say "briefly," I mean I left the show before the audience started showing up in costumes.

In 1989, I joined Dick Clark Productions in series development. And I went to Dick and said, "You know, *Let's Make a Deal* isn't on the air, it's a great show, it has name recognition, and I'm sure Monty would be happy to talk to the two of us." Dick liked the idea, so we reached out to Monty, and everything came together very quickly.

And then Monty, Dick Clark Productions, and NBC got an unexpected offer from the Walt Disney Company. Walt Disney World in Orlando had opened a new movie-themed attraction called Disney/MGM Studios (now called Disney's Hollywood Studios) in 1989. In addition to rides and attractions, Disney/MGM Studios would be a fully-functioning production complex, built to accommodate film, television, and animation.

Disney, hearing that NBC was preparing to mount a new version of a beloved, classic game show, invited the production to use the Disney/MGM Studios facilities, even agreeing to share in the costs of the production. It was a fantastic proposal for everyone. It was an intimidating, massive studio that Disney offered, but within the most popular tourist destination in the world, it was likely that they'd fill all 900 seats for every taping, and probably with a cross-section of America, if not the world, in attendance. On days that the show wasn't taping, Disney would bring local performers into the studio to serve as host and play *Let's Make a Deal* with park visitors for smaller prizes. Disney even offered to build the set, an expense that NBC now didn't need to deal with. That would be the first thing that went wrong. Disney's set was a mammoth, looming two stories high, with four 26-foot neon "waterfalls" framing the three doors. The distance *from stage left to stage right was a sprawling 125 feet. And ironically, it proved to be too small in some critical ways.*

MONTY HALL[cxiv]

They build us a set, not to our specifications, but to their brilliant minds, how a set should be built. No room behind the doors. You needed all that room. You needed 40 or 50 feet to take a car out and bring a car in; to take out these dining room sets and bring in other stuff. No. They had no room behind the doors. You had to go all the way down the studio. You couldn't do that in a two-minute break. You'd go to a commercial and all the prizes had to be taken out through this corridor, and then all the prizes for the next segment had to be loaded in.

PHIL MOORE, audience warm-up man

I have never worked in a studio that size for a TV show, before or since. 900 seats. And they weren't just in front of you, the seats covered the length of the studio. Look to your left, there were people. Look to your right, there were people. Look behind you, there were people. They even had seats installed in the corners and the sides of the studios. The audience members in those sections could only see the show by looking at the overhead monitors.

In addition to the three doors, the new set had a massive video screen looming overhead, plus a large table that could be rolled out in front of the doors for displaying groceries for price-guessing games. Both of these set pieces were in place to fill the void left by Jay Stewart. Monty had the rolling table and video wall installed to replace the portable tray. The thought of finding "the new Jay Stewart" was too much to bear, so the new announcer would only be there to provide voiceovers.

MONTY HALL[cxv]

Now the problem was, who's going to emcee it? In 1990, I said, "No, I don't want to do it any longer. I did 4,700 episodes. Enough."

BOB BODEN

Monty was at a stage in his career where he was more interested in producing shows than being a host. I was an executive at ABC at the time and Monty had pitched a revival of Split Second. We shot the pilot with Robb Weller as host because Monty just wasn't interested in hosting anymore. He wanted to stay behind the scenes and give himself a little more time for doing charity work.

MONTY HALL[cxvi]

Dick said, "I'd like to do the show." I said, "Fine, I'll send you ten copies of the show that you can study over the weekend." He looked at them over the weekend, he called me, and said "I can't do the show. It's too tough. I don't know how you did it, it's too tough for me." So now the search went on. Now we've got to search for an emcee for *Let's Make a Deal*. We put out the word. I can't tell you how many tapes we saw, or how many people we interviewed, or how many people came into the office to be interviewed by me. Or how many run-throughs we did with people. I worked with each one of them.

RON GREENBERG

Monty worked very, very hard at finding exactly the right person to take over the show. You'd come into the office and you'd see Monty, and then you'd see 15 other Montys throughout the day. He was training every one of the people that came in to audition.

MONTY HALL[cxvii]

And when it was over, we narrowed it down to three people. We went to NBC and had a meeting, Dick Clark and myself, and Brandon Tartikoff. They wanted one person, I wanted another. I said, "Look, gentlemen, I know the show, we'll hire Bob Hilton, because Bob Hilton has done *Truth or Consequences*. He's had experience in this arena."

NBC's publicity for the new version was peculiar—many articles about the new show referred to Hilton as "an announcer from Lake Charles, Louisiana," making him sound like a total unknown, when in reality, Hilton's resume as a master of ceremonies and announcer included shows like Truth or Consequences, Tic Tac Dough, The Joker's Wild, The Price is Right, The Newlywed Game, Blockbusters, *and* The Guinness Game. *While Monty Hall repeatedly assured reporters that he had no worlds left to conquer as TV's Big Dealer, it seemed that the show as a whole was hedging his bets; Monty pledged that at some point, he'd make appearances on the new version as "a special guest star."*

The new Let's Make a Deal, *a joint venture of Monty Hall, Dick Clark, Ron Greenberg, NBC, and the Walt Disney Company, premiered on July 9, 1990, with host Bob Hilton.*

Monty passes the box, presumably containing a torch, to Bob Hilton. (Author's Collection)

MONTY HALL[cxviii]

So we go down to Orlando, Florida to do the show. I spent weeks there, working with Bob Hilton, and the crew, trying to teach them how to do the show…and I work with Bob, and I work with Bob, and we go on the air. And we're not doing that well in the ratings. NBC couldn't get a rating in daytime no matter what they put on. If they staged World War III on NBC, it wouldn't get a rating.

PHIL MOORE, audience warm-up

Bob Hilton was so interesting to me because he was such an everyman. I was this young comic and he sat with me during the lunch breaks sometimes. We'd have conversations about football and barbecue. One of the things I've noticed about show business is that once people become successful, they have a swagger about them. It's a certain air. It's not cockiness or arrogance, the people in show business who are nice have this swagger too. It's something in the way they talk and the way they look, it just happens. I noticed it in the way Monty walked, and I noticed it in Dick Clark the one time I met him. And I noticed that Bob didn't have that swagger. He was just a guy. But he was a great host; I thought he did a fantastic job.

MONTY HALL

So after 13 weeks, I get a call from the program director, and she says to me, "You have to take over the show."

I said, "I don't want to take over the show."

She said, "Take it over or we cancel it."

I said, "What if I take it over for a while until we find somebody else?"

"Okay."

So I move down to Orlando and I do 13 weeks.

BOB BODEN

I don't think Monty wanted to work that hard. I don't think he was happy being called into that role. But he was brilliant, and he conducted himself as if it was his first day. He gave all of his energy, even though he was nearly 70 at the time and he had less energy to spare than he did before.

Monty, Bob Hilton, and Dick Clark greet some hopeful contestants at Disney-MGM Studios. (Author's Collection)

A wide shot of the "far too big" set of *Let's Make a Deal* at Disney-MGM Studios. (Author's Collection)]

PHIL MOORE

I was only hired to do audience warm-up so I was never there for meetings or behind-the-scenes stuff. So if you ask me why Bob didn't work out as host, I can only talk about it in terms of theory. I think Monty left too much of an imprint on that show in the years he hosted it, to the point that being a great host wasn't enough. The audience just wasn't ready to accept anybody other than Monty in that role. Jump ahead to 2008, when they revive *Let's Make a Deal* on CBS, I think that's ultimately why they went with Wayne Brady, who is a great host. Now, maybe some guy out there named Steve Wyzanski that nobody's ever heard of would make a better host than Wayne. Maybe Steve Wyzanski would be the best host that show's ever seen. But he'd fail because Monty was so successful in that role that *Let's Make a Deal* is to a point where you can't have someone host it who isn't a name somehow. And I feel bad for Bob if that's the case, because he couldn't control that. Today, if Bob Hilton came along and he wanted to be considered for something, he'd just have to start up a YouTube channel, post videos for a year, get 100,000 subscribers, and the networks would give him more of a shot.

MONTY HALL[cxix]

The worst day of my life was when I had to call Bob Hilton and tell him I had to replace him…He felt very badly about it. He doesn't know how badly I felt.

RON GREENBERG

Bob Hilton got blamed for the show not working. But KNBC, the NBC affiliate in Los Angeles, put us on at 2:00 in the morning. I don't know what kind of ratings they were expecting.

PHIL MOORE

Monty was under a lot of pressure. He was the host and one of the bosses, which meant if he wasn't hosting the show, he had a meeting to attend. He had to talk to the press, he had to oversee production, he had to talk to executives. And then there was the detail that nobody wanted to say out loud: Monty was there to save the show. We all knew that's why he was there but just saying it would have made the mood in the room even more tense. Monty had hired Bob and Monty certainly wouldn't say such a thing, but you knew that was lingering in the back of his head: He had to be here to save the show. He really had a lot on his mind.

Yet, he said hello to me in the hallways, made small talk, smiled at me. What sticks with me was the way Monty looked at me during the show. I'd do my shtick during the commercial breaks while they set up the next game, and then when they were ready to go I'd reintroduce Monty and lead everyone in a round of applause.

I don't need a pat on the back, I'm not desperate for anyone's approval. When you're working on a TV show, the stars of the show have their own stuff to deal with and they're not thinking about you. But when it was time to reintroduce him and start the segment, he would always look right at me, smile, and give me a thumbs-up. Sometimes he'd wink. At the end of the show, he'd give me a pat on the back and say, "Great job." He didn't have to, but it left an impact on me. When impressive people say that you impress them, it means a lot.

One of the things Monty appreciated about me was that I learned how to read him very easily. He had so many other things going on, and I could sense his mood, and I could sense times when he just wanted to be out of there. Sometimes you really work with the audience to whip them into a frenzy, and you build a relationship with them or you have a great comedy bit going and you're running with it. Sometimes Monty gave me a vibe that he just wanted the show to be over and he wanted to get out of there, and whenever I sensed that, I would just do the absolute minimum during a break and then say, "And now, here's Monty Hall again!" He'd give me a smile and he'd nod his head at me, because he understood exactly why I hadn't done very much during that break and he appreciated it.

MONTY HALL[cxx]

The rating goes up a small amount. Michael Eisner, head of Disney…is a powerful man. Disney built the set for us down in Orlando, because it was Disney World. They had a vested interest in the show. They spent a lot of money on a set with steel! They built a set that was much too big. In our 26th week, NBC calls and says "We're gonna give you an extension of five weeks. We're not happy with the show but we'll give you a short extension." Michael Eisner says, "Our contract calls for 26-week [increments]." They say "No." Michael Eisner said, "Tear the set down. No 26 weeks, no deal." We lost the show. I didn't mind. I wasn't going to live in Orlando another day in my life.

On January 11, 1991, "guest host" Monty Hall helmed the final Let's Make a Deal *on NBC daytime, as well as his own final episode. Monty Hall, who 20 years ago was desperately searching for something to do with his life besides host a game show, would never again serve as the regular host of* Let's Make a Deal, *or any other game show, for that matter.*

PHIL MOORE

That job only lasted six months but it's the most important thing that's ever happened to me. In one of the last weeks of taping we did, we had just played the last deal of the main part of the show, then the next segment is the Big Deal of the Day and then we're done and we can go home. In the last deal, the Zonk hidden behind one of the doors was an elephant. We go to the commercial, and I'm kind of giving a goodbye to the audience at that point. "Hey, instead of being out at the park, you spent your day with us, and we really appreciate that, thanks for being here, we hope you had fun." And the director shuts off my microphone and starts talking to me in my earpiece. "Phil, you need to stretch this break out as long as you can. We're not going to be ready for at least 20 minutes."

As it turned out, we had an elephant that wasn't feeling well, and as soon as the segment ended, this elephant just unloaded all over the floor behind Door #3. It's not just a matter of cleaning it; after they clean it, they have to disinfect that entire area, and then they have to deal with the odor. And then we have to wait even longer for them to move the prizes into place for the Big Deal.

So I did every joke and every piece of shtick I had for 20 minutes and just kept it going until we were ready to go again. I told the audience exactly what had happened and the reason for the delay, because it's such a great story, you're crazy if you don't tell the audience that happened. I riffed on that for a while. Dick Clark was in the control room that day and he actually came out of the control room to apologize to the audience for the delay. He had a great line too. "We apologize for the technical difficulty...although I guess this is more of a biological difficulty."

And then he led the audience in a round of applause for me because he was so impressed with how I handled that delay and kept the audience's energy up. The show was cancelled, and I remember the feeling that the show had left me with. All those times when Monty gave me the thumbs-up, gave me the pat on the back, thanked me for the job I was doing...I was happy doing stand-up gigs but those months of working with Monty made me feel like I could do more. I called my agent and said, "I want to have a TV show of my own." And my agent laughed and said "Should I call the Show Fairy for you or what?" I told her I was serious and I said I thought hosting a game show would be the best use of my talents. And watching Monty for the past few months had been an incredible learning experience. What stuck out at me when I stood offstage and watched him was he would actually engage with the contestants. if he was talking to someone who was 4'2" or if he was talking to the Jolly Green Giant, he found something he could relate to in them. Watch the way Monty has conversations with contestants. He's actually invested in the discussion. That's a thing that I spot with game show hosts; you can tell the difference between a host who's just letting the contestant talk and a host who's actually listening.

And the great thing is Monty would use that to build suspense. There's something about his tone of voice when he offers a contestant $500 or whatever's behind the box on the display floor. He says "You can keep that $500" and he gives the contestant this look like what he's really telling him is "That could pay the rent, couldn't it?" A contestant could say they wanted to win a car and Monty would end up making some deal where they'd get a small box of candy, and then suddenly he'd say "Of course, there might be something besides candy in there. I think there's room in that box for a key..." And suddenly this contestant who wanted a car is giving serious thought to whether they should give back that box of candy or not, because Monty bothered listening to them two minutes ago and used that to create this suspenseful moment. Listen to what your contestants are telling you. So learning from Monty and getting all those thumbs up and winks from him made me feel like I could host my own game show. That was January 1991. By December 1991, I was taping *Nick Arcade* for Nickelodeon. I worked with Nickelodeon for years doing different shows for them, as host, as producer, as writer. I did their live tour for a few years. I'm still working for them 28 years later. That's the impact that Monty Hall had on me, personally, but we can take it even further than that. There's a guy named Rubin Ervin. He was a contestant on *Nick Arcade* in our first season. He told me years later it affected him when he got onstage and saw me, the host, for the first time. He's black, like me, and he said, "You were the first person I ever saw in that kind of position on TV, who acted like me, and looked like me. I almost couldn't talk the first time I saw you because I couldn't believe it. It made me feel like I could be myself." Rubin became the announcer for *Family Feud*. He's the announcer for Steve Harvey's talk show. And he told me he wanted to do that kind of work because I inspired him. And I went into my line of work because Monty's encouragement inspired me. So that's two careers that Monty Hall helped make. I'm sure he never thought about me again after *Let's Make a Deal* was cancelled, and he never even met Rubin. But if you're in a position of any kind of power, that is the amount of influence your words and your actions have. One sentence or one gesture can change somebody's entire outlook, their goals, their careers. Monty had that power and he used it to motivate people and to inspire them.

Curiously, even though the show languished at the bottom of the daytime TV ratings for six months, Let's Make a Deal *was propelled back into the public consciousness in 1990 and 1991, in a bizarre way. It wasn't a new version for a network or a cable channel or a syndicate or a foreign country that was grabbing people's attention. Not reruns either. Not a live touring show. Not a home game…It was a math problem. The brouhaha began in September 1990 in* Parade Magazine, *a weekly publication inserted into the Sunday edition of newspapers. A regular feature of the magazine was "Ask Marilyn," penned by Marilyn vos Savant, the woman listed in the Guinness Book of World Records for "Highest IQ." Readers were encouraged to write to vos Savant with logic puzzles, trivia questions, or even philosophical queries, which vos Savant would attempt to answer. In a September 1990 column, she fielded the following brainteaser about a decision to be made on a "game show," although the specific show that inspired the conundrum was unmistakable.*

Suppose you're on a game show, and you're given the choice of three doors: Behind one door is a car; behind the others, goats. You pick a door, say, No. 1, and the host, who knows what's behind the other doors, opens another door, say No. 3, which has a goat. He then says to you, "Do you want to pick door No. 2?" Is it to your advantage to take the switch?

The logical answer to this, in most readers' eyes, is that it doesn't make a difference. Going only by the information presented in the problem, it's a random guess, and with no added help, even if the host opens a door, it's still a random shot, so it's neither advantageous nor disadvantageous. Your odds of winning the car remains the same…right?

That's not what vos Savant said. She said that the contestant would have a better chance of winning the car by switching doors. In the ensuing six months, vos Savant received, by her estimate, 10,000 letters about the problem, nearly all of them lashing out at her for giving such an obvious wrong answer. Mathematicians and scientists wrote in, in some cases insulting her, in other cases, demanding an apology or a retraction.

"You blew it!" wrote a college professor. "Let me explain. If one door is shown to be a loser, that information changes the probability of either remaining choice—neither of which has any reason to be more likely—to one-half. As a professional mathematician, I'm very concerned with the general public's lack of mathematical skills. Please help by confessing your error and, in the future, being more careful."

But Marilyn vos Savant didn't back down. In the months to come, she doubled down, writing additional columns in which she stood firm by her answer and insisted that the odds of winning the car increased by switching doors.

It's worth noting that the Monty Hall Problem existed decades earlier, in a different form. It appeared as early as 1959 in Scientific American as "The Three Prisoner Problem." Columnist Martin Gardner assessed it at that time as "a wonderfully confusing little problem" and said, quite correctly as it turned out, that "in no other branch of mathematics is it so easy for experts to blunder as in probability theory."

The Three Prisoner Problem re-appeared in redressed form in 1976 in the journal American Statistician. Somebody had looked at the problem, a choice involving three like things, and altered it into something more relatable, inspired by a certain game show etched in the American zeitgeist. It was referred to from that point forward as "The Monty Hall Problem," or sometimes "Monty's Dilemma" or "The Monty Hall Paradox."

MONTY HALL[cxxi]

If Monty Hall offers you one of the three doors and one's got a car and two others have goats and he shows you one of the ones that has a goat and you're left with yours that you've selected and an unseen one, should he give you the opportunity to trade again for the unseen one, you should trade.

Well, when that was brought to my attention I said, "What difference does it make?" I never could understand what difference it makes. You make your selection. It's either the one that you've got or the one that's unseen. I got a call from a *New York Times* writer. He said, "I want to talk to you about this Monty Hall Problem."

He came over to my house. He said, "I want to prove to you that you should trade. If they give you a chance to trade, you should trade for the unknown and it works. I don't understand it, but it works."

He printed it, two weeks later, the Sunday *New York Times*, the front page. It started off with an article on the front page; it continued on an interior page. An entire page turned over to this thing.

Reporter John Tierney, a friend of Richard's from Yale, reached out to Monty in search of a story about the problem, and Monty invited him to his home in Beverly Hills for some experimenting. In the dining room, Monty had set up a simulation with three miniature cardboard doors on the table. One was hiding a key (representing the car), the other two hid small snacks (representing the goats).

JOHN TIERNEY

Math problems don't usually trigger a response like this, but this spread the way it did because *Parade* was probably the most widely circulated magazine in the country at that point; it was inserted for free in a lot of Sunday newspapers.

Monty prepared for the simulation by chatting with a mathematician who had seen the outcry over Marilyn vos Savant's assertion. Over the course of a one-hour conversation, the mathematician surprised Monty by agreeing with vos Savant's interpretation and explained why. With that, Monty went into the simulation with a new understanding.

JOHN TIERNEY

Monty was so much fun to be with that day. He loved the fact that he was getting this sudden burst of publicity with no extra effort on his part. He loved that this was going to be on the front page of the Sunday *New York Times*. That was the only time I ever met him, but I remember how happy he was to be there doing these experiments and testing the problem.

Monty had John Tierney run 20 simulations of the Monty Hall Problem. For the first 10 simulations, Tierney chose not to switch and kept his original door. He won the car four times. He won a goat six times. In the second 10 simulations he always switched doors. To his shock, he won eight cars and two goats. Explaining why is a little complicated, but we'll give it a few tries. For our example, let's just say the car is behind door #3.

For your first choice, you pick Door #1. Monty always opens a door that's hiding a goat, so in this example, Monty has to open Door #2. If you switch at that point, you can only have door #3, which is hiding the car. So that's one scenario where you win the car. You could pick Door #2, which means Monty will open Door #1. If you switch, you're left with door #3, which is hiding the car. That's two scenarios where you win the car. If you pick Door #3, the one hiding the car, it really doesn't matter if Monty opens Door #1 or Door #2 now; either one is hiding a goat. And if you switch, you can only end up with the other goat. So now you have two scenarios where you win the car and one scenario where you don't. That's a 2/3 chance of winning the car by switching. Flip that and think about what happens if you choose to keep your original door every time. If you pick Door #1 or Door #2 and choose not to switch, you get a goat. You only win a car if you started at Door #3. So that's a 1/3 chance of winning the car by staying put.

JOHN TIERNEY

I've had to explain this so many times, and after explaining it so many times that I came up with a condensed explanation that seems to work. If you're offered three doors and you're told to pick one, you'll be right one third of the time. That's easy to understand. Since odds of 1/3 aren't in your favor, it would mean that switching wins you the car 2/3 of the time. That's a very simplified version of it but it seems to satisfy most people I talk to.

One of the problems that causes a lot of confusion is that the way the question was phrased in the *Parade* column didn't make Monty's role clear enough. After the contestant selects the initial door, Monty opens one of the unchosen doors. In the *Parade* column, it reads as if he's doing so randomly. The key to the whole problem is that Monty knows where the car is and that he isn't randomly opening one of the other doors. The proper phrasing for the problem is "Monty knows where the car is, and he always opens a door hiding one of the goats."

And then there was the explanation that Monty gave to The New York Times, which Tierney paraphrased. Monty based it on his conversation with the mathematician earlier in the day. You start with an open choice of three doors, and with no help or hint at all, obviously that means the odds are 1/3 that you've picked the right door, or 2/3 that you've picked a wrong door. When Monty opens the door to reveal a goat, it creates an illusion. With two doors remaining, it appears to be a 50/50 shot; this door or that door? But it would only be a 50/50 shot if you had two doors to begin with. Even if two doors are left, you started with a 1/3 chance of picking the right door and a 2/3 chance of picking the wrong door. It's still a 2/3 chance you picked the wrong door even after

Monty has revealed a goat; in essence, that door's odds have been transferred to the other unchosen door. There's a 1/3 chance that your door is correct and a 2/3 chance that the other door is correct. Marilyn vos Savant, writing in defense of her answer, explained that part of the confusion that people felt stemmed from the fact that there were only three doors, which was a small enough range of options that it seemed to be pure luck, and that a key detail was overlooked; Monty knows where the car is, and he always starts by opening a door hiding a goat. That's actually a critical piece of information in understanding the problem.

JOHN TIERNEY

To understand why the host is crucial to the problem, I give people a revised version. I tell them to imagine Monty has spread out a deck of playing cards in front of you and he tells you to pick the ace of spades. So you pick a card, but you don't look at it, you just keep it in front of you and hope that's the ace of spades. So that leaves Monty with 51 cards. The next thing Monty does is he turns over 50 cards that aren't the ace of spades, leaving you with your card and the one card Monty hasn't revealed, and Monty offers you a chance to switch cards. Do you honestly believe that's a 50/50 shot, or do you think it's really, really likely that Monty just gave you a big hint about where the ace of spades is?

Monty saw a flaw in the problem…not so much the core concept of it; the original Three Prisoner Dilemma was fine. Dressing it up in Let's Make a Deal *bothered him because he felt that it oversimplified the show itself.* Let's Make a Deal *wasn't a pure exercise in reason from people calculating probability in their heads. To illustrate the problem that he had with The Problem, Monty ran two more simulations. Tierney nonchalantly selected one of the three doors. Monty promptly opened it, announced, "You've won a goat!" and ended the deal. Tierney, confused, told Monty he made a mistake. Monty explained that contestants aren't told in advance what kind of deals the show will make or how each one will play out. Yes, it's still a random 1/3 chance, but an actual contestant would have given a lot more thought to their first choice if they didn't know the chance to switch was coming. And Monty said that was an important distinction because a real contestant would convince themselves that they had chosen the correct door, which would make the option to switch more of a risk when Monty offered it to them. Monty speculated that in execution, on a real TV show with a real car at stake, contestants would rarely or never switch, because they'd talk themselves into believing they'd picked the right door. Monty ran one more simulation. Tierney, unsure of what Monty was getting ready to do, thought carefully about his choice this time and picked Door #1. Monty threw him a curveball by proceeding with the Monty Hall Problem exactly as stated. He quickly revealed Door #3, revealing a goat.*

Monty asked if he wanted to switch doors. Tierney switched and went with Door #2. And then Monty surprised him by pulling a roll of money out of his pocket. "I'll give you $3,000 not to switch." Tierney asserted that he wanted to switch. Monty upped it to $4,000. Tierney dug in. He still wanted to switch. Monty offered $4,500. Tierney wouldn't budge so Monty crept up to $4,700, then $4,800. Tierney still wanted to switch. Monty made his final offer: $5,000. Tierney would have none of it. He wanted to switch. He won a goat. Monty told him, "Now do you see what happened there? The higher I go, the more you thought the car was behind Door #2. I wanted to con you into switching there, because I knew the car was behind #1. That's the kind of thing I can do when I'm in control of the game. You may think you have probability going for you when you follow the answer in her column but there's the psychological factor to consider." That would always be Monty's objection to the problem; the math was sound. It was definitely a 2/3 chance if you switched. But the problem didn't take into account human emotions, or psychology, or manipulation from a skilled host.

JOHN TIERNEY

The reaction we got at the *Times* was incredible. We had a whole explanation of it in the paper, along with a sidebar and a graphic with multiple explanations of the math. We still got inundated with mail saying "You idiot, it's a 50/50 shot! It doesn't matter!" And I finally sat down and wrote a form letter to mail out to people to explain it in further detail because they still weren't getting it.

CHAPTER TWENTY-FIVE

(Author's Collection)

In 1987, Tom Kennedy, who had so skillfully hosted Split Second *for Hatos–Hall on ABC during the 1970s, got word that his current game, NBC's* Wordplay, *was cancelled. Six months later, Tom, enjoying dinner with his wife at a restaurant, was remarking that he hadn't heard of any new projects from his agent or any of the networks.*

When a waiter approached Tom and saw a mostly empty plate in front of him, he asked, "Are you finished?" Tom smiled at himself and said, "Yeah, I guess I am."

In 1990, ABC introduced a new version of Match Game but deemed the legendary host of that show, Gene Rayburn, unsuited to host the revival at age 72. Monty's best friend, Dennis James, was a pioneer broadcaster, the first host of a regularly-scheduled network game show, way back in 1946. In 1990, Dennis James was 73 years old and hadn't hosted a series regularly since 1977.

Monty was glad not to be in Orlando, doing a version of Let's Make a Deal that proved more stressful for him than he anticipated. And yet, when it was over, he felt a sadness. He was almost 70, and that was reason enough to believe that he was done. Compounding that was that his greatest success had been in game shows, which had experienced ebbs and flows of popularity throughout TV's history. The early 1990s were possibly the worst ebb ever for the game show business.

SHARON HALL (2019)

In our family, we refer to the early 1990s as the "Terrycloth Bathrobe Years." There was a period where my dad referred to himself as retired. We'd walk into the house to visit my parents, and he'd be wearing a white terrycloth bathrobe. It didn't matter what time of day you went over there. He was in his bathrobe. I think he was depressed. He missed the energy and going out there and working.

He was still doing charity events, but in a way, it was too many—there's no such thing as "too many" charity events, obviously. But what I mean is, he began doing so many during those years that you got the impression that he was trying to fill a void.

ROBERT HALL (2019)

I visited his house once and he looked troubled when he looked at the calendar. "Look at this," he says, and he turns ahead a few pages. "September is blank. I don't have anything to do in September. There must be an event going on somewhere. There are charities out there that I've never heard of, but since I've never heard of them, I don't know how to contact them. But what if one of those charities has something going on in September? I could give them a hand."

SHARON HALL (2019)

What brought him back from the brink was having grandchildren. My brother moved back into the area and brought his family with him, and you could see my dad revitalize from having his grandchildren in close proximity.

RICHARD HALL (2019)

I don't know, nor could I imagine, any five children more fortunate than those five grandchildren.

Monty, with a wall covered in plaques honoring his contributions to organizations from every corner of the globe, would show visitors the one he was the proudest of: His "Grandfather of the Year" award, bestowed upon him by his five favorite experts.

SHARON HALL (2019)

The other thing that really brought him back around was he began licensing the *Let's Make a Deal* format for foreign versions, and he loved working with the producers in these countries and consulting with them. That work made him really happy.

Fred Travalena and Monty team up to co-host a comedy special on the TNN cable channel. Monty worked less and less in the 1990s, but the phone did still ring, and he was happy to go in front of the camera again. (Author's Collection)

In the 1990s, Monty Hall was an anomaly among his peers in that, despite his feeling that he was involuntarily retired, his phone still rang quite often. Admittedly, it was with mixed results, but that was the nature of show business. You win some, you lose some. But Monty Hall turned 70 after NBC canceled Let's Make a Deal and he just kept going. Later in 1991, he launched a Let's Make a Deal 900-number, in which recordings of his voice guiding callers through a series of "deals" and games that involved pushing the right buttons on the phone to advance in the game, with a chance to win as much as $2,000. In 1992, Monty was contacted by Dan Farrell, a TV producer about hosting a new series called The Great American Treasure Hunt, an adaptation of a popular British TV show called Antiques Roadshow.

DAN FARRELL

I was living in England in 1981 and I became a fan of the original *Antiques Roadshow* over there. It had premiered two years earlier. I went to the BBC and worked out a deal with them, and I bought the rights to produce the show in America.

It ended up taking me years to get the show on the air. First of all, when I described the show to anybody at an American network or production company, I could see their eyes glazing over the moment I said "Antiques." And everybody connected the word "antiques" with their elderly relatives. They figured that the only people that would watch this show were blue-haired old ladies. Cable TV was starting to thrive in America, but in the 1980s, cable hadn't really started serving niche audiences yet.

All I had to show anybody in the U.S. at that point was a tape of the British version and that was a problem too. I showed it to Dan Taffner, who was the man who brought Benny Hill's series to American TV. He adapted *Three's Company* from a British series called *Man About the House*. I showed him the tape of *Antiques Roadshow* and he said, "It's too British."

I had access to Monty because I was a friend of his son-in-law. I wasn't trying to pitch the show to him, necessarily. I just wanted his opinion of it, and he said the same thing to me. "Dan, this is too British."

Well, finally, in 1990 I decided what I needed to do was tape an American version. I contacted Skinner Auction House and asked if I could bring a crew in to tape during one of their appraisal days. They agreed, so I called Monty on the phone and asked if he'd be my host, and he said yes!

I thought using Monty as host was a brilliant idea, even if it was mine. Also, he was familiar to American audiences. This wasn't *Let's Make an Antiques Deal*. This was a different kind of thing. But Monty could be spontaneous. He could be witty. He could ask questions. And his work ethic was just incredible.

Monty showed up and he was sick as a dog. He had a stomach issue (Crohn's Disease)—and he was in a lot of pain the entire day. But he was an absolute pro. He was there all day, never took a break, never let on that his stomach was hurting so badly.

He was there as the host, but he gave me one great piece of creative input. We were talking with one of the appraisers and they were going to do this Oriental rug on camera.

I said to the appraiser, "Maybe you could explain this by saying…" And Monty taps me on the shoulder and says "Dan, never give them lines. Let people speak the way they're going to speak."

And I always obeyed that. I never tried to give anybody lines again.

We never really made an official pilot. We shot all that footage but never edited the raw tape together. I showed that tape to WGBH…but the executive producer at the time knew how she wanted it to be done and what the elements should be. I gave control of the production to WGBH when they picked it up, even though I'm still involved as consulting producer and I own the rights to the show. But WGBH had control over the show when they decided to pick it up. If I had to guess, I'd say they didn't ask Monty to host when they decided to move forward with the show. They probably couldn't have met Monty's price.

**Monty presents an award to Sumner Redstone on behalf of Variety Club.
(Author's Collection)**

Monty had one last itch to scratch in his career. He had tried film and theater and found he didn't love them like he thought he would. But he still looked back on his decision in 1977 not to host a talk show when he had the chance. At the time, he thought he was risking failure, but he looked back and realized that it had still been an opportunity to try something he really wanted to do.

In 1993, cable TV was booming and expanding in all directions. The industry began catering to niches; Nickelodeon reached out to kids, while MTV sought teenagers. The business at large was still a constant war for viewers aged 18–49, or even better, 18–34. Viewers 50 and older were forgotten. Case in point, two Let's Make a Deal writers, Alan Gilbert & Bernie Gould, spent part of the early 1990s trying to sell production companies on an idea they had for a musical game show aimed specifically at viewers over the age of 50. They were flatly rejected and told to shoot for age 45, tops.

Special Guest Star Monty Hall. Here he joins daughter Joanna Gleason on an episode of *Love and War*. (Author's Collection)

In 1993, a group of former advertising executives in their sixties, feeling pushed out of the industry, teamed up to create their own advertising firm, which they cheekily named Older & Wiser. Older & Wiser combined their resources with Bernie Weitzman, a former executive at Desilu, Lucille Ball's production company, to mount a new cable channel that would serve the interests of 65 million television viewers over the age of 60, who were otherwise totally ignored by the TV business. They named the channel Golden American Television. The schedule would include new shows starring old favorites like Ruta Lee, Peter Marshall, and Army Archerd, as well as a talk show titled Monty & Company. In 1992, Johnny Carson concluded a legendary 30-year run as the host of The Tonight Show at age 67. Now, one year later, Monty Hall would be hosting the first episode of his talk show at the tender age of 71.

Though Monty and Company had a brief run, Monty still found his way into one studio after another. There was The Wonder Years, where he played the part of Monty Hall. Love and War, where he played the part of Monty Hall. And The Nanny, and Sabrina the Teenage Witch and Providence and That '70s Show, every time playing the part of Monty Hall. He got numerous chances to act in the 1990s, decades after he had been begging ABC for the chance. Good things came to he who waited, even if he was typecast.

Monty, a sickly child who wasn't expected to reach 30, had not only lived to see his 70s and beyond, but his face and body seemingly forgot to age. Two generations had watched Let's Make a Deal during its original long run. In the late 1980s and early 1990s, packages of reruns made their way to cable television and introduced a third generation to the game. For viewers, it was fun to see him again because he looked exactly the way he always had. The Monty of the 1990s looked like the Monty Hall of the 1970s, just with a still-full head of hair that had turned a flattering shade of silver once he stopped tinting it. It was like he never left.

Monty had taken on a new agent in the 1990s: Fred Wostbrock, a game show fan who had written to Monty and other hosts as a child, and stayed in touch with them as he reached adulthood, was now taking on all of his childhood idols as clients. He began packaging Monty with other game show icons, like Tom Kennedy, Gene Rayburn, and Wink Martindale, and offering them as guests for daytime talk shows. Geraldo Rivera, Maury Povich, Phil Donahue, and others devoted full hours of their shows to interviewing game show hosts, who'd reminisce about their careers and share their favorite moments, often accentuated with nostalgic photos and video clips. Monty wasn't in demand to sing, dance, or act. And unless one of the talk show hosts suggested doing an actual game with members of their audience, Monty didn't even have to perform as a master of ceremonies. In the 1990s, he just had to show up and be Monty Hall. And time and again, he was the best Monty Hall any show could ask for.

RICHARD HALL (2019)

My dad liked attention more than anything. So, yes, there was a time in his life when he wanted to move on from *Let's Make a Deal*, but it was the thing that brought him the most recognition and the most attention. If some sitcom wanted to do an episode where a contestant had a dream about being a contestant on *Let's Make a Deal*, my dad was happy to come in and do that. He loved it!

And with legend status finally came some recognition. In 1995, he was inducted into the National Broadcasters Hall of Fame, although Monty admitted that time tempered his enthusiasm for recognition from his peers.

TV game show legend Monty Hall. Here he joins fellow legends Gene Rayburn and Wink Martindale on an episode of *Geraldo*. (Fred Wostbrock Collection)

MONTY HALL[cxxii]

I think some of these awards come too late in my life. I have never won an Emmy. And yet, among the people in the business, in all walks of Hollywood, they acknowledge me as the consummate emcee, because I do so much charity work. I'm in a hotel here, like three nights a week doing a benefit. Everybody introduces me as the Number One Consummate Emcee. On television that was the toughest job in the world: *Let's Make A Deal*! Tougher than any of the other jobs where people say "What's the answer to this question?" I had a circus going on. I never got an Emmy. Now, the same thing with being inducted into something. I'm looking at the Television Museum referring to the various decades of what was on the air. They never once in daytime television mention *Let's Make A Deal*! They mention four or five other shows. My show ran longer than any of them by years and years and years. So, you see we've been ignored.

…I know as far as the Emmys were concerned, they always want dignity. They want to be placed like the Oscars. The Tonys may get that prestige but the Emmys will never have the prestige of the Tonys or the Oscars. So, why give it to a show where people come dressed up as Indians and cowboys? It's beneath their dignity to give an award to such a show. We were treated as something not to talk about. Sure, it's one of the biggest three successful shows in history and yet it's ignored. I had to come to grips with that.

When I got into the National Broadcasters Hall of Fame it was okay, but you may be about 10 or 20 years too late. The National Academy of Television Arts and Sciences has yet to recognize me. I dare say if they had an award like the Gene Hershold Award for the Oscars, for philanthropic work, there is no performer that raises one hundredth of what I raise every year and make as many appearances as I do. I do 50 appearances for charity. Besides I head up a golf tournament and a tennis tournament. I work 200 days a year for charity. They should create such an award and I should be the recipient. I'm not talking immodestly. I'm telling you the way it is. I'm ignored by that section of the television people. And yet, when you go around the town and you meet the people in the town, my name stands out very well. I love my reputation. I love the fact that they know I'm Mr. Charity-----but not by the people who give the awards out. So, when you ask me about this award, it's fine, but I wasn't excited as I would've been 20 years ago.

Though he was at peace with being TV's Big Dealer, Monty had reached a point where he was willing to let go of his own creation. He and Stefan Hatos reached an agreement to lease the format of Let's Make a Deal *to another production company, Stone-Stanley, whose game show portfolio included the kids' favorites* Legends of the Hidden Temple *and* Fun House. *For the first time,* Let's Make a Deal *would go into production without either Stefan Hatos or Monty Hall being involved.* Big Deal, *as the new version was titled, would run for only six weeks in 1996.*

Though Monty had leased the rights to the format, he still owned it and was free to do what he wanted. An electronic tabletop home game of Let's Make a Deal *launched, featuring the voice of Monty Hall. He endorsed an auction website, buybidwin.com, and lent his face to a game feature on the site that awarded prizes to visitors.* Let's Make a Deal *slot machines started popping up in Nevada, and state lotteries sold* Let's Make a Deal *scratch-off tickets. Monty even made himself available to corporations and charities that wanted to stage live versions of* Let's Make a Deal *for employees and donors. All they had to do was furnish the prizes and Monty would come in to host the show.*

These ventures may have seemed odd for a man who told Dick Clark in 1989 that he never needed to host Let's Make a Deal *another day in his life, and who had decided in the early 1980s that a live stage production of* Let's Make a Deal *wasn't a workable idea. But* Let's Make a Deal *was a golden goose, and Monty recognized its potential as a means to an end—all the extra income from the slot machines, the tabletop games, and the corporate functions, wisely invested, could do a lot of good for a lot of causes. He had already exceeded his promises beyond Max Freed's wildest dreams, but Monty saw a world that needed help, and saw his own potential to provide Tikkun Olam.*

CHAPTER TWENTY-SIX

(Author's Collection)

STU BILLETT

The business changed in the late 1980s because of Oprah Winfrey. She had been doing a local talk show in Chicago. In 1986, she went national, and she delivered these ratings right away in syndication that nobody could believe. And everybody in the business wanted talk shows. Didn't matter how much clout anyone had built up if they were game show people;

the networks wanted talk shows. Mark Goodson began feeling that squeeze, Bob Stewart felt it, and I think Monty felt it. Executives didn't want new game shows the way they used to. And game shows just really died off during the 1990-91 season while everybody wanted a talk show.

At the same time, the Soviet Union collapsed and disbanded, and all these pieces of the Soviet Union became separate nations. Because they weren't a part of Russia anymore, the television packagers and stations in those parts of the world suddenly needed to start making their own programming. They didn't have much money to work with, and game shows are the least expensive genre to produce, so game shows popped up all over the place in those former Soviet Union countries.

Europe had a boom of game shows and "people shows," as Ralph Edwards would call them, at a time when America wasn't doing them. When a show succeeded in one country, another country would do their own version, so these successful game show formats were created all over Europe in the 1990s. It really altered the business because when America decided to start doing game shows again, it was a different process. Executives didn't want to hear pitches from producers in America who had new ideas. Executives wanted to see an idea that already existed in Europe, and they wanted a graph so they could see the ratings data in Great Britain, and the data from Denmark. Game shows lived on in America, but nobody wanted ideas anymore, they just wanted to adapt things that already had track records.

Monty had been frustrated decades earlier by the major networks' increasing ambivalence toward prime-time game shows. But in the summer of 1999, Monty, along with the rest of the nation, was watching a game-changer called Who Wants to be a Millionaire? *on ABC. Viewers were enamored by the friendly but perpetually bemused Regis Philbin, the trivia questions, the Lifelines, the brooding music. At the end of the season,* Who Wants to be a Millionaire? *ranked #1, #2, and #3 in Nielsen's ratings. The other major networks launched their own games in a vain effort to keep up—Fox's* Greed, *NBC's* Twenty One *revival plus an import from Great Britain called* The Weakest Link.

Writers suddenly began looking back at the old guard of game shows, soliciting interviews for their thoughts on the new trend. Monty's feelings were mixed. He was happy to see game shows succeed, sure, but he really didn't like the new wave of them.

MONTY HALL[cxxiii]

You give away a million dollars, and make the questions so easy that everyone at home says "I could play that game and I could win a million," especially when they ask these questions and four answers come up on the board. If they were going for $8,000, I don't think [audiences would] be watching it. They might watch a little bit because they can play the game.

Along comes *Twenty One* and *Greed* and the others, and they're going for more than a million bucks. Two million. Three million. The next step is to give away the network. Where does entertainment stop and the buying of an audience begin?

CBS, after a slow start, gained a foothold by going in an unexpectedly different direction with a startling offering called Survivor, *in which contestants tried to co-exist while supposedly stranded on an island, voting each other off week by week until only one remained and claimed a million dollars.*

MONTY HALL[cxxiv]

Shows like this, with the voyeurism involved, it's a completely different genre. [The networks] have to come up with something new, and it's not putting on better dramas. If there were no competition for ratings, then you wouldn't see shows like this. You wouldn't see it, because no network official with any decency about him would propose such a show.

Isn't the ultimate one where they kill each other? Isn't that the ultimate game show? I mean, if with *Survivor* right now, because they vote you off the island or whatever it is, the easiest way later on is to kill you.

Surprisingly, not only were the networks rolling out the welcome mats for game shows again, they stayed rolled out. The shows themselves came and went, but prime time game shows weren't a passing fad, as some critics anticipated. In 2002, Monty got a shot at what, deep down, he probably considered retribution. NBC, the network that considered a prime-time version of Let's Make a Deal *to be beneath them, now wanted to air exactly that. NBC negotiated with Monty for a new prime time version of* Let's Make a Deal, *committing initially to five episodes to air on Saturday nights beginning in January 2003, with Monty and his daughter Sharon serving as co-executive producers along with an entirely new staff and a new host.*

MARK MAXWELL-SMITH

When I was hired to work on that show, they hadn't hired a host yet. NBC was very high on, believe it or not, Steve Harvey. Steve Harvey, at that time, had never hosted anything. All we had to go on was his stand-up act. Monty said "No way!" That style was totally wrong.

So we ended up hiring Billy Bush, and in a world where Donald Trump never existed, *Let's Make a Deal* would be remembered as his most embarrassing moment.

Although the show found their new host, though Monty maintained a presence on the new version. A gold coin with Monty's smiling face flashed on the screen at the beginning of each episode. He appeared in a brief segment on the premiere in which he presented Bush with his old microphone, a cute passing of the torch, although he didn't pass it completely. Monty would take over one segment during the five episodes, making a deal with a contestant from the original series.

In the ensuing months, so many things went wrong that Monty couldn't even lay blame on any specific person. Geoff Edwards had aptly called hosting Let's Make a Deal *the hardest job in game shows. When Billy Bush was selected to host, Monty was given only three days to work with him, and then the five hour-long episodes would be taped over the course of three more days. There was too much work to do in too little time.*

MARK MAXWELL-SMITH

That show just always felt like it was doomed. Even in rehearsals, something felt wrong. We had three slot machines set up in the middle of the stage during a rehearsal. And all of a sudden, they just fall over, like a ghost had toppled them. Things like that seemed to happen at the rehearsals.

Once the shows were taped, Billy Bush did publicity, and he said something in an interview about how he did the show without cue cards. Well, yeah, but what he didn't mention was that he had a device called an IFB [Interruptible Foldback] in his ear and he was getting instructions and lines fed to him.

And then there were the deals themselves. NBC, in the wake of the reality TV boom in the early 2000s, suggested making the deals naughtier. It was a notion that Monty hated, but he was willing to compromise. The show's writers came up with deals that were sufficiently edgy. The definitive example was the first deal on the premiere broadcast, in which a female contestant faced three men, dressed respectively in a kilt, a toga, and a grass skirt. Each of them had a small prize hidden underneath their outfits and the contestant chose one to reach under to pull out the prize.

MARK MAXWELL-SMITH

NBC had a very successful game show in prime time at that point called *Dog Eat Dog* which could be very edgy, and NBC wanted a version of *Let's Make a Deal* that would have good parity with *Dog Eat Dog*. That just did not work. You couldn't take what *Let's Make a Deal* was and make it into that. It didn't look right.

I was usually the one tasked with pitching those kinds of deals with Monty and seeing if we could get him to agree to them. Sometimes he did flat-out say no. I was the one who had to pitch the deal with the three skirts to him. The technique for pitching that kind of thing to Monty was to emphasize the psychological element or the game concept to him. When I went in to pitch that idea, I led off by explaining "Mouse in a Box," which was a game we did a lot on *Truth or Consequences* and I told him it was a different spin on that. Monty wasn't thrilled that we had a woman reaching under three men's skirts, but at least this way he could see that there was an actual game there, and you could work with him if he saw that.

Monty, who could be refreshingly honest when giving interviews, openly told any reporter who would listen that he found the concept thoroughly distasteful. The network wanted push the envelope, so he did. He didn't hide that. And if Monty's long-time fans were appalled that he gave in and green-lit that one, all Monty could say in return was…

MONTY HALL[cxxv]
…You should have seen the stuff they tried to put past me.

SHARON HALL (2019)
I was the executive producer. Part of the reason it was so fraught was because I wasn't raised around the show and didn't make a study of it when I was a kid, and I wouldn't know how to produce it. But then I wound up being a producer, and that was a very difficult position for me, because I just kept disappointing my father, and I wasn't used to doing that.

And after the five episodes had taped, NBC abruptly changed their scheduling plans. They held the show until March 2003, and instead of airing it on Saturday nights, they aired it on Tuesdays, in direct competition with Fox's white-hot American Idol. *The new* Let's Make a Deal *delivered a Zonk in the Nielsen ratings, and NBC aired only three episodes. Monty candidly said he didn't care if the other two ever aired.*

It seemed that the old wines were best. As the new Let's Make a Deal *came and went in the blink of an eye, reruns of Monty's years holding the mic endured year after year. Hatos-Hall originally sold a package of reruns to local stations immediately after the original series came to* a close in 1977. After The All-New Let's Make a Deal ended in 1986, the tapes hadn't even started to collect dust when the reruns began airing on USA Network, and later The Family Channel. In 2001, after seven years of on-again, off-again negotiations—Monty knew the value of his property and expected to be paid accordingly—the classic Let's Make a Deal appeared on Game Show Network. As usual, the show was a smash.

Forever young. Reruns of *Let's Make a Deal* became as much of a television institution as the original broadcasts. (Hall Family Archive)

BOB BODEN

GSN licensed several hundred episodes of *Let's Make a Deal* in 2001, shortly before I came to the network as senior vice president of programming. I wanted to rerun the original pilot from 1963. It had never aired in full anywhere. It was such an iconic episode. Partly because of nostalgia value, but also because it was so different from what the show became—no costumes, different announcer, the way Monty presented the deals was somewhat different. I reached out to Monty's agent, Fred Wostbrock, who negotiated the deal to air the pilot as a special. Monty did some press for it and GSN got a lot of attention as a result.

Monty began doing more appearances for us. He attended our press events. The TV Critics Association had an event, and we invited many of the classic game show hosts to attend. My boss at GSN asked me to ask Monty if he'd be willing to do quickie deals with the audience.

I told him, "I don't want to ask an 80-year-old man to go out and work the room for us at a press event. I think it's disrespectful to put him to work for us. I don't think he's up for it. But I'll ask him."

I go to Monty and ask him if he'd make deals with the audience and he says, "Sure, how much time do you need me to fill?"

And then he just went right out there, performed as if he was on the air in front of a national audience. He rose to the occasion, and again, it gave us a lot of good attention in front of a valuable group of people. Monty was just amazing to GSN.

Let's Make a Deal reruns will always be valuable. They'll always be popular because it's the perfect balance of being evergreens and being nostalgic. On reruns of a trivia game, you can kind of date the show by the subject matter of the questions being asked. Reruns of a show like *The Price is Right* have only nostalgic value, not much play-along value, which you want in any game show. That's the point. But if you're watching an episode of *The Price is Right* from 1985, you may not remember that the price of a car at that time was about $7,500.

With *Let's Make a Deal*, they occasionally had price-guessing games, but most of the show was "Do you want this or that?" And even when you're watching an episode from 50 years ago, it's easy to relate to that kind of decision-making. You can still get invested in it and shout at your TV.

CAROL MERRILL

It doesn't matter how old the show is. Monty was and is very appealing. He had that unique and special way of dealing with the traders. He was clever, he was quick-witted, he brought things out of people he talked to, and he made them the stars. And Jay deserves a little credit, and I'll give myself just a little bit. The three of us had synergy. When the three of us were together, each of us was better for it. And I think that's why the reruns hold up.

(Author's Collection)

CHAPTER TWENTY-SEVEN

As Monty got older, it was easy to forget that Monty got older. Every now and then, nature would give him a stern reminder—he quipped in 2002 that the broken hip he suffered that year, at age 81, had taught him that men his age should sit on the edge of the bed instead of standing when they put their pants on.

But the rest of the time, Monty kept up appearances, stepping in front of the camera for guest star spots, and spending meal after meal after meal in the company of friends who wanted to stay in touch. And, Monty would proudly remind everyone, he had driven himself there.

RICHARD HALL (2019)

My parents' social life was incredible. They outlived so many of their dearest friends, but Mom & Dad never got lonely. They just kept going out and making new friends. How many 85-year-olds and 90-year-olds go out to new places to meet new people? My parents did. They just had this massive circle of friends that they kept replenishing as so many other friends died. And so many of their new friends were younger, but my parents were just so outgoing and so open, they could bond with anybody. My parents were never lonely.

STU BILLETT

Monty and I would go to lunch at Hillcrest Country Club. I loved eating lunch with him because no matter how old I got, Monty still called me "Kid." I worked in TV for 50 years, my hair's gray, and Monty greets me at the country club by saying "Hey, kid."

LLOYD SCHWARTZ

Monty went to my parents' anniversary party...I think it was their 55th anniversary. And my dad was getting around the room in a walker. I remember Monty yelling out "Hey, Sherwood! What are you in such a hurry for? Slow down!"

Monty accepts the Ralph Edwards Community Service Award from Game Show Congress, a convention for game show fanatics, in 2005.
(Photo by Jason Hernandez)

CAROL MERRILL

I moved to Hawaii in 1989, but Monty and I stayed in touch. Whenever my husband Mark and I returned to LA, which was usually twice a year, we'd let Monty and Marilyn know, and the four of us would have lunch or dinner together at Hillcrest.

Mark and I moved to Australia for nine years. When I came back, Monty and Marilyn welcomed me back with a dinner at his house, and he invited all of the old staffers, too, so my welcome home was a *Let's Make a Deal* family reunion.

I thought of Monty often. Mark and I volunteered at a school in Australia for children with special needs. I decided we should have a garden there. The children worked with us and we planted a big vegetable garden surrounded by marigolds. One day we were out working, and I look up and I saw a bus with "Variety Club" across the side of it and I thought about Monty. Here I was on another continent and I was seeing this reminder of his work.

Monty was wonderful to me always. When I was on the show working with him, he was wonderful, and he was wonderful after. There was a time when I wanted to do a health & wellness-oriented talk show. It was a new idea at the time; of course, they're everywhere now. I wanted to call it *Opening New Doors with Carol Merrill*. And Monty offered to help me make a demo video to show potential buyers what the show would be like. I came over to his house, and Monty set up a camera in his kitchen. He turned it on, he pulled some chicken out of the refrigerator, and he prepared it while I explained what he should be doing. He didn't ask for anything in return, he just took an afternoon and did that for me.

BOB BODEN
Although we had a professional relationship, Monty and I didn't really have a friendship until the last ten years of his life. I was working at the Fox Reality Channel, and we hired Richard Hall for a series there. I knew Richard, but not very well, but now we're working together. I remember the first time he came in for a meeting at Fox Reality Channel, it made me smile to look at him because he looks so much like his dad.

Richard did a phenomenal job on that show. He and I both moved onto other shows, but I stayed in touch. I e-mailed him one day and said, "I'd love to go to lunch with you and your dad and get to know him better. Would that be possible?"

Within, I want to say, minutes, he got back to me and said "My dad's very fond of you. He'd love to have lunch with you."

We met at Hillcrest Country Club, where Monty was a pillar. When Monty walked into the room, it was literally a standing ovation every time. He was a god at that club. The first lunch went about two and a half hours, and it was Monty holding court and telling stories. In the course of those stories, I appreciated not only the content, but the delivery. He was a master storyteller, and he put his heart and soul into those stories. Stories about his shows, stories about building his company, about his childhood, about the people who worked with him and for him.

What got to me was the pride he took in his staff, who worked with him and for him. He was so dedicated to them. He gave them benefits both financial and emotional, well beyond the standards of any other producers, and many of the key staff members on that show were millionaires when they retired because of the retirement plan that he built for them, and he paid them year-round, 52 weeks a year, every year, whether Hatos-Hall had a show in production or not.

We had such a great time, and from that point forward, he had a lunch every few months.

The biggest event of every year for Monty and Marilyn Hall was Passover Seder.

SHARON HALL (2019)

Passover was the same script year after year after year. My mother would spend days setting a table for 40 people just so. And then on the day of, he would come down and say, "You did it all wrong! Why did you do it like that?" And he'd rearrange everything. She did it a different way every year. And every year, at the eleventh hour, Dad would re-do the whole thing.

It was a very inclusive service. Everyone told stories about their childhood. And it was a long night, but it was always worth it. And he would emcee the dinner like he would a TV show. It was so great.

RICHARD HALL (2019)

We had an amazing brisket, year after year after year. My mother was an amazing cook. As the years went by, she had some health issues, and she would special-order a brisket. And I must say, we really endured some terrible brisket once my mother stopped cooking. But it was a wonderful event. It was as open door as possible. The whole family was invited, but every member of the family could invite anyone they wanted, and friends were asked to come over too. It seemed like we usually had 30 or 40 people at my parents' house for Seder. If you told me there were more than 50 some years, it wouldn't surprise me.

HENRY KOVAL

Monty invited me to Seder one year even though I'm not Jewish. I was the resident goy that night. I remember what an impressive evening it was. He wasn't the center of attention. It wasn't as if he had these people over to watch him be the star of Seder. He hosted the Seder as a way of guiding it. He made sure everyone had a turn to say something and contribute something, so he took command of the whole evening to do that. And I was included in the experience as much as the others.

As part of the Seder traditions, Monty and Marilyn prepared a cup of wine for Elijah. They used a goblet they had found at a flea market during a vacation in Israel. Traditionally, Jews drink four cups of wine during a Seder. When asked what wine he preferred for the custom, Monty remarked, "After the third cup, who cares?"

The cup of wine would be set outside for Elijah. Monty and Marilyn always left the door open during Seder, encouraging visitors to walk in. One year, he set out Elijah's cup and was delighted when a stray dog wandered in.

MONTY HALL[cxxvi]

Passover is a time to ask questions. We stop halfway through the service, discuss a topic of interest; everyone joins in. Sometimes it gets heated—about politics, about Israel. The only subject two Jews agree on is what the third person should give to charity. We stop at different points in the service; we eat gefilte fish, sweet-and-sour herring; we read some more; we stop, we eat chicken soup, matzo balls; we sing. The happening goes on for four hours. Our Seders are wonderful. I'm big daddy, I am what my grandfather was. It keeps the continuity going.

My family has always been close. All my kids are in the business. I didn't get one dentist.

Oldest daughter Joanna Gleason continued her acting career, while her son, Aaron David Gleason, had formed a career for himself as a singer-songwriter. Son Richard had gone into journalism before veering into reality television. And youngest daughter Sharon Hall had produced a number of shows, heading up her own company, Mom De Guerre Productions.

SHARON HALL (2019)

My father was always extremely cautious of the fact that he was a wealthy man raising his children in Beverly Hills. And he really hammered it into us that we had to work for what we wanted. My dad didn't just buy us everything we wanted. We had to work for things. I got into show business without my dad's help. He didn't want me in show business. He wanted me to go to law school. He offered to buy me a condo in Los Angeles if I'd go to law school. Instead I went to New York and joined The Groundlings.

It makes me laugh now when people get to know me. They'll ask, "Were your parents in show business?"

I always laugh and say, "Can you see my face?" Because I look exactly like my father.

My father was always extraordinarily proud of us for doing what we did on our own. If you look at each of our careers, we went into areas of the business where my father really couldn't have helped us.

Monty loved show business. He loved the fame, the financial freedom, the circle of friends. But to say the least, it had a downside that he was extremely aware of.

At a large social gathering, Monty noticed one of his granddaughters surveying the room quietly. He turned to her and said, "Take a look around you. There's only one person in this entire room who isn't in show business. See if you can find that person."

She looked around quizzically, turned to her grandfather, and shrugged. Monty snapped his fingers and said, "It's you, kiddo. And keep it that way."

ROBERT HALL (2019)

I called Monty from Toronto one day and let him know Max Freed was ill. Max was 99 at the time, so this was obviously the end. And Monty dropped everything and flew straight to Winnipeg to be with Max at the end of his life, which I thought was a very noble gesture from my brother.

Monty was 90 and Max was 99. Their final conversation reads more tenderly than it played out; Monty smirked as he recalled the two of them sitting nose-to-nose and yelling in each other's faces. Max was nearly blind and deaf. Violating personal space and raising voices was the only way to communicate in the final days of his life.

Monty got closer to Max's ear and expressed his final words of gratitude to his benefactor. "Max, you gave me a life."

Max Freed corrected him. "No, Monty, you gave me a life."

Max Freed had lived vicariously through Monty in the years since that first encounter with him. He was proud of Monty for holding up his end of the initial bargain, maintaining solid grades and helping his brother with tuition. And Max was doubly impressed when Monty demanded justice for a system that prevented him from attending medical school. But Max could never have anticipated watching Monty bounce all over the planet to raise money for cause after cause after cause, leading trails of hospitals and therapy centers in his wake. He didn't anticipate Monty becoming a celebrity, investing his big paydays wisely, and then donating chunks of his bank account again and again when he felt that asking other people for money simply wasn't good enough.

Max Freed's son once joked to Monty, "I think he loves you more than he loves me!"

But there was a kernel of truth in there, as with most jokes. Monty Hall was the greatest investment Max Freed ever made.

In 2009, CBS introduced a new *Let's Make a Deal*. *FremantleMedia*, the company which was now in charge of the network's enduring game show *The Price is Right*, was now charged with a daily hour-long version of *Let's Make a Deal*. Wayne Brady, actor and

Monty walks the red carpet at the Jerry Herman Awards, a ceremony honoring productions from Los Angeles-area high school theatrical departments. (Courtesy of the Pantages Theater)

improv comic extraordinaire, was chosen from a formidable field of potential hosts—film star Steve Guttenberg and legendary MC Marc Summers auditioned for the gig.

The show was reinvented in Brady's image, so to speak, with songs and characters incorporated into the deals—Wayne was sometimes a superhero or a detective as he guided contestants through their decisions. As of this book's writing, it's lasted over ten years.

RICHARD HALL (2019)

What my dad came to realize was that *Let's Make a Deal* as he had done it worked because it was his show. The show was tailor-made to his strengths. The brilliant thing that the new version has done is that instead of trying to force Wayne into doing my dad's show, they've tailored the show so that it plays to Wayne's strengths, while keeping the core of the show the same. It's a well-done show.

Despite the reinvention, there was always room for Monty Hall. Every now and then, Monty would return to the show to guest-host a segment. Never more than a single segment, though. This was Wayne Brady's show now, and Monty liked what "the new guy" had done with the role.

In 2013, Monty Hall was honored with the Lifetime Achievement Award at the Daytime Emmys. Knowing how much recognition had meant to Monty, and knowing how much he had to fight for it at times, left the Hall family with somewhat mixed feelings about the honor.

BOB BODEN

It was a committee decision to give Monty the lifetime achievement award. There's an east coast contingent, NATAS and the west coast contingent, ATAS. One of the ways they cooperate is that they traditionally alternate making the decision about who should get the daytime lifetime achievement award.

It was our decision on the west coast that year. We considered several longtime contributors, including talent like talk show hosts, soap opera performers, judges…and many producers of those same types of shows. We were torn between two legends in game shows. One, Bob Stewart, had just passed away. The other was Monty.

Bob Stewart got a lot of love from the Academy over the years. *The $20,000 Pyramid* and *The $25,000 Pyramid* won a lot of Emmys. Monty had never gotten an Emmy, and since he was alive, we wanted to give him some recognition.

The plan was to give Monty an award after a speech by Wayne Brady and a beautifully produced and edited retrospective of Monty's career. Wayne said all the appropriate things and was supposed to throw to the tape, and at the end of the speech, he instead said "Ladies and gentlemen, Monty Hall."

Monty gave a beautiful, brilliant, sweet speech with a lot of class. The problem was there were a lot of people in that room who weren't familiar with him, who may have lacked understanding about why he deserved it. That would have been highlighted by the tape.

RICHARD HALL (2019)

The Lifetime Achievement Emmy was nice enough, but it just felt ridiculously overdue. There's no excuse for the way my father was snubbed up until that point. It was, if it doesn't sound too extreme, a miscarriage of TV justice. The National Academy snubbed my dad for years because it's such a political organization and it's been overseen by small-minded people. They expected my dad to play their game and Dad never went along with it, so they just had to show him.

Let's Make a Deal was a hit show year after year, on daytime, on nighttime, on network, in syndication, maintained its audience, and Dad used the popularity to raise over a billion dollars for charity, and the Academy wanted nothing to do with my dad. Honestly, there may have been a time when not getting an award bothered my dad, but once he realized what a joke the process was, he got over it. He didn't care.

So finally, somebody in the Television Academy speaks up and says, "Monty deserves this," but even then, you have no idea how many fucking arms had to be twisted to get that award to my father. It was bullshit, and you can quote me.

SHARON HALL (2019)
My dad was happy to receive the Lifetime Achievement Emmy, but you'll notice he got a little dig in. He joked during his speech, "They couldn't put this in prime time?"

CAROL MERRILL
One of Monty's secrets to a long life was that he ate in moderation. Whenever we ate together, I noticed he would always have a very small meal. We'd go to benefits sometimes, and everyone expects you to eat the catered meal or the buffet that comes with it, but if Monty had already eaten that day, he'd do one of two things. Either he would politely decline to eat, or if they were really insisting on it and Monty felt like he was expected to eat, he'd make a plate of food, but then he'd just push it around on the plate so it looked like he had eaten most of it. Monty really, really limited himself with how much he ate. I also can't remember ever seeing him touch alcohol.

BOB BODEN
Monty's health began to diminish, and it began harder for him to have these lunches with me. Sometimes his stories would get off-track and wavered a bit. Sometimes he repeated the stories—although they were such great stories that it was fine with me, I was happy to hear them again. But those lunches were some of my most cherished memories.

RICHARD HALL (2019)
The last two or three years of my parents' lives weren't fun. They rarely are, for people who see their 90s. If I can find a positive side to this, it's that they didn't have to battle with a major disease. My parents never dealt with cancer, they never—thank God—dealt with

Alzheimer's disease. But they lived into their 90s and naturally, things broke down. They hated it. They were going to Cedars Sinai constantly.

The worst thing for them, I think, was the number of compromises they had to make just to stay alive and move around. That was so difficult for them. Even in their late 80s, my parents went out more nights of the week than I did. They were constantly going to the country club, to restaurants, to the theater, to dinner parties, to Dodger games. To gradually stop doing each of those things was hard for them.

BOB BODEN

In late 2016, Monty's health really started to take a turn. Richard called me and warned me, "We're heading to the end. We're keeping it quiet, but we wanted the key people in Monty's life to know."

As much as I was blessed to be in that circle of friends, I didn't ever think of myself as being close to him. Not close enough to warrant a phone call like that. I asked if there was anything I could do to help.

Richard asked if I would come visit now and then. Visitors helped Monty's mind, he had extra energy whenever he knew he had visitors coming. Monty had full-time nurses taking care of he and Marilyn both. Soon after I started those visits, Marilyn passed away [on June 5, 2017].

RABBI SHARON BROUS
Eulogy delivered at Marilyn's funeral

The obits will tell you that Marilyn started as a radio ingenue for the Canadian Broadcasting Corporation, that she was an acclaimed song writer, and that she won an award for best documentary campaign film. They'll list her television writing credits, including the ABC special *Lights, Camera, Monty* (which I haven't seen, but hear is as charming as it sounds…). They'll tell you about all the shows and movies she associate-produced, produced and executive produced. They may even mention that she co-authored *The Celebrity Kosher Cookbook*.

But as I read all of Marilyn's accolades and honors and achievements, I thought about David Brooks' *Road to Character*, where he writes that there are two sets of virtues, the résumé virtues and the eulogy virtues.

"The résumé virtues are the skills you bring to the marketplace. The eulogy virtues are the ones that are talked about at your funeral — whether you were kind, brave, honest or faithful. Were you capable of deep love?"

These obituaries are incredible lists of resume virtues—and they about the work projects and initiatives that really mattered to Marilyn. She loved her work. It gave her chance to share her voice, explore her purpose, and share creative vision. To produce. But with all respect and love to the people in this room who have fought hard for those achievements, we all know that they don't tell us everything. And actually, they don't tell us what really matters most.

I'm going to try to weave together now just a few of the things you won't read in *Variety* or *Hollywood Reporter* about Marilyn Hall.

It is important to know that Marilyn was a woman ahead of her time. She lived for the present and the future, rarely wanting to revisit the past. At 90—always asking her kids and grandkids what they were working on, listening to, or watching at night. She loved and was so proud of her "Benetton family," multi-racial, diverse and gorgeous. In a world that so often draws harsh dividing lines of inclusion and exclusion, Marilyn loved each and every one of you for exactly who you are, and executed meticulously-prepared scavenger hunts to prove it.

Marilyn had an astonishing capacity to win hearts and minds, beginning with Monty himself, who swore he'd have nothing to do with an 18-year-old (he was 24 at the time), but took one look at her on the train platform and was swept off his feet... And even 70 years later would take her face in his hands and say, "Look at your mother! Look at how beautiful she is!" (And she was.)

With a combination of beauty, charm and sincerity, Marilyn charmed everyone from Monty Hall to Ingrid Bergman and Buzz Aldrin and Shimon Peres and all of us, really. She was Monty's secret weapon.

And here's the kicker: we all know people who know how to light up a room. But Marilyn wasn't just a charmer. She was the real deal. The friendships she built were life-long. She cherished her children and grandchildren, marveled in each one of your triumphs and worried through each one of your struggles. She had girlfriends—many here today—who knew her deepest secrets and whose lives were forever woven into hers. She knew how to entertain: music, food, costume parties, but she also knew how to show up in the quiet moments to give support and love. She knew to climb into bed and snuggle her daughter after surgery. Her big heart was always open.

She was real. If you wonder—as I have—how Monty and Marilyn managed to raise three of the most decent, caring, down-to-earth children right in the eye of the storm (Beverly Hills) and in the eye of the public, the answer is: no showbiz in the house. No privilege in the house.

Some say that we are defined, as people, by the nature of the conversation at our dinner table each night. Sharon once said that the lasting message of her dinner table conversations growing up with Marilyn and Monty Hall as her parents was: your life's work is about giving back. Marilyn and Monty would go to charity events 100 nights a year; organizations and causes they cared deeply for here and in Israel. And make no mistake: their dollars and support were absolutely transformative for these organizations. Joanna, Richard and Sharon grew up knowing that you need to put your money – and your friends' money – on the line for what you believe in.

And it wasn't just the philanthropy that would put your name on the walls. It was showing up at the Jewish home to entertain the old folks—even when she herself was well into her 80s. It was showing up for friends, quietly helping, supporting, sustaining in hard times. It was a rare, basic human decency, which everyone in this room was a recipient of. Monty and Marilyn's approach was simple: We had nothing. We made something. What do you need?

Marilyn was fierce. It's not only that she took her girls—Joanna and Sharon—to the Integration, where she lay with her eyes closed and had mystic revelations. Its' not only that she travelled the world, and befriended strangers all over world. It's important that you know—and if you've ever spoken with Monty for more than 20 seconds you do… Marilyn was the engine behind Monty's career. And she didn't just support him, she believed in him so deeply that she sent him from Toronto, where they lived, to New York, to walk the streets and knock on doors until his dreams were realized. "I'll be the mother and the father for our kids."

And when things got hard, like when Joanna hemorrhaged after a tonsillectomy, she lovingly nursed her back to good health, not even telling Monty what happened because he needed to stay in New York to work.

"It was the bravest thing I ever saw," Monty said.

And during one particularly dangerous snow storm, when Monty was stranded in the city, Marilyn fearlessly put chains on the wheels and drove to the City to pick him up and get him home safely. Monty marvels at her strength, her bravery, her ferocity. "Not once did she say, 'I can't handle this. It's too much.'" She just grabbed life's challenges and gracefully dove in.

Finally, Marilyn was never static. Her life changed many times… Monty gave Sharon great advice on Sharon and Todd's wedding night. He said: "The man you marry today is not the person he will be in 10 years. People change. Learn to love the man he will be." That's good advice—and he knew it because it was the truth of his full love and life with Marilyn. He loved her for more than 70 years, watching her go through many metamorphoses, and loving her through each and every one.

Marilyn was ahead of her time, always real, fierce and loving, always growing and changing… this is the person we remember today. This is the Marilyn we engrave on our hearts.

Sharon has a joke that while the Jewish community's motto is l'dor va'dor—passing values to the next generation, in the Hall family that motto is dor va'dor l'dor Number Three. Rob Eshman wrote a few years ago that the premise of Monty's show—in which contestants would choose to take what's behind one of three doors, and either end up with a valuable prize or a gag—was inspired by the short story *The Lady, or the Tiger?*, in which a man's choices result either in love or death. Rob writes: "I suppose that's what captivated me about the show even as a child: In life, you never know, but you still have to choose."

Monty—your choice was love. That's why this loss is so painful. It is important for you to know now and remember, that ultimately the choice is not between love and death, because real love persists even in death. Or as Sharon Hall has taught us: love is eternal, and Marilyn did not take her love away with her when she left.

Monty, Joanna, Richard & Sharon, Todd & Chris, Jack, Levi, Mikka, Maggie & Aaron Marilyn's sister Peggy…You will find her love now in the blinking of the lights and the swelling of your hearts.

You'll find her love in brunch and in storms, in stories and in silence.

And if the image of Marilyn, at her essence, begins to fade, I pray that you'll imagine her, during a vicious hurricane years ago, with wind and rain pounding on the house, running into the room with a great, big smile, proclaiming, "Isn't this fabulous?!"

Yes, Marilyn—this is fabulous. All of it. The love, the storm, the laughter, the light. We thank you for sharing it with us.

Zikhrona livrakha – may your memory be a blessing.

SHARON HALL
"Yom Kippur Yizkor: Lessons From Monty Hall,"
originally written for *Jewish Journal*

Ten days before my mother died…my sister, brother and I were gathered at her bedside singing the Beatles catalog. She strained to look at us as we harmonized and she seemed to smile when we broke into "Here Comes the Sun."

One of her nurses pulled me aside and said, "You need to let her go. All the attention *has* her attention and she can see that you don't want her to leave and she doesn't want to disappoint you. So figure out a way to say goodbye."

This was a gut punch. I couldn't do it. Neither could my siblings. I said, "Mom, we know that you're still going to be the helicopter mother you've always been, you'll just be here in spirit. Pick your sign to let us know you're still around. Are you going to be a random white feather? Flashing lights? Ringing bells?" She nodded her head and we leaned in.

"Lights," she said weakly. And so it was settled. My mother's presence would be known when light bulbs flickered.

A few days later, at her shivah, we asked Hillel Tigay, our chazzan at IKAR, to play some Beatles music during our silent prayer. My Orthodox cousin from Israel turned to his sister and asked, "Is this a shivah or a summer camp?"

At that very moment, a string of fairy lights embedded in a hedge of ficus trees, lights that had not worked in eight years suddenly came alive. The bulbs flickered in glittering syncopation. Our entire family freaked out. We told the guests about my mother's deathbed agreement. We were all in awe. If my Israeli cousin could have crossed himself, he would have.

In the ensuing days and months, I became strangely attached to that hedge. There were more flashing-light moments. It was like a party trick. It got a little weird. I would embrace the ficus branches like Kevin Costner in his cornfield, trying to conjure her.

Talking to the ficus had become my ritual. It wasn't scary or depressing. It was about light and chlorophyll and oxygen and life. Even with no lights, it was a practice that created a space to see and feel Marilyn Hall's presence — not her absence.

My father died…On Shabbat. On Yom Kippur. Right after Rabbi Sharon Brous' sermon. My phone blew up. I made my way past 1,300 Jews in white when it all faded to white. I don't remember how I got to my father's house to meet the mortuary van. I don't remember much at all about that day.

Many reached out to tell me that dying on a Yom Kippur Shabbat was reserved for holy men, for the pious and exalted. Now, Monty Hall was an amazing guy for lots of reasons, but if you want to know the truth, I think he chose that moment to go because he was trying to dodge Yizkor.

My father was allergic to grief. He was from the "buck up" generation. I never heard him recite the Kaddish out loud. It barely escaped his lips as a whisper. He couldn't metabolize his grief over the death of his beloved wife of 70 years. We understood but we were frustrated that this final chapter would be filled with denial and anger, and for him was devoid of spirituality.

So when I was asked to stand here today, I thought, *yes!* I want to embrace this ritual. I want to take my dad's yahrzeit as a day to make space for grief.

So, Dad, we're not going to dodge Yizkor. You made this day all about you and so you will never miss it again. And you'll get to see Mom, because at IKAR, Neilah always ends with a light show.

BOB BODEN

He and Marilyn had both been going through hard times, and after Marilyn died, Monty began going downhill faster. Richard asked me to bring over anything I could to spark his dad's mind. I dug out all the memorabilia I could. I brought over photos, press releases, press kits, mementos. The visits got much shorter, usually only 15 to 30 minutes. And it got to a point where he could barely speak. I hope those visits meant something to him because they meant a lot to me.

CAROL MERRILL

I made it a point to call Monty every year on his birthday. I called him on August 25, 2017, and I could tell he was feeling low. He had been on dialysis for a few years and that was taking its toll on him. Marilyn had died and I think Monty had just lost his enthusiasm at that point. I mean, they were together for 70 years. Once Marilyn was gone, how could he keep going?

BOB BODEN

For his 96th birthday, I gave him 96 birthday cards. I found a website that allowed you to custom-make and print birthday cards, so all the cards said "MONTY" on the front. I delivered this enormous stack of birthday cards. Richard and Sharon both contacted me and told me their dad was blown away by the cards. He loved them. That day I delivered the cards was my last time seeing him. I was blessed to know him, even in those final days.

I do remember one of my very last conversations with him. It was so hard knowing that we were about to lose him, and I just wanted to make him smile, so as a joke, I got close to him, and I said, "Monty, I was wondering…could you explain the Monty Hall Problem to me?"

Monty looks at me, shakes his head, and says, "I never could understand that damn thing."

On September 30, 2017, Monty Hall, Order of Canada, Order of Manitoba, billion-dollar philanthropist, husband, father, television packager, producer, master of ceremonies, actor, singer, writer, reporter, disc jockey, and butcher shop delivery boy, died at age 96.

CAROL MERRILL

I learned the news from my ex-husband, Tom. He called me that morning to tell me. I was sad, but prepared. And I think Monty was prepared too. I think he was ready to go. He had a long full life, and in those final years, the quality of life he was living was so reduced. I just think he decided he was finished.

The memorial service, at Hillside Memorial Park in Culver City, was held on October 3, 2017. Two days earlier, a crazed gunman had taken the lives of 57 people, and injured over 800 more, at a concert in Las Vegas, Nevada. At Monty's funeral, Rabbi David Baron said that the gunman's act was a sobering reminder of what one person was capable of doing, and expressed hope that the world would longer remember Monty Hall as a greater example of one man's potential for impacting the lives of others. Monty Hall, in his lifetime, had endured physical suffering, religious discrimination, and classism. He reacted to it all with acts of charity that reached so far and wide that even today, recipients of that largesse in hospitals around the world will never know that they owed Monty Hall a thank-you note.

RABBI SHARON BROUS
Eulogy given at Monty Hall's funeral

Grace is a certain kind of love: undeserved love…Monty's death on Yom Kippur will forever associate him with that holy day. I hope you'll all think of him when you say Avinu Malkeinu: וּנְכַלְמ וּנִיבָא. חָנֶנּ וּ וַעֲנֵנוּ כִ ְי אֵ ין בָּ נוּ מַעֲשִׂ ים —be gracious to us, even though we have done nothing to merit it.

    Why should we do acts of kindness toward people we don't know, who don't necessarily deserve them? There's one good reason: we act with grace because we know that we, too, often don't deserve it, but someone else's act of grace—whether God or human—has helped us when we needed it, so treating another with kindness is a cosmic repaying of the debt.

    Monty got that. He would often say that the kindnesses he received were the stimulus for all the things he did later in life. His superpower was that he lived from and with love and grace. He received it, and he gave it, in abundance.

    He always wanted the contestants on the show to win—not because they deserved it, but because he loved people. They'd show up wearing live-bird hats, refrigerator boxes or waving signs pleading, "Pick Me!" What they didn't know, is that they didn't have to wear outrageous costumes to be noticed by Monty; he noticed everyone.

"I'm a people person," he said, and he was.

He worked those telethons and raised all that money and helped all those kids because of love. Because he knew well and understood that he had been the recipient of grace, and he had to pay it forward.

He raised over $1 billion in tzedakah because he knew and understood the power of undeserved love to transform a person's life, as it had both for his grandparents and for him.

One of our first fundraisers for IKAR was at the Friar's Club, Monty emceed. We're taught in rabbinical school that a congregant should never feel comfortable saying a dirty joke in front of you. That night, Monty taught me that there is another way: a way to laugh at ourselves, to bring a kind of lighthearted joy to even the most serious of endeavors, as long as it's driven by love.

One obituary said: "For decades, Hall lived a double life: ebullient game show host and celebrity to millions by day, and, when not on camera, indefatigable fundraiser and philanthropist for Jewish and other causes."

But from what I can tell, that's not exactly right. It was a single life, guided at home and on the screen by one thing: a generous and open heart, an ability to share love.

He was charming and guileless, he didn't judge anyone. Even with all of his celebrity, he was always interested in everyone else's life. "Tell me more about the kids," he'd say. "More! More!"

His greatest joy was sharing what he had earned with others: his parents, his children and grandchildren, strangers on the street. All of this is how he lived, what he called, "a beautiful life."

For many years, mathematicians and statisticians have tried to solve the brainteaser that they called the Monty Hall Problem (even though it wasn't his problem—he knew the answer. It was our problem!): are you more likely to get the dream car if you switch to door #3 or if you stay with door #1?

It turns out there is a dedicated strategy you should follow: switch. But that doesn't matter for us today. Because the real Monty Hall Problem is not how you can increase your likelihood of winning the car, but how can you increase your likelihood of living a beautiful life—like Monty & Marilyn did.

And the answer is: open-hearted, unrepentant love. Grace. Decency. Generosity.

How can you, after 70 years with your beloved, still take her face in your hands and say,

"Look at your mother! Look at how beautiful she is!" That's the dedicated strategy I want in on!

How can you live a life of meaning and purpose—fighting always for what you believe in? Sharon said that the lasting message of dinner table conversations growing up was: your life's work is about giving back. Joanna, Richard and Sharon all grew up knowing that you need to step up for what you believe in. Now that's a dedicated strategy worth studying.

How do you raise three decent, loving, humble, kind children, despite the public eye, despite the celebrity and the privilege? By taking nothing for granted, living with gratitude and enjoying the simplest of moments together. I want that dedicated strategy!

In the priestly blessing, which parents traditionally say to our kids every Friday night, we say: יָאֵר ה וְיָנֻפ דְיָלָא הֲנַחִיו.– May God's light shine upon you and give you grace. May you have a little bit of what Monty had.

Sharon & Todd, Joanna & Chris, Richard & Madudu, Jack, Levi, Mikka, Maggie & Aaron, you have all inherited more than a little of the grace Monty had. You are beloved, and may you continue to live like your father/grandfather did from grace and love every day.

RICHARD HALL (2019)

For my dad, the best way I can phrase this is that the world was a sponge. By the end of his life, he had squeezed it completely dry. He got every drop of life that he could have had.

SHARON HALL (2019)

A lot of the obituaries and tributes made mention of his humanitarian work, which he would have liked. *Let's Make a Deal* brought a lot of joy to a lot of kids who were at home from school with a fever and watched it with their grandmas. But the show was a path for my parents to do what they loved more, which was philanthropy.

HENRY KOVAL

All Monty ever wanted to do was give back. And he did so much of that. And he deserves to be remembered for it.

CAROL MERRILL

His legacy was joy. He brought joy to TV viewers. He brought joy to the people who organized those fundraisers. He brought joy to everyone who benefitted from those fundraisers. Monty brought joy everywhere he went.

KAREN LAPIERRE

There's a theory that I like about the concepts of heaven and hell. The theory is that whenever anybody remembers you or speaks of you, you're called back to Earth to hear what they're saying. And for some people, learning what other people think of you could be hell. For other people, it could be heaven. So everyone gets the same fate, but they'll see it different ways.

I know how I talk about Monty. I know how I'll remember him. Monty's in heaven.

MONTY HALL[cxxvii]

I'd like to be remembered as somebody who cared, who cared for other people, who did his best, who did his best for his family, for his friends, for the community, for the country and continued to do it. I think what you do with your life is your epitaph.

Josh Jacobs Collection

BIBLIOGRAPHY

Amory, Cleveland. "Guess What Monty Hall's Doing? Yep, Another Game Show!" *The Courier News*. 17 Jun. 1977.

Arnold, Janice. "Monty Hall Honored for Humanitarian Work." *Canadian Jewish News*. 11 May 1989.

"Ask Them Yourself." *Florida Today*. Cocoa, FL. 21 Nov. 1971.

Auerbach, Alexander. "Say Monty, Where Did You Get That Zonk?" *Press and Sun Bulletin*. Binghamton, NY. 3 Aug. 1975.

Beach, Susan. "For Variety, Monty Hall Visits St. Mary's." *Palm Beach Daily News*. 25 Jan. 1991.

Beck, Marilyn. "Burt, Star of Girl Won't Team on Screen." *The Shreveport Times*. 19 Apr. 1978.

Beck, Marilyn. "Carol's Busy." *Star Gazette*. Elmira, New York. 16 Sep. 1978.

Biggers, Buck, and Chet Stover. "Dinah Shore Began on Radio." *The Atlanta Constitution*. 16 Jul. 1973.

"Bingo on TV." *New York Daily News*. 18 Feb. 1958.

Buffum, Richard. "The Ability to Give." *The Los Angeles Times*. 10 Sep. 1970.

"Celebrity Resolutions." The Tampa Tribune 28 Dec. 1981

Collins, Don. "Game Show's Bankruptcy Made Even Winners Losers." *The Los Angeles Times*. 6 Nov. 1982.

"Complex Deals Baffle Creditors of Catalena." *The Gazette*. Montreal, Que. 8 Oct. 1981.

Deeb, Gary. "Sirota's Court has Promise of Being Season's Bright Spot." *Dayton Daily News*. 2 Dec. 1976.

Dern, Marian. "Dealing Monty Hall." *Independent Star-News*. Pasadena, California. 23 Jul. 1967.

DuBois, Stephanie. "Dick Clark Lets the Young Do the Dancing." *Wisconsin State Journal*. Madison, WI. 19 Apr. 1981.

Dutton, Walt. "He Wheels, Audience Makes Deals and Everybody's Happy." *The Los Angeles Times*. 5 Aug. 1965.

http://familyhistory.shniers.com/ShnierTree.pdf

Fanning, Win. "Who Watched What on the Fourth." *Pittsburgh Post-Gazette*. 7 Jul. 1976.

Finnigan, Joseph. "Participation Shows Out of Emmy Running." *Pasadena Independent*. 24 Feb. 1964.

"The Four Lives of Monty Hall." *Press and Sun-Bulletin*. Binghamton, NY. 7 May 1966.

"Game Shows Making Strong Comeback." *Broadcasting* Magazine. 24 Jul. 1961.

Gardener, Hy & Marilyn. "Glad You Asked That!" *Daily Record*. Morristown, NJ. 1 Mar. 1981.

Gilbert, Alan, and Bernie Gould. "Execs Love the Show, but It Skews Too Old." *The Los Angeles Times*. 26 Sep. 1994.

Gill, Alan. "How to Smuggle a Celebrity." *The Marion Star*. 20 Aug. 1963.

Gilonna, John M. "Slot Machines That Appeal to Children Criticized." *Reno Gazette-Journal*. 18 Nov. 1999.

Grant, Hank. "Host Monty Hall Lauds Canadian-Born Citizens." *The Indianapolis Star*. 2 Feb. 1964.

Hall, Monty. "Audience Big Park of Let's Make a Deal." *The Bee*. Danville, VA. 26 Jul. 1972.

Hall, Monty. "Daytime Television is That Poor Out-of-Town Cousin Whose Visit is Unwelcome." *Arizona Republic*. Phoenix, AZ. 27 Jul. 1967.

Hall, Monty. "Family Love Remains with Jewish Star." *Austin American Statesman*. 3 Apr. 1976.

Hall, Monty. "What is a Jew?" *The Desert Sun*. Palm Springs, CA. 20 May 1981.

"Hall Wheels and Deals for Many Good Causes." *The Sioux City Journal*. 7 May 1967.

"Hatos-Hall Makes for Bigger Deals." *Broadcasting* Magazine. 16 Oct. 1972.

Heffernan, Harold. "Let's Make a Deal—On Television." *Honolulu Star-Bulletin*. 9 Jul. 1967.

Hoffman, Steve. "Hour of Creed and Its Prophet." *The Cincinnati Enquirer*. 17 Feb. 1970.

"How Well the Games Play on Television." *Broadcasting* Magazine. 9 Sep. 1974.

Humphrey, Hal. "Emmy's Unpopular." *The Akron Beacon Journal*. 10 May 1964.

"Jay Stewart Doesn't Mind Playing the Buffoon." *The Atlanta Constitution*. 22 May 1976.

"Jay Stewart of Zonk Fame." *The San Bernardino County Sun*. 21 Dec. 1975.

"Jewish Women Put on Enjoyable Concert." *The Winnipeg Tribune*. 26 Feb 1940.

"Keep Talking." *The Bristol Daily Courier.* Bristol, PA. 16 Jul. 1958.

Kleiner, Dick. "Hollywood Today." *Standard-Speaker.* Hazelton, PA. 16 Nov. 1967.

Knapp, Dan. "Deal is No. 2 and Trying Harder." *The Los Angeles Times.* 20 May 1970.

Kreiling, Ernie. "Ernie Calls Monty Hall Television's Big Dealer." *The Pantagraph.* Bloomington, IL. 24 Aug. 1965.

Krier, Beth Ann. "Let's Make a Deal Called TV's Best Daytime Drama." *Star-Gazette.* Elmira. NY. 22 Sep. 1973.

Levin, Ann. "Jewish Fur Traders? And Ranchers Too?" *The Marion Star.* 20 Dec. 1993.

Love, Myron. "New Winnipeg Street Renamed for Monty Hall." *Canadian Jewish News.* 19 Jun. 1986.

Lungen, Paul. "Bob Hall Gives Lesson in Humility." *Canadian Jewish News.* 13 Nov. 1986.

MacMinn, Aleene. "Monty: His Biggest Deal." *Detroit Free Press.* 2 Jul 1967.

Maksian, George. "Monty Hall Warms Up for TV Variety Debut." *New York Daily News.* 4 Jun 1972.

Markoutsas, Elaine. "Work's Still a Big Deal for Monty Hall." *The Dispatch.* Moline, IL. 24 Sep. 1975.

"Monty Appreciates Schedule Change." *Fort Lauderdale News.* 16 Jan. 1970.

"Monty Hall Dedicated to Community Services." *Clarion-Ledger.* Jackson, MS. 7 May 1967.

"Monty Hall Declines Appointment." *Santa Cruz Sentinel.* 23 Jan. 1981.

"Monty Hall Does First Acting in 15 Years." *Fort Lauderdale News.* 10 Oct. 1969.

"Monty Hall Made a Deal with ABC." *The Tampa Tribune.* 1 Aug. 1976.

"Monty Hall Will Host TV Specials." *News Record.* North Hills, PA. 25 May 1974.

"The Name of the Game is Game Shows." *Broadcasting Magazine.* 16 Apr. 1984.

"NATPE Off to a Rousing Start." *Broadcasting Magazine.* 13 Feb. 1984.

"New Let's Make a Deal Premieres." *The Leaf-Chronicle.* Clarksville, TN. 10 Jun. 1990.

https://www.newsfromme.com/2009/02/09/todays-video-link-35-3/

O'Brian, Jack. Bingo at Home on TV Called Dull, Cheap, and Drab." *Cumberland, Evening Times.* 18 Feb. 1958.

"On Television." *The Marshall News Messenger.* Marshall, TX. 9 Jun. 1964.

Oppenheimer, Peter J. "TV's Monty Hall: Two Women in My Life Who Made Me Lucky." *Lansing, MI.* 27 Aug. 1972.

Pack, Harvey. "Keynotes: Monty Hall Makes a Deal." *The Morning Call.* Allentown, PA. 11 Dec. 1968.

Pack, Harvey. "Monty Hall Has Loot, Seeking Another Deal." *Dayton Daily News*. 25 Dec. 1971.

Peterson, Bettelou. "Cavett's Down but Not Out, and Here's What May Happen." *Detroit Free Press*. 6 Jul. 1972.

"Psychology at Noon Provides Hot Menu in New Video Game." *The Philadelphia Inquirer*. 20 Aug. 1963.

"The Quizzes." *Broadcasting Magazine*. 28 July 1958.

Resnik, Bert. "Bert's Eye View." *Independent Press-Telegram*. Long Beach, CA. 4 Aug. 1963.

Resnik, Bert. "Let's Make a Deal Hit the Road Before the Air." *Independent Press-Telegram*. Long Beach, CA. 25 Apr. 1965.

Riste, Tom. "Let's Make a Deal Star Had to Sell His Idea First." *Arizona Daily Star*. Tucson, AZ. 1 Oct. 1970.

Roessing, Walter. "And Behind This Curtain—Monty Hall." *The Ottawa Journal*. 4 Oct. 1969.

Royal, Don. "Game Shows Return to Prime Time." *The Courier*. Waterloo, IA. 28 May 1969.

Sanchez, Alicia. "Monty Hall is Always on the Go." *The Tampa Tribune*. 26 May 1974.

Scott, Vernon. "He's the Host of Let's Make a Deal." *Courier-Post*. Camden, NJ. 7 Oct. 1967.

Shull, Richard K. "Unloading Preposterous Prizes." *The Baltimore Sun*. 18 Apr. 1971.

Silberman, Belinda. "Working For Our People Hall's First Concern." *Canadian Jewish News*. 5 Jun. 1986.

"Some Deal." *The Ottawa Citizen*. 11 Sep. 1981.

Starr, Eve. "Inside Television." *The Mercury*. Pottstown, PA. 20 Jan. 1965.

Stewart, D.L. "Monty Hall…No Big Deal." *The Journal Herald*. Dayton, OH. 18 Sep. 1976.

Sudlow, Dina. "Tom Jones Prepares New TV Series." *The Ottawa Citizen*. 27 Mar. 1981.

Tiede, Tom. "TV's Game Shows: Physical Test." *Marshfield News Herald*. 8 Aug. 1975.

Tierney, John. "Profs are Goats in Puzzle." *Arizona Republic Sun*. Phoenix, AZ. 21 Jul. 1991.

Thompson, Ruth. "Show Host Made a New Deal." *The Sentinel*. Carlisle, PA. 22 Jan. 1972.

Tusher, Will. "Lucy's Studio Switch Spurred by Film Deal." *Ducannon Record*. 27 May 1971.

"TV's Big Dealer Craves New Deal." *Star Tribune*. Minneapolis, MN. 9 Nov. 1969.

Unger, Arthur. "Hired a Hall for Best Deal on TV." 30 Jun. 1974.

Van Slyck, Edith. "A Game Show with Hysterical Party Air." *The Baltimore Sun*. 29 Dec. 1968.

Wetzig, Mina. "Bingo's on the Air." *New York Daily News.* 4 May 1958.

Whitbeck, Charles. "Monty Hall's a Wheeler Dealer." *The Journal News.* White Plains, New York. 22 Jan. 1964.

Whitbeck, Charles. "Second Banana on Let's Make a Deal." *The Miami News.* 29 Nov. 1975.

"Young Viewer's Dream is One Box Top Away." *The Morning Herald.* Hagerstown, MD. 27 May 1961.

Willis, John M. "Monty Hall Bids Adieu to Let's Make a Deal." *The Courier News.* Bridgewater, NJ. 31 Dec. 1976.

http://www.aish.com/jw/s/Lets-Make-a-Deal.html

ENDNOTES

i. Polah, Maralyn Lois. "Interview: Monte Hall—Is He Really a Big Deal?" *The Philadelphia Inquirer*. 7 Mar 1976.
ii. Rasky, Frank. "Halls Always Make a Good Deal When Charity Calls." *The Canadian Jewish News*. 7 Apr. 1983.
iii. Hall, Monty. "The Fragile Legacy." *Guideposts Magazine*. September 1975.
iv. Ibid.
v. Whitney, Christy. Interview with Monty Hall. Yiddish Book Center. 11 Mar. 2014.
vi. "Storytime with Monty Hall – Los Angeles Video Production." https://www.youtube.com/watch?v=NC0BlVZUx6E
vii. Whitney, Christy. Interview with Monty Hall. Yiddish Book Center. 11 Mar. 2014.
viii. Rasky.
ix. Ibid.
x. Leiderman, M. (Writer). (1999). Monty Hall [Television series episode]. In *Biography*. A&E.
xi. Holston, Noel. "Canada's Gift to the US Lays His Cards on the Table." *The Orlando Sentinel*. 26 May 1974.
xii. Buck, Jerry. "Monty Hall Peddles Dreams." *Florida Today*. Cocoa, FL. 10 Mar. 1974.
xiii. Maron, Mark. "Monty Hall." *WTF* (podcast).
xiv. Grant, Hank. "Host Monty Hall Lauds Canadian-Born Citizens." *The Indianapolis Star*. 2 Feb. 1964.
xv. Maron.
xvi. Shostak, Stu (host/producer). 2011 May 18. *Stu's Show* [internet radio]. Chatsworth, CA.
xvii. "Monty Hall Prefers to Emcee TV Shows." *Asbury Park Press*. 4 May 1962.
xviii. Schott, John, director. *Deal*. 1978.
xix. Behar, Joe. 2003 October 29. Personal interview with Jennifer Howard on behalf of the Archive of American Television.
xx. Hall, Monty. 2002 February 15. Personal interview with Fred Wostbrock on behalf of the Archive of American Television.
xxi. Ibid.
xxii. Sagi, Douglas. "You May Get a Prize—Or It Might Be a Zonk." *The Gazette*. Montreal, Quebec. 24 Dec. 1971.
xxiii. Shostak.
xxiv. Hall, Monty. Interview by L. Wayne Hicks. http://www.tvparty.com/gamemonty2.html
xxv. Kreiling, Ernie. "A Closer Look." *Valley News*. Van Nuys, CA. 16 Apr. 1965.
xxvi. Rizzo, Joan. "Thrills Per Square Nickel." *Democrat and Chronicle*. Rochester, NY. 8 Mar. 1970.
xxvii. Sagi, Doug. "You May Get a Prize—Or It Might Be a Zonk." *The Gazette*. Montreal, Quebec. 24 Dec. 1971.
xxviii. Dern, Marlene. "Dealing Monty Hall." *Independent Star-News*. 23 Jul. 1973.
xxix. Wostbrock.

xxx. "Game Show Like Obstacle Course." *The Ottawa Citizen.* 19 Apr. 1975.
xxxi. Howard.
xxxii. "Game Show Like Obstacle Course." *The Ottawa Citizen.* 19 Apr. 1975.
xxxiii. Hicks.
xxxiv. Steger, Pat. "Jay Stewart Made a New Deal with Himself." *The San Francisco Examiner.* 7 Aug. 1977.
xxxv. Heffernan, Harold. "Kisses Too Much for TV Emcee." *Orlando Evening Star.* 24 May 1967.
xxxvi. Heimer, Mel. "Surprises Make Deal Popular." *The Journal News.* White Plains, NY. 9 Apr. 1969.
xxxvii. Mary, W.B. "What's Monty Hall Reeeely Like?" *Journal and Courier.* Lafeyete, IN. 11 May 1966.
xxxviii. "Hall Wheels and Deals for Many Good Causes." *Sioux City Journal.* 7 May 1967.
xxxix. Ibid.
xl. Ibid.
xli. Buffum, Richard. "The Ability to Give." *The Los Angeles Times.* 10 Sep. 1970.
xlii. "The Four Lives of Monty Hall." *Press and Sun-Bulletin.* Binghamton, NY. 7 May 1966.
xliii. Rasky.
xliv. Whitney, Christy. Interview with Monty Hall. Yiddish Book Center. 11 Mar. 2014.
xlv. Hall.
xlvi. Ibid.
xlvii. "Monty Hall Puts Story in a Book." *The Anniston Star.* 16 Mar. 1974.
xlviii. Keating, Micheline. "Hall Kicks Off KZAZ's Season." *Tucson Daily Citizen.* 25 Sep. 1970.
xlix. Severson, Jack. "Monty Hall: A Millionaire on the Run, By Choice." *The Philadelphia Inquirer.* 3 Feb. 1979.
l. Kleiner, Dick. "Monty's Not All Wheeling and Dealing." *Journal Gazette.* Mattoon, IL. 22 Mar. 1974.
li. Buck, Jerry. "Monty Hall Peddles Dreams." *Florida Today.* Cocoa, FL. 10 Mar. 1974.
lii. Personal interview. June 2006.
liii. Rizzo.
liv. "Monty Hall Will Deal in New Version of Game Show." *The Ottawa Journal.* 25 Jul. 1980.
lv. Dodd, Mike. "Monty Hall Looks for a Deal." *The Cincinnati Inquirer.* 22 Mar. 1984.
lvi. Howard.
lvii. Keaton, Bob. "Jay Stewart: Let's Make a Deal Can Be Fun as Well as Frantic." *Fort Lauderdale News.* 26 Oct. 1975.
lviii. LeBlanc, Jerry. "Even Monty Hall Can End Up Zonked." *Detroit Free Press.* 24 May 1976.
lix. Polak, Maralyn Lois. "Interview: Monty Hall—Is He Really a Big Deal?" *The Philadelphia Inquirer Sun.* 7 Mar 1976.
lx. Unger, Arthur. "Hired a Hall for the Best Deal on TV." *Honolulu Star Bulletin.* 30 Jun. 1974.
lxi. "Audience Makes Deal Success." *Abeline Reporter-News.* 9 May 1971.
lxii. Polak.
lxiii. Adler, Dick. "Monty's Touchy About Game Show Criticism." *The Ithica Journal.* 20 Dec. 1975.
lxiv. Ibid.
lxv. Wostbrock.
lxvi. Scott, Vernon. "No Matter How You Slice It, It Still Comes Out Monty Hall." *St. Louis Post Dispatch.* 16 Jun. 1974
lxvii. Hall, Monty. "My Favorite Jokes." *The Sioux City Journal.* 19 Oct. 1975.
lxviii. O'Brien, Jim. "Monty Hall Makes a Charitable Deal." *Philadelphia Daily News.* 2 May 1975.
lxix. Wostbrock.
lxx. http://www.curtalliaume.com/lets-make-deal/
lxxi. Hicks.
lxxii. Ibid.
lxxiii. "Monty Says Cut Games, Add Variety." *Courier-Post.* Camden, NJ. 19 Apr. 1975.
lxxiv. Kleiner, Dick. "Local TV Plays Flop for Flop." *Ames Daily Tribune.* 7 Aug. 1975.

lxxv.	Camper, John. "Guess Who Objects to Lack of Variety." *Arizona Daily Star*. Tucson, AZ. 28 Sep. 1975.
lxxvi.	"How Well the Games Play on Television." *Broadcasting* Magazine. 9 Sep. 1974.
lxxvii.	Jones, Paul. "Game Shows: The Great TV Escape." *The Atlanta Constitution*. 18 Jan. 1975.
lxxviii.	Camper.
lxxix.	Rizzo, Joan. "Thrills Per Square Nickel." *Democrat and Chronicle*. Rochester, NY. 8 Mar. 1970.
lxxx.	"Game Show Like Obstacle Course." *The Ottawa Citizen*. 19 Apr. 1975.
lxxxi.	http://emceesteve.tripod.com/column_9_4_00.htm
lxxxii.	Wostbrock.
lxxxiii.	"Curtain Comes Down for Daytime Deal." *Broadcasting* Magazine. 12 Jul. 1976.
lxxxiv.	Hack, Richard. "Rumors of Retirement Aren't True." *Democrat and Chronicle*. Rochester, NY. 20 Mar. 1977.
lxxxv.	Shister, Gail. "Hall has a New Deal in Store." *The Philadelphia Inquirer*. 17 Sep. 1984.
lxxxvi.	Kleiner, Dick. "Announcer Jay Stewart Found Job, Himself." *Daily Press*. Newport News, VA. 26 Dec. 1978.
lxxxvii.	Ibid.
lxxxviii.	Wostbrock.
lxxxix.	Ibid.
xc.	TVParty.
xci.	Lewis, Dan. "Monty Hall's New Deal." *The Evening Review*. East Liverpool, OH. 26 Aug. 1977.
xcii.	Scott, Vernon. "Old Dream Works Best for Monty Hall." *The Orlando Sentinel*. 9 Oct. 1980.
xciii.	Ibid.
xciv.	Severson.
xcv.	Baber, David. *Television Game Show Hosts: Biographies of 32 Stars*. McFarland and Co. Publishing. Jefferson, NC. 2008.
xcvi.	Gardner, Marilyn & Hy. "Once He Got a Microphone in His Teeth." *The Times*. Shreveport, LA. 1 Mar. 1981.
xcvii.	Scott.
xcviii.	Beck, Marilyn. "Hollywood Flings Cash." Gannett News Service. 19 Dec. 1982.
xcix.	Charkow, Cindy. "The Halls." *Canadian Jewish News*. 25 Mar. 1993.
c.	Gasner, Cynthia. "Hall's Wife Carving a Name for Herself in Television." *Canadian Jewish News*. 5 Jun. 1986.
ci.	Whitney.
cii.	"Monty Hall at the Improv." *The San Bernardino County Sun*. 22 May 1983.
ciii.	Heller, Marilyn. "The Big Dealer." *The Philadelphia Inquirer*. 5 Dec. 1988.
civ.	Ibid.
cv.	Shister.
cvi.	Shister.
cvii.	Fine, Marshall. "Hall Can't Make Deal for New Idea." *Green Bay Press Gazette*. 19 Feb. 1984.
cviii.	Haithman, Diane. "Ordinary People, Come On Down!" *Detroit Free Press*. 17 Oct. 1985.
cix.	Jacobs, Joshua. Personal interview with Monty Hall. 2015.
cx.	Baber.
cxi.	Alexander, Joan. "Reena Dinner Honoring Monty Hall Raises $75,000." *Canadian Jewish News*. 5 Nov. 1981.
cxii.	Ibid.
cxiii.	Wostbrock.
cxiv.	Ibid.
cxv.	Ibid.
cxvi.	Ibid.
cxvii.	Ibid.
cxviii.	Ibid.
cxix.	Ibid.
cxx.	Ibid.
cxxi.	Hicks.

cxxii. Hall, Monty. Interview by Gary James. http://www.famousinterview.ca/interviews/monty_hall.htm
cxxiii. Johnson, Allan. "Monty Hall Says Current Quizzers are Simply Buying the Audience." *The Anniston Star.* 11 Jun. 2000.
cxxiv. Ibid.
cxxv. Baber.
cxxvi. Levitt, Beverly. "Behind Door No. 1: Family, Faith, and Passover." *Tampa Bay Times.* 31 Mar. 2004.
cxxvii. https://jewishjournal.com/hollywood/225241/monty-hall-co-creator-host-lets-make-deal-dies-96/

www.ingramcontent.com/pod-product-compliance
Lightning Source LLC
Chambersburg PA
CBHW050828230426
43667CB00012B/1921